A TREASURY OF XXth CENTURY MURDER

The Lindbergh Child

cloth: ISBN 10: 1-56163-529-4
ISBN 13: 978-1-56163-529-0
paperback: ISBN 10: 1-56163-530-8
ISBN 13: 978-1-56163-530-6
©2008 Rick Geary
Printed in China

5   4   3   2   1

Comicslit is an imprint and
trademark of

NANTIER · BEALL · MINOUSTCHINE
Publishing inc.
new york

THE LINDBERGH CHILD

THE SENSATIONAL CASE THAT TRANSFIXED THE NATION.

THE QUESTIONS THAT REMAIN TO THIS DAY.

THE ATROCIOUS KIDNAPPING AND MURDER OF THE INFANT SON OF AMERICA'S HERO Col. CHARLES A. LINDBERGH

THE HOUSE AT HOPEWELL, NEW JERSEY

WRITTEN AND ILLUSTRATED by RICK GEARY

NBM ComicsLit

Also available by Geary:
A Treasury of Victorian Murder:
Jack The Ripper pb.: $9.95
The Borden Tragedy, pb.: $8.95
The Fatal Bullet, pb.: $9.95
The Mystery of Mary Rogers
hc.: $15.95
The Beast of Chicago pb.: $9.95
The Murder of Abraham Lincoln
pb.: $8.95, hc.: $15.95
The Case of Madeleine Smith
pb.: $8.95, hc.: $15.95
The Bloody Benders
pb.: $9.95, hc.: $15.95

P&H: $4 1st item, $1 each addt'l.

We have over 200 titles, write
for our color catalog:
NBM
40 Exchange Pl., Suite 1308,
New York, NY 10005
see our website at
www.nbmpublishing.com

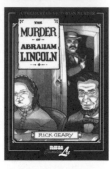

THE LINDBERGH CHILD

BIBLIOGRAPHY

Behn, Noel, *Lindbergh: The Crime*. (New York, Atlantic Monthly Press, 1994)

Douglas, John and Mark Olshaker, *The Cases That Haunt Us*. (New York, Scribner, 2000)

Fisher, Jim, *The Ghosts of Hopewell, Setting the Record Straight in the Lindbergh Case*. (Carbondale IL, Southern Illinois University Press, 1999)

Linbergh, Anne Morrow, *Hour of Gold, Hour of Lead*. (New York, Signet Books, 1974)

Mappen, Marc, *Murder and Spies, Lovers and Lies: Settling the Great Controversies of American History*. (New York, Avon Books, 1996)

Waller, George, *Kidnap: The Story of the Linbergh Case*. (New York, The Dial Press, 1961)

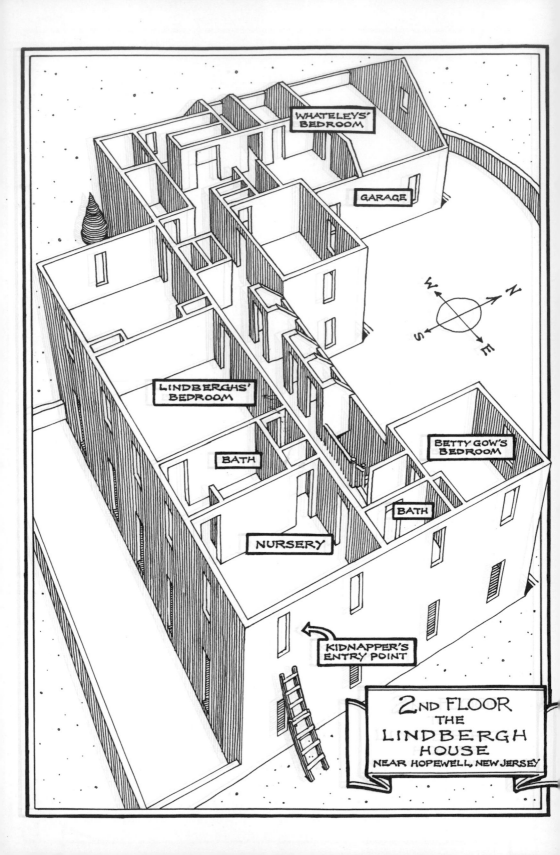

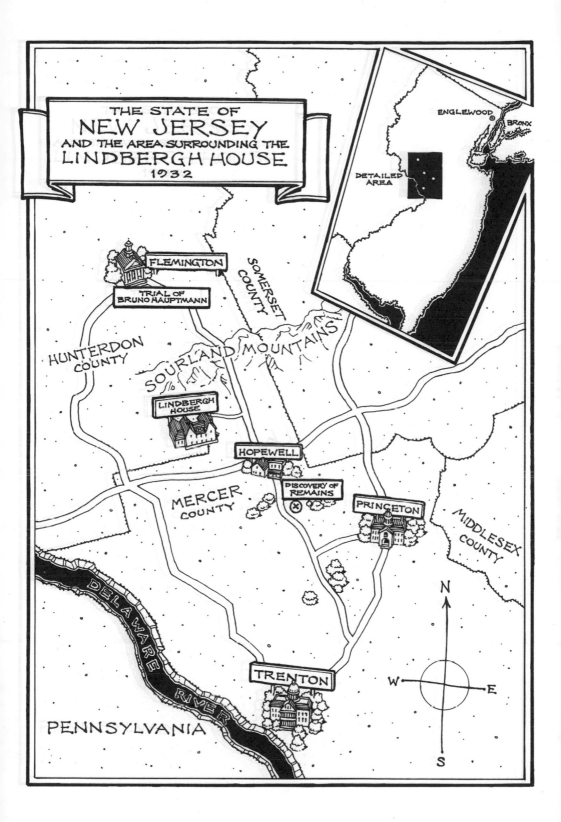

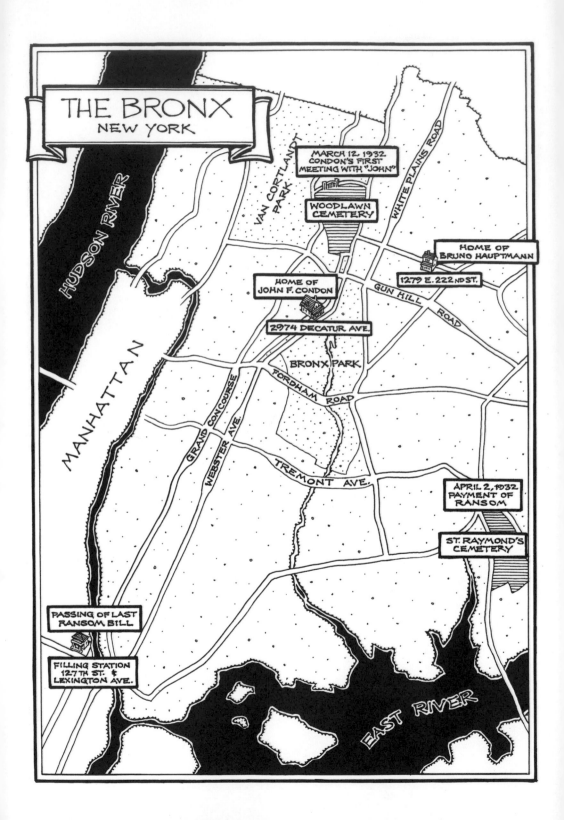

PART ONE
THE LONE EAGLE

SATURDAY, MAY 21, 1927
CHARLES A. LINDBERGH BECOMES THE HERO
OF THE AGE WITH HIS COURAGEOUS SOLO FLIGHT
ACROSS THE ATLANTIC.

LATER IN THE YEAR, THE LINDBERGHS PURCHASE A TRACT OF 360 ACRES NEAR THE VILLAGE OF HOPEWELL, NEW JERSEY — BELOW THE SOURLAND MOUNTAINS, ABOUT 15 MILES FROM PRINCETON.

ENGLEWOOD

NEW JERSEY

NEW YORK

NEXT DAY HILL

HOPEWELL

PENN.

HERE, THEY BEGIN CONSTRUCTION ON A LARGE HOUSE — THEIR SANCTUARY.

AS CONSTRUCTION NEARS COMPLETION IN 1932, THE FAMILY SPENDS ITS WEEK DAYS 50 MILES AWAY, AT NEXT DAY HILL, THE MORROW ESTATE IN ENGLEWOOD, NEW JERSEY.

ANNE IS AT WORK ON A BOOK OF HER ASIAN TRAVELS, WHILE CHARLES TRAVELS DAILY TO HIS OFFICE IN NEW YORK CITY.

WEEKENDS FIND THEM IN RESIDENCE AT THEIR NEW HOME, THOUGH MUCH OF THE INTERIOR REMAINS UNFINISHED.

THE SOLITUDE OF THEIR LOCATION, THE BLEAK BEAUTY OF THE COUNTRYSIDE, PROVIDE THE PEACE AND RESPITE THEY LONG FOR.

THEIR PERSONAL STAFF CONSISTS OF THREE INDIVIDUALS.

THE ENGLISH BUTLER, ALOYSIUS "OLLY" WHATELEY AND HIS WIFE, ELSIE, WHO SERVES AS COOK AND HOUSEKEEPER.

AND THE BABY'S NURSEMAID, BETTY GOW, AGE 25, A RECENT IMMIGRANT FROM SCOTLAND.

PART TWO
THE CRIME

THE WEEKEND OF FEBRUARY 27-28, 1932,
FINDS THE LINDBERGHS, ACCORDING TO RECENT
CUSTOM, AT THEIR NEW HOME.

DURING THIS TIME, CHARLES, JR. DEVELOPS A
SERIOUS COLD, AND ON MONDAY, FEBRUARY 29
MRS. LINDBERGH DECIDES NOT TO RETURN TO
ENGLEWOOD.

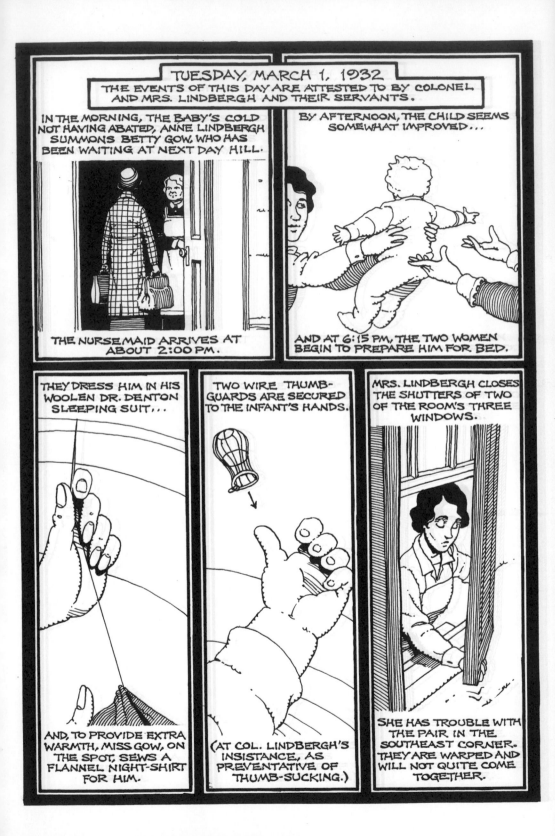

TUESDAY, MARCH 1, 1932

THE EVENTS OF THIS DAY ARE ATTESTED TO BY COLONEL AND MRS. LINDBERGH AND THEIR SERVANTS.

IN THE MORNING, THE BABY'S COLD NOT HAVING ABATED, ANNE LINDBERGH SUMMONS BETTY GOW, WHO HAS BEEN WAITING AT NEXT DAY HILL.

THE NURSEMAID ARRIVES AT ABOUT 2:00 PM.

BY AFTERNOON, THE CHILD SEEMS SOMEWHAT IMPROVED...

AND AT 6:15 PM, THE TWO WOMEN BEGIN TO PREPARE HIM FOR BED.

THEY DRESS HIM IN HIS WOOLEN DR. DENTON SLEEPING SUIT,...

AND, TO PROVIDE EXTRA WARMTH, MISS GOW, ON THE SPOT, SEWS A FLANNEL NIGHT-SHIRT FOR HIM.

TWO WIRE THUMB-GUARDS ARE SECURED TO THE INFANT'S HANDS.

(AT COL. LINDBERGH'S INSISTANCE, AS PREVENTATIVE OF THUMB-SUCKING.)

MRS. LINDBERGH CLOSES THE SHUTTERS OF TWO OF THE ROOM'S THREE WINDOWS.

SHE HAS TROUBLE WITH THE PAIR IN THE SOUTHEAST CORNER. THEY ARE WARPED AND WILL NOT QUITE COME TOGETHER.

SHE LEAVES THE ROOM AT 7:30, AS MISS GOW SECURES THE BABY IN HIS CRIB BY MEANS OF TWO LARGE SAFETY PINS.

THE NURSEMAID REMAINS IN THE ROOM UNTIL SHE IS CERTAIN HER CHARGE IS ASLEEP...

LEAVING AT ABOUT 8:00 PM TO JOIN ELSIE WHATELEY IN THE SERVANT'S SITTING ROOM.

THE EVENING HAS TURNED COLD AND BLUSTERY AS COL. LINDBERGH ARRIVES HOME AT ABOUT 8:30 PM.

AFTER A FULL DAY OF APPOINTMENTS, HE HAS FORGOTTEN AN IMPORTANT ENGAGEMENT THIS EVENING. HE WAS TO BE GUEST OF HONOR AT NEW YORK UNIVERSITY'S ALL-ALUMNI CENTENNIAL DINNER.

TWO THOUSAND ATTENDEES AWAIT HIM AT THE WALDORF-ASTORIA HOTEL.

AS THE LINDBERGHS SIT DOWN TO DINNER, BETTY GOW TALKS ON THE TELEPHONE TO HER BOYFRIEND, HENRY "RED" JOHNSEN.

REGRETABLY, SHE HAS TO BREAK THEIR DATE FOR THIS EVENING.

AFTER DINNER, HUSBAND AND WIFE RELAX IN THE IN THE LIVING ROOM.

AT ONE POINT, THE COLONEL HEARS A NOISE FROM OUTSIDE—A SHARP SOUND LIKE BREAKING WOOD.

NOTHING IS THOUGHT OF THIS, SINCE THE NIGHT IS UNUSUALLY WINDY.

AT 9:30 PM, THE LINDBERGHS CLIMB THE STAIRS TO THEIR BEDROOM.

SHORTLY THEREAFTER, CHARLES RETURNS DOWNSTAIRS TO WORK IN THE LIBRARY...

WHICH IS SITUATED DIRECTLY BELOW THE NURSERY.

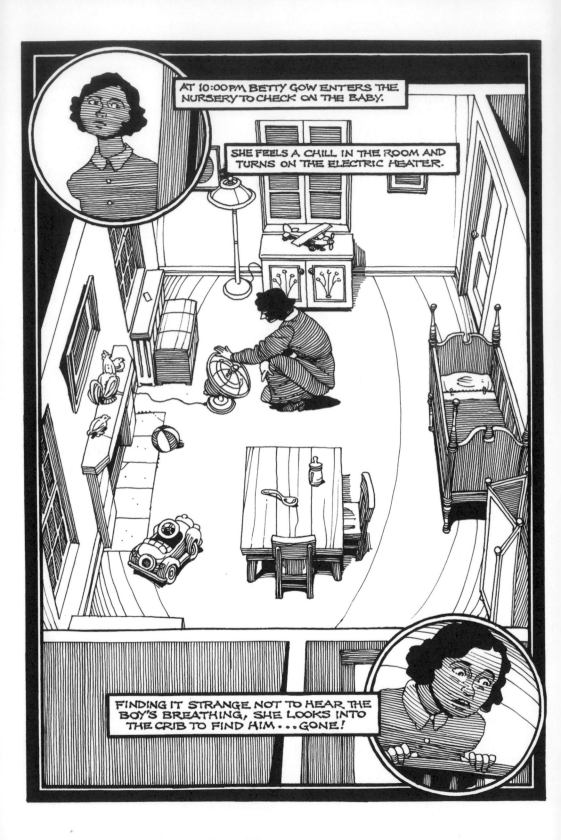

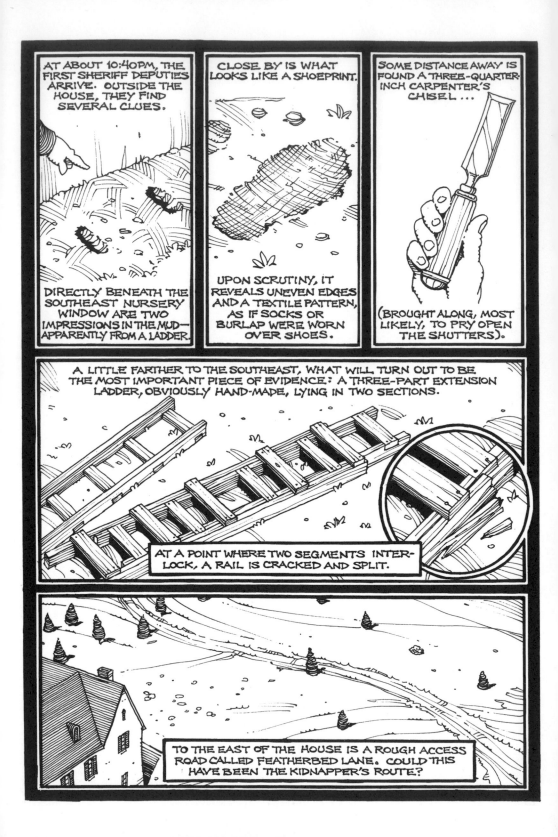

AT ABOUT 10:40PM, THE FIRST SHERIFF DEPUTIES ARRIVE. OUTSIDE THE HOUSE, THEY FIND SEVERAL CLUES.

DIRECTLY BENEATH THE SOUTHEAST NURSERY WINDOW ARE TWO IMPRESSIONS IN THE MUD—APPARENTLY FROM A LADDER.

CLOSE BY IS WHAT LOOKS LIKE A SHOEPRINT.

UPON SCRUTINY, IT REVEALS UNEVEN EDGES AND A TEXTILE PATTERN, AS IF SOCKS OR BURLAP WERE WORN OVER SHOES.

SOME DISTANCE AWAY IS FOUND A THREE-QUARTER-INCH CARPENTER'S CHISEL ...

(BROUGHT ALONG, MOST LIKELY, TO PRY OPEN THE SHUTTERS).

A LITTLE FARTHER TO THE SOUTHEAST, WHAT WILL TURN OUT TO BE THE MOST IMPORTANT PIECE OF EVIDENCE: A THREE-PART EXTENSION LADDER, OBVIOUSLY HAND-MADE, LYING IN TWO SECTIONS.

AT A POINT WHERE TWO SEGMENTS INTER-LOCK, A RAIL IS CRACKED AND SPLIT.

TO THE EAST OF THE HOUSE IS A ROUGH ACCESS ROAD CALLED FEATHERBED LANE. COULD THIS HAVE BEEN THE KIDNAPPER'S ROUTE?

BACK IN THE NURSERY, THE ENVELOPE FOUND BENEATH THE WINDOW IS CAREFULLY OPENED.

THE NOTE INSIDE, CRUDELY-WORDED IN AN UNCERTAIN HAND, LEAVES NO DOUBT AS TO THE NATURE OF THE CRIME.

"DEAR SIR, HAVE 50,000$ REDY..."

"AFTER 2-4 DAYS, WE WILL INFORM YOU WHERE TO DELIVER THE MONY..."

"WE WARN YOU FOR MAKING ANYDING PUBLIC OR FOR NOTIFY THE POLICE..." (UNFORTUNATELY THIS WARNING COMES TOO LATE.)

"THE CHILD IS IN GUT CARE..."

"INDICATION FOR ALL LETTERS ARE SINGNATURE AND 3 HOLES."

THE "SINGNATURE" IS ACTUALLY A HAND-STAMPED SYMBOL: TWO INTERLOCKING RINGS, A RED CIRCLE IN THE SPACE THEY OVERLAP, AND THREE HOLES PUNCHED INTO THE PAPER.

ALL AGREE THAT THIS APPEARS TO BE THE WORK OF A PERSON UNFAMILIAR WITH THE ENGLISH LANGUAGE.

WEDNESDAY, MARCH 2 — BY MID-MORNING, THE NEW JERSEY STATE POLICE HAVE SET UP A HEADQUARTERS INSIDE THE LINDBERGHS' GARAGE.

THE INVESTIGATION IS HEADED BY THE STATE POLICE SUPERINTENDENT, COL. H. NORMAN SCHWARZKOPF.

THE JUSTICE DEPARTMENT'S BUREAU OF INVESTIGATION, DIRECTED BY J. EDGAR HOOVER, OFFERS ITS ASSISTANCE...

ALTHOUGH AT THIS TIME, THERE IS LITTLE, BY LAW, THAT IT CAN DO.

BY MID-DAY, THE ROADS INTO HOPEWELL ARE JAMMED.

JOURNALISTS AND THE CURIOUS PUBLIC ROAM FREELY ABOUT THE LINDBERGH PROPERTY...

UNTIL THEY ARE AT LAST CLEARED AWAY BY THE POLICE.

FORENSIC EXAMINERS CAN FIND NO FINGERPRINTS ON THE RANSOM NOTE, THE LADDER, THE CHISEL, OR ANYPLACE IN THE NURSERY—NOT EVEN THOSE OF THE FAMILY.

THIS IS DEEMED STRANGE BY ALL.

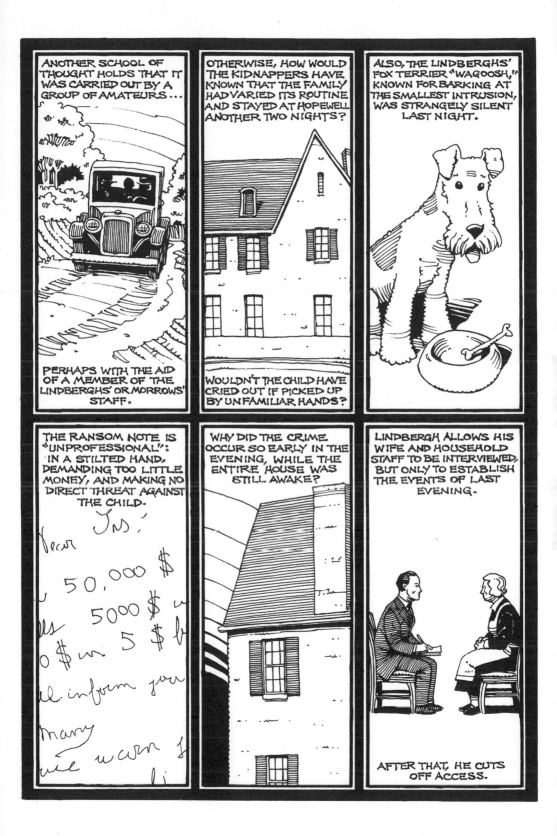

ANOTHER SCHOOL OF THOUGHT HOLDS THAT IT WAS CARRIED OUT BY A GROUP OF AMATEURS...

PERHAPS WITH THE AID OF A MEMBER OF THE LINDBERGHS' OR MORROWS' STAFF.

OTHERWISE, HOW WOULD THE KIDNAPPERS HAVE KNOWN THAT THE FAMILY HAD VARIED ITS ROUTINE AND STAYED AT HOPEWELL ANOTHER TWO NIGHTS?

WOULDN'T THE CHILD HAVE CRIED OUT IF PICKED UP BY UNFAMILIAR HANDS?

ALSO, THE LINDBERGHS' FOX TERRIER "WAGOOSH," KNOWN FOR BARKING AT THE SMALLEST INTRUSION, WAS STRANGELY SILENT LAST NIGHT.

THE RANSOM NOTE IS "UNPROFESSIONAL": IN A STILTED HAND, DEMANDING TOO LITTLE MONEY, AND MAKING NO DIRECT THREAT AGAINST THE CHILD.

WHY DID THE CRIME OCCUR SO EARLY IN THE EVENING, WHILE THE ENTIRE HOUSE WAS STILL AWAKE?

LINDBERGH ALLOWS HIS WIFE AND HOUSEHOLD STAFF TO BE INTERVIEWED, BUT ONLY TO ESTABLISH THE EVENTS OF LAST EVENING.

AFTER THAT, HE CUTS OFF ACCESS.

A PETTY CRIMINAL NAMED MORRIS "MICKEY" ROSNER, WHO CLAIMS TO HAVE CLOSE CONTACTS IN THE UNDERWORLD, OFFERS HIS SERVICES AS A GO-BETWEEN.

HE INTRODUCES TO COL. LINDBERGH TWO SYMPATHETIC BOOTLEGGERS: SALVATORE "SALVY" SPITALE AND IRVING BITZ.

THESE MEN ARE CERTAIN THAT, AMONG THEM, THEY CAN SECURE THE RELEASE OF THE CHILD.

FROM HIS CELL IN THE COOK COUNTY JAIL IN CHICAGO, THE NATION'S MOST NOTORIOUS GANGSTER OFFERS HIS HELP.

AL CAPONE SYMPATHIZES WITH THE YOUNG FAMILY AND IS CONFIDENT THAT HE CAN RETURN THEIR SON IF THE GOVERNMENT WOULD GRANT HIM HIS FREEDOM. THE OFFER IS RESPECTFULLY DECLINED.

SPITALE AND BITZ ESTABLISH A HEADQUARTERS IN A NEW YORK SPEAK-EASY.

THEY ARE GIVEN TRACINGS OF THE RANSOM NOTE TO AID THEM IN THEIR INQUIRIES.

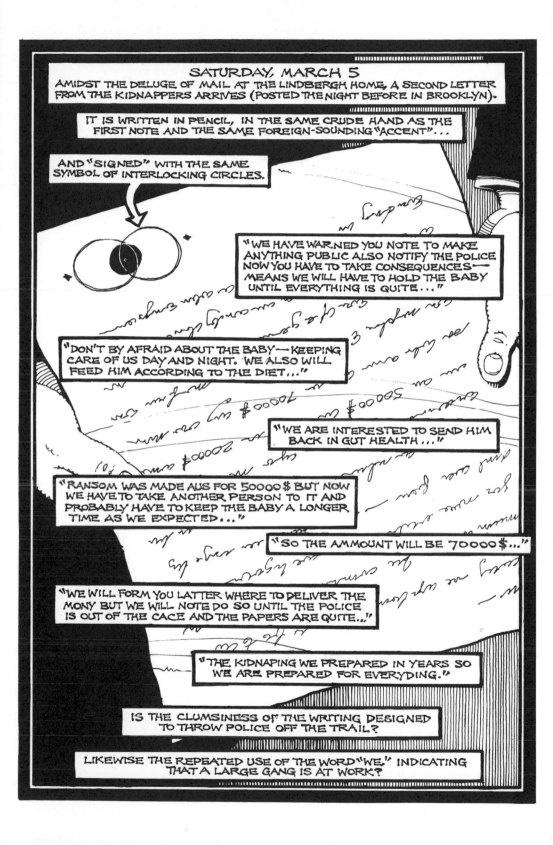

HE IS PARTICULARLY HORRIFIED TO LEARN THAT COL. LINDBERGH IS RELYING UPON PROFESSIONAL CRIMINALS TO FIND HIS CHILD.

HE HAS SUBMITTED A LETTER TO THE LOCAL DAILY NEWSPAPER, THE BRONX HOME NEWS, WHICH IS PUBLISHED IN TODAY'S EDITION.

IN IT, HE ADDRESSES THE KIDNAPPERS, OFFERING HIMSELF AS GO-BETWEEN.

TO SWEETEN THE OFFER, HE PLEDGES $1000 OF HIS OWN MONEY ADDED TO THE RANSOM.

WEDNESDAY, MARCH 9 AN ANSWER ARRIVES AT THE CONDONS' DOOR.

MR DOCTOR JOHN F. CONDON 2974 DECATUR AVENUE NEW YORK

CRUDELY LETTERED IN PENCIL, THE NOTE ACCEPTS CONDON AS GO-BETWEEN, WARNS HIM NOT TO NOTIFY THE PRESS OR THE POLICE AND INSTRUCTS HIM TO PLACE AN ANONYMOUS NOTICE IN THE NEW YORK AMERICAN WHEN THE MONEY IS READY.

A SEALED ENVELOPE ACCOMPANIES THE NOTE, THE CONTENTS OF WHICH, IT SAYS, ARE FOR COL. LINDBERGH'S EYES ONLY.

AS COL. LINDBERGH FOLLOWS THE RANSOM NOTES, POLICE FOLLOW DIFFERENT AVENUES OF INVESTIGATION.

OF PARTICULAR INTEREST IS THE BOYFRIEND OF BETTY GOW, FINN HENDRIK JOHNSEN, KNOWN AS HENRY "RED" JOHNSEN, A NORWEGIAN SEAMAN...

WHO WAS TOLD BY HER ON THE NIGHT OF THE KIDNAPPING THAT THE LINDBERGHS WOULD BE REMAINING AT HOPEWELL.

IT TURNS OUT THAT HE HAS WORKED ON SEVERAL LUXURY YACHTS AND IS IN THE UNITED STATES ILLEGALLY...

AND HE DRIVES A GREEN CAR.

IN THIS CAR IS FOUND AN EMPTY MILK BOTTLE. HE EXPLAINS THAT HE OFTEN DRINKS MILK WHILE DRIVING.

HIS WHEREABOUTS UPON THE NIGHT IN QUESTION— AT HIS BROTHER'S HOUSE IN WEST HARTFORD, CONNECTICUT—SEEM TO BE FIRMLY ESTABLISHED.

THURSDAY, MARCH 10
NEWARK POLICE INTERVIEW THE 29-PERSON STAFF OF NEXT DAY HILL.

ALL OF THEM ARE FOUND TO BE CO-OPERATIVE, EXCEPT FOR MISS VIOLET SHARPE, AN ENGLISH WOMAN, AGE 28, EMPLOYED AS A HOUSEMAID.

SHE IS SAID TO BE ROMANTICALLY INVOLVED WITH THE HEAD BUTLER, SEPTIMUS BANKS.

FOR HER INTERVIEW, SHE APPEARS NERVOUS AND INDIGNANT: WHY SHOULD THE POLICE BE PRYING INTO HER PRIVATE LIFE?

AS TO HER ACTIVITIES ON THE EVENING OF MARCH 1, SHE IS AT FIRST EVASIVE.

SHE THEN RELATES AN IMPLAUSIBLE STORY ABOUT GOING OUT TO A PICTURE SHOW WITH A GROUP OF PEOPLE SHE HAD ONLY MET THAT DAY.

NO, SHE COULD NOT RECALL WHAT PICTURE... OR THE NAMES OF THE PEOPLE SHE WAS WITH.

FRIDAY, MARCH 11
A CLASSIFIED AD APPEARS IN THE NEW YORK AMERICAN.

I ACCEPT.
MONEY IS READY.
JAFSIE.

THE CODE NAME "JAFSIE" IS MADE UP OF JOHN F. CONDON'S INITIALS.

A REPLY ARRIVES THIS VERY DAY IN THE FORM OF A TELEPHONE CALL. A GUTTURAL VOICE INSTRUCTS DR. CONDON TO REMAIN AT HOME EVERY NIGHT, 6PM TO MIDNIGHT, AND SOON HE WILL RECEIVE ANOTHER NOTE. FOLLOW THE NOTE'S INSTRUCTIONS PRECISELY.

DURING THIS CONVERSATION, CONDON HEARS ANOTHER VOICE IN THE BACKGROUND. TO HIM, IT SOUNDS ITALIAN: "STATTI CITTO!" ("SHUT UP!")

HENRY BRECKINRIDGE TAKES UP RESIDENCE AT THE CONDONS' HOME, AWAITING THE KIDNAPPERS' NEXT MOVE. IT COMES ON THE EVENING OF:
SATURDAY, MARCH 12.

AT 8:30 PM, A TAXICAB DRIVER ARRIVES AT THE HOUSE AND HANDS OVER AN ENVELOPE.

IT WAS GIVEN HIM, HE SAYS, BY A SHADOWY MAN ON THE STREET.

THE NOTE DIRECTS CONDON TO AN ABANDONED HOT DOG STAND ON JEROME AVENUE. HE IS DRIVEN THERE BY HIS FRIEND AL REICH.

ON THE PORCH, HE FINDS ANOTHER NOTE.

IT DIRECTS HIM FURTHER ALONG JEROME AVENUE, TO 233RD ST. AND THE ENTRANCE TO WOODLAWN CEMETERY.

233 RD ST.

VAN CORTLANDT PARK

WOODLAWN CEMETERY

JEROME AVE.

(HE FEELS HE MUST PROCEED TO THIS MEETING, DESPITE THE FACT THAT THE MONEY IS NOT YET READY AND THE BOX FOR IT NOT YET CONSTRUCTED.)

SUNDAY, MARCH 13

POLICE BRING TO THE LINDBERGH HOME DR. ERASMUS M. HUDSON, PHYSICIAN AND FINGERPRINT EXPERT, IN THE HOPE THAT HE CAN FIND PRINTS WHERE THE POLICE TECHNICIAN DID NOT.

DR. HUDSON SPRAYS THE BABY'S TOYS WITH A FINE MIST OF SILVER NITRATE, AND THEN EXPOSES THEM TO THE SUN.

SEVERAL HUNDRED PARTIAL PRINTS EMERGE, OF WHICH THIRTEEN ARE IDENTIFIABLE AS THOSE OF THE CHILD.

THE KIDNAP LADDER UNDERGOES THE SAME PROCESS. OVER 500 SMUDGES ARE FOUND, OF WHICH 200 ARE USABLE PRINTS...

ATTESTING TO THE NUMBER OF OFFICIALS WHO HAVE SULLIED THIS IMPORTANT ITEM OF EVIDENCE.

PAINSTAKING SCRUTINY OF THE NURSERY REVEALS NO PRINTS FROM THE LINDBERGHS OR THEIR HOUSEHOLD STAFF.

THE SURFACES OF THE ROOM, IN FACT, APPEAR TO HAVE BEEN WIPED CLEAN.

TUESDAY, MARCH 15

ON THIS DAY, A PARCEL ARRIVES AT THE CONDON HOME. HENRY BRECKINRIDGE HURRIES THERE TO OPEN IT.

INSIDE IS A BABY'S SLEEPING SUIT — UNDOUBTEDLY THE "TOKEN" PROMISED BY THE MAN IN THE CEMETERY.

COL. LINDBERGH — IN DISGUISE — ARRIVES EARLY THE NEXT MORNING.

THE GARMENT HAS APPARENTLY BEEN LAUNDERED, BUT HE THINKS THAT, IN ALL PROBABILITY, IT IS HIS SON'S.

A NOTE IS ENCLOSED WITH THE SUIT DEMANDING THAT AN AD BE PLACED IN THE NEW YORK AMERICAN WHEN THE MONEY IS READY. THEN...

"AFTER 8 HOURS WE HAVE THE MONY RECEIVED, WE WILL NOTIFY YOU WHERE TO FIND THE BABY. IF THERE IS ANY TRAPP, YOU WILL BE RESPONSIBLE FOR WHAT FOLLOWS"

WEDNESDAY, MARCH 16
A SECOND CLASSIFIED AD RUNS IN THE NEW YORK AMERICAN.

I ACCEPT
MONEY IS READY.
JOHN, YOUR PACKAGE
IS DELIVERED AND
IS OK. DIRECT ME.
JAFSIE

DURING THIS TIME, COL. LINDBERGH HAS BEEN SELLING STOCKS AND BONDS, CLOSING OUT ACCOUNTS TO ACCUMULATE THE NECESSARY CASH.

A WOODEN BOX, BUILT TO THE KIDNAPPERS' SPECIFICATIONS, HAS BEEN COMPLETED BY A LOCAL CABINETMAKER.

MONDAY, MARCH 21
A LETTER IS AT LAST DELIVERED TO DR. CONDON...

"YOU AND MR. LINDBERGH KNOW OUR PROGRAM. IF YOU DON'T ACCEPT DEN WE WILL WAIT UNTIL YOU AGREE WITH OUR DEAL."

"WE WILL TELL YOU AGAIN: THIS KIDNAPPING CACE WAS PREPARED FOR A YEAR ALREADY SO THE POLICE WON'T HAVE ANY LUCK TO FIND US OR THE CHILD."

DID THE KIDNAPPERS MISS LAST WEEK'S AD? THEY SEEM TO THINK THAT LINDBERGH DOES NOT ACCEPT THEIR TERMS.

CONDON AND BRECKINRIDGE COMPOSE ANOTHER AD...
IT RUNS IN THE NEW YORK AMERICAN AND THE BRONX HOME NEWS FOR THREE CONSECUTIVE DAYS.

THANKS.
THAT LITTLE PACKAGE YOU SENT ME WAS IMMEDIATELY DELIVERED AND ACCEPTED AS THE REAL ARTICLE. SEE MY POSITION. OVER FIFTY YEARS IN BUSINESS AND CAN I PAY WITHOUT SEEING THE GOODS? COMMON SENSE MAKES ME TRUST YOU. CASE UNDERSTAND MY
JAFSIE.

THE CASH IS COLLECTED INTO THE DENOMINATIONS DEMANDED BY THE KIDNAPPERS.

ALSO IN ACCORDANCE WITH THEIR WISHES, COL. LINDBERGH REFUSES TO HAVE THE BILLS MARKED IN ANY WAY. HE IS CONVINCED, HOWEVER, BY AGENTS OF THE BUREAU OF INVESTIGATION TO HAVE THE SERIAL NUMBERS RECORDED.

ALSO AT THIS TIME, A NEW AVENUE TO THE KIDNAPPERS EMERGES, IN THE PERSON OF JOHN H. CURTIS, AGE 43, A WEALTHY AND RESPECTED BOAT-BUILDER OF NORFOLK, VIRGINIA.

TUESDAY, MARCH 22.

HE COMES TO THE LINDBERGH ESTATE IN THE COMPANY OF TWO LIKEWISE RESPECTABLE CITIZENS: ADMIRAL GUY BURRAGE AND THE REVEREND HAROLD DOBSON-PEACOCK, BOTH OF THEM ACQUAINTANCES OF THE LINDBERGH AND MORROW FAMILIES.

CURTIS RELATES TO COL. LINDBERGH A STRANGE AND COMPELLING STORY...

IT SEEMS THAT, BACK ON MARCH 9, HE WAS ACCOSTED BY A MYSTERIOUS MAN CALLING HIMSELF "SAM."

THE MAN EXPLAINED THAT HE WAS AN ASSOCIATE OF THE SCANDINAVIAN GANG THAT HAD STOLEN THE LINDBERGH BABY...

AND THAT THEY HAD CHOSEN CURTIS TO ACT AS A CONDUIT TO COL. LINDBERGH.

CURTIS WAS SHOCKED AND SPENT A NIGHT OF INDECISION.

THE NEXT MORNING, HE TOLD "SAM" THAT HE WOULD ACCEPT THE TASK.

COL. LINDBERGH HAS DOUBTS ABOUT THE STORY. COULD THESE BE THE SAME PEOPLE WHO CONTACTED DR. CONDON?

STILL, HE DOES NOT WANT TO CLOSE OFF ANY POSSIBILITY. HE ASKS CURTIS TO DEMAND FROM "SAM" PROOF THAT THE CHILD IS WELL—SUCH AS A RECENT PHOTOGRAPH.

AS THE MONTH OF MARCH CLOSES, YET A THIRD CONNECTION TO THE KIDNAPPERS IS IN PLAY...

INITIATED BY GASTON B. MEANS, AGE 53, A FORMER PRIVATE DETECTIVE AND AGENT FOR THE BUREAU OF INVESTIGATION.

THOUGH OF UNSAVORY REPUTATION, HE HAS MANAGED TO GAIN THE TRUST OF THE WEALTHY WASHINGTON HOSTESS EVALYN WALSH McLEAN, A FRIEND OF THE LINDBERGHS.

MEANS HAS TOLD HER OF HOW, BEFORE THE CRIME, HE WAS APPROACHED BY THE KIDNAP GANG AND ASKED TO JOIN THEM.

HE REFUSED, BUT WAS NOW APPOINTED TO HANDLE THE NEGOTIATIONS.

WITH COL. LINDBERGH'S APPROVAL, MRS. McLEAN HAS HANDED OVER $50,000 OF HER OWN MONEY TO PAY THE RANSOM.

THIS IS SHORTLY RAISED TO $100,000.

MEANS HAS COLLECTED THE FULL SUM FROM HER, IN CASH — PLUS FURTHER AMOUNTS FOR HIS EXPENSES.

MRS. McLEAN NOW WAITS PATIENTLY WHILE HE GIVES HER EXCUSE AFTER EXCUSE AS TO WHY THE EXCHANGE CANNOT BE MADE.

FRIDAY, APRIL 1
WHILE WALKING ABOUT THE ESTATE, BETTY GOW AND ELSIE WHATELEY MAKE A SURPRISING DISCOVERY:

ONE OF THE BABY'S THUMB-GUARDS, LYING ALONG THE EDGE OF THE GRAVEL DRIVEWAY LEADING TO THE HOUSE.

DOES THIS MEAN THAT THE KIDNAPPERS USED THE MAIN DRIVEWAY AS THEIR ESCAPE ROUTE, RATHER THAN THE WOODS TO THE EAST?

FURTHER, COULD THE THUMB-GUARD HAVE LAIN THERE UNNOTICED FOR SO LONG BESIDE THE HEAVILY-TRAVELLED DRIVEWAY?

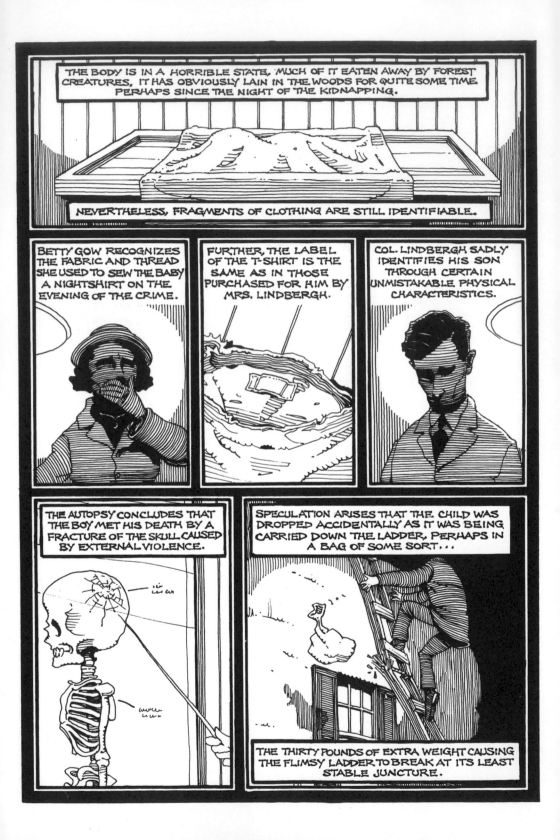

PART FOUR
THE MANHUNT

THE SHOCKING NEWS SPREADS THROUGHOUT THE WORLD.
THE CASE OF KIDNAPPING IS NOW ONE OF MURDER.

COL. LINDBERGH NOW RELINQUISHES HIS LEADING ROLE IN THE
INVESTIGATION. HE AND HIS WIFE — NOW PREGNANT WITH
THEIR SECOND CHILD — GO INTO DEEP SECLUSION.

THE MANHUNT IS NOW TAKEN UP IN EARNEST BY THE
NEW JERSEY STATE POLICE, COMMANDED BY COL.
H. NORMAN SCHWARZKOPF, ASSISTED BY LOCAL
AGENCIES OF A SEVERAL-STATE AREA.

TUESDAY, MAY 17
UNDER PROMPTING BY THE POLICE, JOHN H. CURTIS CONFESSES THAT HIS ENTIRE SCENARIO WAS A HOAX.

HE WILL EVENTUALLY BE TRIED FOR FRAUD.

GASTON MEANS WILL ALSO BE PUT ON TRIAL FOR HIS DEVIOUS EXTORTION OF MONEY FROM MRS. EVALYN McLEAN.

THE LADY WILL SEE ONLY A FRACTION OF IT RETURNED TO HER.

THE UNFORTUNATE VIOLET SHARPE COMES TO A BAD END.

THURSDAY, JUNE 9
SHE IDENTIFIES A PHOTOGRAPH OF A TAXI-SERVICE OPERATOR NAMED ERNEST BRINKERT AS THE MAN WITH WHOM SHE WENT TO THE ROADHOUSE.

SHE THEN BECOMES HYSTERICAL AND REFUSES TO ANSWER ANY FURTHER QUESTIONS.

FRIDAY, JUNE 10
VIOLET SHARPE COMMITS SUICIDE BY SWALLOWING A MIXTURE OF WATER AND CYANIDE CHLORIDE, IN THE FORM OF A POWDERED SILVER POLISH.

POLICE PLAN TO RETURN THE NEXT DAY, BUT BEFORE THEY CAN...

HER ACTIVITIES ON THE NIGHT OF THE KIDNAPPING ARE LATER FOUND TO HAVE BEEN PERFECTLY INNOCENT, LEAVING ANOTHER MYSTERY AMONG THE MANY IN THIS CASE.

DURING THE SUMMER OF 1932, THE LINDBERGHS LEAVE THE HOUSE AT HOPEWELL, NEVER TO RESIDE THERE AGAIN.

WEDNESDAY, JUNE 22 CONGRESS PASSES THE "LINDBERGH LAW," MAKING KIDNAPPING A FEDERAL CRIME — ALTHOUGH TOO LATE TO HELP IN THIS CASE.

TUESDAY, AUGUST 16 IN NEW YORK CITY, ANNE LINDBERGH GIVES BIRTH TO THEIR SECOND CHILD, A SON THEY NAME JON.

THE WRITTEN MESSAGES FROM THE KIDNAPPER — THIRTEEN IN ALL — HAVE BEEN PLACED UNDER THE SCRUTINY OF SEVERAL HANDWRITING EXPERTS...

INCLUDING PROF. ALBERT OSBORNE, CALLED THE DEAN OF AMERICAN FORENSIC GRAPHOLOGISTS.

THEIR CONSENSUS IS THAT THE NOTES WERE ALL WRITTEN BY THE SAME HAND. THE MISSPELLINGS AND GRAMMATICAL ANOMALIES ARE CONSISTENT THROUGHOUT.

THE WRITER IS MOST LIKELY GERMAN.

THE MESSAGES ARE ALSO STUDIED BY A NEW YORK PSYCHIATRIST, DR. DUDLEY SCHOENFELD.

HIS CONCLUSIONS:

THE KIDNAPPER IS A MAN WITH DELUSIONS OF OMNIPOTENCE, WHO NEVERTHELESS OCCUPIES A LOW STATION IN LIFE...

AND BLAMES OTHERS FOR HIS FAILURES AND INADEQUACIES.

THIS MAN FOCUSES ALL OF HIS ANGER AND FRUSTRATION ON COL. LINDBERGH, THE UNIVERSALLY ADORED HERO, AND SCHEMES TO OUTSMART AND HUMILIATE HIM.

SUCH A MAN WOULD WORK ALONE AND TAKE GREAT PERSONAL RISKS.

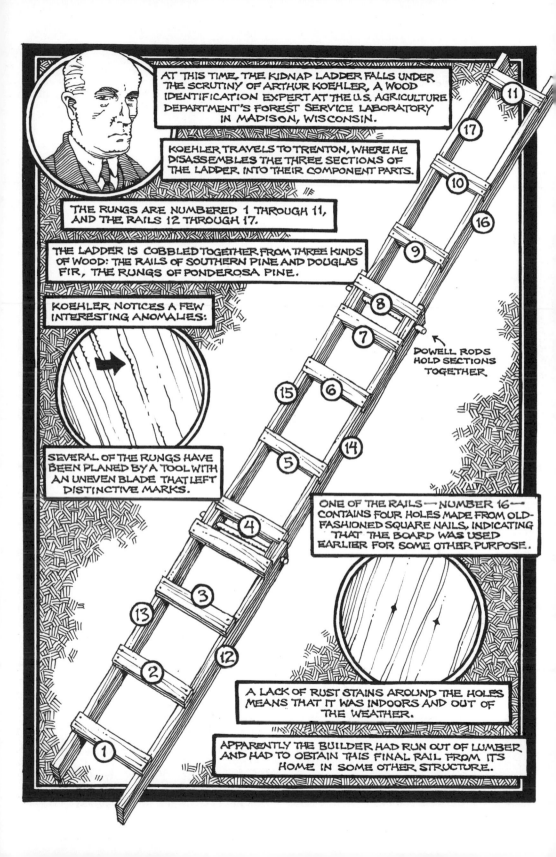

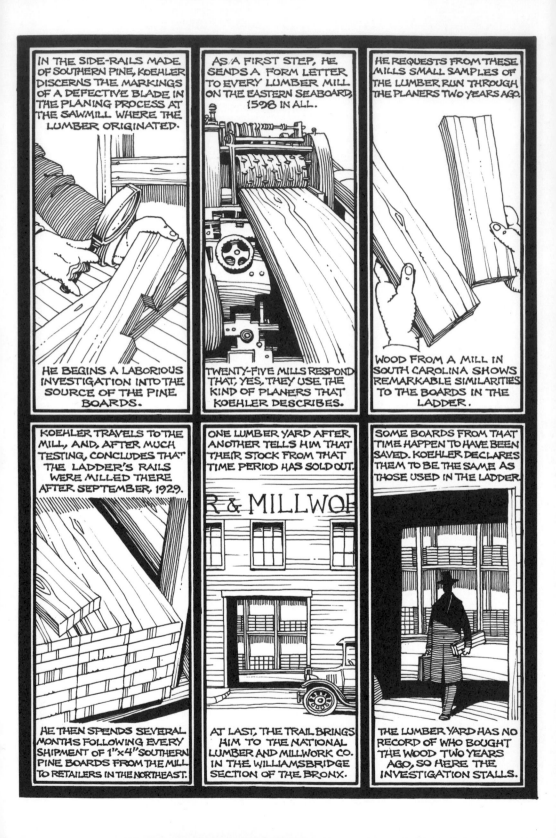

IN THE SIDE-RAILS MADE OF SOUTHERN PINE, KOEHLER DISCERNS THE MARKINGS OF A DEFECTIVE BLADE IN THE PLANING PROCESS AT THE SAWMILL WHERE THE LUMBER ORIGINATED.

HE BEGINS A LABORIOUS INVESTIGATION INTO THE SOURCE OF THE PINE BOARDS.

AS A FIRST STEP, HE SENDS A FORM LETTER TO EVERY LUMBER MILL ON THE EASTERN SEABOARD, 1598 IN ALL.

TWENTY-FIVE MILLS RESPOND THAT, YES, THEY USE THE KIND OF PLANERS THAT KOEHLER DESCRIBES.

HE REQUESTS FROM THESE MILLS SMALL SAMPLES OF THE LUMBER RUN THROUGH THE PLANERS TWO YEARS AGO.

WOOD FROM A MILL IN SOUTH CAROLINA SHOWS REMARKABLE SIMILARITIES TO THE BOARDS IN THE LADDER.

KOEHLER TRAVELS TO THE MILL, AND, AFTER MUCH TESTING, CONCLUDES THAT THE LADDER'S RAILS WERE MILLED THERE AFTER SEPTEMBER, 1929.

HE THEN SPENDS SEVERAL MONTHS FOLLOWING EVERY SHIPMENT OF 1"x4" SOUTHERN PINE BOARDS FROM THE MILL TO RETAILERS IN THE NORTHEAST.

ONE LUMBER YARD AFTER ANOTHER TELLS HIM THAT THEIR STOCK FROM THAT TIME PERIOD HAS SOLD OUT.

R & MILLWOR

AT LAST, THE TRAIL BRINGS HIM TO THE NATIONAL LUMBER AND MILLWORK CO. IN THE WILLIAMSBRIDGE SECTION OF THE BRONX.

SOME BOARDS FROM THAT TIME HAPPEN TO HAVE BEEN SAVED. KOEHLER DECLARES THEM TO BE THE SAME AS THOSE USED IN THE LADDER.

THE LUMBER YARD HAS NO RECORD OF WHO BOUGHT THE WOOD TWO YEARS AGO, SO HERE THE INVESTIGATION STALLS.

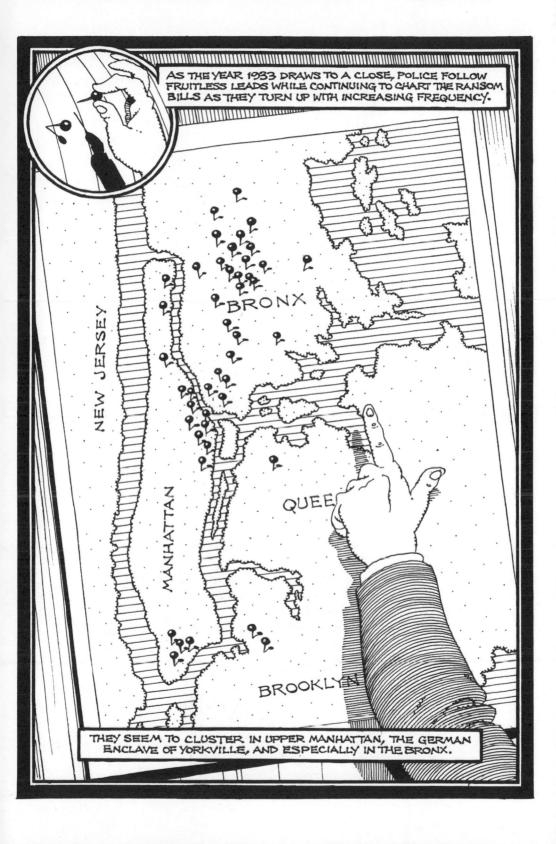

PART FIVE
THE ACCUSED

WEDNESDAY, SEPTEMBER 19, 1934
NEW YORK POLICE HAVE TRACED THE OWNER OF THE CAR TO A
HOUSE AT 1279 E. 222ND STREET IN THE BRONX.

THE UPPER FLOOR IS THE HOME OF
RICHARD HAUPTMANN, AGE 35, A CARPENTER BY TRADE.

OFFICERS SURROUND THE HOUSE IN THE EARLY MORNING, WATCHING
FOR ANY MOVEMENT.

IN THE AFTERNOON, HAUPTMANN IS BROUGHT DOWNTOWN TO THE NYPD'S 2ND PRECINCT STATION AT 130 GREENWICH STREET FOR A THOROUGH INTERROGATION.

THIS WILL INCLUDE A CERTAIN AMOUNT OF PHYSICAL "PERSUASION."

NEVERTHELESS, THE MAN FORCEFULLY DENIES HAVING HAD ANY PART IN EITHER THE KIDNAPPING OR THE EXTORTION OF THE RANSOM MONEY.

HIS FULL NAME IS: BRUNO RICHARD HAUPTMANN.

HE IS AN IMMIGRANT FROM GERMANY AND SPEAKS WITH A HEAVY ACCENT.

HE PREFERS TO BE CALLED RICHARD OR DICK.

HE SUBMITS SAMPLES OF HIS HANDWRITING IN A TEST DEVISED BY ALBERT S. OSBORNE.

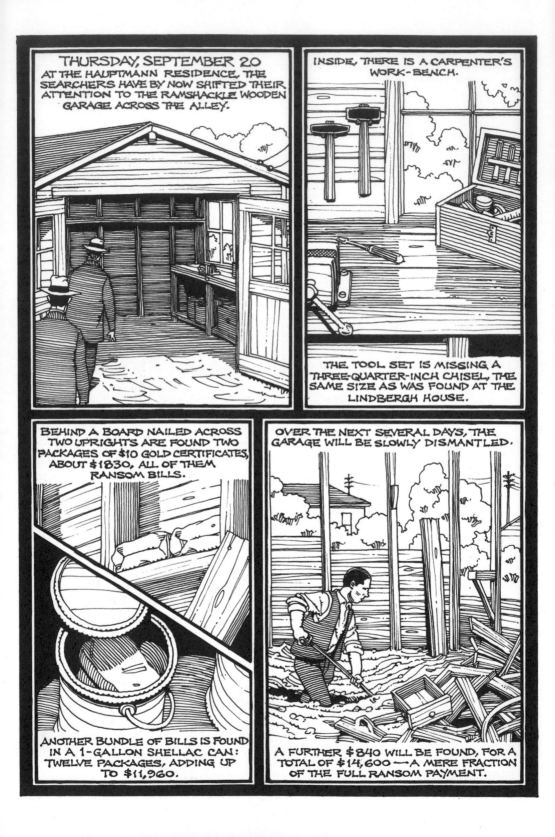

THURSDAY, SEPTEMBER 20
AT THE HAUPTMANN RESIDENCE, THE SEARCHERS HAVE BY NOW SHIFTED THEIR ATTENTION TO THE RAMSHACKLE WOODEN GARAGE ACROSS THE ALLEY.

INSIDE, THERE IS A CARPENTER'S WORK-BENCH.

THE TOOL SET IS MISSING A THREE-QUARTER-INCH CHISEL, THE SAME SIZE AS WAS FOUND AT THE LINDBERGH HOUSE.

BEHIND A BOARD NAILED ACROSS TWO UPRIGHTS ARE FOUND TWO PACKAGES OF $10 GOLD CERTIFICATES, ABOUT $1830, ALL OF THEM RANSOM BILLS.

ANOTHER BUNDLE OF BILLS IS FOUND IN A 1-GALLON SHELLAC CAN: TWELVE PACKAGES, ADDING UP TO $11,960.

OVER THE NEXT SEVERAL DAYS, THE GARAGE WILL BE SLOWLY DISMANTLED.

A FURTHER $840 WILL BE FOUND, FOR A TOTAL OF $14,600 — A MERE FRACTION OF THE FULL RANSOM PAYMENT.

AT THE PRECINCT HOUSE, AFTER NEARLY 24 HOURS OF "GRILLING," HAUPTMANN CONTINUES TO MAINTAIN HIS INNOCENCE.

HE HAS GIVEN THE POLICE HIS ALIBIS FOR THREE IMPORTANT DATES...

NO HIRING TODAY

ON TUESDAY, MARCH 1, 1932, THE DAY OF THE KIDNAPPING, HE WAS IN MANHATTAN, SEARCHING FOR WORK AT VARIOUS BUILDING SITES.

AT 7:00 PM, HE MET HIS WIFE AT HER PLACE OF EMPLOYMENT, FREDERICK'S BAKERY IN THE BRONX.

THEY ATE DINNER THERE AND THEN WENT HOME TO BED.

ON SATURDAY, APRIL 2, 1932, THE NIGHT OF THE RANSOM PAYMENT, HE WAS AT HOME ENJOYING A MUSICAL EVENING WITH HIS FRIEND HANS KLOPPENBURG.

THEY GET TOGETHER ON THE FIRST SATURDAY OF EVERY MONTH TO PLAY AND SING THEIR FAVORITE GERMAN SONGS.

SUNDAY, NOVEMBER 26, 1933, THE NIGHT THE MYSTERIOUS PATRON TOSSED THE FOLDED BILL TO THE THEATRE CASHIER, HAPPENED TO HAVE BEEN HAUPTMANN'S BIRTHDAY.

HE CELEBRATED AT HOME WITH HIS WIFE AND A FEW FRIENDS.

HOW DID HAUPTMANN SUPPORT HIS FAMILY, HE IS ASKED, SINCE HE QUIT HIS JOB, IN APRIL OF 1932, AT THE MAJESTIC APARTMENTS IN MANHATTAN?

HOW DID HE AFFORD SUCH RECENT INDULGENCES AS A NEW VICTROLA AND A TRIP TO GERMANY FOR HIS WIFE?

THE PRISONER EXPLAINS THAT HE BEGAN TO INVEST IN THE STOCK MARKET AROUND THAT TIME...

STREET JOURNAL

AND HAD DONE SO WELL THAT THE FAMILY COULD LIVE DECENTLY ON THE EARNINGS.

HOW DID HAUPTMANN COME INTO POSSESSION OF SO MUCH OF THE LINDBERGH RANSOM MONEY?

HE SAYS THAT HE FOUND IT AMONG SEVERAL BOXES OF PERSONAL ITEMS LEFT TO HIM BY HIS FRIEND AND BUSINESS PARTNER ISADOR FISCH.

FISCH

HE AND FISCH ENGAGED IN SEVERAL VENTURES TOGETHER, INCLUDING THE FUR-IMPORTING ENTERPRISE.

BUT FISCH, SUFFERING FROM TUBERCULOSIS, RETURNED TO GERMANY IN DECEMBER OF 1933, AND DIED IN LIEPZIG ON MARCH 29, 1934.

ONE OF THE BOXES WAS STORED BY HAUPTMANN ON THE TOP SHELF OF A KITCHEN CLOSET...

UNTIL ONE DAY, DURING A HEAVY RAIN, A LEAK IN THE ROOF SOAKED THE CONTAINER.

INSIDE, HE WAS SHOCKED TO FIND STACKS AND STACKS OF CASH!

IN AUGUST OF 1934, HE DECIDED THAT HE WAS ENTITLED TO SPEND SOME OF THE MONEY, SINCE FISCH LEFT THE COUNTRY OWING HIM $7000.

DESPITE HIS DENIALS, THE PRISONER IS CHARGED THIS AFTERNOON WITH EXTORTION.

BUT COL. SCHWARZKOPF BELIEVES THAT THE STATE OF NEW JERSEY WILL BE ABLE TO NAB HIM FOR THE GREATER CRIME.

MONDAY, SEPTEMBER 24 OFFICERS STILL SEARCHING THE HAUPTMANN HOME COME ACROSS A NEW PIECE OF EVIDENCE.

THE ADDRESS AND TELEPHONE NUMBER OF JOHN F. CONDON ARE FOUND WRITTEN IN PENCIL ON THE DOOR FRAME INSIDE A BEDROOM CLOSET; ALSO THE SERIAL NUMBERS OF TWO OF THE RANSOM BILLS.

HAUPTMANN RESPONDS THAT HE DOESN'T RECALL HAVING WRITTEN THE NUMBERS... BUT HE MIGHT HAVE, SINCE HE WAS FOLLOWING THE CASE AT THE TIME.

NYC POLICE
12822
9 2 34

WEDNESDAY, SEPTEMBER 26
HAUPTMANN IS INDICTED FOR EXTORTION BY A BRONX GRAND JURY. LATER IN THE DAY, OFFICERS OF THE NEW JERSEY STATE POLICE, WHILE SEARCHING THE ATTIC OF THE PRISONER'S HOME, FIND A PUZZLING DISCREPANCY

ONE OF THE FLOOR-BOARDS IS MISSING... APPARENTLY SAWN AWAY.

SEVERAL OFFICERS HAVE LOOKED HERE ALREADY, BUT NONE NOTICED THIS GAP IN THE FLOOR. IS IT SIGNIFICANT?

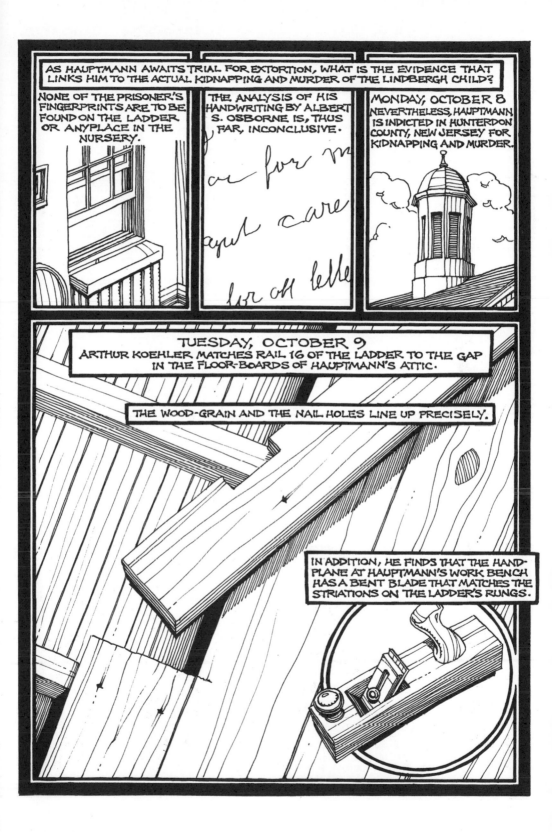

AS HAUPTMANN AWAITS TRIAL FOR EXTORTION, WHAT IS THE EVIDENCE THAT LINKS HIM TO THE ACTUAL KIDNAPPING AND MURDER OF THE LINDBERGH CHILD?

NONE OF THE PRISONER'S FINGERPRINTS ARE TO BE FOUND ON THE LADDER OR ANYPLACE IN THE NURSERY.

THE ANALYSIS OF HIS HANDWRITING BY ALBERT S. OSBORNE IS, THUS FAR, INCONCLUSIVE.

MONDAY, OCTOBER 8 NEVERTHELESS, HAUPTMANN IS INDICTED IN HUNTERDON COUNTY, NEW JERSEY FOR KIDNAPPING AND MURDER.

TUESDAY, OCTOBER 9 ARTHUR KOEHLER MATCHES RAIL 16 OF THE LADDER TO THE GAP IN THE FLOOR-BOARDS OF HAUPTMANN'S ATTIC.

THE WOOD-GRAIN AND THE NAIL HOLES LINE UP PRECISELY.

IN ADDITION, HE FINDS THAT THE HAND-PLANE AT HAUPTMANN'S WORK BENCH HAS A BENT BLADE THAT MATCHES THE STRIATIONS ON THE LADDER'S RUNGS.

TUESDAY, OCTOBER 16
THE NEW YORK EXTORTION CHARGES ARE SET ASIDE, AND HAUPTMANN IS TRANSPORTED TO NEW JERSEY, WHERE HE RESIDES IN THE HUNTERDON COUNTY JAIL IN FLEMINGTON.

JERSEY

VANIA

⊙ FLEMINGTON

⊙ HOPEWELL

FRIDAY, NOVEMBER 2
HE ACQUIRES A HIGH-PROFILE DEFENCE ATTORNEY IN THE PERSON OF THE FLAMBOYANT VETERAN EDWARD J. REILLY OF BROOKLYN...

WHOSE SERVICES ARE PAID FOR BY WILLIAM RANDOLPH HEARST'S NEW YORK JOURNAL — IN EXCHANGE FOR MRS. HAUPTMANN'S EXCLUSIVE STORY.

REILLY WILL BE ASSISTED BY THREE NEW YORK ATTORNEYS: C. LLOYD FISHER, FREDERICK A. POPE AND EGBERT ROSECRANS.

THE REMAINDER OF THE DEFENSE CASE CONSISTS OF SEVERAL DUBIOUS WITNESSES AND "EXPERTS."

THESE INCLUDE CHRISTIAN AND KATIE FREDERICKSON, PROPRIETORS OF FREDERICKSON'S BAKERY, AND CERTAIN OF THEIR CUSTOMERS, WHO CLAIM TO HAVE SEEN HAUPTMANN THERE ON THE EVENING OF MARCH 1, 1932.

TWO GENTLEMEN, BEN LUPICA AND WILLIAM BOLMER, WERE IN THE VICINITY OF THE LINDBERGH ESTATE ON THAT NIGHT.

THEY EACH DESCRIBE HAVING SEEN A MYSTERIOUS CAR CONTAINING A MAKESHIFT-LOOKING LADDER, AND DRIVEN BY A MAN WHO LOOKED NOTHING LIKE THE DEFENDANT.

FRIENDS OF THE HAUPTMANNS, INCLUDING HANS KLOPPENBURG AND GRETA HENKEL TESTIFY AS TO THE DEFENDANT'S GOOD CHARACTER...

AND REPORT HAVING SEEN ISADOR FISCH IN HIS COMPANY UPON SEVERAL OCCASIONS.

THE DEFENSE CALLS ITS SINGLE HANDWRITING AUTHORITY IN THE PERSON OF JOHN TRENDLEY.

HE INSISTS THAT HAUPTMANN DID NOT WRITE THE RANSOM NOTES, DISPLAYING SEVERAL POINTS OF DISSIMILARITY.

LIKEWISE A LONE "WOOD EXPERT," CHARLES DE BISSCHOP, A LUMBERMAN, NURSERYMAN AND GENERAL CONTRACTOR.

HE MAINTAINS THAT RAIL 16 DOES NOT MATCH THE FLOOR-BOARD IN HAUPTMANN'S ATTIC.

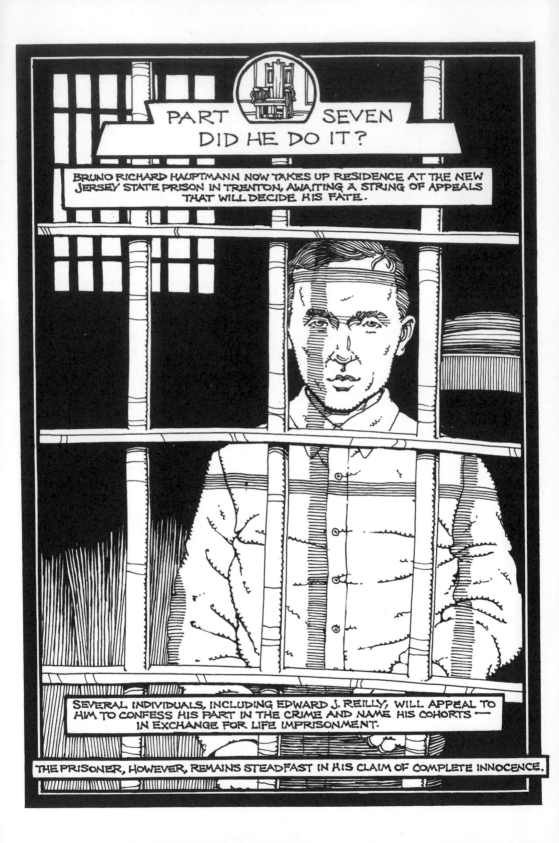

PART SEVEN
DID HE DO IT?

BRUNO RICHARD HAUPTMANN NOW TAKES UP RESIDENCE AT THE NEW JERSEY STATE PRISON IN TRENTON, AWAITING A STRING OF APPEALS THAT WILL DECIDE HIS FATE.

SEVERAL INDIVIDUALS, INCLUDING EDWARD J. REILLY, WILL APPEAL TO HIM TO CONFESS HIS PART IN THE CRIME AND NAME HIS COHORTS — IN EXCHANGE FOR LIFE IMPRISONMENT.

THE PRISONER, HOWEVER, REMAINS STEADFAST IN HIS CLAIM OF COMPLETE INNOCENCE.

OF THE DEFENSE TEAM, ONLY C. LLOYD FISHER REMAINS LOYAL TO THE CONVICTED MAN. HE PREPARES A BRIEF CITING INSTANCES OF PROSECUTORIAL MISCONDUCT.

...DONE BY THE PROSECU... AND HINDER THE DEFENSE.
1. DEFENSE WAS DENIED AN UP-TO-THE MINUTE COPY OF THE TRIAL TRANSCRIPT.
2. DEFENSE WAS NOT GIVEN ADEQUATE OPPORTUNITY TO EXAMINE THE RANSOM NOTES AND OTHER HANDWRITING EXHIBITS.
3. DEFENSE COUNSEL WAS DENIED PRIVATE CONFERENCE WITH THE DEFENDANT.
4. (a) DEFENSE WAS DENIED ACCESS TO THE HAUPTMANN HOME.
   (b) DEFENSE WAS DENIED ACCESS TO THE LINDBERGH HOUSE AND GROUNDS.
5. CROWDING THE PROSECUTION TABLE WITH ...D INFLUENTIAL AND WELL-KNOWN ... THE STATE'S CASE

THE NEW JERSEY COURT OF APPEALS, HOWEVER, DENIES HIS PETITION, AND THE U.S. SUPREME COURT DECLINES TO REVIEW THE CASE.

HAUPTMANN'S CAUSE IS TAKEN UP BY NEW JERSEY'S NEW GOVERNOR, HAROLD HOFFMAN, WHO PUBLICLY STATES HIS BELIEF THAT THE LINDBERGH CASE IS STILL NOT SOLVED.

SUNDAY, JANUARY 12, 1936
HE GRANTS THE PRISONER A 30-DAY REPRIEVE AND ORDERS THE STATE POLICE TO RE-OPEN THE CASE.

ELLIS PARKER, SENIOR DETECTIVE OF BURLINGTON COUNTY, AND THE STATE'S MOST FAMOUS CRIME-BUSTER, SHARES THE GOVERNOR'S DOUBTS ABOUT HAUPTMANN'S GUILT.

PARKER'S THEORY IS THAT THE REMAINS FOUND IN THE WOODS WERE ERRONEOUSLY IDENTIFIED AND THAT THE LINDBERGH CHILD IS STILL ALIVE...

AND IN THE HANDS OF THE ACTUAL KIDNAPPER, A DISBARRED TRENTON ATTORNEY AND EX-CONVICT NAMED PAUL H. WENDEL.

WEDNESDAY, FEBRUARY 13
PARKER AND A GROUP OF OTHERS ABDUCT WENDEL AND BEAT A CONFESSION OUT OF HIM.

BUT UPON HIS RELEASE SEVERAL WEEKS LATER, WENDEL RETRACTS THE CONFESSION, AND PARKER WILL LATER, IRONICALLY, BE TRIED FOR KIDNAPPING.

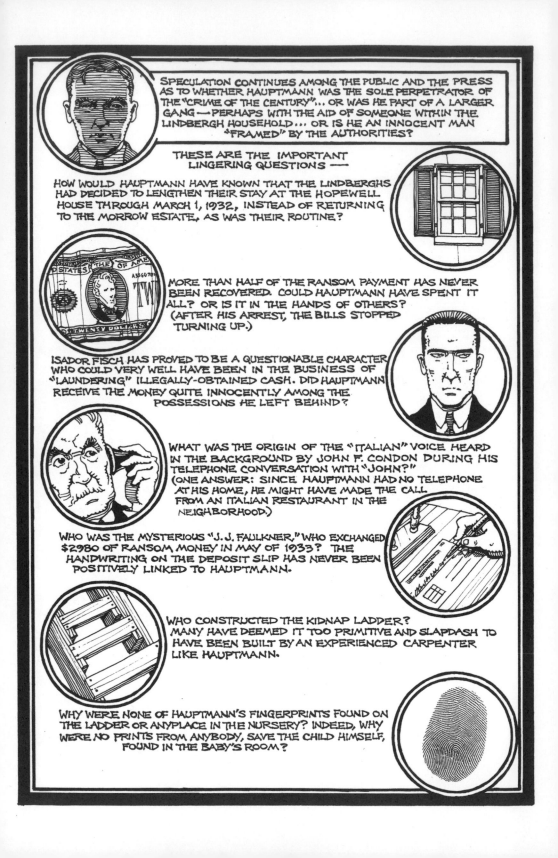

SPECULATION CONTINUES AMONG THE PUBLIC AND THE PRESS AS TO WHETHER HAUPTMANN WAS THE SOLE PERPETRATOR OF THE "CRIME OF THE CENTURY"... OR WAS HE PART OF A LARGER GANG — PERHAPS WITH THE AID OF SOMEONE WITHIN THE LINDBERGH HOUSEHOLD... OR IS HE AN INNOCENT MAN "FRAMED" BY THE AUTHORITIES?

THESE ARE THE IMPORTANT LINGERING QUESTIONS —

HOW WOULD HAUPTMANN HAVE KNOWN THAT THE LINDBERGHS HAD DECIDED TO LENGTHEN THEIR STAY AT THE HOPEWELL HOUSE THROUGH MARCH 1, 1932, INSTEAD OF RETURNING TO THE MORROW ESTATE, AS WAS THEIR ROUTINE?

MORE THAN HALF OF THE RANSOM PAYMENT HAS NEVER BEEN RECOVERED. COULD HAUPTMANN HAVE SPENT IT ALL? OR IS IT IN THE HANDS OF OTHERS? (AFTER HIS ARREST, THE BILLS STOPPED TURNING UP.)

ISADOR FISCH HAS PROVED TO BE A QUESTIONABLE CHARACTER WHO COULD VERY WELL HAVE BEEN IN THE BUSINESS OF "LAUNDERING" ILLEGALLY-OBTAINED CASH. DID HAUPTMANN RECEIVE THE MONEY QUITE INNOCENTLY AMONG THE POSSESSIONS HE LEFT BEHIND?

WHAT WAS THE ORIGIN OF THE "ITALIAN" VOICE HEARD IN THE BACKGROUND BY JOHN F. CONDON DURING HIS TELEPHONE CONVERSATION WITH "JOHN?" (ONE ANSWER: SINCE HAUPTMANN HAD NO TELEPHONE AT HIS HOME, HE MIGHT HAVE MADE THE CALL FROM AN ITALIAN RESTAURANT IN THE NEIGHBORHOOD.)

WHO WAS THE MYSTERIOUS "J. J. FAULKNER," WHO EXCHANGED $2980 OF RANSOM MONEY IN MAY OF 1933? THE HANDWRITING ON THE DEPOSIT SLIP HAS NEVER BEEN POSITIVELY LINKED TO HAUPTMANN.

WHO CONSTRUCTED THE KIDNAP LADDER? MANY HAVE DEEMED IT TOO PRIMITIVE AND SLAPDASH TO HAVE BEEN BUILT BY AN EXPERIENCED CARPENTER LIKE HAUPTMANN.

WHY WERE NONE OF HAUPTMANN'S FINGERPRINTS FOUND ON THE LADDER OR ANYPLACE IN THE NURSERY? INDEED, WHY WERE NO PRINTS FROM ANYBODY, SAVE THE CHILD HIMSELF, FOUND IN THE BABY'S ROOM?

IS HAUPTMANN THE INNOCENT VICTIM OF A "FRAME-UP?"

IF SO, IT IS THE PRODUCT OF A MASSIVE POLICE CONSPIRACY, PERPETRATED BY MANY OFFICERS OF COMPETING AGENCIES...

OR COULD A SMALL CABAL HAVE MANAGED IT ALL?

REGARDING RAIL 16 OF THE LADDER: CERTAIN WITNESSES CLAIM TO HAVE SEEN NO NAIL HOLES IN THE WOOD WHEN IT WAS FIRST RECOVERED.

FURTHER, THE RAIL IS CONSIDERABLY SHORTER AND NARROWER THAN THE PLANKS IN HAUPTMANN'S ATTIC.

WOULD IT NOT HAVE BEEN EASIER FOR A KIDNAPPER TO PURCHASE THE CORRECT-SIZED BOARD, RATHER THAN TO LABORIOUSLY PRY ONE FROM THE ATTIC, CUT AND PLANE IT TO FIT?

WAS THIS CRUCIAL PIECE OF EVIDENCE MANUFACTURED WHEN NOTHING ELSE EMERGED TO PLACE THE DEFENDANT AT THE CRIME SCENE?

REGARDING THE ADDRESS AND TELEPHONE NUMBER OF JOHN F. CONDON, FOUND INSIDE A CLOSET DOOR-FRAME AT HAUPTMANN'S HOUSE...

HE AT FIRST ADMITTED THAT HE "COULD HAVE" WRITTEN IT, BUT LATER DENIED IT.

IT IS LATER CLAIMED TO HAVE BEEN PUT THERE BY AN UNSCRUPULOUS NEW YORK JOURNALIST— AS A PRANK THAT WENT AWRY...

AT LEAST THAT IS HOW THE MAN HIMSELF TELLS THE STORY.

THERE IS LITTLE DOUBT THAT HAUPTMANN RECEIVED BRUTAL TREATMENT AT THE HANDS OF THE NEW YORK AND NEW JERSEY POLICE...

AND THAT HIS TRIAL WAS TAINTED BY MISCONDUCT ON THE PART OF THE STATE.

IF, AS THE WEIGHT OF THE EVIDENCE SUGGESTS, HAUPTMANN IS THE SOLE PERPETRATOR — HOW DID HE DO IT?

AS HE STATES IN THE RANSOM NOTES, THE PLAN HAS BEEN IN THE WORKS FOR ONE YEAR.

ENGLEWOOD

THE BRONX

HUDSON RIVER

MANHATTAN

GEO. WASHINGTON BRIDGE

THAT TIME WAS SPENT SCRUTINIZING THE MORROW ESTATE IN ENGLEWOOD, JUST ACROSS THE HUDSON RIVER FROM THE BRONX.

HE GETS TO KNOW THE COMINGS AND GOINGS OF THE FAMILY.

THE 3-PART LADDER, WHEN EXTENDED TO ITS FULL LENGTH, REACHES TO THE SECOND-STORY WINDOW OF THE BABY'S NURSERY.

ON THE EVENING OF MARCH 1, 1932, HAVING HEARD THAT COL. LINDBERGH WILL BE IN NEW YORK ALL EVENING, HE DRIVES TO ENGLEWOOD...

FULLY INTENDING TO WAIT INTO THE NIGHT TO MAKE HIS MOVE.

ALONG THE WAY, HOWEVER, HE CATCHES A STRAY BIT OF GOSSIP, PERHAPS FROM AN EMPLOYEE OF THE HOUSE: THE LINDBERGHS ARE STILL AT HOPEWELL.

BUT NOW HE CANNOT BACK AWAY — HE HAS WORKED HIMSELF INTO A FEVER. TONIGHT HAS TO BE THE NIGHT!

SO HE DRIVES THE 50 MILES TO THE HOPEWELL ESTATE (WHICH HE HAS NO DOUBT VISITED BEFORE).

AND HERE HE SEIZES THE MOMENT.

DOES HE INTEND TO KILL THE CHILD? IF NOT, WHERE WOULD HE KEEP IT? NO ANSWER HAS YET ARISEN.

IN ANY CASE, THE MAN'S ARROGANCE WILL PREVENT HIM FROM EVER CONFESSING TO THE CRIME.

DR. JOHN F. CONDON RELATES HIS ADVENTURES ON THE LINDBERGH CASE IN A 1936 ACCOUNT SERIALIZED IN LIBERTY MAGAZINE.

HE DIES IN 1945 AT AGE 85.

OTHERS WHO WRITE OF THEIR ASSOCIATION WITH THE CASE INCLUDE —

- NEW JERSEY GOVERNOR HAROLD HOFFMAN
- DEFENSE ATTORNEY C. LLOYD FISHER
- MRS. EVALYN WALSH McLEAN
- KIDNAP VICTIM PAUL H. WENDEL
- FINGERPRINT EXPERT ALBERT S. OSBORNE
- ANNE MORROW LINDBERGH, IN TWO VOLUMES OF HER LETTERS AND JOURNALS

AFTER THE TRIAL, CHARLES LINDBERGH MOVES WITH HIS WIFE AND SON TO ENGLAND.

HE AND ANNE WILL PRODUCE FOUR MORE OFFSPRING.

THE LONE EAGLE NEVER SPEAKS OF THE KIDNAPPING FOR THE REMAINDER OF HIS LIFE. HE DIES ON AUGUST 25, 1974 AT AGE 72....

AND IS BURIED ON THE HAWAIIAN ISLAND OF MAUI.

HIS WIDOW, AGE 94, DIES IN 2001.

ANNA HAUPTMANN, STILL MAINTAINING HER HUSBAND'S INNOCENCE, DIES IN 1994, AT AGE 95.

AS WITH HER HUSBAND, HER REMAINS ARE CREMATED, THE ASHES SCATTERED IN AN UNDISCLOSED LOCATION.

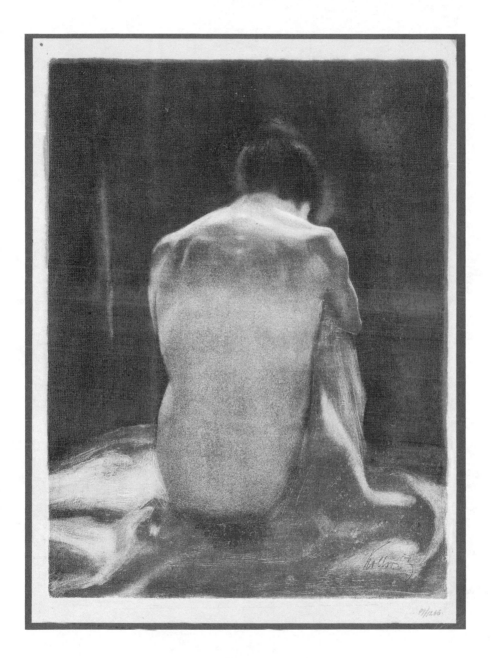

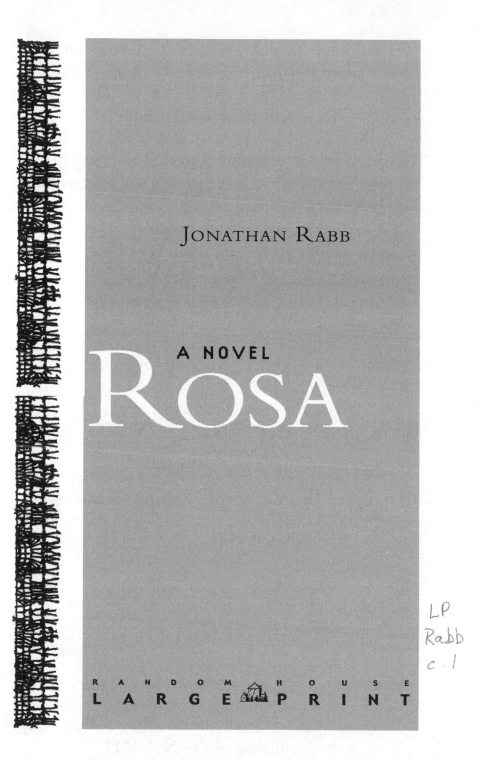

Jonathan Rabb

A NOVEL

ROSA

RANDOM HOUSE
LARGE PRINT

The Library of Congress has established a Cataloging-in-Publication record for this title.

0-375-43447-x

www.randomlargeprint.com

FIRST LARGE PRINT EDITION

10   9   8   7   6   5   4   3   2   1

This Large Print edition published in accord with the standards of the N.A.V.H.

FOR ANDRA

ACKNOWLEDGMENTS

I am indebted to Professors David Clay Large and Peter Fritzsche for their help in bringing to life the Berlin of 1919. I also thank Peter Speigler and Sean Greenwood for their wise advice and encouragement on the earliest drafts of the book—more so for their friendship—and Professor Abraham Asher for his expertise on the German Revolution and its aftermath. As ever, Byron Hollinshead and Rob Cowley brought seasoned eyes to the later drafts. And for her wonderful renderings of the lace patterns, I am also grateful to Anne Auberjonois.

Once again, Matt Bialer and Kristin Kiser kept me on the right course with good humor, insight, and enthusiasm. All writers should have such agents and editors.

And finally I would like to thank my family, and especially my wife, Andra, who make it all worthwhile.

In the last days of the First World War, socialist revolution swept across Germany, sending Kaiser Wilhelm into exile, and transforming Berlin into a battleground. Order returned only when the two leaders of the movement—Karl Liebknecht and Rosa Luxemburg—were hunted down and assassinated on the fifteenth of January, 1919. Liebknecht's body was discovered the next morning; Luxemburg's body, however, remained missing until the end of May

Speculation about Rosa's fate during those months continues to this day.

This is one possibility.

PART ONE

Berlin, 1919

Kepner's
House

Zoo

KaDaWe

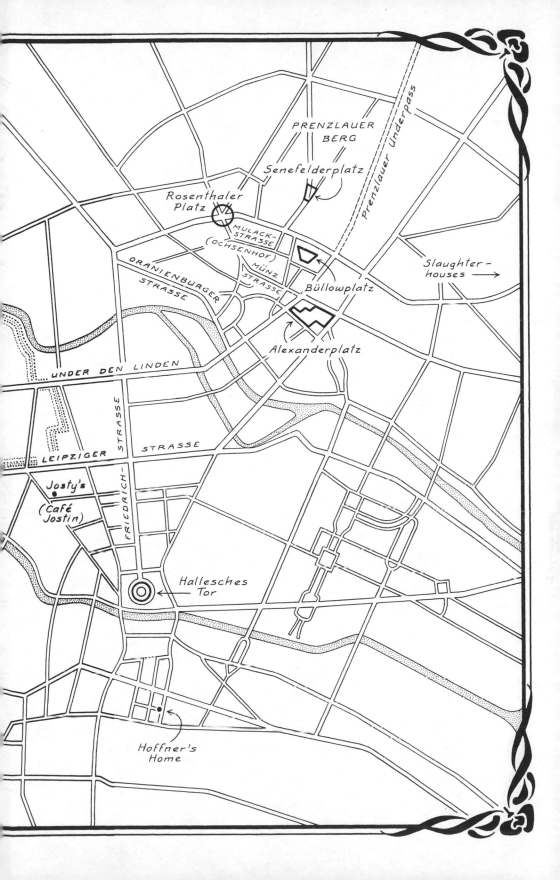

ONE

⊰ 1919 ⊱

Berlin in December, to those who know her, is like no other place. The first snows take on a permanence, and the wide avenues from Charlottenburg to the Rondell breathe with a crispness of Prussian winter. It is a time when little boys drag their mothers away from the well-dressed windows at KaDeWe or Wertheim's or the elegant teas at the Hotel Adlon and out to the Tiergarten and the wondrous row of marble emperors along the Siegesallee. Just as dusk settles, as the last flurries of the day swirl through the leafless trees, you can steal a glimpse of any number of little eyes peering up, hoping, just this once, to catch a stony wink from an Albrecht the Bear, or a Friedrich of Nuremberg with his large ears and dour expression. Just a wink through the snow to tell him that Christmas will be kind to him this year. "There,

Mama, did you see! Do you see how he winked at me!" And the pride that next morning, bundled up beyond measure, racing out from his fine house on Belziger or Wartburg Strasse to tell his friends of his triumph. "Yes, me, too! Me, too!" Berlin in December.

This, however, was January, when the snow had turned to endless drizzle, so raw that it seemed to penetrate even the heaviest of layers. And whatever civility they might still be clinging to elsewhere, here on the east side of town, all the way up to the flophouses in Prenzlauer Berg, people had little time or patience for such gestures. Christmas had brought nothing, except perhaps the truth about how the war had been lost long before the summer, how the generals had been flimflamming them all the way up to the November capitulation. Oh, and of course, the revolution. Christmas had brought that, a thoroughly German revolution, with documents in triplicate, cries from the balconies, demonstrations and parades, tea still at four o'clock, dinner at seven, and perhaps a little dancing afterward up at the White Mouse or Maxim's. Shots had been fired, naturally, a few hundred were dead, but the socialists—not the real socialists, mind you—were straightening everything up.

Still, it was the weather that had most people on edge. The rain just wasn't giving in, and it was why Nikolai Hoffner, rather than waiting out on the tundral expanse of the Rosenthaler Platz, had snuck off to Rücker's bar for something warm to drink. Years of experience had told him that nothing of any significance was going to happen today: later on, he would come to regret that arrogance. So, with a knowing smile, he had left the ever-eager Hans Fichte up on the square; at the first sign of trouble, Fichte knew where to find him.

Hoffner sat with a brandy ("I'd walk a mile for Mampe's brandy, it makes you feel so hale and dandy!"), the early edition of the **BZ am Mittag** in front of him. He had not sat like this in weeks, a quiet read to clear the mind. And not because of the nonsense that had been going on out at the stables, or up at the Reichstag: all the pretty uniformed men had managed to disrupt traffic too many times, now, to recount. No, Hoffner had been up to his ears in real violence, genuine terror, hardly the kind plotted in Red pamphlets or designed in back rooms by overfed burghers calling themselves socialists. They played at revolution; he knew another kind. But for today—orders from on high—he was told to leave that alone and join the rest of his breed in the streets to make sure "nothing untoward" would come to pass.

Hoffner finished off the last of his drink and nodded to the barman to bring him another. As he was one of only three people in the place—a man at a corner table, his head tilted back against the wall, his mouth gaped open in sleep; a woman with a beer and bread, her business at one of the nearby hotels temporarily interrupted—the service was unusually prompt. The barman approached with the bottle.

"This, I'm sad to say, will have to be the last."

Hoffner looked up from his paper. "I'm sad to hear." He had a steady, reassuring voice.

"It's this damned rationing," said the man. "This and another bottle's all I've got for the day. My apologies."

Hoffner half smiled. "What do you care if the money's coming from me or from someone else?"

"Simple economics, **mein Herr.** No brandy, fewer people in here to buy my sausages before they rot." The man opened the bottle. "It's called the distribution of capital, or something like that. You understand."

Hoffner's smile grew. "Completely."

"And"—the man nodded as he poured—"the money's not coming from you. It never does. So why don't you be nice to me today and let someone else pay for the brandy?"

Hoffner reached into his coat pocket and produced a ten-pfennig coin. He placed it on the table.

The man smiled again as he shook his head. "No, no. I like that you don't pay. You like that you don't pay. We may be governed by socialists now, but it's better that you hold on to your money."

The man popped the cork back into the bottle and headed for the bar. "Time to wake up, Herr Professor **Doktor,**" he said as he moved past the man in the corner. The man at once opened his eyes, looked around in a daze, and then, in one fluid movement, pawed out his beard, picked up his umbrella, and stood. Upright, he seemed far more impressive, though from the look of his clothes, one had to wonder how much sleep he had gotten in the last few days. He peered over at Hoffner. "Is it safe out there, **mein Herr**?"

Hoffner continued to read his paper. "Safe as can be, Herr Professor **Doktor.**"

"Excellent." The man turned to the barman. "My thanks, Herr **Ober.**" And, placing his hat on his head, he started for the door, stopping momentarily to bow to the lady. "Madame." He then glanced quickly through the windows, and was gone.

Hoffner scanned through several stories, all of which were doing their best to assuage a devoted readership. The Reds were dead: good old Liebknecht had gotten his in the park, little Rosa in the clutches of a murderous mob, though her body was still missing; Chancellor Ebert could be trusted with the government; business was on the rise, so forth and so on. And yet, even within the lines meant to pacify, the **BZ** had that remarkable capacity to stir up a kind of subdued panic:

Reichs Chancellor Ebert, with the full cooperation of a diligent military, has declared the streets once again safe for the men and women of Berlin. Hurrah! With the National Assembly election only days away, we must thank this provisional

government for the speed with which it has put down the Bolshevik-inspired insurgency, and hope that it is equally tireless in its efforts to hunt down the deluded lone sharpshooters who still infest our city. Those living in the area between Linienstrasse and the Hackescher-Markt are advised to remain indoors for the next twenty-four hours.

The woman at the table laughed lazily to herself. Still pretty at twenty-two, twenty-three, she jawed through her bread. She was wearing the unspoken uniform of those girls who sell roses and matches at the restaurants along Friedrichstrasse—the silk-thin dress, ruffles along the low collar and cuffs, the dark cloche hat with its front trim tucked up, just so—except hers was well past its prime, the sure indication that she, too, had progressed. All pretense long gone, she spoke her mind. "It's so easy to spot one of you," she said, not looking up. "Long brown coat, brown shoes, brown hat, brown, brown, brown."

Hoffner flipped to the next page. "One might say the same of you, Fräulein."

She bit into a wedge of bread. "But you won't. As a gentleman."

"No, of course not. As a gentleman."

The woman started to laugh again as she picked at the remaining slab of bread, her fingers like little bird beaks pecking at the crust. "Another glass of brandy for my friend, Herr **Ober**," she said, her eyes fixed on the bread. "We must make sure to keep our men of the Kripo warm and happy. Who will protect us from the Russian hordes?" Another laugh.

Hoffner folded his paper and placed it on the table. "Alas, Fräulein, but the Russians are out of the **Kriminalpolizei**'s jurisdiction. We deal only with the Berlin hordes."

The man at the bar smiled quietly and retrieved the bottle, but Hoffner shook his head and pushed back his chair, a bit farther than he had anticipated needing. His wife was pleased that he was having no trouble keeping the weight on, a testament to her culinary skills amid all the shortages. Not that he was fat, but Hoffner had a certain image of himself that he was, as yet, unwilling to part with: good height, deep eyes, dark hair (he had gotten the latter two from his Russian mother, likewise the first name), reasonably fit, and with a thin scar just beneath the chin, a worthy reminder of championship days as a **Gymnasium** fencer. At forty-five, however, several centimeters had vanished to the slight roll in his shoulders; the depth of his eyes had relocated south to a pair of ever-widening bags; and while the hair was still full, dark most certainly would have been a stretch. As to the rest, more like distant friends than close companions.

"Thank you, Fräulein," said Hoffner. "But I'm guessing you've got better things to do with your hard-earned money."

The front door opened and a pocket of chilled air

quickly made the rounds. There, slick from the rain and out of breath, stood Hans Fichte, his eyes on Hoffner.

"Shut that door," barked the barman as he placed the bottle back on its shelf.

Fichte did as he was told, and moved quickly to Hoffner's table. "You're needed back in the square, Herr **Kriminal-Kommissar.** It's—" He glanced around, then leaned farther in over the table. "It's important we get back." Fichte spoke as if he actually thought someone other than Hoffner might have any interest in what he was saying.

Fichte was a large man, over two meters tall, and with wide, thick shoulders. A strip of flaxen hair, matted in sweat and rain, held to the top of his brow, and his usually gray/white cheeks were blistered in odd blotches of red. A single drop—let it be perspiration—clung to the tip of his nose, which was too long for his narrow face, and which always gave him a look of mild disdain. At twenty-three, Fichte still had a boyish smoothness to his complexion, though the ordeal of the last six weeks was beginning to dig out some distinguishing lines: hardly what one would call character, but it was something.

The fact that Fichte had reached twenty-three—uncrippled and completely unconnected with any of the convalescence asylums that had recently surfaced throughout the city and the Reich—made him something of an anomaly. Fichte had been fit enough to serve his Kaiser in 1914, or at least up through the second week of September 1914, when, in a moment of profound stupidity, he had volunteered during a drill to demonstrate how to use one of the early gas masks, those chemically treated masks that required wetting with a special activating agent immediately prior to use. Hans had not known about the need for the wetting. The gas had come on, he had inhaled, and from that moment on, he had ceased to be fit enough to serve his Kaiser.

Damaged lungs, however, were just fine for the **Schutzmannschaft** (municipal beat cops), and after three years of stellar duty, Fichte had applied and won transfer to the Kripo. He had been presented to Hoffner two and half months ago as his **Kriminal-Assistent** (detective in training), a replacement for a partner of twelve years who had volunteered and then gone missing in 1915. Victor König had come as close to a friend as Hoffner had permitted, and his death had taken some time to get over. With the choices on the home front greatly diminished, the **Kriminaldirektor** (KD) had been kind enough to let Hoffner work alone for the better part of four years. Hans Fichte was now the price for that kindness.

"So important," Hoffner said as he got to his feet, "that you've decided to leave the square yourself?" He was waiting for a response. "In the future, Hans, find a boy—there's always one roaming about—and send him to get me. Yes?"

Fichte thought for a moment, a mental note etched across his face. When it was properly filed, he nodded, and then headed for the door.

Hoffner followed, stopping as he reached the bar. "One more for my friend," he said. He pushed a coin along the uneven surface, then turned to the young woman's table and placed several more in a neat stack next to her glass. She continued to stare at her bread.

"It'll cost you a lot more than that, Herr Detective," she said.

Hoffner slowly pulled his hand away. "No—I think umbrellas go for about that much in this weather, Fräulein."

She looked up. A kind, if sparing, smile curled her lips.

Hoffner turned back to the bar to find two small glasses filled with brandy. "Come on, Fichte. It'll do you good. Whatever's up on the square can wait while you get a bit of warming-up."

Fichte hesitated, then strode to the bar and downed the brandy in one swift movement. He stood there, awaiting his next assignment. Hoffner did his best to ignore the deferential stare as he sniffed at the liquid and then tossed it back. He placed the glass on the bar. "You're welcome, Fichte."

Another moment to consider. "Oh . . . yes. Thank you, Herr **Komm** . . . Hoffner."

"And to you as well, Herr Economics." Hoffner tipped his hat to the young lady and motioned Fichte to the door. Together they stepped out into the street.

The brandy, as it turned out, was no match for the city's infamous **Berliner Luft,** a smack of frigid air just the thing to set Hoffner's eyes tearing. He turned up his coat collar and pulled his hat down to his face. His wife had insisted he take a scarf, but he had left it back at the office: Martha would find a certain pleasure in that later tonight. Hoffner noticed Fichte was sporting a nice thick woolen muffler. And who's been taking care of him, Hoffner wondered.

They turned right, the rain spraying up at them through the wind tunnel that was the block of tenements. The street was deserted, its gray stone merely a façade for the life that lay hidden beyond. Too many times, Hoffner had been forced to venture into the inner courtyards, each dripping with laundry—Turkish, Polish, German—endless lines of clothes that spoke to one another in a kind of ragged semaphore. And within the crumbling buildings, the squalor grew only more oppressive, dank hallways leading blindly from one hovel to the next, each filled with the smell of rotting cabbage. The worst was the **"Ochsenhof"** ("cattle yard"), with its dozen entrances and twenty stairways, all leading nowhere, pointless escapades in search of criminals all too secure within its walls. It was a vast, silent place to the men of the Kripo, indecipherable and thus impregnable.

Outside, however, all was serene. The stones blended effortlessly into the darkened haze of sky, only those occasional passersby bold enough to peek

out from under the brims of their hats able to determine where one left off and the other began. Hoffner
was not one of these: he pressed his head farther
down to meet the wind. By the time he and Fichte
had made it to the square, his pants were once again
damp through from the knees down: at least the exertion was helping to keep him warm.

Surprisingly, the wind was taking no interest in
Rosenthaler Platz. People were jumping on and off
trams without the least sign of aerial difficulty, and
whatever Fichte had thought demanded his immediate attention, Hoffner could find nothing that was
even remotely out of the ordinary: like a painted
newsreel clip, the square buzzed in accelerated activity. There was the requisite line outside the win-
dowed cafeteria that was Aschinger's, the hawkers of
neckties and sponges and fruit brandies in front of
Fabische's on the corner ("A suit, **mein Herr**? Take
one, Ready-To-Wear!"), and the usual mayhem of
cabs, horsedrawn carts, and pedestrians darting in
and out of one another's ways. Rosenthaler Platz had
taken no time off to breathe during the revolution;
why should it do so now?

"Well," said Hoffner as they maneuvered their way
through the crowd, "I can see why you raced back to
get me."

"The building site, Herr Inspector."

Fichte led Hoffner up toward the subway excavations. The fencing around the northern tip of the

square had been there for almost a year, a promise from the Kaiser that his capital would be home to the finest trams and underground trains in Europe. Few Berliners took notice anymore of the wooden slats that sprouted up around the city, most **Städters** resigned to the ongoing renovations that had been a part of their lives for the past twenty-five years. Wilhelm's insecurity about his chosen city had led him, over time, to reinvent her as a paean to grandeur in the architecture of her monuments, churches, government buildings, stores, hotels, and, yes, railway stations. It was said of Berlin that even her bird shit was made of marble.

Then again, the slats did make for nice advertising space. A large placard of a cigar-smoking goblin peered down at Hoffner as he followed Fichte toward the site. The lime-green skin against the cerise background, at first off-putting, quickly became hypnotic. The creature had an almost maniacal smile, the cigar evidently just that good to take him to the edge of sanity, although why a goblin would need any kind of stimulus for that sort of behavior had always puzzled Hoffner. A cigar, though, would have been nice right about now.

Fichte and Hoffner moved out into the square, jumping the tram rails as they sidestepped a cab, its goose-squawk horn eliciting a growl from Fichte. A single patrolman stood guard atop the wooden ramp that led up to what, until recently, had been the boarded-up entrance to the pit behind the fencing. He put out a hand as Hoffner and Fichte approached.

"It is forbidden, **meine Herren.**" The man's German had the precision of working-class Berlin, the extended roll of the **r**'s a pompous display of office. He kept his woolen short-coat buttoned to the neck, its band collar sporting the single stripe of a constable, his lip-brimmed helmet topped by the ubiquitous silver imperial prong. "Please turn around—" The man caught himself as soon as he recognized Fichte. "Ah, Herr Detective." There was nothing apologetic in the tone.

Hoffner knew this type, a Schutzi-lifer who considered the very existence of the Kripo a slap in the face, even if, every year for the past fifteen years, he had applied and been rejected for transfer. Still, it was the chain of command. Order had to be preserved. The man stepped aside.

Hoffner nodded. "Patrolman."

A white-gloved finger smoothed through a perfectly pruned moustache. "Detective."

Hoffner moved past the man and began to make his way down a second ramp behind the fencing. As he did so, he turned his head and corrected, "Detective **Inspector.**"

Inside, the building work was far more extensive than one might have imagined from the square. An area, perhaps twenty meters by ten, extended to the far fencing, most of it still earth. Closer in, however,

stood the top staging of a tower of wooden scaffolding that dug deep into the ground. From their vantage point, Fichte and Hoffner could see only a
fraction of the edifice, its depth apparent only once
they stepped out from the ramp and moved to the
ladder at its center. A second patrolman stood directly behind the small hole of an entrance. Hoffner
looked at the man, then peered down the shaft.
"Must be a good fifteen meters," he said. Police
lamps, recently attached, hung along the rungs, all
the way down. Hoffner looked back up, a thoroughly
disingenuous smile on his lips. "May we?" The man
said nothing as Fichte took hold of the top rung and
started down. Hoffner followed.

The air quickly thickened, and the smell of damp
earth—at the top quite pleasant—gave way to something less inviting as they descended, familiar, yet
nondistinct. It was only when he reached the bottom
and stepped away from the ladder that Hoffner recognized the odor. Human feces. Muted, but
undeniable.

The two Kripomen were now standing in the first
of a series of man-made caverns, wide mining shafts
that spoked out from the central area. The subway
station at Rosenthaler Platz had evidently been chosen to house an underground arcade—shops, cafés—
the skeleton of which had been near to completion
before the work had been shut down. All that remained by way of construction material, aside from
the timber and steel supports, was the odd piece of

wiring and the scrawl on the wooden slats, measurements and the like penned in a dull charcoal. A few of the slats had gone missing, though Hoffner recognized that they had been well chosen; none of the gaps looked to be threatening the pit's structural integrity. He had to hand it to the poachers.

He never imagined, however, that these poachers would be standing directly behind him, or rather sitting. And yet there, along a narrow wooden bench in an adjoining cavern, sat an utterly unexpected foursome—husband, wife, and two sons of perhaps eight and ten. They were all neatly dressed, considering the circumstances, the man in a worn coat and tie, the woman in a long dress in need of a good cleaning, all with overcoats folded in their laps. The gaunt faces stared straight ahead as if, with a kind of macabre persistence, they were waiting for a train. Off to the side were what looked to be two well-worn feather beds sitting atop several of the absent slats, a small wooden table, a bucket, and a camping fire. A steel trunk rounded out the furnishings.

Two more patrolmen stood at either end of the bench. A third—a sergeant, from the braiding on the brim of his helmet—stood by the fire. He took a step toward Hoffner. "Herr Detective, I am—"

"Yes, I'm sure you are," said Hoffner as he turned to Fichte. "I think my partner can fill me in."

The attention seemed to catch Fichte by surprise. When Hoffner continued to stare, Fichte finally said,

"Apparently they live down here. The man was an engineer—"

"Division Two, **Firma** Ganz-Neurath." The voice came from the father. Hoffner turned. "I am a designer for this site," the man continued in an accent tinged with something other than German. "Under the direction of Herr Alfred Grenander. We have only been living here. Nothing else. Nothing else." There was a wavering sincerity in his tone, one that Hoffner recognized all too well. It was usually reserved for the third or fourth hour of interrogation, that time when a man tries to convince himself of his own innocence. "I am not ashamed to be here."

Hoffner kept his gaze on the man, then turned to Fichte. "He's not ashamed to be here," he echoed wryly.

Fichte nodded. "From what we can make out, he lost his position. They had a choice. Either hold on to their flat, or eat. They decided to eat. It's actually pretty livable down here. It's dry, warm, and except—"

"Yes," said Hoffner. "I can smell it."

Again, Fichte nodded.

"And the boys?"

"On the rolls at a nearby school. They haven't missed a day."

Hoffner looked back at the family. Again, he waited. "Why am I standing down here, Herr **Kriminal-Assistent**?" Before Fichte could answer, Hoffner continued, enjoying his audience: "He seems like a nice-enough fellow, decent. Amid all the shortages, war, revolution, he's managed to find a way to keep a—well, to keep something over his family's head. He sends his children to school. He's been an engineer with Ganz-Neurath, Division Two, under the tutelage of the great Grenander himself. What more can we ask of him?" Hoffner peered over at the sergeant, then slowly moved toward him. "But, of course, for the Schutzmannschaft, this poses a problem. Criminals everywhere, and they choose to spend their time on—"

"We have no interest in this man," said the officer.

Hoffner had not expected the response. For a moment he said nothing. Then, with an audible sigh, he turned to Fichte and said, "Why am I down here, Hans?"

Even in the dim light, Hoffner recognized the slight tensing in the younger man's expression. With a jabbed thumb over his shoulder, Fichte said, "This way." And without further explanation, he picked up a lamp and started toward the central tunnel. With no other choice, Hoffner did the same.

The air grew still heavier as they made their way deeper into the maze. Fichte stopped at one point to pull a small glass inhaler from his coat pocket, the nebulized liquid making a sharp puffing sound each time Fichte sucked in. Hoffner had learned not to notice these brief episodes; the shame in Fichte's face was something he didn't care to see. Hoffner slowed and waited until Fichte had picked up the pace again.

Two caverns on, they stopped. A lone patrolman
stood at the entrance.

It was the odor that gave it away. Decomposing
flesh, when kept moist, takes on a scent not unlike
rotting fruit with a bit of sulfur thrown in. Hoffner
had actually experimented with various mixtures
some years ago. He had kept a number of covered
bowls in a remote area of the cellar at police headquarters, all filled with different concoctions. It had
taken him nearly two weeks to hit on the right combination. When asked why he was doing this, Hoffner had explained that it could be used to train
detectives how to sniff out hidden or buried corpses:
take the bowl, place it behind some boards, etc. They
had all gotten a good laugh out of it until a young assistant detective by the name of Bauman had cracked
the infamous Selazig case of 1911 by nosing around
the man's office. Selazig had been in the pickled-
herring business and believed that the smell of his
cannery could hide anything he might be keeping behind the walls of his office. Detective Bauman had
been doing a routine check of the man—the disappearance of his wife and son, missing money, Herr
Selazig distraught beyond all measure—when he
happened to detect something of a familiar scent
coming from behind a large filing cabinet. So acute
was Bauman's nasal prowess that he had actually distinguished the smell of rancid pears, so he described
it, from that of three-day-old fish. The bodies had

been found within a small chamber behind the wall, each laid out perfectly on an altar of sorts, bits and pieces of arms and legs having been nibbled away. Selazig had gone to the gallows, Bauman to **Kriminal-Bezirkssekretär** (detective sergeant), and Hoffner back to his experiments, along with a short article titled "The Odor of Death" published in **Die Polizei,** August 11 issue, a framed copy of which still hung in his office.

"It's just here," said Fichte as he moved through the cavern and knelt down in front of a mound by the far wall. He placed his lamp to the side and waited for Hoffner to draw closer. He then began to pull back the tarp.

Hoffner leaned over. "I'm surprised he didn't post another moustache back here."

"He tried," said Fichte. "I told him that wouldn't be advised."

"Good. Who found it?"

"The older boy. He was rummaging."

Hoffner crouched down and drew his lamp closer in to the corpse. Fichte had learned to take careful note of his partner at these moments. Gone was the waggish smile. In its place, a concentrated gaze lingered over the body and the areas just around it, every inch cataloged for later use. Without warning, the eyes would dart to a wall, or the space by the entrance, hold for a moment, then return for more probing. Fichte knew to say nothing.

Hoffner's first inclination was to flip her over, check

her back, look for the markings that had been so much a part of his life—their lives—since that first grisly discovery in early December. But this woman was too young to have anything to do with that. Strange to feel relief at the side of a murdered woman, he thought. "So," said Hoffner, his tone matching his focus, "how many have been back here?"

"The boy and the father, and one or two of the patrolmen."

"One or two?"

"They're not convinced it's our case. Keeping their mouths tight. They're waiting for a **Leutnant** to arrive. That's why I was in such a hurry."

"Right. We'll need shoe molds from each of them to match against all of this. And photos of everything before the body is moved." Fichte jotted down a note in his pad as Hoffner continued to speak. "The boy, the father. They've seen no one else down here?"

Fichte shook his head. "It turns out there might actually be another three or four ways down into the site. It's impossible to know how many, or where. According to our ex-engineer, the station promenade was to have extended as far east as Bülowplatz."

"Bülowplatz? That's over half a kilometer. Wonderful."

The clothes were in surprisingly good shape. In cases like these, they were either missing entirely—the motive for the killing—or had succumbed to the elements—caked-on mud, gnawing rats, etc. Not so here. The woman's skirt and bodice looked almost new, and she was wearing a pair of intricately woven lace gloves. That seemed odd. "And nothing's been moved?" said Hoffner.

"As far as I can tell, no. The boy said he saw her, then ran for his father. They brought the moustache. I followed."

Hoffner nodded slowly. "And how long do we guess she's been down here?" He took a pen from his coat pocket and brushed the hair back from her face.

"Rate of decay, rats. I'd say about a week, week and a half."

"Good." Hoffner liked it when Fichte got something right. He moved farther down the corpse. "But the clothes say otherwise." Hoffner used his pen to lift the hem of her dress and examine the legs. What he saw momentarily startled him. The flesh on the legs was almost entirely rotted through, with a small puddle of worms and crawling ants camped in between her knees. In an odd way, it looked as if they had been placed there, caged by the legs, and given free rein to go about their business, but only as far as the mid-thigh. There, Hoffner noticed something slick on the flesh, something that was keeping the worms at bay.

Fichte had seen it, as well. It was as if they were looking at two entirely different corpses, one a week postmortem, the other at least six. For several moments Hoffner said nothing as he stared at the strange sheen.

"Someone's been taking care of her," he finally said.

He let the hem fall back. "Flip her over," he said as he stood.

Fichte peered up at him. There was a momentary plea in the boy's eyes, as if to say, They told us we were off this today. Then, with a conscious resolve, Fichte reached under her shoulders and slowly pulled her over.

"Oh God" was all he could get out.

FROM THE LANDWEHR CANAL

Police headquarters were a disaster.

Hoffner hopped out of the ambulance and motioned for the medic to continue driving through the main gate, or at least what was left of it. For a place he had been coming to six days a week for the past eighteen years, it was almost unrecognizable. The once-imposing line of redbrick archways looked ashamed of itself. Four days removed from the final assault, and the crumbling masonry—chalk-white— was doing little to hide the naked slats of wood that pockmarked the façade. Worse were the iron gates that skulked behind, all at wild angles, bent like spoons for a child's amusement. And along the lower floors, turreted windows peered out blindly from empty sockets, shards of broken glass still clinging to their disfigured panes. Such was the crowning achievement of Alexanderplatz in the wake of revolution.

A trio of soldiers stood lazily by the gate, guns rest-

ing on the ground, their collars pulled up tight to
fight back the chill. Each sucked on a cigarette,
though the tobacco—where they had managed to
scavenge that was anybody's guess—was clearly too
harsh for their young lungs. For a fleeting moment
Hoffner thought of his own boys, younger still. He
would have to teach them how to smoke properly
one of these days. None of the soldiers took even a
moment's notice as the ambulance moved past them.

Hoffner had lost track of the different uniforms
now strewn about the city—Guard Fusiliers Regiment, **Republikanische Soldatenwehr,** Section
Fourteen of the Auxiliary, so forth and so on—the
names and insignia all melding into one another. The
majors and colonels who had once led them no
longer seemed to matter. These were simply boys
with guns in a once-civilized city.

The trouble had all begun quite innocently some
ten weeks ago, when the sailors and stokers in Kiel
had decided that they, like the great General Ludendorf, had had enough. Ludendorf had fled to Sweden
at the end of October. They, unwilling to suffer
through another humiliation at the hands of the
British, had simply left their ships. On the fourth of
November—in a moment of genuine socialist spon-
taneity—they formed a Workers' and Sailors' Council and took their defiance beyond the naval base to
the city hall. Naturally, soldiers were sent in to sup-
press the uprising, but when the boys arrived—for
they were mostly boys, after all—they discovered that

it was not a wild mob that they had come to destroy, but a group of the dedicated proletariat. And so the soldiers joined them, and the word spread: Munich, Bremen, Hamburg, Dresden, Stuttgart. By the time the Kaiser declared the armistice on the eleventh, Germany was already comfortably ensconced in revolution.

Berlin, of course, was not one to miss out. On the ninth, Karl Liebknecht—son of the late socialist leader Wilhelm, and himself a recent political guest of Luckau prison—took to the streets with a legion of striking workers behind him. They marched under the banner of Spartakus—the new communist party—and declared the birth of the Free Socialist Republic from the balcony of the Royal Palace. Within days, Rosa Luxemburg was with them. She had spent the better part of four years in Breslau prison, her virtual isolation having done nothing to shake her devotion to the cause. There had been rumors—bouts of hysteria, the possibility that little Rosa had slipped off into madness while caged at the far reaches of the Empire—but she showed none of it on her return to Berlin. She had come to take the revolution as far left as humanly possible, and it was there that the real difficulties had begun.

Had the revolutionaries been of one mind, thousands of innocents might have been spared the fighting. But the revolutionaries were socialists: Karl and Rosa wanted the genuine article, workers of the world rising as one, the death of capitalism, so forth

and so on; Chancellor Ebert and his Social Democrats—terrified of a Soviet-style putsch—wanted a
National Assembly, elections, and perhaps even a bit
of help from various capitalist concerns so as to get
the country up and running again. They might have
called themselves socialists, but they were a peculiar
breed willing to bring back the monarchy—in name
only—in the hopes of restoring order. And then there
were the sailors—the People's Naval Division—just
back from the front, leftists through and through, so
long as they got their pay.

Revolution, however, matters only when the soldiers decide to take sides. In early December Prince
Max von Baden and the General Staff chose Ebert,
and while there were brief moments of hope for
Spartakus after that—Christmas Day on the Schloss
Bridge, cannons at the ready, hundreds of armed
civilians forcing the government troops into retreat;
January sixth, thousands more marching along
the broad Siegesallee toward the War Ministry—they
were only moments. Karl and Rosa made speeches
and printed articles and convoked meetings, but in
the end they were left to live on the run and on bor-
rowed time. Troops had been spilling in from the
front like so much dirty scrub water since late November. They were hungry for a fight, and needed
someone to blame for their recent defeat. Who better
than the Soviet-styled Spartakus? Oddly enough, it
was Police President Emil Eichorn who was the one
to give Ebert his opportunity to mop everything up.

Eichorn's allegiance to the Spartakus movement had never been much of a secret. The new government could ill afford that kind of official opposition, and so, on the eleventh of January, it was Eichorn's politics that ultimately turned the police buildings on Alexanderplatz into the last battleground of the revolution. Refusing to leave his desk after receiving his dismissal papers—and with a group of Spartacists on hand to defend him—Eichorn gave Ebert no choice but to send in a battalion. It was only yesterday morning that the morgue had removed the last of the corpses.

The men of the Kripo had been elsewhere on the fateful day: they had known what was coming and had left Eichorn alone with his revolutionaries. Even so, there was still bad blood between the government soldiers and the men of police headquarters. It was why Hoffner now chose not to meet them head-on.

He sidestepped his way through several clumps of fallen brick and, turning right with the building, headed down Alexanderstrasse. Hoffner pulled open the outer gate and then made his way to the third door down. The building had lost power on the twelfth, the corridors once again lit by gas lamps. Hoffner followed his shadow to the back stairwell and headed up.

It was on the third floor that he finally ran across another human being. As it turned out, first contact came in the form of Ludwig Groener, distant nephew or cousin or something of the great General Wilhelm

Groener, who had played so pivotal a role in December by placing the army in Ebert's hands. Unlike his epic forebear, however, Groener the lesser marched to the rear, still a detective sergeant at fifty-one, with fewer and fewer cases coming his way. He had become quite proficient with paperwork, and now rarely left the building. Not that he was unpleasant, or embittered by his place in the grand scheme: he was, but that wasn't the problem. Groener simply had the most notoriously foul breath. It seemed almost inconceivable that such a small man could produce so overwhelming a stench. Hoffner kept to his side of the hall as they passed.

"I hear you've found another one." Groener's voice trailed after him.

Hoffner stopped and turned around. Groener had gotten the hint over the years: he kept at a healthy distance during these conversations. "Really?" said Hoffner. "And who'd you hear that from?"

"The KD wants to see you."

"The KD? Dropping off some files, were you, Groener? Overheard a little something?"

Groener ignored the comment. "He's waiting in his office."

Hoffner turned and headed down the corridor. "Then it's lucky I ran into you," he said over his shoulder. "Otherwise I would have been completely at a loss."

The men of the Kripo—known within police circles as Department IV—worked entirely out of the third floor, all four sides around the great courtyard given over to their offices, examination rooms, and archives. Hoffner's office was along the back of the building, tucked safely away within the one spot that had managed to avoid the two-day battle for headquarters.

Stepping into the cramped space now, it was as if the first weeks of January had never taken place at all. Everything was as it had been, as it would be: open files littered the desk; bound casebooks, along with assorted editions of statutes and codes, stood in high columns along the bookshelves that ran the length of the far wall; two plaster casts of battered human skulls—evidence for upcoming court appearances—nestled between a stack of newspapers and two odd volumes of Brockhaus's **Konversations-Lexikon,** for some reason Hoffner having taken a specific liking to the encyclopedia's **E** and **S** installments; and, rounding it all out, a cup of something stale and cold—coffee was his best guess, but the color was wrong—sat at the center of his desk. Hoffner would have loved to have blamed his office on the revolution; he just couldn't.

The one piece of perfect coherence in the room stretched the length of the wall across from his desk. It was a map of Berlin, clean, crisp, its few markings penned in a surprisingly neat hand. This was a custom with Hoffner: a new map for each new case. In that way he could allow the city to assert herself, fresh each time, her moods invariably the single most important clues to any crime. Each district had its own temper, a personality. It was simply his task to watch for the variations, find what did not belong, and allow those idiosyncrasies to guide him. Berlin called for deviation, not patterning. It was something so few in the Kripo understood. To his credit, young Hans Fichte was slowly not becoming one of them.

Hoffner stood in the doorway, as yet unable to see the incongruity in the four pins sticking out from the map: the Münz Strasse roadwork, the sewer entrance at Oranienburger Strasse, the Prenzlauer underpass, and the grotto off Bülowplatz. And now another in the Rosenthaler Platz station. There was something odd to that one—as he had known there would be—the feel of it forced as he drove the pin through the paper. He stared at it for nearly a minute before moving to the desk.

The place was still an icebox as he pulled his notebook from his pocket: someone had promised a delivery of coal by the end of the week, but Hoffner knew better. Picking up the cup on his desk, he sniffed at the contents and then took a sip: something to mask the brandy. With a wince, he swallowed and headed for the corridor.

The KD was behind his desk and on the phone when Hoffner pulled up and knocked at the open door. **Kriminaldirektor** Edmund Präger looked up and motioned Hoffner inside. Like his own appearance, Präger kept his large office sparse: a long wooden desk—phone, blotter, and lamp—with two filing cabinets at either end, and nothing more. More striking, though, was the absence of anything that might have indicated that a battle had been fought on these floors in the last week. Whatever remnants might still be in piles of debris around the rest of the offices, here there were none. Präger had insisted on it. If the revolution was over, it was over. He had no desire to be reminded of it.

Hoffner watched as Präger continued to nod into the receiver, an occasional "Yes, yes, of course," or "Quite right," poking its way into the conversation. Another half-minute and Präger again motioned to Hoffner. Not knowing what to do, Hoffner moved over to the window and gazed out, his eyes wandering across the wreckage in the square below.

Willingly or not, Hoffner now saw the Alex as if through a sheet of fine gauze, all of it familiar, real, yet profoundly not. In a single moment it had changed forever. Whether over hours, days, weeks, Hoffner had discovered that, in revolution, the passage of time is instantaneous, the reality of the sequence irrelevant and irrevocable: perspective made the sensation only more acute. He had felt something similar to this once before, the same distortion, the same jarring disbelief. Then, he had not thought himself capable of striking Martha—he wasn't—and yet, in that one infinite moment, he had sent her to the ground, his oldest boy watching in horror, the reality of it now lost, only its shame lived over and over: one moment, all as it was, as it had been; the next, fine gauze, and with it a sense of helplessness so deep as to make it almost illusory.

"She has the same markings?" said Präger.

Hoffner turned. The KD was off the phone and was busy writing on a pad as he spoke. "Yes," Hoffner answered. "Identical."

A nod.

"You've heard the rumor, of course," said Hoffner. "We're due for another new chief, any day." He moved toward the desk. "What does that make—four, five in the last month?"

Still preoccupied, Präger said, "And when were you planning on starting this rumor?"

Hoffner smiled quietly to himself. "As soon as all the bets were in." He thought he saw the hint of a grin.

"So this makes five," said Präger as he flipped through the papers.

"Yes."

"And that makes your maniac rather special, doesn't it?" Präger stacked the pages, then placed them in perfect alignment along the top right-hand corner of his desk.

"Yes." Hoffner waited for Präger to look up. "This one looks to be his first. She might even have had a personal connection with our friend."

"Personal?"

"He's preserved her. My guess is at least six weeks. That makes her different."

"Different is good. And how's Fichte working out?"

"Fine. He's with the body."

"Yes, I know. Allowing someone else to take care of your evidence. How far we've come, Nikolai."

"A brave new world, Herr **Kriminaldirektor.**"

Präger motioned to the chair by the desk. "I need you to finish this one up."

Hoffner sat. "I don't think he meant for us to find this woman," he said, as if not having heard the request. "The others, yes. This one, no." Hoffner pulled open his notebook and flipped to a dog-eared page. "Preliminary guess is that she was asphyxiated like the others, then—"

"How close are we, here?"

Hoffner looked up. That wasn't a question one asked in cases like these. In cases like these, one had to let it play itself out, each one unique, like the men and women who committed the crimes: degree was never an issue, and Präger knew that. Hoffner did his best to let the question pass. "As I said, we might have someplace to go with this one—"

"I need this finished," Präger cut in. He waited. "Do you understand what I'm saying, Nikolai?"

Hoffner remained silent. "No, Herr **Kriminaldirektor,** I do not."

Präger began to chew on the inside of his cheek: it was the one lapse in composure he permitted himself. "Almost half a dozen mutilated women in just over a month and a half," he said, his tone more direct. "I'm not sure how long we can keep this out of the press. The distractions of revolution are beginning to fade."

"They're also not going to be getting in the way of an investigation anymore. And," Hoffner continued, "correct me if I'm wrong, Herr **Kriminaldirektor,** but we've always been very good at using the newspapers to our advantage."

"As you said, Nikolai, a brave new world."

For the first time today, Hoffner was genuinely confused. "You're going to have to make that a little clearer, Herr **Kriminaldirektor.**"

Präger's tone softened. "Once in a while, Nikolai, you need to consider the world outside of homicide. You need to consider the repercussions."

Hoffner had no idea where Präger was going with this, when the KD suddenly stood, his gaze on the door. "Ah." Präger moved out from behind his desk. "Herr **Kriminal-Oberkommissar,**" he said. "I wasn't expecting you quite so—promptly."

Hoffner turned to see a tall, angular man in an expensive suit stepping into the office: a chief inspector with a thin coating of meticulously combed jet-black hair atop a narrow head. Hoffner stood. He had never seen the man before.

Präger made the introductions. "**Kriminal-Oberkommissar** Gustav Braun, this is—"

"**Kriminal-Kommissar** Nikolai Hoffner," said the man, a strangely inviting smile on his lips. "Yes, I know your work well, Inspector. A most impressive résumé."

With a slight hesitation, Hoffner nodded his acknowledgment. "I wish I could say the same of you,

Chief Inspector." Hoffner then added, "I mean, that I know your work well. I don't."

Still coldly affable, Braun said, "No, no, of course not. We tend to keep ourselves to ourselves, upstairs."

And there it was, thought Hoffner. "Upstairs." Of course.

A step up from the **Kriminalpolizei,** both by floor and autonomy, were the detectives of Department IA, the political police. Hoffner had never figured out whether they had been created to combat or augment domestic espionage. Whichever it was, he had learned to keep his distance from the men on the fourth floor. Their influence, never lacking under the Kaisers, had grown by leaps and bounds during the last few months. It was simply a question of how far it would ultimately take them. Why they should be showing any interest in his case, however, was not at all clear. The first four bodies had been those of a sales clerk, two seamstresses, and a nurse, no connections among them—except perhaps that they had all lived solitary, isolated lives—but nothing to pique the curiosity of the Polpo: unless the boys upstairs knew something about number five that Hoffner had failed to see, which meant that Präger was obviously in on the secret.

"Yes, well," said Präger, predictably less poised: seniority of rank never seemed to matter when IA was involved. "I can assure you that the Chief Inspector has an equally impressive record, Herr Detective Inspector. Although, of course, one never knows how

much more has been left out of the file that would be
even more impressive had it been in the file"—Hoffner enjoyed watching Präger flounder—"but, of
course, it couldn't be—coming from upstairs." Präger
nodded once, briskly, as if to say he had finished
whatever he had been trying to say, and that, whatever he had been trying to say, it had been good.
Very good.

Unnerved still further by the ensuing silence,
Präger awkwardly motioned toward the door. "We'll
go down, then. At once." Präger nodded to Braun,
who headed out. He then turned to Hoffner and,
with a strained smile, indicated for him to follow. No
less confused—though rather enjoying it all—Hoffner moved out into the corridor.

The morgue at police headquarters—more of an
examination room, and nowhere near as extensive as
the real thing across town—sat in the sub-basement
of the southwest corner of the building, in better days
a quick jaunt across the large glass-covered courtyard, and then down two flights. For the trio of
Präger, Hoffner, and Braun, however, it was more of
a trek, the courtyard having taken the brunt of the recent fighting. Mortar fire had shattered several sections of the glass dome, allowing individual columns
of rain to pour down at will, the echo, in spots, over-
powering. Cobblestone, where it remained, was per-
ilously slick; elsewhere, one was left to navigate
through tiny rivulets of mud. Herr Department IA
seemed little inclined to get his boots dirty.

"I could always carry you," said Hoffner, under his breath.

"Pardon?" said Braun as he hopped gingerly from one spot to the next.

"What?" said Hoffner innocently.

"I thought you said something."

"No, nothing, Herr **Kriminal-Oberkommissar.**" Hoffner looked at Präger. "Did you say something, Herr **Kriminaldirektor**?"

Präger quickened his pace and, still a good ten meters from the door to the lower levels, stuck out his arm. "Ah, here we are," he said. "That wasn't so bad."

Three minutes later, all three stepped into the morgue's outer hallway, the air thick with the smell of formaldehyde. An officer sat at a desk. He nodded them on.

Visible through the glass on the far doors were six tables in a perpendicular row along the back wall. Sheeted bodies occupied the two tables at the far ends; the four inner ones remained empty. Along the other walls, bookcases displayed a wide array of instruments and bottles, the latter filled with various liquids and creams. Above, the old gas lamps had once again been called into service. Hans Fichte was by one of the shelves, holding an open bottle in his hands—sniffing at its contents—as the three men pushed through the doors and stepped into the room. Momentarily startled, Fichte tried to get the lid back on as quickly as possible. "Ah, Herr **Kriminaldirektor**," said Fichte, "I didn't expect—"

"You've been down here alone?" asked Präger.

"Yes, sir," answered Fichte, still having trouble with the lid. "Except for the medic. But he left once the body . . . Yes, sir. As you directed. Alone."

"Good."

"Thank you, sir."

Hoffner leaned into Fichte as he passed by him. "Hand in the cookie jar?" It was enough to stem any further fidgeting.

Präger led Hoffner and Braun toward the body on the far right table. He was about to pull back the sheet when Fichte interrupted. "No, no, Herr **Kriminaldirektor.**" All three looked over at him. For a moment Fichte seemed somewhat overwhelmed, as if he had forgotten why he had stopped them. Then, moving toward the table on the left—bottle still sheepishly in hand—he said more quietly, "Ours is this one here."

Präger continued to stare at Fichte. "No," said Präger, his tone almost apologetic. "It's not, Herr **Kriminal-Assistent.**" He then turned to Hoffner. "The repercussions, Nikolai. Fished from the Landwehr Canal this morning." Präger pulled back the sheet.

There, lying facedown on the table—with the all-too-familiar markings chiseled into her back—was the lifeless body of Rosa Luxemburg.

⟜ THE DIAMETER-CUT ⟝

It was a good hour and a half before Fichte placed the bottle back on the shelf, and then wiped his hands on his pants. His nose had gone a nice pink from the chill in the room.

"You were holding it the whole time they were here," said Hoffner, who was peering over Rosa's body. He was in shirtsleeves rolled to the elbow, with thick rubber gloves extending halfway up his forearm.

Fichte sniffed at his fingers as he walked back to the examining table. "Well, I couldn't have stepped away."

"With the lid open." Hoffner continued to trace the incisions on her back with what looked to be a thin steel pointer.

Fichte took a moment to answer. "Yes."

Not looking up, Hoffner added, "Feeling a bit faint, are you?"

"No. Why?"

"You might want to read a label now and then, Hans. Sniffing isn't actually a science."

"I did read it."

Hoffner bent over a particularly intricate patch. "Really?" He nodded to himself. "So you're comfortable inhaling a solution of arsenious acid. Glad to hear it."

Fichte was about to sniff at his fingers again; he thought the better of it.

"It's actually illegal now," Hoffner continued, his eyes fixed on the series of narrow grooves. "Even at that dilution. But, of course, you knew that." Fichte said nothing as Hoffner dabbed at a bit of swelling. The skin had retained a surprising elasticity. "Used to be that arsenic was a wonderful thing for preserving a body. I suppose there were too many of those side effects, though. Bleeding mouth, sores, vomiting. Don't know why it's still on the shelf."

Fichte's face turned a shade paler. ". . . Right."

Hoffner stood upright. He wanted some confirmation. "There's something different about these." He used the pointer to draw a circle in the air above several of the slices. "You see what I mean?" Fichte was off in his own thoughts. Hoffner enjoyed the teasing, even if Fichte always took it too seriously, but Hoffner needed the boy to see the corpse, not the woman. Over the last two months, Luxemburg had been a mainstay on the front page of every newspaper in town. This morning they claimed that she had been dragged off by an angry mob. The markings on her back, however, said otherwise. "You'll be fine, Hans. I promise. Now, put on some gloves."

Fichte looked over and did as he was told. With a newfound caution, he leaned in over the body and cocked his head to the side so as to get a better angle.

Hoffner waited. "Well," he said, trying not to sound impatient. "What do you make of them?"

After several false starts, Fichte finally looked up

from across the body. "They're . . ." He chose his words carefully. "More jagged. On an angle."

"Which?"

"Which cuts?"

"No"—a hint of frustration in his voice—"which is it, jagged or at an angle?"

Fichte stood upright. His eyes remained on the body as if he thought it might twitch one way or the other with the answer. "I think—both."

Hoffner would have liked to have heard more conviction in the voice, especially when Fichte had gotten it right. Instead, he leaned in and scanned across the carvings: he could sense Fichte's gaze following his own. Shifting his attention to the far table, Hoffner stood and moved over to victim number five, today's discovery. A nice glob of the preserving grease, which still covered most of her upper body and thighs, sat in a jar at the edge of the table. Hoffner handed the jar to Fichte, then turned up the overhead lamp. He pulled back the sheet. "Make sure it's properly labeled," he said as he bent over to examine the back. "We'll need someone to take a look at it tomorrow morning."

Fichte handled the jar with great care as he placed it on a nearby shelf. He jotted a few words of detailed description on the label, then wiped his gloved hands on his pants.

Hoffner continued to scan along the grooves. "That's a nice eye, Hans. This one's smooth all the way across." Hoffner shifted his perspective. "As it was with ladies one through four." He stood and peered over at Rosa. "But not with our Fräulein Luxemburg," he said as if to himself. "Why?" It was not the only dissimilarity Hoffner had seen: Rosa had not been asphyxiated like the other victims, and there was a nice crack to the top of her skull. It might have been from a rifle butt, but Hoffner was only speculating there.

Fichte stared at Hoffner as Hoffner stared at Rosa. After several seconds, Fichte said, "She was pulled out of the canal. Maybe—"

"No," said Hoffner, no less intent on her corpse. "The water's not going to have made that kind of a difference."

"A different knife, then?"

Again, Hoffner shook his head as he moved back to Rosa. This time he used his gloved little finger to highlight the most dominant marking on her back, a straight rut of perhaps eight or nine centimeters in length, a centimeter in width. All the other rivulets spoked out or crisscrossed this central line, which ran between her shoulder blades. Hoffner had come to call it the "diameter-cut." "It's got the same little bumps every two centimeters"—he pointed with his finger—"here, here, and here. The same flaw in the blade." He shook his head. "No, it's the same knife."

Fichte moved to the other side of the table and both men stood peering down at Rosa's back. "Maybe," said Fichte hesitantly, "he realized who she was after he'd killed her. He panicked and rushed the artwork." When Hoffner said nothing, Fichte added, "It does have that kind of forced look to it."

The word "forced" struck Hoffner. He looked up with sudden interest. "Why do you say that?"

Fichte nearly beamed at the encouragement. "Well," he said, tracing a section. "These bits here. Our boy's usually much neater in this part. See how the line lightens up and runs off just at the end."

Fichte was right. Up by the left shoulder blade, one of the incisions seemed to tail off to the right as it joined the diameter-cut: not in keeping with the strict precision of the other lines.

"Here, as well." Fichte pointed to another section.

Hoffner had noticed it fifteen minutes ago while under the watchful gaze of Herr **Kriminal-Oberkommissar** Braun. It was only now, though, hearing the word "forced," that he began to see something else. His eyes moved along the ruts as he spoke: "Bring over a bottle of the blue dye and a thin brush," he said distractedly as he leaned closer into the body. "And grab one of those short blades."

Fichte quickly found the items and brought them back to the table. Hoffner dipped the brush into the dye and gently ran it along the areas Fichte had just traced. As he got to the tail-off point—where the dye brought out the detail of the lighter strokes—Hoffner's eyes widened. For several seconds he held his hand out over the area, his palm facing up. He stared at his own hand.

With a sudden urgency, Hoffner stepped farther down the body and drew a wide circle of blue on Rosa's untouched thigh. He held the knife out to Fichte. "All right, Hans," he said. "I want you to hold it in your open palm, with the blade facing away from you, your thumb on the knife's midpoint. And with the flat of the blade parallel to your palm. As if you were going to jab it at me." He waited until Fichte held it correctly. "Good. Now, carve out a small rut inside the circle." Hoffner pointed to two spots on the thigh. "Start here, end here. Carve up and away from yourself."

Fichte stared at him incredulously. "You want me to disfigure the body?"

"She won't mind," said Hoffner, his eyes still on the thigh. "Trust me." He made a sweeping movement with his hand. "Up and away. Keeping the flat of the knife against the skin. Anytime, Hans." The discussion was over.

This was not the first time that Fichte had been handed his fate. With no other choice, he slowly placed his free hand just above the back of Rosa's knee and, pulling the skin taut, began to carve out a rut. The sensation was strangely calming, the cold flesh giving way easily to the run of the knife. To Fichte's surprise, the sliced skin held together like pencil shavings, curling upward, then spiraling down over the thigh before crumbling onto the table. Reaching the endpoint, he stood back and placed the knife next to the body. Hoffner was already leaning in, staring up along the newly made groove.

"Good," said Hoffner. He stood upright, keeping his eyes on Rosa. "Excellent."

Fichte was not sure what to answer. ". . . Thank you."

Hoffner looked over, not having been listening. "What?" Almost instantly, he added, "Oh, yes. Good. You're welcome." He looked back at Rosa. "Now, I want another rut," he said, tracing a second line on her thigh, "right next to the first one—"

"What exactly are we doing?" said Fichte, his tone a bit more aggressive than either of them expected.

Hoffner stopped and looked at him. "Cutting out ruts," he said calmly. "Is that all right with you?" After a moment's hesitation, Fichte nodded. "Good," said Hoffner; he waited until Fichte had the knife. "This time," he continued, "hold it with the blade facing into you, with your thumb at the back, as if you were going to jab it into your own stomach. Again, with the flat of the blade parallel to your palm." Fichte positioned the knife. "Now carve down and toward yourself, between the same points, the same length as before. **Exact** same length. You understand?" Hoffner waited for a nod and stepped back.

It was a bit tougher going this time, but Fichte eventually created a parallel line. Again, Hoffner leaned in to examine the results. When he stood, he was nodding to himself.

"What?" said Fichte.

Hoffner thought a moment longer, then turned to Fichte. "Clean it out, and see for yourself."

Fichte took a cloth, dipped it into a jar of alcohol, and swabbed out the ruts. He then drew to within a few centimeters of the body. When he had finished examining his handiwork, Fichte pulled back and smiled, tracing the first line with his finger. "Smooth," he said; he then traced the second. "Angled and jagged. How did you know?"

"I didn't," said Hoffner, "until I watched you." He took the blade and held it just above the new markings. "Look." Fichte bent in closer as Hoffner demonstrated. "That second time, when you were cutting downward, toward yourself, the natural inclination is to carve at a raised angle, which means that the stroke becomes clipped and slightly forced. You see? And, at the bottom, in order to intersect the point without going past it, the stroke shortens, making the wrist inadvertently twist inward, thus making the blade curl just a touch. Like this." Hoffner exaggerated the movement. "Hence the lighter markings to the side, here and here." Fichte nodded. Hoffner shifted the blade. "Cutting upward, the angle is flatter, less severe, the motion a continuous stroke, smooth. You see? That's why there was no need to twist to keep it from going past the point at the top." He extended the blade to Fichte, the lesson complete. "I couldn't do it myself because I knew what I wanted to see. It would have altered my hand. Not so with you."

Fichte waited, then took the knife. "So, when do I start seeing all of these things for myself?"

Hoffner picked up the can of dye and walked it back to the shelf. "I don't know. When you start looking for them?"

"That's encouraging."

"Really," said Hoffner. "It wasn't meant to be." He waited, then laughed quietly. "Don't worry, Hans. It'll come. The question is"—he moved back to the table—"does it help us? We now know how they're different. We still don't know why."

"So maybe I was right. Maybe he panicked. He was in a rush."

"And he decided to cut up his latest victim in a way he's never done before? Does that make any sense to you?" Catching Fichte in mid-breath, Hoffner added, "Think before you answer, Hans." Fichte waited, then shook his head slowly. "So, what's the most obvious answer? Two different strokes, so—"

Fichte needed another few seconds. "Two different men?" he said, completely unsure of himself.

"Exactly. A second carver." Hoffner took a cloth and began to wipe off the brush. "And suddenly our world is far less simple."

Fichte started to say something but stopped. He looked puzzled. "I'm not sure I'd describe what we've been working with so far as 'simple.'"

"Maybe," said Hoffner as he finished with the brush and headed for the shelf. "But remember, simple isn't always the most helpful of things. It's plain, fixed, consistent." Hoffner was at the tray, ordering the brushes by size. "Look at us. It's been simple for the past six weeks, and we're still finding bodies."

Fichte was not convinced. "So going from one madman with four anonymous victims to multiple killers with a victim whom everybody knows—not to mention another one who's been preserved for six weeks—makes our lives better?"

"Better, worse, that's not the point." Hoffner put the finishing touches on the brushes. "It gives us more to play with, highlights the deviation. And that"—he made his way back to the table—"is always to our advantage." He pulled the sheet over Rosa and took off his gloves. "Something to think about. Yes?" Hoffner moved to the sink and began to rinse his hands. He had trouble remembering whether this was the third or fourth time he had tried impressing this point on Fichte. No matter. Someday it would stick. "And progress always deserves a drink." He brought his hands to a full lather. "How about it, Hans? Have we spent enough time with the ladies for one day?"

Fichte was still mulling over the impromptu lesson. "Shouldn't we bring the KD up to speed?" he said.

"Hans"—Hoffner rinsed off the last of the soap, trying not to sound too dismissive—"the Herr **Kriminaldirektor** has been home for the past hour, sitting in front of a nice fire with a far better brandy than you or I will ever drink. He knows these ladies will be here tomorrow. He knows we'll be here tomorrow.

His only concern is that we don't find any more of them to play with." Hoffner shook out his hands, turned off the tap, and took a towel. "Unless you want me to drink alone?"

Fichte hesitated. "Well, no," he said. He moved to the far table and covered up victim number five. "It's just"—he began to take off his gloves—"I was meeting someone, and—" Fichte struggled to finish the thought.

"Ah," said Hoffner, saving him the trouble: the prospect of facing dinner at home without something of a distraction beforehand was far more deflating than Fichte's awkward brush-off. "A different kind of deviation." The joke was lost on Fichte. "Never mind," said Hoffner. "Another time." He pressed a small white button by the sink, and a bell rang beyond the doors to inform the orderlies that the bodies were ready for the ice room.

"No." Fichte was suddenly more animated. "You should come. I'd like you to come." Still more steam. "Yes, come. Lina's even asked about you."

"Lina," said Hoffner.

"A friend. A girl."

"Oh, a girl," said Hoffner, stating the obvious. He tossed the towel onto the counter. "Then I should definitely **not** come."

"No, no. It's nothing like that," said Fichte, even more insistent. "Well, I mean it is like that, but it'll be for a drink. One drink. We can talk about working together. You know."

"'Working together,'" Hoffner echoed.

"As detectives."

"Right," said Hoffner, more skeptically. "I can tell her what a fine partner you are, the great work you're doing."

"Exactly," said Fichte. "We'll have some fun." He continued to gain momentum. "She's great, my Lina. No. You have to come now. She won't forgive me if I show up without you."

"I see." Hoffner stepped aside. He sat against the counter, arms crossed at his chest, as Fichte started in at the sink. "How can I deprive your Lina of my re-markable company?"

"Yes. Exactly."

Hoffner watched as Fichte sniffed at his lathered hands. There was something reassuring about this particular fixation of his. Fichte completed his in-spection and, finding nothing, rinsed off.

"So," asked Hoffner, "how long has she been sell-ing flowers along Friedrichstrasse?"

"About three months," said Fichte offhandedly. He then looked over at Hoffner in complete surprise. "How did you know that?"

Hoffner smiled. "I was also once a twenty-three-year-old **Kriminal-Assistent,** Hans. Mine was called Celia."

Fichte shook his head as he turned off the tap and picked up the towel. "No, my Lina's a nice girl."

For several seconds, Hoffner stared down at the floor, trying to recall his Celia. He could almost see her, the long, slim frame, the wirelike fingers, the small breasts, all of it, except for the face. He tried to find it—bad skin, pretty—but no, only a vague outline: an endless array of thieves and murderers clear as day, but no Celia. "A nice girl," he said, still distant. He looked at Fichte. "And what makes you think mine wasn't?"

Fichte saw the change in Hoffner's expression. He stopped drying his hands. ". . . I didn't mean—"

Instantly, Hoffner started to laugh. "Well, you're right. She wasn't." When Fichte smiled sheepishly, Hoffner pushed himself up from the counter and said, "All right, one drink, Hans. But anything to impress your Lina will cost you extra."

Ten minutes later, after having retrieved his coat and having jotted down a few notes, Hoffner joined Fichte out on the square. The rain was misting in tiny drops of water visible only as haloes around the street lamps.

Fichte was enjoying a cigarette; he offered Hoffner a drag, but the smell of the smoke was enough to put anyone off a tasting. Fichte had a girl: he needed to save his pfennigs. Hoffner had always reasoned that the cheaper the tobacco, the greater the capital required to grease the way. From the expression on Fichte's face each time he inhaled, few came more chaste than little Lina.

There was no reason to ask where they were heading. If Fichte was playing it well—and from the tobacco, he clearly was—he would have progressed to old Josty's in Leipziger Strasse by now, over in the west, a step up: the café was fancy enough so that the girl would feel Fichte was showing her the proper respect, lively enough to know that respect wasn't really what he was after. Fichte had probably asked one of the boys at headquarters where to take her, someone reliable. Hoffner felt a bit tweaked that Fichte had gone elsewhere for the advice.

"She's quite popular, is she?" said Fichte as they continued to walk. Hoffner had no idea what Fichte was saying. "Or at least she was."

"Was what?" said Hoffner. "Who?"

"At the lab. Luxemburg. She was popular."

"Ah, Luxemburg. I suppose that depends on who you are." Hoffner pulled up the collar of his coat. "You fancy yourself a Red, then?"

Fichte laughed awkwardly. "Certainly not."

"So you're more for the oppression of the masses. The inscrutable certainty of capitalism."

"The what?" said Fichte.

Hoffner smiled quietly. "Yes. She was popular, Hans."

Fichte nodded and then said cautiously, "You're . . . not a Red, are you, Herr **Kriminal-Kommissar**?"

Hoffner dug his hands deeper inside his coat pockets. "And what did you have in mind?"

"Well, you know . . ." Fichte had been given the go-ahead. "Blowing up buildings, marching in the streets, chaos, that sort of thing."

"'That sort of thing,'" Hoffner echoed. "Sounds a bit more like anarchy, don't you think?"

"Anarchy. Socialism. Same thing."

"I'll leave the distinctions to you, shall I?"

Fichte hesitated. "She was a Jew," he said with surprising certainty.

Hoffner nodded to himself. "Well, then, there you have it. The complete picture." They ducked in behind a cart and headed across the street. Hoffner said, "You know, your anarchist wasn't always waving her fists from balconies, Hans, but then you're probably too young to remember that." Hoffner hopped up onto the curb.

"Really?" said Fichte, following.

"Really."

They continued to walk in silence until Fichte managed, "How so?"

The boy was genuinely keen on the subject. Hoffner said, "It might do you to pick up a newspaper now and then, Hans."

Fichte nodded. "It might, Herr **Kriminal-Kommissar,** but then I've always got you if I don't."

Hoffner had never heard Fichte's playful side: the prospect of seeing his girl was evidently working wonders. "Fair enough," said Hoffner. "It was before the war, around the time they hanged that Hennig fellow for the Treptow murders. You remember the case?" Fichte nodded. "Fräulein Luxemburg printed an article in one of her papers, something about how the average soldier was being mistreated by his officers. Not that this was any great news to anyone, but she claimed that it had gotten out of hand. Lots of press after that. A Red coming to the aid of the army's downtrodden. Powerful stuff."

Fichte was skeptical. "Luxemburg did that . . . for the soldiers?"

"She wasn't trying to scrap the whole business, Hans—she wasn't angling for them to disband the army or hang the culprits—she just wanted a bit of fair play."

"Oh," Fichte conceded.

"Naturally, the General Staff didn't like it. They said that she'd insulted the entire breed—from the lowest scrub all the way up to General von Falkenhayn himself—so they put her on trial. Wanted to teach her a lesson, show her how easily a little Red could be crushed by the might of the Imperial Army. Except the soldiers started showing up in droves to give testimony, and all of them saying that she'd gotten it right. Something of a humiliation for the boys on top."

"I don't remember hearing—"

"**Reading,** Hans. It required a bit of reading. Anyway, Rosa came out of it the most popular girl in town. First the workers, then the soldiers. She had a little army behind her, this little Jewess with the funny walk. That's why they threw her in prison when the war broke out. And why those same boys she'd helped all those years before were so eager to hunt her down once the war was over. They were officers by then. Not terribly appreciative, were they?"

Fichte waited before answering with a grin, "You're sure you're no Red, Herr **Kriminal-Kommissar?**"

Hoffner smiled with him. "It's not all wild Russians and unwashed masses, Hans. There was a bit of courage in what she did—even for a socialist—and you have to respect that."

The two walked past the darkened shops of Konigsstrasse and up alongside the walls of the Royal Palace—recent victim of its own revolutionary clash, and now forced to play the role of impotent relic. This, thought Hoffner, was to be the home of the new government. Already it seemed to be screaming out "bureaucracy!" to the socialist upstarts champing at the bit—rococo and baroque ousted by the dull gray furnishings of reform. From a certain angle, the four-block behemoth actually looked like a massive legion of filing cabinets. Maybe the social democrats knew more than they were letting on?

Wilhelmine Berlin reemerged as they crossed the Platz and started down the always-vibrant Unter den Linden. Hoffner marveled that, even in the aftermath of revolution, the avenue maintained an almost pristine elegance: trams, buses, people, were all decorously in tune with each other. Not a single tree within the dual column at its center had fallen—to battle or to firewood—although a few limbs had snapped under the push of onlookers during those first wild forays in late December. Those not lucky enough to have merited access to the upper floors of the various stores and hotels—or who had simply been daring enough to venture outside—had been forced up into the bigger branches for their vantage points. Thus had the twin line succumbed to the weight of rebellion. Still, Hoffner had to concede that, socialist or not, Berliners had known themselves well enough to leave the avenue in one piece. It was, after all, far more than just another rendering of the grand European boulevard. It was—it would always be—the city's conduit between east and west, between the grind of labor and the gate of privilege, between his own world and the world of nobility. Revolution or not, Hoffner knew that that line could never be broken. It had made a certainty of defeat even before the first shots had been fired.

Unbreakable, however, was not the way the avenue presented itself to him tonight. Where stone and light and trees sprouted, Hoffner saw only the rising shoulder blades of the Alex and the Brandenburg Gate, the crisscrossing carvings of the well-lamped Friedrich and Spandau and Charlotten Strassen; even the elfin spire of Hedwig Church seemed now like a jagged imperfection dug out by a flawed blade. Hoffner gazed at the passing bodies, trams, automobiles, all of them caught inside the impenetrable pattern of a madman's imagination, their movements dictated by the sudden twists and turns, and all perfectly synchronous and smooth. Variations in speed, angle, and direction faded as the avenue breathed life into the design. And within it walked Nikolai Hoffner, a willing speck in its circulation. He had allowed himself to believe that the pattern would rise up, reveal its meaning, if only he could maintain the ruse, convince it that he, too, belonged on the diameter-cut.

A child darted away from its mother; a man dropped to his knee; a tram screeched to a stop. And the pattern dissolved.

The Brandenburg Gate—once again stone—loomed above, and Hoffner heard words. Fichte was saying something. Hoffner continued to walk: he decided to let Fichte's droning die out on its own.

As it turned out, Fichte was merely pointing out a tram and, expecting no response, had raced off to hold the door. It took another moment for Hoffner to catch on before he put some life into his legs, ran up, and jumped on. He was greeted by several muted hrumphs from the seated passengers. A flash of his badge to the conductor quieted any further commentary.

Hoffner moved to the back of the car and gazed out at the receding avenue. He tried to find the pattern again, but it was gone. Another lost opportunity, he thought. He closed his eyes and let his body sway to the tram's motion as Fichte checked his watch.

It was another fifteen minutes before Hoffner felt a tug on his sleeve. He opened his eyes to see Fichte moving to the door, the lighted sign of Café Jostin growing nearer and nearer through the tram's window. They had arrived in Potsdamer Platz. Two uniformed Schutzis stood at either end of the square's traffic circle, trying to impose order. Hoffner smiled at their ineptitude: even the buses seemed to be ignoring them. He moved toward the door where Fichte was waiting impatiently. The tram came to a stop and the two hopped off.

"I didn't know the badge gets us a free ride," said Fichte, quickening his pace as they crossed the square.

"Only mine," said Hoffner, aware that Fichte was too far ahead to hear him.

Hoffner let Fichte lead the way as they approached the café's large front windows, several long panes of glass that stretched nearly half a block. The bodies inside were packed in tightly, standing and sitting, an amorphous mass on view for the curious passerby. Pieces of conversation spilled out onto the street with each opening and closing of the door, at this hour in constant flux from the young clerks and salesgirls recently unchained from their posts at Wertheim's and the other stores along the avenue. A slightly rougher crew—those who had left carts and other street-front enterprises—milled about around the bar. By eight o'clock it would be a different crowd altogether, a touch more sophisticated and with a few extra marks in their pockets for the second page of the menu. Until then, however, beer, not wineglasses, sat atop the marble tables; paper napkins served in place of the cloth; and those immaculately bleached white coats remained on their hooks—the long, if slightly dingy, waiters' aprons sufficient for the early clientele.

From the eagerness in his stride, Fichte was clearly

hoping to escape the changing of the guard. By then, if all had gone well, Hoffner expected him to have little Lina on his arm for a walk in the Tiergarten, her coat too thin for the cold, a needed arm around her shoulder—better yet—around her waist. Hoffner saw the evening's performance playing out in Fichte's eyes as his young assistant stepped over to the door.

"You go on in," said Hoffner, still lagging behind. "I'm going to have a quick smoke." Before Fichte could answer, Hoffner had a cigarette in his hand. "Come on, Hans. She'll want a minute or two alone with you. You have to give her that, don't you?" Fichte's confusion gave way to a look of reluctant appreciation. Maybe an old detective inspector had more to offer than Fichte realized, than any of the young guns back at headquarters realized? If not, at least Hoffner was feeling himself back in the game. Or vindicated. Or not.

Fichte shrugged with a nod, opened the door, and moved inside. Hoffner watched him go as he tongued the end of his cigarette, lit it, and stepped over to the window, just out of reach of the lights. Taking in a long draw, he peered in from the shadows.

He saw her almost at once, even before Fichte did, impossible to miss her by the side wall. She was seated alone, with a small glass of beer perched at the edge of her table. She could have been any number of girls—a younger version of this morning's encounter, perhaps—but Hoffner knew better. This one had a

long way to go before stepping up to those ranks, her
reputation clearly still her own. Even so, it was a
plain face that gazed out, small nose, full mouth,
with a curling of brown-blond hair pulled back and
parted at the side. Her shoulders, slouching forward
just enough, gave her slight bosom some depth, and,
with her coat draped over the back of her chair, her
slender arms lay bare as they disappeared into her lap.
She sat, neither charmed nor daunted by the affectation all around her. Fichte had chosen well: maybe he
would be the one to save her? From the look of her,
she might even save herself.

She took a sip of beer, licked her lower lip—the
tongue lingering just an instant too long—and sat
back. She caught sight of Fichte and raised an arm,
and Hoffner realized that perhaps he had underestimated her. The face transformed with a smile.
Her eyes, unremarkable to this moment, sparked at
the sight of Fichte, not with an adolescent excitement, but with something far more self-possessed. It
gave her entire face a brightness. It would have been
difficult to call it beauty, but it was no less riveting.
Hoffner watched as Fichte maneuvered his way
through the tables, as he leaned down to kiss her
cheek, and sat beside her. She offered him her beer.
He looked around for a waiter. When none could be
found, Fichte coyly accepted the glass and began to
speak between sips.

There was something fascinating in the way she
watched Fichte talk, something Hoffner had not ex-

pected: she was leaning back. There was no need to perch forward, no attempt to show her undying interest, no sudden laughter, no distractions to sate her vanity. That scene was playing itself out at too many of the other tables. Here, she was actually listening. When she finally spoke, it was with a genuine conviction that, to Hoffner, was as out of place as it was compelling. He found himself drawn in, watching her speak, her every word, closer and closer to the glass, until, with a start, he saw her staring back at him. He stood there, suddenly aware of the shadows no longer around him.

A piece of ash dropped from his cigarette: it glanced off his hand and he flicked it away. It was only then that he noticed Fichte signaling for him to join them. Hoffner wondered which of the two had spotted him first.

Hoffner took a last drag, then tossed the cigarette to the ground. It fizzed in the puddled pavement as he stepped over to the door and pushed his way through.

The din of chatter rose up at once as if personally welcoming him, an imagined "Nikolai!" drawing his attention to a swarm of bodies off to his right. Hoffner turned back and pointed his way past the maître d' as he made his way over to the table and Fichte, who was standing. Hoffner waited for Fichte to present her, and then offered a short bow. "Fräulein." Before Lina could respond, Hoffner had lassoed a waiter and was ordering three glasses of Engelhardt's. Fichte moved around to the other side of the table and allowed Hoffner to take his chair. The two men sat. "I'm sure your girl can do with a glass of her own," said Hoffner. He placed his hat on the empty seat across from her.

Lina said, "You didn't have to smoke outside, Herr **Kriminal-Kommissar.**" Her voice was low and inviting, and just as self-assured as Hoffner had imagined. "I wouldn't have minded."

"No," said Hoffner, reaching in his pocket and retrieving the pack, "I don't think you would have, Fräulein." He took a cigarette for himself, then offered one to Fichte. "The rain's let up. I thought I'd take advantage of it." He saw Fichte's hesitation. "Come on, Hans. Better than that **müll** you've been smoking. Do us all some good." Fichte looked at Lina, smiled sheepishly, and took the cigarette. "Can't understand why he smokes them," said Hoffner, striking a match and lighting Fichte's. Not giving her time to answer, Hoffner said, "Must have some reason, eh, Fräulein?" He lit his own and tossed the match into the ashtray.

Fichte cut in quickly. "I don't usually smoke around Lina."

"That's a noble fellow," said Hoffner. He picked at a piece of stray tobacco on his tongue.

"She says she doesn't mind," said Fichte. "Naturally, I can do what I like."

"Well," said Hoffner, "that's very open-minded of you, Fräulein."

"Thank you, Herr **Kriminal-Kommissar,**" she said. "Hans tells me your case is getting more and more interesting. That must be exciting."

The word "exciting" had never sounded so raw. Hoffner smiled. "Nikolai. Please. For such a close friend of Hans."

Fichte perked up. "Thank you, Herr **Krim . . .** Hoff . . . Nikolai."

"And you must call me Lina," she said, her eyes fixed on him.

Hoffner felt her gaze as he tapped out a head of ash into the tray. "That's very kind, Fräulein Lina."

"Not at all, Nikolai."

Again, he peered at her. Hoffner wondered if Fichte knew what he was dealing with here.

The beers arrived. Fichte tossed back what remained of his first glass and handed the empty to the waiter. He then picked up his new glass and proposed a toast. "To . . ." It was as much as he had prepared.

"To new friends," said Lina.

"Yes," said Fichte enthusiastically. "New friends."

Hoffner raised his glass, then took a sip. He placed his glass back on the table and said, "So, you've never told me how the two of you met."

It was all the prompting Fichte needed; with an occasional "Really, Hans—an ice-skating rink?" Hoffner had bought himself another few minutes to study Lina.

He now realized that the view from the window had not come close to doing the girl justice. Not that she was all that much more attractive. True, there were a pair of rather nice legs that had been lost under the table—her dress had risen to just above the knee and hinted at an even greater loveliness higher up the thigh—but it was nothing so mundane as a physical reappraisal that intrigued Hoffner. Lina had an energy, instantly perceptible, that told of a past and a future filled with daring and, above all, conquest, none of it garish or cheap, but intensely real, like the eyes that stared across at Hans and his stories of their recent present. The only mystery for Hoffner was why she had lighted upon his assistant, his well-meaning, young, very young, Hans as her escort.

"Hans exaggerates that part," said Lina as she took his hand. "It was a little jump, and I almost fell."

"She was magnificent, Nikolai," said Fichte. "Truly."

It was the first time Hoffner had heard Fichte sound comfortable using his name: remarkable thing, the touching of hands.

Hoffner took a long swig of beer. He stopped for breath, finished off the glass, and then placed it on the table. "It all sounds very romantic," he said as he patted at his pockets for some coins. "Sadly . . ."

"Oh, no," said Fichte. "You're not going yet. And you're certainly not paying when you do." It was clear Fichte was already feeling the effects of the alcohol. Before Hoffner could stop him, Fichte was on his feet. "We have to find you some company. We can't share Lina, you know, if we're going dancing."

Fichte was lost to the melee of tables and waiters before Hoffner could put out a hand to stop him. Even so, Hoffner swatted at the air before sitting back.

"He knows you won't stay," said Lina. "But he wants to make the effort."

Hoffner started looking for a waiter. "Another mouth to feed."

"You don't have to do that, Nikolai."

The mention of his name stopped Hoffner. The sound of it now felt wrong, not that hearing it had ever stopped him in the past. A waiter appeared. "Four more glasses," said Hoffner.

"Three," said Lina.

"Three," said Hoffner, "and a dish of ice cream, vanilla, for the lady." He turned to her. "Do you like nuts?"

"We have no nuts, **mein Herr,**" said the waiter.

Hoffner continued to stare at Lina. "Then we don't want any." Lina smiled. Hoffner tried not to enjoy it as much as he did.

The man seemed confused. "But we don't—"

Hoffner turned back to the waiter. "Just the ice cream, then," he said, relieving the man of any further mental anguish. When the waiter had gone, Hoffner turned again to Lina. "Ah," he said, and shook his head. "I should have asked for chocolate sauce. You do like chocolate sauce?"

"Yes. They wouldn't have had any."

Hoffner retrieved his cigarette from the ashtray.

"No," he said as he watched the line of smoke peel upward. "I'm surprised they had the ice cream." He took a long pull on the cigarette. "You're nineteen. Give or take."

"Give or take."

"Funny, you don't seem nineteen."

"No. I don't." She waited, then brought her wrist up toward him. "Hans gave me this. For my birthday."

Hoffner leaned over and admired the cheap little bracelet, a thin silver plate chain. He made sure to keep his eyes on the trinket. He could feel her eyes on him. "Very handsome." He sat back, took another pull, then crushed out the remaining cigarette. "He'll make a good detective," said Hoffner, continuing to play with the stub. He had no idea why he had volunteered the information when he didn't believe it himself.

"He'll like to hear that," said Lina.

"Then you mustn't tell him."

She laughed: there was nothing coy or timid about it. Hoffner wanted to laugh, as well. Instead, he released the cigarette and brushed off his hands. "And it seems you're fascinated with police investigations."

"I wouldn't say fascinated."

"Excited, then."

"Not really. Hans wanted me to ask you."

Hoffner nodded slowly. "I see." She had given in too quickly. "Clever boy, our Hans." He took a sip of beer. Lina did the same.

"He thinks a great deal of you, you know," she said.

"Of course he does." Hoffner placed the glass back on the table. "I'm his detective inspector."

"No. I mean a great deal."

"He'll get over it." Hoffner felt something fast approaching from behind him. His sense of relief was equally palpable. "Aha," he said. "What's she look like?"

Lina immediately peered past him. Her eyes widened as she gave in to a grin and spoke under her breath. "You don't want to know."

"Then I'm sorry for you. You'll have a tough time getting rid of her once I'm gone."

Lina's eyes told him that Fichte was almost upon them. "Don't worry," she said. "We'll get rid of her." Hoffner had no doubt of it.

"Look who I've found," came Fichte's too-loud voice from behind as he drew up.

Hoffner turned. A short redhead, dyed almost to the roots, had an arm around Fichte's waist; her other was reaching out for Hoffner. She was, by conservative estimates, a good 120 kilos, something of a miracle given the food situation in Berlin. And she was clearly proud of her heft. Her age was anybody's guess.

"Fat Gerda!" barked the woman as she managed to slap a paw onto Hoffner's shoulder. "That's who he's found for you, you lucky boy!"

The smell of alcohol was equally aggressive, a bit much even for the pre-eight-o'clock crowd. "Just my type," said Hoffner as he stood.

"I knew it," said Fichte, a lilt to his voice that told them he had had another pop at the bar during his search. Hoffner recalled the first time he had gone out drinking with the boy, the night after he had introduced Fichte to the "cattle yard" and his first abandoned baby. The stench had been enough to lead them directly to the flat; they had both needed a drink after that. By the third beer, Fichte had been singing, a remarkably quick drunk for such a big man. Hoffner had pinned it on the lungs. Better to think that everything stemmed from that one defect than to consider the larger Fichte picture.

"I've seen your wife, Nikolai," said Fichte. "This one's perfect!" He laughed loudly and Gerda joined in. Lina did her best to enjoy them from a distance.

"Can't argue with that, now can I?" said Hoffner as he retrieved his hat and stood. His own Martha may not have been as trim as little Lina, but she was still a few fighting classes removed from Gerda. "That's inductive reasoning at its finest, Hans," he said. "You're really showing me something here, tonight. Very impressive."

Fichte flopped down onto the chair across from Lina. He looked more than dazed. "Hello, Lina," he said.

"Hello, Hans," she answered.

"Mine's old," said Gerda. Hoffner was praying she was referring to him. She was trying to find a seat for herself but was having trouble squeezing in behind Fichte. "I don't like this Lina person," she said to no one in particular. Gerda suddenly burst out laughing and bumped Fichte into the table. Forcing her way through, she lowered herself onto the chair: seated, she virtually lunged across at Lina. "I didn't mean it," said Gerda, her words as undulating as the thick flesh on her arms. "You know I didn't mean it. You're such a sweet little pretty thing for your young man. Even if he came to find me." She did her best to shake out her hair, her massive chest jiggling with the movement. It was an odd blend of the coy and the vulgar. "He's yours, you know," she added. "Not mine. Yours." She peered up at Hoffner, then took a playful swipe at him across the table. "That's mine."

Lina smacked Gerda across the face, a lithe, swift movement. A nail scraped and Gerda's cheek bled.

For several seconds, Gerda remained motionless. Only when she sat back did she bring her hand to her face. She looked at her fingers, saw the blood, and her disbelief turned to rage. Again she lunged.

Almost without effort, Hoffner caught her wrist, twisted, and pinned her to the table. It was remarkable to see that much size incapable of movement. "Don't," was all he said.

Through it all, Lina didn't so much as flinch. Fichte tried to follow the proceedings, but it was too much for him. No one at the surrounding tables showed the least bit of interest. In a calm, quiet voice, Hoffner said, "You might want to move over by Hans, Fräulein." Lina got up and stepped to Fichte's side.

Still manipulating the wrist, Hoffner got Gerda to

her feet and moved her around to the other side of the table. He was standing between the two women when he released her. He handed Gerda a napkin. "It's not so bad, is it?" he said. Gerda tried to look past him to Lina, but Hoffner shifted his weight so as to block her view. "Is it?" he said again. Gerda looked up at him. She shook her head slowly. "No, I didn't think so," he said. He reached into his pocket and pulled out a few coins. "No reason for you to come back, is there?"

It took Gerda a moment before she pocketed the money. Again she shook her head. Then, stepping slowly away, she continued to peer around Hoffner. "That's not right, you know," she said. "That's not right at all." At a safe distance, she looked at Hoffner. "I know Pimm." She continued to move away, a finger wagging back at him. "Pimm doesn't stand for that sort of thing."

Hoffner knew the name well, a top boy with one of the larger syndicates: fencing, pimping. Gerda needed a friend like that, although she should have been a bit better with her geography. Pimm's terrain was back near the Landsberger Allee. East. This was more Sass brothers' territory. Still, he appreciated the effort. Hoffner reached into his coat pocket and produced his badge. He placed it on the table. Gerda's expression changed instantly. "You tell Pimm I'll keep that in mind," he said.

Gerda looked as if she might say something. Instead, she turned and quickly moved off. Hoffner waited until she was a few more tables on before turning back. He kept his profile to Lina. "Not much of a dancer," he said.

"No," said Lina quietly.

Hoffner knew there would be nothing more by way of explanation, not that he needed one. He placed his hat on his head and retrieved the badge from the table. He then peered down at Fichte. "Probably best to take your walk a little early tonight, Hans. You could use the air."

Fichte looked up. His eyes were anything but focused. He did his best with a nod.

Finally, Hoffner looked at Lina. He knew he would see nothing in the girl's eyes to hint at what had prompted the sudden entertainment. She was, at that moment, completely unknowable. Hoffner nodded once. "Fräulein," he said.

She swayed slightly to stop him from going "We should do this right, sometime," she said. She then placed a hand on Fichte's shoulder. "You, me, and Hans."

Hoffner held her gaze. "Good night, Fräulein." He then slapped a hand at Fichte's arm. "Tomorrow morning at eight, Hans. Wouldn't want to disappoint the KD."

The ice cream arrived; Hoffner was already off in the crowd.

By eight, he was back at the block of flats on Friesen Strasse, following the echo of his own steps

across the vast and empty stone courtyard and into the
entryway marked D. He still had to remind himself it
was D: they had lived in F for almost twelve years, up
until a year ago when the larger place had come available. Martha had insisted he use his position as a Kripo
detective to make sure they got it. Who was he to argue? Two or three families on the floor still refused to
talk to him, though Martha seemed to find a kind of
vindication in their bitterness. He had preferred F.
Nicer carpeting on the stairs up.

The long walk south to Kreuzberg had done little
to make sense of the minor drama at Josty's. Hoffner
wondered how much of it he had provoked himself:
he knew entirely, but his ego was allowing him a little
leeway. Why shouldn't she want to impress him? The
problem was, why was he so desperate to be impressed? He had managed to keep himself in check
since Victor's death, a poor attempt at gallantry in
the name of a fallen comrade, but even Hoffner was
having trouble these days convincing himself that
lethargy was particularly noble. As he passed the
third floor, he realized the point was moot. Fichte
was probably off somewhere staking his claim, right
now. It had been that kind of an evening. Then
again, Hoffner remembered the tobacco. She might
just be putting up a good fight. He made his way up
to the fourth floor and let himself in.

The smell of boiled cabbage and some distant relative of meat greeted him at the door. It would taste
better than it smelled; it always did with Martha. His

youngest, Georgi—Georg to his friends, now that he had reached the advanced age of seven—was waiting for him in the front hall, his slippered feet dangling above the carpet, his long nightshirt lapping at his shins. His head, drooped to his chest, sprang instantly to life as Hoffner stepped through the doorway. Georgi held a piece of paper in his hands. He raced over and hugged his father around the waist. Just as quickly, he held the paper up to Hoffner's face. "It's two weeks from Sunday," he said. "And the tickets are very reasonable."

Hoffner took the paper. Very reasonable, he thought. Evidently, Georgi had gotten to Martha first.

It was an advertisement for an air show out at Johannisthal, a political maneuver masquerading as a father-and-son afternoon outing. The profile of a handsome young sky pilot filled much of the page, with tiny aeroplanes and zeppelins swarming about his head and chest. One actually seemed to be flying up his nose. To his credit, the young pilot was standing firm.

The Ebert government was being clever, thought Hoffner, taking everyone back to the gentler days. Hoffner had gone several times with his older boy, Sascha, when Georgi had been too little. The shows had stopped, for obvious reasons, and Georgi had spent the last three years reminding anyone who would listen of his considerable deprivation. It had not helped that Sascha had kept several posters of the

Deutscher Rundflug—the monthlong rally across Germany—plastered above his bed. "You're sure you want to go?" said Hoffner with feigned surprise. "It looks like it's just some old Albatros D-threes, maybe a few Halberstadt C-types. But if that's all right with you—"

"Papi!" said Georgi with a look of total incomprehension. He grabbed the paper back and began to scan it with ratlike intensity. His tight dark curls bobbed as he read. Again, he thrust it at Hoffner. "Six-cylinder, liquid-cooled in-line engine! A Fokker D-seven!"

"A D-seven, you say?" said Hoffner. "Well, then we really have no choice, do we?" He handed back the sheet and set off down the hall. Georgi seemed to dance his way behind.

The living and dining rooms were dark as father and son passed them along their way to the kitchen, twenty years of accrued furnishings—an amassed life—erased by the shadows, leaving only soulless outlines. Martha preferred it that way.

She was at the sink, cleaning up the last of the boys' dinner, her own small plate of potatoes and meat just off to the side, when Hoffner stepped into the kitchen. Her hair was pulled up in a bun, a few stray wisps tickling at her neck. It was still a fine neck, white and soft, in strict contrast to the hands that ran through the steaming water: the one sign of her age—not in the face, not in the full, strong shape of her figure—only in the hands. They had become oddly rough.

A bowl of brown soup and a loaf of bread awaited him on the table. Hoffner tossed his coat onto an empty chair and sat. Georgi was right behind him.

"I thought I told you to get into bed," said Martha without turning around.

Hoffner thought of something clever to say; instead he picked up his spoon and started in on the soup. It was already cold.

"Papi said we can go," said Georgi, sidling up to her.

Martha shook out a plate and placed it on the rack. "I told you he would. You weren't supposed to wait up for him."

Georgi looked back at his father for help. Hoffner nodded sympathetically, but said nothing. It seemed to take the air out of the little man. Georgi's shoulders slunk forward and he started slowly for the door. "I just wanted to tell you, that's all," he said with exaggerated dejection.

"Good night, Georgi," said Martha.

"Good night," he said. Just as he was at the door, he raced over to his father and hugged him tightly. He whispered in his ear. "I knew you would, Papi. I just wanted to show it to you, that's all."

Hoffner squeezed the little body into his own. The boy's back was wonderfully bony. Hoffner wondered how many more of these embraces he would be allowed. He kissed Georgi on the neck then whispered back, "I'm glad you waited for me, too."

Georgi was gone by the time Martha joined him at the table. Hoffner concentrated on his soup. "Where's Sascha?" he asked.

"Was she worth the struggle?" said Martha, calmly focusing on peeling back the skin of one of her potatoes.

Hoffner looked up, mildly perplexed.

"Your hand, Nicki," she said, still with the potato. "Glad to see you didn't feel it."

Hoffner looked at the back of his hand. Two thin scratch marks ran across the veins, undeniably a woman's nails. They had begun to scab. He laughed quietly. "Fichte's got a girl," he said as he dabbed at them with a bit of saliva. "We went for a drink. He wanted to get a friend for me." Hoffner went back to the soup. "I wasn't inclined—this time." Over the bowl, he saw the hint of a smile in her eyes.

"Pretty?" said Martha.

"Not the one with the nails." When he saw the full smile, he added, "She's all right. Too thin."

"Do you want them for dinner sometime?"

"Not if we can help it." He continued with the soup. "Where's Sascha?"

Martha looked up from her food and peered over at the door.

Hoffner turned to see his older boy standing there. Sascha was in his school uniform—short pants and tie—his jet-black hair combed crisply, his expression quietly defiant. Had he been wearing the jacket, Hoffner might have mistaken him for an adolescent **Kriminal-Oberkommissar** Braun—a slightly rounder face, but an equally dismissive stare. As for the jacket, it had already been hung up in the bathroom. Martha was convinced that the steam-pipe air was keeping it somehow fresher. It had become a nightly ritual.

"Hello, Father." The boy addressed him as if he were one of his school instructors. Probably Herr Zessner, thought Hoffner. He taught physics. Sascha hated physics.

"Hello there, Sascha." Hoffner had given up trying to diffuse these first few moments, terrifying as they were. He turned back to his near-empty bowl and did his best to find a last few drops with his spoon. "We're off to Johannisthal two weeks from Sunday," he said. "You're welcome to join us, if you like." When Sascha failed to answer, Hoffner pulled off a wedge of the bread. The boy continued to stand in silence.

"You know he doesn't like that anymore," said Martha, her voice with the hint of a reprimand. Hoffner knew it was for Sascha's benefit.

"Doesn't like what?" said Hoffner, knowing exactly what she was referring to. "Air shows?"

It had been a slow process, this, the losing of a son. Hoffner would have loved to point to the most obvious moment for its origin—Martha on the ground, Sascha staring at him in disbelief—but, if he was being honest, he knew he needed to go back further than that. The choice to remain faithful to his wife had sapped Hoffner of something vital. Rather than simply narrowing the focus, it had eliminated the beam entirely: he had shut it all down. In an odd way, that moment of infinite regret had been the final dousing of the flame. Sascha had even forgiven him for it, but by then Hoffner had become unreachable. He might have convinced himself that it was to keep the temptations at bay. He did, for a while, but even Hoffner knew better than that. It had only been a matter of time before the boy had given up trying. Recent events had simply taken Sascha over the edge.

"He wants to be called Alexander," said Martha. "He's asked you several times."

"That's right," said Hoffner, nodding as if he only now remembered. "I must be losing track with all these name changes around here. Georg, Alexander." He turned to Sascha. "But yours has nothing to do with age. You're simply ashamed of your Russian past."

The boy held his ground. "I'm surprised you're not, Father." His voice sounded more like his mother's than he had wanted; the sharpness in his tone, however, more than made up for the pitch.

Hoffner almost let himself get drawn in. Instead he turned back, took the wedge of bread, and dunked it in the tiny puddle of soup. "No, that's true. We Bolsheviks do like to stay together." He took a bite.

"Don't make fun of him, Nikolai," said Martha. "You don't have to go to that school every day."

Hoffner looked across at her, the first hint of frustration in his eyes. He swallowed. He could sense that Sascha, too, was unhappy that his mother had come to his defense. "Yes," said Hoffner, his tone now more pointed as he mopped up the last of the soup, "I suppose giving in to them is the best choice."

Sascha had reached the limits of his self-control. His cheeks flushed; his large eyes grew larger still. "You think you know, but you don't," he said with as much restraint as he could. "You think you can laugh about it, like you laugh about everything else. Well, I'm glad they killed them. I'm glad they killed those Reds. I'm a German. A **German.** I'm not like them. I'll never be like them."

Sascha saw his mother start toward him; with a look, he stopped her. He waited for his father to turn. When Hoffner continued to stare into his bowl, Sascha bolted from the room. Martha stood to go after him, but Hoffner quickly reached out and held her back. She turned to him. She said nothing.

The ring of the telephone startled them both.

It was a recent addition. Headquarters had been insisting for years that Hoffner have one installed: a detective inspector needed to be reached. Hoffner saw it otherwise: the one at the porter's gate was sufficient; nothing could be that pressing. Präger, however, was not to be denied. So, with the new flat had come the new device. To Hoffner's way of thinking, they might just as well have removed the building's

walls: anyone could break through now, so what difference did it make?

In the year they had had it, the telephone had rung
twice: the first at a prearranged minute so that Hoffner could sing to Georgi on his birthday; the second
for a misconnection. Neither time had the ring occurred later than four in the afternoon.

Hoffner let go of Martha's arm, jarred if not slightly
relieved. The look on her face had turned to panic.
He gave her a reassuring shake of the head, stood,
and headed out into the hall, she behind him, stopping at the living room door as he found a light and
moved across the room to the telephone. She waited
in the hall. Georgi was already at her side as Sascha
appeared from behind the two of them.

Hoffner said, "Go back to your room, boys." It was
a tone of voice he rarely used. Georgi and Sascha
quickly moved back down the hall and Hoffner
picked up the receiver. "Hello?" It was Fichte. He
sounded frantic. "Yes, it's me," said Hoffner.

"She's missing," came the rasped voice over
the line.

"Calm down, Hans," said Hoffner. "Who's missing? Where are you?"

There was a pause. Fichte tried to control himself.
"At headquarters. The morgue. No one's here."

It took Hoffner a moment to digest the information. "Headquarters? What are you doing at the
morgue? Calm down."

Another pause. "Lina wanted to see."

"You took the girl—" He stopped himself. Again, he needed a moment. Then, in a strong, controlled voice, he said, "This is a police matter. Anyone on the line, please disengage." The sound of the operator's click brought him back to Fichte. Again, Hoffner spoke very deliberately. "You need to explain to me, Hans, why you took Lina to the morgue, and then you need to tell me who is missing."

"We'd come before," said Fichte, his panic mounting. "It was nothing. The guard let us look around."

Hoffner had trouble believing what he was hearing. With a practiced calm, he said, "All right. And who is missing?"

There was a long pause on the line. Finally Fichte said, "No one's here. No guard. And the body—"

"Which body, Hans?" Hoffner cut in. He could hear Lina in the background. "Not a name, Hans, just left or right."

Another silence. It was clear Fichte was trying to orient himself. "Right," he said. "Right is missing."

"All right," said Hoffner. "Send the girl home. She's to say nothing. You understand?" A muted "Yes" crackled on the line. "Stay there. I'll be there as soon as I can." He paused. "You're not to do a thing."

Hoffner placed the receiver in its cradle. He stood there staring at it for several seconds. Missing. What was Fichte—the thought turned his stomach. Hoffner looked at Martha. She was already holding his coat.

The first cabs began to appear up by the Hallesches Gate: at this hour, the great marble Peace Column at its center—a nod to a way of life the German people had yet to grasp—stood as the outermost edge of the city's nightlife. The few cabs that did venture this far south raced around the bright-lit obelisk at speeds of almost forty-five kilometers an hour, all too eager to get back north and the possibility of a fare out to the rarefied air of Charlottenburg. Hoffner had no choice but to stand out in the middle of the roundabout, his badge held windshield high, before he finally flagged one down.

At the Alex, a trio of seasoned **Soldaten** had replaced the boy-soldiers from this afternoon; the night shift around headquarters evidently required a sterner face. Hoffner produced his badge, then his papers—a necessity in the city these days—and impatiently waited while they slowly pored over them. "New evidence, just in," he said. "A murder case." At once, all three looked up at him.

Hoffner always found this strangely amusing, if not slightly disturbing: hardened men, who in the last five years had witnessed more death than he had seen in his twenty with the Kripo, never failed to flinch at the mention of murder. Until a few weeks ago, he had seen it as a kind of vanity, the nobility of their own art—the defense of a nation's honor—sneering down at the dirty business of pure killing. He wondered, however, how far the revolution had gone to shake that certitude.

"Good," said the oldest of the three as he slapped the papers into Hoffner's chest. "All is in order here. You may go in."

The entrance atrium was empty, a cavernous corridor that ran the length of the building. An older sergeant—Fliegmann or Fliegland, Hoffner could never remember which—sat behind the now superfluous security desk at its center, the dim gaslight overhead just enough to give the newspaper in his hands the pretense of focus; no doubt Fichte and Lina had snuck by without too much of an effort.

"Good evening, Sergeant," said Hoffner, momentarily startling the man.

FliegFlieg's recovery was instantaneous. "Good evening, Herr **Kriminal-Kommissar,**" he said, laying the paper on the desk. "I wasn't told you'd been called back in."

"Lots of activity tonight?" said Hoffner as he signed the sheet. He noticed Fichte's name was nowhere on the page.

The question seemed to confuse **Der Flieger.** "No, Herr Inspector. Quiet enough. I suppose those boys outside have something to do with that." He waited, then took the offensive. "Is there someone you want me to contact for you?" He reached for the phone.

"A scarf, Sergeant," said Hoffner as he started past the desk and toward the courtyard doors. "I'll be sleeping on the floor tonight if I come home without it."

FliegFlieg let go of the receiver with a nod. "Can't have our detective inspectors sleeping on the floor, now can we?"

The sound of tobacco-laced laughter followed Hoffner out into the courtyard, which was now dotted in tiny pools of reflected moonlight; they gave the impression of countless cats' eyes peering up at him as he made his way across the cobblestones. He quickly reached the door to the sub-basement, and was pulling it open, when the ring of the phone back at the sergeant's desk stopped him: instinctively, Hoffner tried to make out what the man was saying, but it was too far off, the echo too thick under the dome. Hoffner let it pass and stepped through to the stairs. At once he found himself in near pitch blackness.

Odd, he thought as the door clicked shut behind him. Fichte would have left the lights on. Or maybe the boy had just been overly cautious? Better yet, maybe he had been setting a mood, although what kind of mood Fichte had learned to fashion in a morgue was anybody's guess. Hoffner considered the unsettling, if mildly titillating, image as he traced his hands along the wall in search of the lights: the touch of cold steel, he thought. The smell of formaldehyde. Why not? Hoffner located the knob for the lamps and headed down.

Two floors on, he again found himself in virtual darkness. Luckily the light from the stairwell was spilling out just enough to give a sheen to the blackened glass of the morgue's windows at the far end of the hall; the desk sat empty and there was no sign of Fichte. Hoffner moved down the corridor, his hand along the wall to guide him. To his surprise, he discovered that the doors were locked. He did his best to peer in through the windows, but could see nothing.

Hoffner never felt uneasy in moments like these; he never let the dark create what wasn't there. Instead he focused on what was out of place, and that was the locked doors. Fichte had been here alone, or at least alone with Lina. He had clearly been inside the ice room to see that a body had gone missing, which meant that he had been beyond these doors. Yet Fichte had no keys for the morgue, no way to lock them. Hoffner again peered in through the glass. "Hans," he said in an unconvincing whisper.

The sound instantly dissolved into the void beyond. The silence grew more acute and made the sudden ring of the telephone on the desk like a kick to the ribs. It snapped Hoffner's head to the side as he waited for a second, then a third ring. He stepped over and slowly placed his hand on the receiver—the feel of the vibration in his palm—before picking up. Hoffner listened through the silence.

"Yes?" he finally said; it was more a question than an invitation.

"**Kriminal-Kommissar** Hoffner?"

Hoffner did not recognize the voice. "Yes," he repeated with greater conviction.

"Would you be so kind as to join us on the fourth floor. **Zimmer vier-eins-sechs.**"

"Who is this?" said Hoffner.

"Room four-one-six," the voice repeated. "**Kriminal-Assistent** Fichte is with us." The line disengaged.

For the second time in the last hour, Hoffner found himself staring at a silent receiver. The fourth floor, he thought. The Polpo. Hoffner placed the phone back in its cradle and began to tap at it in the dark. Wonderful.

Locked doors and shadows notwithstanding, his current situation was now crystal clear. Even so, Hoffner felt a first twinge in his gut: this wasn't what he needed. The deviations he sought—those fine quirks that he had come to recognize—populated a world that, for him, respected the inviolability of truth and falsehood. Naturally, the span between them was where most everything played itself out, but the boundaries themselves remained fixed, and thus tangible: deviation made sense only if there was something genuine to deviate from. That, however, had never been the case with the men of the Polpo: they saw no edges, no discernible absolutes. Even the way they had summoned him—"**Zimmer vier-eins-sechs . . . Kriminal-Assistent** Fichte is with us"— reeked of obfuscation and the **dramatique.** Hoffner pictured a group of university toffs in robes and cowls teaching each other solemn oaths and hand signs, secret societies for the adoration of bad beer and oak tables and girls they knew they would never have. He had seen such groups firsthand in his days at Heidelberg, their trips to the **Schwarzwald** in the dead of winter so as to run naked through the trees while proclaiming their own divinity, the none-too-subtle markings on their arms or chests or wherever they had chosen to burn the insignia into their flesh, all of it to make certain that their associations, though wrapped in mystery, were at least well enough on display to provoke envy. Hoffner had always felt little more than mild amusement when in their company. He had even been asked to join one of the more exclusive **Geheimkreisen** in his second year. When he had politely declined, he had been presented with looks of mild shock. He doubted a refusal to join the boys on the fourth floor would elicit a similar response.

Hoffner stood catching his breath on the final landing, the extra flights on either end of his usual three-floor climb having taxed him to his limits. He knew he was in poor condition; he just preferred not to be reminded of it. He mopped a handkerchief across the back of his neck and waited for his heart to dislodge from the base of his throat. No wonder the boys up here were always in such a foul mood.

There was little to distinguish the corridor from its counterpart on the third floor: the intervals between offices were identical; the wood creaked with equal regularity; and the smell of lavatory disinfectant and stale cigarettes lingered in the air. It was all too familiar, except for the little 4s that appeared on each of the office doors. A trivial detail, thought Hoffner, yet monumental: their stark angularity was so contemptuous as compared to the soft curves of the 3s below. In his twenty years with the Kripo, Hoffner had ventured up—or rather, had been summoned up—half a dozen times, always to the same office, always to the same clerk for the mundane exchange of files, yet even the clerk, in his role as bland bureaucrat, had maintained an air of impenetrability, as if he, too, drew strength from those dismissive 4s. There was no such thing as "mild amusement" on the fourth floor.

Room 416 looked to be like any other on the hall. Hoffner heard voices through the door: he knocked once, the din stopped, and a moment later the door opened to reveal **Kriminal-Oberkommissar** Braun.

"Good evening, Herr Inspector," said Braun, still immaculately combed and pressed. In a strange twist, he, too, had lost his jacket; Hoffner wondered if there might be a steam pipe somewhere in the vicinity.

"Kriminal-Oberkommissar," said Hoffner. Braun nodded once and ushered him in.

Two other men stood to the left by a long desk; a third was seated behind. The gaslight was keeping the office as bright as possible. Hans Fichte was by himself in a chair at the far end of the room, bits and pieces of him lost to the shadows. He sat up eagerly as Hoffner entered.

"Kriminal-Assistent," said Hoffner with a look to keep Fichte where he was.

Fichte seemed slightly disappointed; he settled back into his chair. "Herr **Kriminal-Kommissar,**" he replied quietly.

"Ah, here we are, Nikolai," said the man from behind the desk. "Nice to see you again."

Polpo **Kriminaldirektor** Gerhard Weigland stood and offered his hand. He had aged considerably since Hoffner last saw him: the hair was virtually gone except for a neat ring of curly white at the temples; the beard had grown long and full, stained a mucinous yellow around the chin and moustache from decades of cigarettes; and the face had thickened, pressing the eyes deep into the twin cavities above the gray-red cheeks. Never tall, Weigland seemed squatter still from the added weight. His hand, though, remained powerful. The knuckles drove up through the flesh as if the fingers intended to squeeze the life out of anything they touched.

Hoffner peered at the two other men, then stepped over and took the PKD's hand. "Herr **Kriminaldirektor,**" said Hoffner.

"It's been a long time, Nikolai," said Weigland; he released and sat. "Only a floor above and—well, a long time."

"Yes, Herr **Kriminaldirektor,**" said Hoffner, who remained standing at the edge of the desk.

"It seems your man was in the midst of giving a little tour," said Weigland through a half-smile.

Hoffner said, "Hans is very enthusiastic, Herr **Kriminaldirektor.**"

"As we discovered," said Weigland with a laugh. The other men laughed, as well.

Hoffner waited. "I'm sure that's not why we're here, Herr **Kriminaldirektor.** After all, we were all **Assistenten** once."

Weigland stared up with a smile that claimed to know Hoffner better than it did: everything about Weigland claimed to know more than it did. "Always right to it," he said. "A lesson for us all, eh, Herr **Oberkommissar?**"

Braun, who was now at Weigland's side, seemed to grow tauter still. "Indeed, Herr **Direktor.**"

"We needed a bit more time with the Luxemburg body," said Weigland in an equally casual tone. "You understand."

"We?" said Hoffner, peering again at the two other men.

Weigland followed Hoffner's gaze. "You know **Kommissaren** Tamshik and Hermannsohn?"

"No, Herr **Kriminaldirektor.**"

"Ah," said Weigland. "My mistake." He made the introductions. "They've been brought in, now that it's a political case."

Ernst Tamshik had the look of the military about him, the way he kept his hands clasped tightly behind his back, the way his broad shoulders hitched high so as to keep his back ramrod straight. There might even have been something protective to him had it not been for the expression on his face: he was a bully, and a particularly brutal one, judging from the child's sneer in his eyes, an ex–sergeant major, Hoffner guessed, who had reveled in the terrorizing of his young recruits. But, like all bullies, he had learned to play the innocent while under his mother's watchful gaze. Hoffner had yet to figure out which of the two, Weigland or Braun, had assumed that role.

Walther Hermannsohn was far less graspable. He was slighter, though just as tall, and had no need for Tamshik's stifled violence or Braun's clipped affectation. He projected nothing and, for Hoffner, that made him the most dangerous man in the room.

"A political case?" said Hoffner. "That seems a bit premature, don't you think, Herr **Kriminaldirektor**?"

Weigland was momentarily confused. "Premature? Why do you say that?"

Hoffner explained, "Luxemburg has the same markings as the other homicides. Why assume that it wasn't simply bad luck for her and poor timing for us—or, rather, for you, Herr **Kriminaldirektor**?"

Weigland tried another unconvincing smile. He shifted slightly in his chair. "It's just **Direktor** now, Nikolai. **Direktor, Kommissar, Oberkommissar.** We've dispensed with the **Kriminal** up here."

Hoffner waited before answering. "That's convenient." Weigland showed no reaction. "Then, my mistake, Herr **Direktor.**"

Weigland's smile broadened. "No mistake, Nikolai. Just a bit of new information."

Hoffner nodded once. "Is it also new Polpo policy

to take Kripo bodies from the morgue in the middle of the night?"

Weigland was unprepared for the question. Tamshik, however, was not so reticent. He spoke with a clumsy arrogance. "It wouldn't be the first time."

The look from Braun told Hoffner where the teat lay.

"If," Braun said calmly, "this is a political case—as the **Direktor** has just said—then your confusion, Herr **Kriminal-Kommissar,** seems unwarranted."

Hoffner continued to look at Weigland. "And the body would simply have found its way back to the morgue by tomorrow morning? Or would my confusion have begun then?"

Braun answered with no hint of condescension: "There are things here you can't fully understand, Herr **Kriminal-Kommissar.** Luxemburg's been our case since she got back to Berlin in early November. A Kripo officer happens to find her body in mid-January and you think she's no longer ours? You must see what little sense that makes."

"Yes," said Hoffner. "I'm beginning to see the lack of sense. Did you have a man waiting for her outside the prison gates, Herr **Oberkommissar,** or does the Polpo leave the distant edges of the empire to some-one else?"

Braun said, "Frau Luxemburg was a threat no mat-ter where she was, Herr **Kriminal-Kommissar.** Bres-lau, Berlin, it makes no difference. That's why she spent the war inside a cell. The last few months should have made that obvious, even to you."

"I see." Hoffner saw how pleased Braun was with his answer. "Funny," said Hoffner, "but I thought the last few months were all about how the generals and politicians were divvying up what the Kaiser had left behind when he ran off to Holland. I wasn't aware that one little crippled woman had played so important a role. Unless the game was charades."

Braun's jaw tightened. "And I wasn't aware that officers in the Kripo had sympathies for such extremists."

"Just for pawns, Herr **Oberkommissar,**" said Hoffner. Braun said nothing. "May I see the body?"

Braun said, "And what would be the reason for that?"

Hoffner waited. Braun's expression told him nothing. Hoffner turned to Weigland. "I assume the body will not be coming back to us tomorrow."

"No," said Braun.

Hoffner continued to speak to Weigland: "I didn't know the fourth floor had storage and examination facilities, Herr **Direktor.**"

"A recent addition," said Braun.

Hoffner kept his gaze on Weigland. "Can I assume the markings on the back will go untouched?"

Braun said, "Again, I'm afraid we can't promise that, Herr **Kriminal-Kommissar.** But we'll do our best. For your case, of course."

Hoffner finally turned to Braun. "Of course," said Hoffner. The room became silent as the two men stared at each other.

"Why not simply take her this afternoon?" The voice came from behind them. Hoffner turned. It was Fichte from the corner; he showed no fear at all. "I mean, if it was your case, Herr **Oberkommissar,**" Fichte continued. "Why not take the body then?"

Hoffner stared at his young **Assistent.** It was the first time he had felt pride in him.

Braun had also redirected his attention. "A courtesy, Herr **Kriminal-Assistent,**" he said coolly. "We do, after all, work in the same building."

"I see," said Hoffner, retaking the reins. "A courtesy that runs out at, what, seven-thirty, eight o'clock? Is that about the time Frau Luxemburg made her way up to the fourth floor? And, forgive my confusion, Herr **Oberkommissar,** but how did you know Herr **Kriminal-Assistent** Fichte was down in the morgue if you already had the body?"

For the first time, Braun hesitated. "There were tools we needed—"

"Tools?" Hoffner countered. "I see. And what exactly were you planning to do with our body, Herr **Oberkommissar?**"

"I find it strange," said Braun, "that you should have such an interest in this one body when you have yet to make sense of the other five. Surely the pattern should be clear enough, by now?"

"Clear as day," said Hoffner, "if we could be certain that those bodies wouldn't go missing in the middle of the night, Herr **Oberkommissar.** Will our ice room be empty in the next week, in the next two weeks? I'm just asking so as to minimize any confusion."

Weigland suddenly thumped his hand on the desk. "Let's have a walk, Nikolai," he said amiably. "You and I." He stood and stepped out from behind the desk. "A walk would be good, yes?"

The suggestion was as inappropriate as it was unexpected. Hoffner felt like the class idiot about to be ushered from the room. Tamshik seemed to be enjoying the moment immensely.

Hoffner said in a quiet tone, "If that's what you'd like, Herr **Direktor.**"

"Absolutely," said Weigland as he put a hand on Hoffner's shoulder and started to move him toward the door. "There should be a pot of coffee at the end of the hall. A coffee would be nice, don't you think?" Tamshik had the door open. "See if Herr **Assistent** Fichte would like something, as well," said Weigland as he passed Tamshik.

Hoffner found himself out in the corridor, the door closed behind him. Weigland kept his hand on Hoffner's shoulder: it helped to maintain the surreal quality to the little jaunt. "Your boys are what, six and ten now, Nikolai?" said Weigland as they slowly made their way down the hall.

"Seven and fifteen, Herr **Direktor.**"

"That's right. Seven and fifteen. Very nice." Weigland continued to walk. "I lost a grandson in the war, you know. Not much older."

"Yes. I was sorry to hear, Herr **Direktor.**"

"Yes." They walked a bit more before Weigland released Hoffner's shoulder. "This business with Luxemburg," he said. "Best to let it work itself out, don't you think? She's not crucial to your case, and I'm sure whatever Herr Braun feels is of such vital importance is . . ." Weigland seemed to lose the thought.

"Of such vital importance?" said Hoffner.

Weigland laughed to himself. He patted another knowing hand on Hoffner's shoulder. "It's that mouth of yours that kept you out of the Polpo, you know."

"It might have been that I never filed an application, Herr **Direktor.**"

Weigland nodded as if having been caught out. "I suppose that might have had something to do with it, yes."

They reached the end of the corridor and stepped into a kitchen, of sorts: table, icebox, sink. A kettle of coffee sat on a small iron stove. Weigland found two cups and placed them on the table. The two sat and Weigland poured. "Your father would have made an excellent Polpo officer," he said as he set the kettle on the table.

Hoffner was unsure where Weigland was going with this. He answered, nonetheless. "He always thought so, Herr **Direktor.**"

"But then there was all that business with your mother, which made it impossible." Weigland took a sip. He kept his eyes on the cup as he placed it on the table. "Jewish converts weren't exactly popular at the time."

Hoffner watched Weigland for a moment; the man was so obvious in his baiting. Hoffner brought the cup to his lips; he said nothing. This was not a topic he discussed.

Weigland looked up. "You never had any trouble with that, did you? The Jewish issue, I mean. Even if you are technically one of them."

Hoffner placed his cup on the table. "I was raised a Christian, Herr **Direktor.**"

"Lutheran?"

"No idea."

Again, Weigland laughed. "That sounds like your father." Hoffner nodded. "It was your mother's idea, I think?" said Weigland. "For his career."

"I imagine it was."

Again, Weigland focused on his cup. "We came up at the same time, you know, your father and I." He continued to stare at the cup until, with a little snap of his head, he looked up at Hoffner. "I had no idea, of course. None of us did. Not until it came out."

Hoffner took another sip. He had no interest in Weigland's excuses. Hoffner placed his cup back on the table and said, "So, you want me to let this one go."

Weigland nudged a bowl of sugar cubes Hoffner's way. "Go on. Take one. They're real." Weigland clawed out three and dropped them into his cup. "We pulled them out of a shipment Pimm was smuggling in from Denmark. He would've made a fortune on the black market."

Hoffner picked out a cube and slipped it into his

cup. "I didn't know the syndicates were Polpo juris-diction."

"Neither did Pimm." Weigland took a fourth cube and popped it in his mouth. "Look, Nikolai," he said, "you're making a good name for yourself in the Kripo. You solve this one and the papers will turn you into a nice little celebrity. You'd probably make chief inspector."

"This one, but without Luxemburg."

Weigland sucked for a moment on the cube. "Why would you want to drag yourself into all of that?" He shook his head. "Honestly, I have no idea why she had, as you say, the bad luck to run into your maniac. But for you, she's just one more body. To the rest of Germany, she's Red Rosa, the little Jewess who tried to bring Lenin's revolution to Berlin. Your case will get lost in all of that. Braun's right. You don't know how these things work. You're a very capable detec-tive, Nikolai. So why not do what you do well, and leave·this other piece to us."

Hoffner reached over and took two more cubes; he slipped them into his pocket for Georgi. "And if Herr Braun needs another body from the morgue?"

"I'm sure he thought he was doing all of us a favor. Think about it. If your man doesn't come back in tonight, no one's the wiser."

"You really think I wouldn't have noticed?"

"Fine," Weigland conceded, "I'm sure you're just that good." He waited, then said more emphatically, "This is a touchy business, Nikolai. Ebert's still not on firm ground. You don't want to make the same kind of mistake your father did."

And, like a slap to the face, Hoffner understood. It required every ounce of restraint to answer calmly. "And what mistake was that, Herr **Direktor**?"

There was nothing comforting in Weigland's tone: "Understand the situation, Nikolai. Luxemburg, a Jew. Your mother, a Jew. And a Russian, to boot. Times haven't changed all that much."

Hoffner nodded slowly. He thought to correct Weigland: Luxemburg had been a Pole. Instead, he pushed his cup across the table and stood. "Thank you for the coffee, Herr **Direktor.**"

Weigland reached out and grabbed Hoffner's forearm; the grip was as impressive as Hoffner had imagined it would be. "People make mistakes, Nikolai, and the rest of their lives are filled searching for penance." Weigland continued to squeeze Hoffner's arm. "Understand that, and do what I'm asking you to do."

Hoffner felt the blood pulsing in his hand. He twisted his arm slightly and Weigland released it. "Technically, Herr **Direktor,** I'm not sure I'm in a position to give or receive absolution." Not waiting for a response, Hoffner turned and walked back down the hall. He opened the door to the office and poked his head in. "We're done here, Hans." He turned to the rest of the room. "Gentlemen." None of the three said a word.

Unsure for a moment, Fichte stood and moved

across to the door. He then turned back with a little bow. "**Oberkommissar, Kommissare.**"

Hoffner pulled the door shut behind him, and the two headed back down the stairs. They walked in silence until they reached the courtyard, where Fichte finally managed to get something out. "I'm—sorry for all that, Herr **Kriminal-Kommissar.**"

"You've nothing to be sorry about," said Hoffner.

"I shouldn't have been trying to impress Lina."

"No. That was stupid. Don't do that again." Hoffner began to button his coat. "As for the rest, you were fine, Hans. You handled yourself very well."

Fichte's concern gave way to genuine appreciation. "Thank you, Herr **Kriminal-Kommissar.**"

They passed through the door to the atrium. FliegFlieg was dozing; Hoffner didn't bother to sign out. Out in the drizzle, the soldiers barely gave them a second glance.

When they had moved out of earshot, Hoffner said, "You didn't mention anything about today's discovery, did you?" They continued to walk. "Nothing about the woman in the Rosenthaler station?"

"No, Herr **Kriminal-Kommissar.**" Fichte was doing his best to keep up. "Absolutely not. Nothing."

"Good." They reached the middle of the square. Hoffner stopped and turned to Fichte. "Go home, Hans. Take a cold bath. We start in at eight tomorrow morning."

"Yes, Herr **Kriminal-Kommissar.**" Fichte was about to head off when he said, "The PKD, Herr

Kriminal-Kommissar. You know him well, don't you?"

Hoffner stared at his young **Assistent.** "Good night, Hans."

Five minutes later, Hoffner watched as the Peace Column flew past his window, the cab racing him south to Kreuzberg.

The scarf, he thought. I forgot the damn scarf.

TWO

❦ MECHLIN RÉSEAU ❦

The wail of a siren reached up through the bath-room window and momentarily drowned out the street sounds of early morning. Hoffner tapped his cigarette into the basin, retrieved his razor, and set to work on the stubble just under his chin.

The fires were still burning out in Treptow, where, up until a few days ago, a "unit" of university stu-dents had been fighting with epic naïveté. The last of them had fallen on Tuesday to a roving band of **Garde-Kavallerie-Schützen-Division** men who had pulled the three boys out into Weichsel Square and beaten them to death. On a whim, the right-wing thugs—only the uniforms made them sol-diers—had then lit up the place. According to the papers, the fire brigades had thus far recovered the remains of two children who had been burned alive.

Hoffner listened as the scream of the siren faded to nothing.

"And he still won't admit it?" said Martha from the bedroom. "Even after all this time."

Hoffner waited while another siren passed. "Of course not," he said. For some reason he was having trouble with the angle this morning: his neck was sore. He did what he could, then unplugged the drain. He was wiping off the last of the shaving soap when Martha brushed by him with a pile of clean towels. She placed them in a cupboard by the tub. Hoffner tossed his into the hamper.

"You can use them more than once, you know," said Martha.

Hoffner picked at a piece of raw skin on his cheek. "I thought I had."

She retrieved the towel and hung it on a rack. "Did he mean it as a threat, do you think?"

Hoffner continued his examination. "He's never been that clever." He splashed some cold water on his face.

"Then why bring it up?"

"Make things right," he said. "I don't know. He's an old man." Hoffner dried off, put on his shirt, and started in on his tie as Martha knelt down to rub a damp cloth over the tub. He said, "You know, I think he was actually asking for my forgiveness."

"For something he claims he never did?" She shook her head and pushed herself up. Hoffner said nothing. "You shouldn't work with those people, Nicki. Especially now."

"Not my choice."

Nudging him to the side, she wrung out the cloth in the sink. "Sa—" She caught herself. "Alexander has a match this afternoon. Four o'clock." She hung the cloth next to the towel. "You should be there."

The morning had been progressing so nicely, thought Hoffner, talk of Weigland notwithstanding. Now he felt a knot in the pit of his stomach: why was it that she could never understand he would be the last person Sascha would want to see at a match?

"I'll try," he said.

"Try hard, Nicki."

She moved past him and into the hall. Hoffner was left alone to sort out the mess he had made of his tie.

Hans Fichte was waiting for him outside his office when Hoffner got to headquarters. The boy's face was bloated from last night's alcohol, and his inhaler seemed to be doing double duty. Fichte was in the midst of a good suck when Hoffner walked up.

"Glad to see you're here early," said Hoffner, busying himself with his coat so as to give Fichte a moment to recover. He stepped into the office, tossed his hat onto the rack, and settled in behind the desk. "Come in, Hans. Close the door." Fichte did as he was told. "You're not a drinker, Hans. Try to remember that. Take a seat."

Fichte moved a stack of papers from a chair. "Yes, Herr **Kriminal-Kommissar.**" He sat.

"Your girl get home all right?"

"Yes. Thank you for asking, Herr **Kriminal-Kommissar.**"

"Good." Hoffner watched Fichte's expression; the boy had no idea what he had signed on for with this Lina. Hoffner wondered if he had been any less thickheaded at Fichte's age. He hoped not. With a smile, Hoffner leaned back against the wall, his elbows on the chair's armrests, his hands clasped at his chest, and said easily, "So. What exactly do you think we learned last night?"

Fichte thought for a moment and then said, "That I shouldn't bring Lina—"

"Yes," Hoffner cut in impatiently. "We've been through all that. What about from upstairs?"

This took greater concentration. "That—this is a political case and we shouldn't overstep our bounds?"

"Exactly right," said Hoffner. Fichte's surprise was instantaneous. "Something wrong?" said Hoffner coyly.

"Well"—Fichte showed a bit more fire—"I didn't think you—we—would back down so easily." He waited for a reaction. When Hoffner said nothing, Fichte added, "It is our case, after all."

"It is, isn't it." Hoffner sat staring across at Fichte.

Uncomfortable with the silence, Fichte said, "I'm not sure I understand, Herr **Kriminal-Kommissar.**"

Hoffner sat forward. "You need to ask yourself, Hans: Is Luxemburg an element of our case?"

"Of course," said Fichte.

"According to the Polpo?"

"I suppose not, no."

The response provoked several quick taps of Hoffner's fingers on the desk. "And so their focus will be—" He waited for Fichte to complete the thought.

"Luxemburg."

"And ours?"

Fichte was anxious not to stumble, having come this far. "Everything else . . . ?" he said tentatively.

"Exactly. For the time being, we're no longer concerned with Frau Luxemburg, with her forced, angular ruts, or with her second carver. You understand?"

"Yes, Herr **Kriminal-Kommissar.** I do."

"Good. Does this mean she's no longer an element of the case?"

Without hesitation, Fichte said, "No, Herr **Kriminal-Kommissar,** it does not."

"Excellent, Hans." Again, Hoffner smiled. "Maybe a drink for you, now and then, isn't such a bad idea. Full marks this morning." Fichte looked pleased, if slightly embarrassed. "All right," said Hoffner. "So what do we do now?"

"We—look at everything else."

When nothing by way of detail followed, Hoffner explained, "The morgue, Hans. I need you to go down and retrieve that bottle of preserving grease. The one from yesterday's victim. No one's to see you

leave with it, you understand? And then I want you
to meet me outside in the square. Is all of that possible?"

"Yes, Herr **Kriminal-Kommissar.**"

"Good."

The Kaiser Wilhelm Institute for Physical
Chemistry and Electrochemistry sits on what was
once the Prussian Royal Estate of Dahlem in the
southwest section of town. It stretches over a thousand acres of prime riding land, and was the gift of
one of those unremarkable Junker princes who, rec-
ognizing the need for "something useful in this city
of ours," ceded it to a growing Berlin. Naturally he
had wanted a racecourse, or perhaps a garden "for
young ladies to stroll about at their leisure," but in
the end prudence had won out. He had been happy
enough to let someone else make the decision, especially when they had come to him for a little cash for
the project. "Land is the greatest treasure," he had
said: it was up to the Prussian Ministry to come up
with anything else. As it turned out, one member of
the Ministry had voted for the racecourse; it happened to be the prince's cousin. The rest had opted
for a different kind of "useful." The doors to the Institute had opened in October of 1912, and since
then the place had been home to some of the more
innovative breakthroughs in German chemical engi-
neering and physics. Many attributed its success to
the man at the top. The **Direktor,** however, took

little credit. He had always enjoyed horse racing himself and sometimes wondered if they had all not somehow missed out on a wonderful opportunity.

Getting to the Institute from Alexanderplatz requires two transfers, first on the No. 3 to Potsdamer Platz, then on the Nord-End 51 to Shmargendorf Depot, and finally on the No. 22A, which stops directly in front of the university's central library. Students who fall asleep on the bus after a late night slumming it "up east" find themselves out in Grunewald before they know it, at which point most of them have no choice but to spend the night in the park and curse fate for their misadventure. Hoffner and Fichte took a cab.

"I thought about university, at one point," said Fichte as they moved across the plaza toward the Institute's entrance. It was a massive building of five floors, with an ersatz Greek front of four thick columns and pediment tacked onto the façade; odder still was the circular tower that seemed to be standing sentry duty at its far right. Its roof resembled a vast Schutzi helmet—made of Thuringian slate—along with its very own imperial prong rising to the sky: an unflinching Teuton at the gates of the Temple Athena, thought Hoffner. So much for chemistry. "Not much of a student, though," Fichte continued. "More what my father wanted me to do, I suppose. Luckily the war came along and, well, you know the rest."

Hoffner nodded, not having been listening, and

began to mount the steps. He had to remind himself that yammering enthusiasm was a part of the Fichte-away-from-the-office days. He watched as the boy raced by to open the door for him.

According to the wood-carved listing in the entry hall, Herr Professor **Doktor** Uwe Kroll was to be found on the third floor. Hoffner remembered roughly where Kroll's office was; even so, it took them a good ten minutes to locate Kroll in the lab across from his office.

Kroll was wearing a white lab coat, and sat staring intently at a slide beneath his microscope when the two men stepped into the room. There was nothing at all to distinguish Kroll: he projected the perfect image of the scientist, except without the eyeglasses. Fichte had always associated myopia with science. He estimated Kroll to be in his late forties.

"That was quick, Nikolai," said Kroll, still perched in concentration. "I didn't expect you for another half-hour."

"We took a cab."

"Ah," said Kroll, looking up. "The deep pockets of the **Kriminalpolizei.**"

Hoffner introduced Fichte.

Kroll said, "You should know, Herr **Kriminal-Assistent,** that your Detective Inspector would have made a pretty fair chemist himself. Didn't like the symmetry, though, wasn't that it, Nikolai? Too much coherence." Kroll held out his hand. "All right, let's have a look at it, this great mysterious goop of yours that's too complex to be seen by my esteemed colleagues at police headquarters."

Fichte produced the bottle and handed it to Kroll, who brought it up to the light and watched as the contents oozed slowly from side to side. Kroll then brought it to his lap, unscrewed the lid, and sniffed. "You said on the telephone that it was used to preserve flesh. Are you sure it wasn't used as an inhibitor?"

"I don't know what you mean," said Hoffner.

"As something to keep the elements of decay—animals, moisture, that sort of thing—from getting to the skin. Rather than as an agent that works **with** the skin. You see what I'm saying?"

"A repellent," said Hoffner.

"Exactly. That would make my work much easier. On the other hand, if it is something that actually interacts with the flesh and creates a reaction, then it becomes far more complicated."

"And your guess is?"

Kroll looked over at Fichte with a grin. "And now you see where the two of us go our separate ways, Herr **Kriminal-Assistent.** No guesses, Nikolai. I can let you know in a few days." When Hoffner nodded, Kroll placed the jar on his table and said, "And am I right in thinking you'll be the one to get in touch with me?"

"Yes."

"'Yes,'" repeated Kroll knowingly. "Must be interesting times at Kripo headquarters, these days."

Hoffner waited before answering. "Yes."

"'Yes,'" Kroll repeated again. "And should anyone come calling from the Alex, I know nothing about this little jar. Is that right?"

"Is that a guess, Uwe?" Without giving Kroll a chance to answer, Hoffner added, "You see, Hans? Even a chemist can show the makings of a pretty fair detective."

Out on the plaza, the rain had returned as freezing drizzle; it slapped at the face like tiny pieces of glass, but did little to dampen Fichte's enthusiasm.

"You saw what he did?" said Fichte eagerly. "When he opened the bottle?"

Reluctantly, Hoffner said, "Yes, Hans. I saw. He sniffed at it." Hoffner pulled his collar up to his neck: how difficult was it to remember a scarf?

"You see," said Fichte, his coat still unbuttoned. "I have an instinct for these things."

"An instinct. That must be it. Then tell me, Nostradamus, where are we heading next?"

"KaDeWe's." Fichte spoke with absolute certainty. He brushed a bit of moisture from his nose. "To see about the gloves." Hoffner nearly stopped in his tracks as Fichte continued, "I checked on the body this morning—number five, in the morgue. The gloves were missing. The Polpo doesn't know about them, so I assumed you'd taken them. KaDeWe is the best place in town for lace."

And just like that, thought Hoffner, Fichte was actually becoming a detective.

"**A** darker beige and a powdered blue," said the man behind the counter. He stared across at the woman who looked to be incapable of making a decision. She pulled the glove snug onto her hand and gazed at it in the mirror. She flexed her fingers and then reangled her head. All the while, the man stood with a sliver of smile sewn onto his lips. After nearly half a minute he glanced furtively at Hoffner, who had edged closer to the glass. "Just another minute, **mein Herr**," he said impatiently, but with no change in his expression. "Thank you, **mein Herr.**"

In his finely pressed suit, the man looked like the perfect twin of every other clerk on the floor, or perhaps the perfect "light" twin, as they seemed to come in three distinct shades: blond, brunette, and gray. The creases in his trousers were another nod to his perfection, as was the slip of blue handkerchief that peeped out from his breast pocket. The delicacy of his hands was also something remarkable, pale and soft as they graced the waves of satin.

"You will find none more exquisite in the city, Madame," he said, equally transfixed by the gloves. "Feel them against your skin. Lovely."

It was clear from Fichte's expression that he had never been inside Kaufhaus des Westens, or KaDeWe, as it had come to be known: the high temple of capitalism, undaunted by threats from either socialists or shortages. Utterly self-assured, the place was alive with consumption, and Fichte seemed unable to take it all in fast enough. There was the endless sea of scarves and blouses, soaps and colognes, each department with its own distinct color and feel. Even the size of the clerks seemed to change from one area to the next: long, elegant men to clothe the customer, squatter ones to perfume her, thick-necked boys for her sporting equipment. And somewhere in the distant reaches, men's ties and shirts filled the glass-topped rows; they, however, were lost behind a wall of ever-moving flesh. Above it all, the din from countless conversations crested in an orchestral echo that, to Fichte's ear, sounded as if it were tuning. He had played the violin as a boy, poorly, but had always enjoyed that collective search for pitch.

Looking up, he followed a network of wires that crisscrossed the vaulted space; the lines were only a stepladder's climb from him, but they seemed to soar high above as they rose to a squadron of desks on the mezzanine level: this was where all transactions were consummated; money was never kept at the counters. In a constant whir of tramlike efficiency, tiny boxes whizzed overhead, carrying receipts and payments back and forth. This had been the way at KaDeWe since its opening; modern mechanisms had yet to infiltrate. Fichte had to wonder if a pluck on one of the cables might produce a perfect A-flat.

"Oh, well," said the woman as she removed the glove. "Not today." She thanked the clerk and moved off. The man nodded politely, replaced the two sets of gloves beneath the glass, and then turned to Hoffner and Fichte. He needed only a glance to take stock of the two men: Fichte was still gazing upward. It was enough for the clerk to know that his frustrations would continue.

"And now, **mein Herr,**" he said to Hoffner with icy civility. "How can we be of assistance today?"

Hoffner pulled from his pocket a small parcel wrapped in brown paper. He opened it and placed the contents on the counter. "I'm wondering," he said, "where I might get a pair like these for my wife." The voice and attitude were unlike anything Fichte had ever seen or heard coming from Hoffner before. There was something almost apologetic, even puny, to him. It was an astonishing transformation. The wonder of KaDeWe instantly faded to the background.

"For your wife," said the man, as he glanced indifferently at the muddied gloves. "Yes, **mein Herr.**"

"The dog got into the bureau," said Hoffner sheepishly. "Made a complete mess of them. All my fault."

"Yes," repeated the man. He took in a long breath, then picked up one of the gloves. Almost at once his demeanor changed. He quickly brought the glove up to his face and began to examine it closely.

"Is there—something wrong?" said Hoffner.

The man looked across at him. "Oh, no, no, no, **mein Herr,**" he said, now the model of fawning ser-

vility. "It's just—I couldn't tell the remarkable quality, what with all the staining."

"I see," said Hoffner with a bland smile.

The clerk continued to pick his way through the
lace. "Wonderful," he said. "May I ask where **mein
Herr** originally purchased them?"

"A gift," said Hoffner. "From an aunt, I believe."

"I see," said the man. He placed the glove on the
counter and pointed behind him to two large volumes. "May I?" he said.

Hoffner nodded his assent.

The man pulled the second of the books from the
shelf and, placing it on the counter, began to leaf
through. It was clear he knew exactly what he was
looking for. "It's an extremely intricate pattern, **mein
Herr,**" he said as he continued to flip through the
pages. "Quite rare. We don't carry it ourselves, but
we'd be happy to order it for you. Ah, yes," he said,
stopping on a page. "Here it is." He flipped the book
around so that Hoffner could see the drawing.
"Mechlin Réseau de Bruges," said the man as he
watched Hoffner scan the page. The clerk then
picked up the glove and began to illustrate for Fichte.
"It's like the Brussels mesh," he said as he dusted off
the palm. "But here you see the four threads are
plaited only twice, instead of four times, on the two
sides, while the two threads are twisted twice, instead
of once, on the four sides." The clerk stared at the
glove with almost spiritual devotion; it was as if Hoff-

ner and Fichte had disappeared. "Marvelous crafts-manship."

Fichte had no idea what the man was saying; he nodded nonetheless.

"It's Belgian?" said Hoffner, looking up from the book.

"Yes, **mein Herr.** And made only in Bruges. As I said, we can order it for you."

"From this firm, here," said Hoffner, pointing to a name on the page.

"Edgar Troimpel et Fils. Yes, **mein Herr.**"

"Do you make such orders quite often?" said Hoffner.

"All the time, **mein Herr.**"

"To this particular firm in Belgium?"

The man seemed momentarily confused. "Well—no, **mein Herr,** but our couriers are excellent."

"No, of course," said Hoffner. "I'm just wondering if you've placed an order with them in, say, the last few months?"

Again, the clerk seemed slightly put off. "Not that I recall, **mein Herr.** Not with the war. But that shouldn't be a problem at all now. They know us quite well. Since before the war."

Hoffner knew he had hit the point of retreat. Clerks like this wanted to be coddled, not prodded. Still, Hoffner needed a little more information. He smiled and took a final, harmless swipe. "Of course," he said. "I imagine KaDeWe is the only store in Berlin they work with."

As if on cue, the man's face tightened. "No, **mein Herr.**" His words were now clipped. "I'm sure Wertheim's or one of the lesser stores has contacts with the firm. I can't address the quality of their service—"

"No, of course not," said Hoffner with a penitent smile. "I was only inquiring." He decided to throw the man a bone. "Rest assured that when I order them, I will order only from the best and most respected. KaDeWe."

The man softened as he beamed. "That's very kind of you, **mein Herr,** and may I say, I think a wise choice. Shall I get the order form?"

"I'll need two pairs of the gloves." Hoffner saw the Reichsmarks dancing in the man's eyes. "The second for my sister. Unfortunately, I haven't brought her size with me. I didn't want to get her hopes up if I didn't know I could find them. You understand."

"Absolutely, **mein Herr.**"

"You are here until—"

"Six o'clock, **mein Herr.**"

"Then I will be back before then." Hoffner retrieved the package.

"Excellent, **mein Herr.**"

"Come, Reiner," Hoffner said to Fichte with sudden determination. "We mustn't keep your bowel doctor waiting."

Three minutes later, Hoffner ordered two coffees before making his way over to a table and Fichte, who had settled in by one of the café's outdoor heaters: the long, iron-encased lamp was working at full capacity to create a pocket of toasted air. Ten or so other lamps littered the space under the wide awning; even so, most of the clientele had opted for seats inside. Hoffner, on the other hand, liked being out on the street; he liked the occasional spray of rain that seemed to defy all logic by attacking from the side and not from above; most of all, he liked that Fichte was getting the brunt of it. Across the avenue, KaDeWe loomed like an enormous troll.

"All right," said Fichte. "So, now that we're sitting down, why the performance, riveting as it was, Herr **Kriminal-Kommissar**?" For the first time, the title seemed to carry less than its usual reverence: Hoffner liked the change. He tossed his hat onto an empty chair.

"Riveting?" he said. "You're too kind."

"Yes. My bowels and I are great aficionados."

Hoffner laughed a nice full laugh. "Your expression was priceless."

Fichte bowed his head once submissively. "I'm glad we could be so amusing."

"Very. Actually, Victor once had his—" Hoffner stopped himself. He saw the anticipation in Fichte's eyes. There was nothing threatening in it; still, Hoffner felt a moment's betrayal. He waited, then explained, "The Polpo, Hans." Hoffner took a napkin and began to wipe off the mud that had splattered onto his pant leg. "If I bring out my badge, our clerk can tell anyone nosing about that two Kripomen have been in there asking about a pair of gloves. We don't need that kind of attention."

"But the Polpo wasn't interested in the gloves. If they were, they would have taken them."

"True." Hoffner was struggling with a particularly resilient stain. "Except they weren't interested because they didn't know about them." Hoffner finished with the napkin and tossed it next to his hat. "I've had the gloves with me since we brought the body in yesterday."

"You've had the gloves?" This was new information to Fichte. "Why?"

"Last night wasn't the first time someone's gone through our evidence." The coffees arrived. "Don't look so surprised, Hans." Hoffner took a sip; he had expected better from a place like this, especially in this part of town: he could taste the chicory. "It just happened to be the first time they were caught."

Fichte waited for the waiter to move off. "And you knew it was the Polpo?"

"No. I thought maybe the KD was getting anxious. I even thought you might have been putting in some extra hours, bizarre as that might sound." Fichte ignored the comment. "Either one would have been preferable." Fichte let this all sink in as Hoffner suffered through a few more sips. "It means," said Hoffner, "that you'll have to be just as careful this afternoon." Hoffner looked for a sugar bowl. There was none to be found.

"This afternoon? What are we doing this afternoon?"

"**We** aren't doing anything." Hoffner settled on a spoonful of cinnamon: for some reason, cinnamon was making it through to Berlin in truckloads. "**You** are hunting down all the places in town that do business with Monsieur Edgar Troimpel."

"All?" said Fichte.

"Relax, Hans. There can't be more than ten in the entire city that handle this kind of lace." Hoffner tried another sip; the combination of cinnamon and chicory was truly dreadful. "And I don't want any of them thinking that someone from the Kripo has been asking them questions. **Comprends**?"

Fichte sat slightly amazed. "You want me to do this on my own?" Before Hoffner could answer, Fichte said, "I mean, of course I can do it on my own. I just want to make sure that's what you meant."

"Surprised, Hans? I would have thought your instinct would have seen this coming a long way off."

Again, Fichte let the comment pass. "And what exactly will the Herr **Kriminal-Kommissar** be doing while I'm racing around town?"

Hoffner stood and placed a few coins on the table. "Mechlin Réseau. Write it down, Reiner." He then picked up his hat, ducked under the awning, and stepped out into the rain.

⟻ *IM SÜDENDE* ⟼

Her last known address was a matter of record; it
took Hoffner less than two hours to find it. Even so,
Luxemburg had spent too many years in and out of
prison to make anything completely verifiable: five
out of the last seven, from what he had read. There
was the flat on Cranachstrasse that she had shared
with a Leo Jogiches, but the lease there had run out
in June of 1911. She had reappeared later that year in
police postal records for the South End section of
town, but, given the war and recent events, it was
anybody's guess how often she had called Number 2
on the tree-lined Lindenstrasse her home. Probably
better that way: less chance that someone might be
taking an interest in Hoffner's unannounced visit.

The building was typical for this part of town, five
or six stories, a flat on each floor, comfortable bour-
geois living. Hoffner had imagined Red Rosa in
something grittier. In fact, he remembered how
he and Martha had thought about this part of town
for themselves, but had found it too expensive.
Maybe he had chosen the wrong profession, he
thought. Hoffner mounted the steps and rang the
porter's bell.

Characteristically efficient, the man had wasted no
time in attending to the nameplate for the top-floor
flat. A lone **L** and **u** were all that remained of the torn
strip of paper.

The door opened and an older woman appeared

from the shadows. She was painfully thin, and the wisps of her gray, bunned hair seemed to create a small halo above her head. She looked gentle enough, though the last weeks had evidently taken their toll. "Yes?" she said tentatively.

"So sorry to trouble you, Madame, but I was hoping to take a look at the top-floor flat. You are the landlady?"

"My husband is the porter. That flat is not available." She started to close the door, when Hoffner reached into his coat pocket and pulled out his badge. He kept it close to his body as he showed it to her. Her discomfort grew. She stared at the badge, then up at Hoffner. For some reason, she brought her hand up to her neck. It seemed to calm her. "My husband isn't here," she said. "He said you wouldn't be back for another few days."

Hoffner showed no sign of surprise. "Other policemen were here this morning?" he said as he returned the badge to his pocket.

The woman looked confused. "No. A few days ago. I told them Frau Luxemburg hasn't been here in weeks. We—" She stopped. "May I see your badge again?"

Hoffner reached into his pocket. "Of course," he said, and handed it to her. She examined it closely. "Would it be better if I came inside?" he said. "Out of the rain?"

She seemed torn between apprehension and decorum. She quickly found what she was looking for and handed the badge back to Hoffner. "Forgive me," she said. "Of course. Please come in."

The hall had a few touches to liven it up—a small table by the stairs, a lamp with a colored glass shade—but it remained a rather bleak introduction to the building. Behind her, the door to her own flat stood ajar.

"So you say Frau Luxemburg hasn't been here in several weeks," said Hoffner.

"She was living closer in to town—near to where her newspaper was published, I think." The hand returned to her neck. "I don't know. I don't know the address." Her discomfort grew. "I told this all to the other men."

"Yes," said Hoffner calmly. "But it's always good to hear it again. Make sure you haven't remembered something new in the meantime." This seemed to make sense to her. "Did the men take a look upstairs?" Again she nodded. "I'll need to do that, as well."

Luxemburg's flat was as large as his own, although the decor tended to stifle the space under a thick, middle-class charm: dark velvet curtains and oriental rugs followed him from room to room, as did endless rows of photographs and books that were placed along the shelves and bureaus; pillows of every size, color, and origin seemed to be lounging on whatever surface was available—twin settees, chairs, window seats, even by the fireplace; and the smell of dried wood hung in the air. This, thought Hoffner, had been a home for gatherings, a place of deep warmth.

It emanated most vividly from the faces in the pictures, a few of which he recognized—Karl Liebknecht, Franz Mehring—but most told of a life unseen by the newspapers: laughter, a kiss, things incompatible with the iron stare of socialist zeal. He noticed, too, that Luxemburg had had a taste for things Japanese, a silk screen in her bedroom, a series of candid photos in kimono and jaunty parasol. Even so, it felt odd seeing her like this. Not that Hoffner was new to spending hours rummaging through the lives of any number of victims, but this was his first taste of one so public. It made even a cursory investigation seem somehow indiscreet.

He moved from dining room to parlor, then back to the bedroom, unsure what it was that he had come to see. He looked in her closet: he noticed that a suitcase's worth of clothing was missing; the rest hung neatly in rows. He leafed through several stacks of papers and books on her desk—from what he could tell, the bound drafts of speeches she had never delivered—and then made his way to the kitchen. The cabinets were reasonably well stocked; a teacup sat in the sink. The decision to live closer into town had obviously been a last-minute one.

The porter's wife remained by the front door, waiting nervously as Hoffner made his way from room to room. She said nothing; she could barely bring herself to look inside. As he passed by her for a second time, Hoffner thought that perhaps the prospect of entering the house of the dead—the newspapers had said as much—was too much for her. On closer examination, however, he saw it was something far less primal: this was where the end of her Germany had been plotted, where revolution and destruction and terror had first been conceived, and as much as she wanted to believe that Frau Luxemburg's absence over the last weeks had mitigated her own responsibility, she could not. Hoffner sensed how much the flat's untouched gentility served only to compound her guilt.

He was about to say something when he suddenly realized what it was that was out of place: nothing. The rooms were exactly as they had been the day Luxemburg had left them. And yet, if the Polpo had been here only a few days ago, there should have been some trace of their visit: at least the papers should have gone missing. Hoffner spoke as he walked toward her: "How long were the policemen here the other day?"

The sound of his voice momentarily startled the woman. She peered in through the doorway. "I don't know. My husband—"

"Five minutes?" he cut in bluntly as he drew up to her. "Ten? An hour? You were here, weren't you?"

The woman began to nod nervously. "Yes. Of course I was here, but my husband let them in."

Hoffner kept at her: "Did he stay with the men while they were up here?"

"Of course."

"To lock the door after them."

"Yes."

"Did they take anything?"

She looked confused. "The men?"

"Yes," said Hoffner. "Did they take anything?"

The woman became more flustered. "I don't—no. They took nothing."

"You're sure of that?"

"Yes, yes." The nodding became more insistent. "I would have seen. My husband would have seen."

"So how long was he up here?"

The nodding became a shaking of the head. "My husband? I don't know. Five minutes?" Her eyes went wide. "Yes, five minutes. No more than that. Why is this of any importance?"

"And you haven't been up to the rooms since?"

Once again she began to shake her head vigorously. Her answers became clipped. "No. Of course not. Why should I come—"

"And neither has your husband? To straighten up, remove anything?"

"No."

"You're sure of that?"

"Yes. Of course. Why would he come up to this flat?" She had reached her limit; her words spilled out of their own accord. "We did what we were told to do. We took the name away. We've been to the post office and to the local precinct to tell them that she no longer lives here. Why would we come up to these rooms? We're to wait until her family writes us about the furnishings, the clothing, everything else. Until then, we're to touch nothing."

The orders had been precise, thought Hoffner: the

woman and her husband had followed them to the letter. Hoffner knew why, but he asked anyway. "You were told," he said, his tone less strident.

"Yes."

"Who told you?"

She hesitated. "The men who came." There was a hint of defiance in her voice, as if their very mention exonerated her. "They told us."

It was clear that even the name frightened her. Hoffner decided to make things easier. "The Polpo," he said.

With a short, swift nod, the woman said, "Yes."

"And they'll be back in a few days."

"Yes. A few days. I don't know."

Hoffner knew it was best to let it go. He could see the conversation still spinning in her eyes. He waited, then said quietly, "I see." He then turned back into the flat and let his eyes wander from space to space.

Five minutes, he thought. What could they have wanted with only five minutes? And why days **before** her disappearance? That made no sense. And why nothing since then? More than that, why announce that they'd be back? Not like the Polpo, at all.

Hoffner felt suddenly ashamed of the way he had treated the woman. She had been hiding nothing, except perhaps her own fear, and even that had been too much for her. He considered an apology, but knew that would only embarrass her. Instead, he turned and, with a warm smile, slowly reached out for her hand. Uncertain for a moment, she let him

take it; he cupped it in his own and said, "Thank
you, Madame." His tone was once again reassuring.
"You've been very helpful." Still uneasy, she nodded.
"Extremely helpful." There was a genuine tenderness
in the way he spoke to her. "Especially given how difficult it is these days to know everything that goes on
inside a building. Not like the old days." Again she
nodded. He said, "Who could expect you to know
everything that goes on?"

The woman tried to find the words. "That's right,"
she said, convincing herself as much as agreeing with
him. "I can't know everything."

"How could you?" Hoffner said kindly. "So I want
to thank you for being so perceptive, even when it's
not your job to know everything that goes on inside
these walls." For the first time, she smiled. "Even before all of this, Madame," he said with greater em-
phasis. "That wasn't for you to know, either. Or for
you to do anything about." He paused and then
squeezed her hand. "You understand?"

She stared up at him. For a moment it looked as if
she might say something. Instead she pulled a handkerchief from her dress pocket and turned her
head away.

Downstairs, she insisted he stay for a cup of coffee—a real coffee, she said. Hoffner thanked her, but
instead headed for the front door.

Twenty minutes on, the dense, sweet smell of
adolescent exertion filtered through as Hoffner made

his way along the corridors of Sascha's school. The walls were dotted in a row of saluting wooden pegs, half of them buried under the hanging clumps of boys' athletic gear. Hoffner had forgotten how quiet the place could be in the late afternoon; its stillness and scent walked with him like old friends. Even the memories of untold torments within its walls—those simple cruelties that all boys endure, yet which seem so uniquely pointed at the time—blurred into a larger sense of belonging. What was here remained fixed, his—for good or ill—and even Hoffner could take solace in that. Martha was convinced that they had sent Sascha here for the fine education, the family ties—even if it was out of the way—but Hoffner knew otherwise: survive this and survive anything. Already, Sascha was doing a far better job at it than his father ever had.

As he approached the **Sports Halle** doors, Hoffner heard the familiar clink of foil on foil, along with the occasional cheer and applause for a touch. He checked his watch: he was over forty minutes late. He had gone to Luxemburg's flat because of its proximity to the school. He now knew that had been a mistake. What Hoffner was still debating was how conscious a mistake it had been.

One or two spectators—seated along the hall's risers—peered over as the groan from the doors' hinges announced his arrival. Hoffner ignored the stares and instead scanned the line of boys sitting in full gear off to the side; Sascha was the second one in. It was clear he had already fenced: his hair was matted in sweat, and his cheeks were flushed. He sat staring at the bout in progress. Even so, Hoffner could tell that his son had seen him come in: Sascha's eyes were too intent on the action as Hoffner continued over to the stands. He found a seat in the front row, sat, and, for a few minutes, allowed himself to slip into the easy rhythm of the match.

It was the footwork he had always enjoyed most. The rest—**mano di ferro, braccio di gomma** (iron hand, rubber arm)—had never really been his strength. What had set him apart was his uncanny ability to keep just enough space between himself and his opponents: close enough for the quick touch; nimble enough to make that closeness disappear instantly. Over the years, Hoffner had often wondered how much of that talent he had taken with him beyond the fencing strip.

A hit. The boys on the bench stamped their feet; they shouted out for their teammate. Hoffner applauded politely with the rest of the crowd, one of whom was clapping loudly enough to draw his attention. Instinctively, Hoffner glanced over his shoulder. What he saw nearly made him blanch: there, staring directly down at him from three rows behind, sat Polpo **Kommissar** Ernst Tamshik. Neither man showed the least reaction. Tamshik stopped clapping. The two exchanged a cold nod, and Hoffner turned back to the match.

For the next several minutes, Hoffner did his best

to follow the movements on the strip, but his mind was racing to images of Luxemburg's flat, the porter's wife—he was sure he had been careful there. He pieced through the details of last night's conversation, anything that might have brought the Polpo to Sascha's school. A message? Was Weigland's little chat insufficient? And here: why?

Hoffner forced himself to refocus on the boys, both clearly too green to do much damage. As if divinely inspired, the smaller of the two suddenly tripped on the matting and unwittingly managed something resembling a hit. For a moment the director stood motionless, unsure what to do. Then, with a look of genuine relief, he raised the flag and awarded a point to the boy. It gave him the bout, and gave Sascha's side the match. There was another chorus of foot-stamping—along with a mighty cheer and the requisite handshakes—before the two teams dispersed to the waiting crowd.

Hoffner decided to follow protocol: without a thought for Tamshik, he headed over to Sascha. The boy was packing up his gear when Hoffner approached. "The squad looks strong," said Hoffner.

Sascha remained in a crouch; he was busy fitting his foil into its canvas bag. "Not really," he said. "The other school was weak."

"Still," said Hoffner. "A victory's a victory. Always worse to lose to the weak ones."

Sascha pulled the bag together and stood. "I suppose." He looked directly at his father. Up until this moment, Hoffner had never realized how tall Sascha had grown. They were standing nearly eye to eye.

"So," said Hoffner. "You won your bout?"

"Yes. Fifteen to two."

"Impressive."

"I'm second on the team now, Father."

"Yes. Your mother told me. Excellent."

This only seemed to make things worse. Sascha said, "It means I fence second, Father." Sascha knew his father already understood this. At fifteen, however, he was still impatient with the subtlety of his jabs. "That means early, Father," he said. "Did Mother fail to tell you that?"

Sascha might still have believed that, with enough goading, he could provoke a response. Somewhere along the way, however, Hoffner had seen his son lose sight of that hope and instead settle for cruelty. Given the setting, it seemed only fitting; besides, Hoffner knew he deserved it. "She didn't mention it, no."

Sascha looked as if he had something else to say. Instead he brought the bag up to his shoulder and waited; father and son quickly slipped into silence, which Hoffner took as his cue to glance back for Tamshik: he saw him standing with a small boy, smaller even than the recent victor on the strip. Nodding over, Hoffner said, "Do you know that boy?"

Sascha looked over. "Why?" Hoffner repeated the question. "Krieger," Sascha said grudgingly. "Reinhold Krieger. Hasn't even made it into a junior match yet. Terrible. Why?"

"Let's go over."

Sascha let out a forced breath. "I have to get out of my gear, Father, and I'm meeting—"

"Come on, Alexander," Hoffner said, and started to walk. "Let's go say hello." It might have been the surprise at hearing his full name, but Sascha gave in without another word. When they were within earshot, Hoffner called over, "Herr Tamshik?"

Tamshik looked up. He did what he could with a smile and said, "Herr Hoffner. What a coincidence."

"Yes." Neither man believed it. Hoffner motioned to Sascha. "This is my son Alexander. Second year."

Sascha snapped his head with an efficient bow.

"An excellent fencer," said Tamshik. "You must have been sorry to miss it."

Hoffner wondered how long it took a man to develop so acute a sense of viciousness. Tamshik made it seem effortless; perhaps he had simply been born with it. "Yes," said Hoffner. "I was."

"You were a fencer, as well? As a boy?" said Tamshik.

Hoffner did his best to hide his surprise; Tamshik had evidently done his homework. "I was."

"Easy to tell. Something like that gets passed on. The flair." Tamshik nodded to the other boy. "This is my nephew. Reinhold Krieger. First year. My sister's son."

Hoffner could hardly have imagined a less likely duo. Tamshik's physical power, apparent in his every gesture, seemed capable of crushing the boy simply by its proximity. Reinhold was tiny. He tried his best to mimic Sascha, but on one so small and awkward, the quick drop of the chin gave the impression of a marionette fighting against its twisted strings. Hoffner knew the boy would be hopeless as a fencer. He could only guess at whose insistence he had signed on for his imminent torture.

"Reinhold is small," said Tamshik, staring down at the boy without the least thought for his feelings. "And quite weak. But he has an agile mind. I think the one can help the other, at least on the fencing strip. Isn't that right, Reinhold?"

"Yes, Uncle." To his credit, the boy seemed equally dedicated to the ideal of improvement.

"And a strong will," said Tamshik. "Which the boy has." He looked at Hoffner. "Something he shares with your Alexander."

Hoffner nodded. He was not quite sure how to answer. "Alexander is very dedicated," he said.

"That much is clear." He turned to Sascha. "Your footwork is most impressive, young Hoffner."

"Thank you, **mein Herr.**"

"Herr **Kommissar,**" Hoffner corrected.

"Herr **Kommissar,**" said Sascha.

"Not at all," said Tamshik. "A pleasure to give such a compliment."

Reinhold spoke up: "If I could watch or train with someone like you, Hoffner, I'm sure I would become much better."

Hoffner senior wondered how many versions of the

script Tamshik had worked on before coming up with this one. At least Reinhold was remembering his lines. That notwithstanding, the prospect of a direct link between his own son and a Polpo surrogate—no matter how junior—hardly sat well with Hoffner, especially after last night. He was about to make some excuse, when Sascha spoke up.

"All right," said Sascha casually. "If you want. You can watch."

The answer stunned Hoffner.

"You mean it?" said Reinhold, equally dumb-founded.

"Why not?" said Sascha. "Maybe you'll pick up a thing or two. I don't know."

"Thank you, Hoffner," said Reinhold eagerly. "Thank you, indeed. I'll certainly try. I'll give it my best effort." He was back on script.

"That's very good of you," said Tamshik to Sascha. He turned to Hoffner. "You have a fine boy there."

"Yes," said Hoffner, still mystified by Sascha's response. "I do."

Almost at once, Tamshik found a reason to break up the little gathering: mission accomplished, Hoffner imagined. The good-byes were brief. Out in the corridor, as father and son headed for the changing rooms, Hoffner said quietly, "Do you mind telling me what that was all about?"

"What what was all about?"

"The sudden generosity of Herr Alexander Hoffner."

"The what?" Sascha said coolly.

Hoffner spoke more deliberately: "Little Krieger? Your new training partner?"

"I said he could watch."

"Yes, I heard. You don't have five minutes for your own brother, who asks about it every day, but for Krieger, suddenly he could 'pick up a thing or two'?"

"I said he could watch," Sascha repeated.

Hoffner heard the first strain of irritation in his son's voice. "You know what I'm saying."

Sascha stopped as they reached the entryway. He looked at his father: the boy was well beyond irritation. "Are you joking?" he said defiantly. When Hoffner failed to answer, Sascha said, "I did it because I thought that's what you wanted me to do, Father."

It was the last thing Hoffner had expected to hear. "What **I** wanted you to do?"

"You **are** joking." When Hoffner again said nothing, Sascha said, "What did you think, Father? That I actually cared about some first-year **stümper**? We went over so you could make good with your Kripo friend. I thought you'd be happy."

Hoffner had no idea what to answer. He was trying to figure out which was worse: the fact that his son thought that he had been using him, or Sascha's conviction that going along had been his only way to please his father. Neither left Hoffner with much to say. "He's not Kripo," said Hoffner. "He's Polpo."

The word seemed to spark an immediate interest. "The fellows who got rid of the Reds?"

"Among others. Yes."

"And he's a friend of yours?"

The sudden level of enthusiasm troubled Hoffner. "No. I just wanted to know what he was doing here."

As quickly as it had come, Sascha's fascination vanished. "And that's the reason you came today?" he said with renewed venom.

It took Hoffner a moment to follow the boy's train of thought. "No, of course not," he said, trying to dismiss the absurdity. "I had no idea he'd be here."

Sascha stared at his father. He then said, "I have to go." He started for the door.

Hoffner moved to block his path. "I can wait. Take you home." The silence returned. "If you like."

Sascha's eyes had gone cold. He said, "Today's Friday, Father. There's a concert. After that, I'm at Kroll's house for the night. Mother knows all about it."

Hoffner nodded as if he had just now remembered: he had never been told. "I saw his father today," he said for some reason. When Sascha continued to stare at him blankly, Hoffner said almost apologetically, "You know you don't have to help with that Krieger boy, now. No reason for you to waste your time on some **stümper.**" The word sounded so forced on his tongue.

In a strangely detached tone, Sascha said, "No, I think I'd like to, Father. Who knows? Could be fun." He brought the bag back up to his shoulder. "But I really do have to go now. Kroll's waiting. I'll see you tomorrow. Thank you for coming, Father."

Before Hoffner could answer, Sascha had side-stepped his way to the door and was pushing his way through. Hoffner was left to face the corridor alone.

Idiot, he thought as he began to walk. Pushed him right into Tamshik's hands, didn't I? Sometimes Hoffner wondered if it might not have been better never to have met Martha at all.

⇒ ASCOMYCETE 4 ⇐

It was Wednesday when he finally got back to head-quarters. The weekend had disappeared into a Schwarzschild black hole of family commitments: Martha's sisters on Saturday, his mother on Sunday. Sascha had been present for both events and had worn his potential Tamshik-connection like a light summer cardigan: casually draped over his shoulder in a posture of smug defiance. Hoffner had sat through the long afternoons hoping for a ring of the telephone. It had never come. Monday and Tuesday had found him at the Reichstadt Court giving expert testimony and presentation of evidence for three sep-arate cases. By himself, Hoffner had sent two men to the gallows. The third, a minor trafficker in Pimm's organization, had gotten off with a slap on the wrist. Evidently, Weigland enjoyed his sugar cubes more than he was letting on.

In the meantime, Fichte had found nothing among the various stores that dealt with Monsieur Edgar Troimpel et Fils; not that Hoffner had been expecting anything. The trade lines between the former Central and Entente powers were just now beginning to resurface: French cheese was finding its way to Salzburg, Umbrian wine to Cologne. Given that everyone's focus was on Paris and the peace talks, the lace market remained slightly less pressing. On the helpful side, Hoffner's fawning friend at KaDeWe—Herr Taubmann—had been kind enough to take a stab at when the gloves had been made: kind enough once Hoffner had ordered a single pair for himself. They had cost him nearly half a week's salary. He would, of course, cancel the order in a few day's time. Still, the money was out of pocket until then, but the information had been worth it.

Herr Taubmann had estimated that, given the lower-than-usual quality of the dye, the gloves had been produced in the last six months: the war had forced everyone to cut corners, which meant that the gloves had been purchased no earlier than the summer of 1918. The question of where was equally limited: before the war, Troimpel et Fils had sold in Berlin, Milan, London, and Paris, and, of course, Brussels and Bruges, but given Belgium's fate during the first few weeks of the war, export to friend or foe had been out of the question. A pair or two might have been brought back to Berlin by a soldier on leave, but the chances of an officer's gift—and a rather pricey one at that—ending up on the hands of, at best, a middle-class girl were beyond remote.

The gloves had been purchased in Belgium, that

much was clear. And, given the girl's unique character-
istics when compared with those of the other victims—
her age, her clothes, the preserving grease—Hoffner
was guessing that she, too, had originated elsewhere.
He had sent out a wire to both the Brussels and Bruges
police on Monday before leaving for the courts.

On the unlikely chance that he was wrong, however, Hoffner had sent Fichte out this morning to the
Missing and Displaced Persons Office in Hessiche
Strasse. For some reason, the powers that be had decided to set up the bureau directly across the street
from the morgue: someone's idea of efficiency, no
doubt. There was still the possibility that a photo or
description of the girl had come in sometime in the
last six weeks: a slim one, thought Hoffner, but at
least it was giving Fichte a chance to familiarize himself with one of the more depressing offices in town,
and one of the busiest since the revolution.

Hoffner picked up the telephone and dialed the
Kaiser Wilhelm Institute. The KWI operator was infamous for misdirecting calls, and Hoffner spent a
good ten minutes waiting for her to find the right extension. He was still adrift in static when a messenger
appeared at his door, holding a small envelope. Hoffner ushered the boy into his office just as Kroll was
picking up the line.

"Uwe Kroll here."

Hoffner took the envelope, then motioned for the
boy to wait. "Uwe, hello. Any news?" There was an
unexpected silence on the other end. "It's Nikolai."

"Yes," said Kroll. "I know who it is." Again, Kroll seemed content to leave it at that.

"Is this a bad time?" Hoffner said skeptically.

"You're calling about the material."

Hoffner stated the obvious: "Yes."

Kroll paused. "You're going to need to come down to the Institute, Nikolai. All right?"

There was something odd in Kroll's voice. Hoffner had been bringing him goops and oozes to analyze for years, and not one of them had ever provoked more than a playful curiosity. This, however, had the ring of seriousness to it. Hoffner considered pressing for more, but knew better. "All right," he said. "An hour?"

"Fine," said Kroll. "I'll see you then."

Hoffner hung up and he turned to the boy. "From the wire room?"

"No, Herr **Kriminal-Kommissar.**"

"No? . . . Interesting." Hoffner peered at his own name written across the front of the envelope. There was no return address, no office number, just the name. The boy started to go. "Wait," said Hoffner. The boy planted himself by the door as Hoffner opened the envelope. The note was brief, and to the point. It read:

You should go back to the flat, Detective Inspector.

It was signed "K" and nothing else.

Hoffner flipped the card over and scanned it more

closely. There was nothing distinctive to it: a card to be found in any stationers in Berlin. He rubbed his finger across the ink. Luxemburg's flat, he thought. He felt the little ridges of raised cloth. Someone other than the landlady knew he had been there.

"How are you, Franz?" said Hoffner, his eyes still on the card.

The boy seemed genuinely pleased at the recognition. "Very well, Herr **Kriminal-Kommissar.**"

Hoffner had always held a soft spot for these runners, the boy messengers who were as old a tradition at the Alex as any he could recall. The installation of telephones—along with the recent child labor laws—had helped to thin their numbers, but for boys with no hope of schooling beyond the age of nine or ten, this was one of the few chances they had to get themselves off the streets. There were even a few beds up in the attic where the most promising, and most desperate, spent their nights.

Hoffner gazed over. He knew this boy well; he had worked with him before: always the same placid stare. Hoffner imagined that Franz could have blended in to any background. The boy saw Hoffner staring at him; his expression remained unchanged. Hoffner found that rather impressive. Going on a year, guessed Hoffner, maybe longer. A few more months, and Franz might find himself assisting a junior clerk, or even in filing, if none of the syndicates had lured him away by then. "So, tell me, Franz—who received the note?"

"The security desk, Herr **Kriminal-Kommissar.**"

"From whom?"

The boy was momentarily at a loss. "I don't know, Herr **Kriminal-Kommissar.** I could find out."

"Yes, why don't you do that." Before the boy was through the door, Hoffner stopped him again. "Just to the security desk and back. And not too many questions. If they don't remember who brought it in, they don't remember. All right?"

"Yes, Herr **Kriminal-Kommissar.**"

"Good." Hoffner nodded him out and then sat back. He again turned to the note.

There was nothing aggressive in its tone, nothing leading, or mocking. It was a simple suggestion. Though neat, the handwriting was clearly that of a man. The **s** was too compressed, and the **K** too severe, to have come from a woman's pen. More than that, the ink was thick, the point heavy, not like the delicate line produced by a woman's narrower nib. There was also nothing of the pathological in the script. Hoffner had seen too many messages from maniacs not to be able to discern the subtle shadings in the angle and height of the letters. The language was also wrong for that. No, this had come from an educated man—no doubt a secretive one, from his method of delivery—but aside from that, Hoffner had little to go on. The phrase "Detective Inspector" struck him as odd. There might even have been something encouraging in that.

Hoffner stood and moved over to the map. He located Luxemburg's flat and stared at the little street for nearly a minute. He then looked up at the area where his pins were sprouting: over six kilometers away. There was no connection. He was about to return to his desk when he realized that he had yet to put a pin into the spot along the Landwehr Canal where Luxemburg's body had been discovered. He picked one up from the box on the shelf and held it in his fingers as he traced the canal's winding path. It cut across most of the city: impossible, naturally, to determine where the body had gone in. What, then, was the point of marking where it had come out, he thought. He continued to stare. Maybe that was the point.

The boy reappeared, slightly out of breath. He stood waiting at the door until Hoffner motioned him in. "They think a man with a beard, Herr **Kriminal-Kommissar.**"

"They think?"

"It was busy, Herr **Kriminal-Kommissar.** The letter was dropped at the desk. The Sergeant thinks he saw a man with a beard around the time it came in."

"Nothing else?" said Hoffner.

"No, Herr **Kriminal-Kommissar.**"

Hoffner nodded slowly, then said, "All right, Franz. You can go."

The boy bobbed his head in a quick bow, and was almost out the door, when Hoffner again stopped him. "Wait." Hoffner reached into his pocket and pulled out a pfennig. He held it out to the boy. The men of the Kripo were strictly forbidden to give

taschgeld to the boys, but Hoffner had never seen the harm in a little pocket money. Franz hesitated; he, too, knew the rules. Hoffner brought his finger up to his lips as if to say it would be their secret. Again the boy hesitated; he then took the coin and, just as quickly, was gone.

Hoffner turned back to the map and dropped the pin into its box. Another time, he thought. He checked his watch and, placing the card in his pocket, grabbed his coat and headed for the stairs.

This time, Kroll was in his office when Hoffner knocked. A quick "Come" ushered him in: Kroll looked up from behind his desk and immediately stood. From the abruptness of the movement, he seemed oddly tense. "Hello, Nikolai," he said as he stepped out to extend a hand. It was all far more formal than Hoffner had expected. Not sure why, and not wanting to break the mood, Hoffner took his hand.

"Uwe."

No less forced, Kroll said, "We saw your Alexander, Friday. Charming boy, Nikolai. Really. He's grown into quite a young man."

For a fleeting moment, Hoffner wondered if the tone on the telephone, and now here, had something to do with Sascha's visit to the Krolls. Had something been said? Was there a reason for the two fathers to talk? That would be unpleasant. Worse than that, Hoffner couldn't for the life of him remember Kroll's boy's name. There was no way to return the compliment and move on quickly. "Thank you," said Hoffner. "Yes. Sascha couldn't stop talking about the lovely evening he had."

"Good, good. Johannes really enjoys the time they spend together."

"Johannes," said Hoffner, doing his best not to show his relief. "Yes. I haven't seen him in years. Also a wonderful boy."

"Yes . . . Thank you."

The two men stared at each other for several seconds. Finally, in a moment of sudden recollection, Hoffner blurted out, "The **Deutscher Rundflug.** The four of us went to the opening to see König fly. My old partner."

"Yes," said Kroll, remembering eagerly.

Hoffner had no inkling why they had slipped into this bizarre little scene. He had known Uwe for far too long. Nonetheless, he continued to watch as his friend nodded uncomfortably: it quickly became apparent that Kroll's behavior had nothing to do with either of the boys. Finally, Hoffner said, "The material, Uwe. Is there something I should know?"

Kroll stopped nodding. "The material," he repeated distractedly. "Yes." He pointed to a chair and headed back behind his desk. "Why don't you have a seat, Nikolai."

Hoffner sat. Kroll sat, his mood more serious. "About the material. I ran a few tests." He seemed unsure how to explain what he had found. "It's military."

This was the one thing Hoffner had hoped not to hear. "Military," he repeated.

"Yes. Used during the war and, not surprisingly, developed here, at the Institute. There are files that are very"—Kroll tried to find the right word—"selective. I haven't been able to look at all of them, but I've made an appointment for us to go up and see the **Direktor.** I've told him who you are, the work you do. He's agreed to talk with us, but with the understanding that any information will remain strictly . . ." Again Kroll had trouble finishing the thought.

"Selective," said Hoffner.

"Yes. Exactly." Kroll stood and motioned to the door. "Shall we?"

Hoffner hesitated. "You mean now?"

"Yes." Kroll was already out from behind the desk. "He's expecting us. Please."

The glass on the fifth floor office had the word DIREKTOR stenciled across it: Kroll knocked, then stepped through to an anteroom fitted with desk, chairs, and several filing cabinets. A plump woman, with her hair pulled back in the tightest bun Hoffner had ever seen, was seated behind the desk: he was amazed that the skin had yet to tear on her forehead. She stood.

"Good afternoon, Frau Griebner," said Kroll, with a quick click of the heels: his anxiety had mutated into a strict Germanic decorum.

"Good afternoon, Herr **Doktor** Kroll." She offered

an equally perfect nod: her manner was as efficient as her hair. She took no notice of Hoffner. "I will tell the Herr **Direktor** you are here." She stepped out from behind her desk and disappeared through a second door. Almost immediately she returned. "The Herr **Direktor** will see you now, Herr **Doktor**." Hoffner followed Kroll into the office.

The room was large and filled with lamps, though the light seemed inclined to shine on only a few select areas. The rest of the space lay in half-shadows, less the result of poor positioning than of an ominous afternoon sky that hovered outside the four vast windows. The gloom seemed to be drawing the light out through the glass: Hoffner wondered if closing the drapes might, in fact, have helped to brighten the place up.

The **Direktor** had done his best to construct a small preserve of light for himself across the room. He got to his feet. "Herr **Doktor** Kroll," he said. "Hello, hello." He came out into the shadows to greet them. The **Direktor** was much younger than Hoffner had expected, a man of perhaps forty with a somewhat unruly moustache beneath a wide nose and basset hound eyes. Even more unexpected was the remarkable smile that seemed so out of place in the impressive, though dour surroundings.

"Herr **Direktor**," said Kroll. "Allow me to present Herr **Kriminal-Kommissar** Nikolai Hoffner. Herr Hoffner, this is Herr Professor **Doktor** Albert Einstein."

Hoffner recalled Kroll having mentioned Einstein once or twice, over the years. The man had come up with some theory that Kroll had described as either ludicrous or genius. Hoffner couldn't remember which. The three shook hands and retreated to the desk. Einstein did his best to expand the pocket of light; even so, Hoffner and Kroll were forced to lean in over the edge of the desk in order to escape the shadows.

Einstein reached down and opened the bottom drawer. He pulled out a thin file with the word RE-STRICTED in bold type across its front. There was also a long paragraph describing the penalties for disseminating the material, written in much smaller print below. "This is for a criminal case?" said Einstein.

"Yes, Herr **Direktor**," said Hoffner.

Einstein nodded. "I've always been fascinated by criminal cases. They're like little puzzles. Quite a bit like what we spend our time on."

"Except no one ends up dead, Herr **Direktor**."

Again Einstein nodded. "How little you know about science, Herr **Kriminal-Kommissar**." He paused, then added, "Anyway, you wanted to hear about something that was meant to be helpful on the battlefield." He slid the dossier over to Hoffner. "It was called Ascomycete 4. One wonders what happened to numbers one through three." Einstein was the only one to enjoy the joke.

Hoffner took the folder and opened it. Kroll quickly interrupted: "That's all very technical stuff,

Nikolai. Formulations and so on." Kroll reached over and flipped to the last few pages. "The gist of the thing is at the back. This bit here." Again, Hoffner began to read, and again Kroll cut in. "It was developed for trench fatalities," said Kroll. "And, on occasion, no-man's-land retrievals."

Hoffner looked up. Evidently there would be no need for reading. "For men already dead," said Hoffner, inviting more of the lesson.

"Yes," said Kroll. "During the beginning of the war—and later on, during the worst of the fighting—it was impossible to transport the dead back to the field hospitals in order to prepare them for burial. Too many bodies were rotting on the front. Not only was contagion an issue, but morale, as well. Men needed to know that if they went down, at least an entire corpse would be returned to their families. The military decided that it needed something to keep the bodies as fresh as possible so that, during those periods of isolation, they could minimize the distraction and disease produced by the corpses, and also treat the dead with as much decency as possible. So they came to the Institute."

"And"—Hoffner scanned the front page—"to **Doktors** Meinhof and Klingman."

"Two very capable chemists," said Kroll. "They came up with the solution. Meinhof is now in Vienna, at the Bielefeld Institute. Klingman passed away about a year ago."

"So how did you know it was this"—again Hoffner read—"Ascomycete 4 from the sample I gave you?"

"Actually," said Kroll, "it didn't take me that long. Once I separated out the components, there were trace elements of an unguent I'd seen only once before. It was in a sample that I'd been asked to analyze during the war."

"A military request?" said Hoffner.

"Yes. How did you know?"

"You made the connection and it brought you to the restricted files."

Now Einstein was impressed. "You're very good at this, Herr **Kriminal-Kommissar.**"

"No, Herr **Direktor,**" said Hoffner, "just impatient." He turned to Kroll. "And the components were the same?"

"Identical."

Hoffner flipped to the back of the file; he scanned a few of the paragraphs. Kroll had been right to give him the condensed version. "And this compound," said Hoffner. "It's now available outside the military?"

"That's where the difficulty lies," said Kroll. "All of this is still under lock and key here at the Institute. More than that, the research was discontinued in the middle of 1917. They stopped producing it. I won't ask you where you got your sample."

"Stopped?" said Hoffner. "Why?"

"Because they discovered that too much of it, if inhaled, acted as a very potent hallucinatory stimulant."

This seemed to perk Einstein up a bit. "Not a bad little side effect, eh, **Kriminal-Kommissar?**"

Kroll continued: "Once the men on the line discovered its other use—well, how can you blame
them, really? The General Staff did its best to restrict
access—select doctors were the only ones who could
get hold of the stuff—but then it no longer served
the purpose for which it had been designed."

"For a time," added Einstein, "it actually became
more popular than morphine. You can only imagine
the embarrassment Meinhof and Klingman went
through."

"I'm sure," said Hoffner as he tried to digest all of the
information.

Einstein said to Kroll, "You know, it just now occurs
to me that that was probably the same problem you
were looking into when they gave you the original
unguent to analyze. The hallucinogenic side effects."

Kroll nodded, considering it for the first time himself. "That's probably true, Herr **Direktor.** I never
thought of that."

"Yes," said Hoffner, interrupting the riveting side-
bar. "But would they have destroyed the stock they
still had?"

Einstein said, "Oh, I doubt that. Too much potential as a weapon, don't you think? The chance to develop it into a hallucinatory gas, that sort of thing."

Unfortunately, Hoffner knew Einstein was right.
"And would one slathering keep a body fresh indefi-
nitely?"

"That was another problem," said Kroll. "It had to

be reapplied quite frequently. Hence the large quantities and the hallucinations."

"How frequently?" said Hoffner.

"**Very** frequently," said Kroll. "At least two or three
times a day."

"So, how much of the stuff would one need to keep
a body fresh for, say, six weeks?"

"Six weeks?" Kroll said incredulously. "Not possible. You're talking liters and liters. Vast amounts."

Hoffner was pleased to hear it. "So nothing your
average officer would have been able to ferret away?"

"Impossible," said Kroll with complete certainty.
"It was designed to insulate the flesh for two, maybe
three days, and that with constant supervision. And
even that became impractical. Too many bodies to
manage. The whole thing proved to be a disaster."

Hoffner sat back and again let the information settle. At least the lone army psychopath was no longer
a possibility, not that the alternative was all that
much more appealing. "And you're sure that what I
gave you is this same compound?"

"Absolutely. The chemical makeup is unique. It's
like a signature. Meinhof and Klingman might just as
well have attached their thumbprints to it. It's
Ascomycete 4, Nikolai. No question."

The three men sat in silence for nearly half a
minute. Hoffner could tell that Einstein wanted to
ask a few questions of his own, but was choosing not
to venture out of his own realm. Maybe the posi-

tioning of the light was more than just bad happenstance. Insulation could be so very comforting.

Hoffner spoke to Einstein: "I could demand all the relevant files, Herr **Direktor.** This is, after all, a Kripo investigation."

"Yes, Herr **Kriminal-Kommissar,** you could, but then I would have to get in touch with the Office of the General Staff—" Einstein stopped himself. "There is still an Office of the General Staff, isn't there?"

"Yes, Herr **Direktor,**" said Hoffner.

"Good," said Einstein, mildly relieved. "One doesn't always know these days, what with the revolution. Anyway, given the peculiarity of this case, I'm not sure you'd want them to hear that you're looking into it, just yet." The knowing smile returned. "I could be wrong, but that's up to you, of course."

Hoffner nodded. "Point well taken, Herr **Direktor.**"

Again, the room grew quiet. Einstein said, "I imagine this only complicates your case, Herr **Kriminal-Kommissar.**"

"Yes, Herr **Direktor,**" said Hoffner. "It does."

Einstein nodded coyly. "That's not always such a bad thing."

"I know, Herr **Direktor.** But right now it doesn't make things any easier."

The air outside was pleasantly dry as Hoffner lit a cigarette and stepped onto the plaza. It made the cold all the more piercing and gave the smoke a certain crispness as it raced down into his lungs.

Kroll had been nice enough to run through the remaining files with him, but there had really been nothing more to see. The names of the officers on the General Staff had been omitted, as had any firms that had been used to transport or produce the compound in any large quantities. It was all just science, and that, as Kroll had pointed out, was probably of little use to the Kripo.

"Herr **Kriminal-Kommissar.**"

Hoffner turned around. To his complete surprise, he saw Hans Fichte heading toward him. Hoffner tried to remember if he had left a note for Fichte back at the Alex. He knew he hadn't, which made Fichte's appearance all the more puzzling.

Fichte was eating something out of a brown bag. He tossed both it and the bag into a dustbin, and quickly made his way over. "Herr **Kriminal-Kommissar,**" he repeated.

"Hans. What are you doing here?"

"They told me you were with the **Direktor.** I didn't want to disturb you."

"Or interrupt your lunch."

"That, too."

Hoffner stared at Fichte. "So . . . Are you going to explain how you found me here, or do I have to guess?"

Fichte's face brightened. "A wire came in for you back at the Alex. It was marked 'urgent.' On the off chance, I checked the switchboard logs to see if you had made any telephone calls today. There was the one to Herr **Doktor** Kroll late this morning, so . . ." Fichte left it at that.

Hoffner reached into his coat pocket, pulled out his cigarettes, and offered one to Fichte. "Nicely done, Hans." Fichte took the cigarette; Hoffner used his own to light it, and they began to walk. "So what's so urgent?"

Fichte coughed several times, unaccustomed to the quality of the tobacco. "Two things. First, a wire came in from Bruges. They're putting through a call to you at one o'clock this afternoon. I didn't want you to miss it."

The Belgians were also full of surprises, thought Hoffner: he had been hoping to hear from them by next Monday at the earliest. "So, nothing at Missing Persons?" The two continued across the plaza.

"Pleasant little spot," said Fichte. "They actually laughed when I mentioned Brussels. They're dealing with close to twelve hundred Berliners who've gone missing since November. I had no idea."

"Then let's hope our girl isn't from Berlin." Fichte nodded and Hoffner continued, "You said two things."

There was a hesitation as Fichte reached into his coat pocket and pulled out a folded newspaper. "I trust you haven't seen this." He handed the paper to Hoffner. "This afternoon's edition."

It was a copy of the **BZ.** Hoffner took it and scanned the front page.

"Page four, at the bottom," said Fichte.

Hoffner flipped it open. It took him no time to find it. When he did, he stopped and stared in disbelief. Fichte could see the anger rising in his eyes. "That son of a bitch," was all Hoffner could get out.

It took them forty minutes to get back to the Alex, enough time for Hoffner to cool off. Even so, he headed straight for the KD's office as Fichte trailed behind.

Without knocking, Hoffner pushed open the door. Luckily, Präger was alone: he looked up calmly as Hoffner bore down on him. "Something I can do for you, Nikolai?"

Hoffner planted the article in front of him. "Have you seen this, Herr **Kriminaldirektor**?"

Präger continued to look up at Hoffner; he then slowly picked up the paper and began to read. The telltale chewing of the inner cheek told Hoffner that he had not.

After nearly a minute, Präger said, "I love how they say 'sources in the Kripo.' That always gives it such a nice ring of truth."

"And we have no idea how this got out," said Hoffner.

Präger shook his head as he reread several of the passages. "It's obviously from someone who knows something about the case," he said, still scanning. "At least two victims. A vague reference to something on the back, though no mention of a knife." He looked up at Hoffner. "This reads more like a teaser. I'm guessing they've got more information than they're letting on."

"Agreed," said Hoffner. "You know we had a nice little chat with Weigland last week."

"Yes," said Präger, with just a hint of reproach. "**Kriminal-Oberkommissar** Braun stopped in to ask me to make sure you understood the parameters of the case." With mock sincerity, Präger said, "You do understand the parameters of the case, don't you, Nikolai?"

"It's just **Oberkommissar** now," said Hoffner. "That's the way they like it upstairs."

"Well, we're not upstairs, are we?" Präger handed the paper back to Hoffner. "The Polpo likes its turf, Nikolai, but there's no reason they would do this. Just consider yourself lucky there wasn't any mention of Luxemburg."

"Yes, I'm feeling very lucky." Hoffner knew Präger was right: the Polpo had nothing to gain by it. No one wanted the hysteria this might produce. Still, Hoffner had his doubts. "They've got Luxemburg," he said. "Of course she wouldn't be mentioned."

Präger disagreed. "This isn't the way they'd go about it. Also, there are too many other possibilities—a family member of one of the victims, someone downstairs. Any one of them could have let this out. It's the **BZ,** Nikolai. This story didn't come cheap." Präger turned to Fichte. "So, Herr **Kriminal-Assistent,** what do you think? Is this the Polpo?"

Fichte stood motionless. The KD had never asked his opinion on anything. "Well," Fichte said with as much certainty as he could find, "any leak might lead back to Luxemburg, Herr **Kriminaldirektor.** I don't think they'd want that."

Präger smiled and turned to Hoffner. "That's a very good point, Herr **Kriminal-Assistent.** Don't you think, Nikolai?"

Hoffner said, "You know I'm going to look into this personally, Edmund. And I'm going to want a note sent out to every Kripo office. A general reminder on discretion."

Präger knew there would be no fighting Hoffner on this one. "Fine. Just don't let it get in the way."

"It won't."

Fichte cut in. "The telephone call, Herr **Kriminal-Kommissar.** We should get back to the office."

Hoffner turned to Fichte. He tried not to sound too cavalier. "Have you been paying attention, Hans? We're not going back to the office."

The switchboard operator stared defiantly at Hoffner, who stood hovering above her. This, he knew, was the surest way to keep the lines of communication as restricted as possible. Fichte agreed: Thursday's late-night encounter had opened him up to an entirely new world at the Alex. And while

Fichte had been strangely intrigued by it at the out-set, Hoffner had quickly set him straight: these were uncharted men, the source of speculation and deri-sion from a distance, but far more treacherous up close. Whatever arguments there were to the con-trary, Hoffner made it clear that the Polpo never merited the benefit of the doubt. Fichte now under-stood that.

Electricity had come back to the Alex sometime on Monday. The lights from perhaps ten unattended calls flashed in frantic patterns across the board; Hoffner continued to keep the woman from answering them: she was doing little to hide her disapproval. Fichte stood by the door.

"This is highly unusual, Herr **Kriminal-Kommissar,**" she said as the board begged for atten-tion. "I really need to take care of these. I can easily forward the call to your office when it comes in."

Hoffner nodded. "Yes, I know, Fräulein. I just feel more comfortable receiving it here."

"The international line is no difficulty, Herr **Kriminal-Kommissar.**"

"Well, I don't want to tie up any more of your wires than are necessary, Fräulein."

The woman insisted, "You wouldn't be tying up—"

"Let's just wait for the call, shall we?" Hoffner checked his watch. It was coming up on one o'clock. At eight seconds to, the international line began to flash. Hoffner nodded and the operator made the connection. She confirmed the caller and then handed the earpiece to Hoffner. Without any hesitation, she retrieved a second earpiece and sat back.

"Could you wait outside, Fräulein?" said Hoffner.

The woman looked up in disbelief "Excuse me, Herr **Kriminal-Kommissar**?"

"This won't take more than a few minutes, Fräulein."

The woman spoke as if to a child. "I can't leave my post, Herr **Kriminal-Kommissar.** All of these calls—"

"Can wait." Hoffner's tone made sure she understood. "Time for a coffee break, wouldn't you say, Fräulein?" Hoffner nodded to Fichte to open the door. The woman's gaze grew more hostile until, with a practiced civility, she slowly stood, nodded to both men, and headed for the door.

At the door, she turned back to Hoffner bitterly. "This will be reflected in my report to the **Kriminaldirektor,** Herr **Kriminal-Kommissar.**"

"Yes, I'm sure it will, Fräulein **Telephonistin.**"

Fichte shut the door, and Hoffner brought the receiver up to his ear. "Detective Inspector Nikolai Hoffner here," he said in French.

"One moment, Monsieur." Hoffner waited through the silence. He nodded to Fichte to stay by the door.

"Inspector Hoffner?" The voice was distant but audible. "This is Chief Inspector van Acker, Bruges police."

"Chief Inspector. I appreciate the speed of your response."

"Not at all," said van Acker. "I do need to ask, is this the same Inspector Hoffner who published a piece titled "The Odor of Death" in **Die Polizei,** eight, maybe nine years ago?"

For a moment, Hoffner thought he had misheard; he had a hard time believing that anyone still remembered the article, less so that it's "fame" had ever extended beyond a five-block radius of the Alex. "Yes," said Hoffner, not quite convinced. "You know it?"

"Of course," said van Acker. "Pretty standard reading here, Inspector. In Brussels, as well."

"Really?"

"Truth be told, I probably wouldn't have set up the telephone call except, well, I thought it might be my only chance to talk with you in person."

"Really, I'm—flattered," said Hoffner. Fichte looked over. Hoffner shook him off.

"Nice little feather in my cap," said van Acker. "Anyway, about your wire, Inspector. I'm not sure how helpful we can be, but we might have a little something."

"You've got a missing girl, then?"

"Your description was a bit vague, but the time frame is about right for a case we've been looking into. May I ask how you knew to contact us?"

Hoffner told him about the gloves.

"It might also be Brussels," said van Acker.

"Yes. I've got a call in."

"Of course. The problem is, I'm not sure the girl

we've got in mind could have afforded a pair of Troimpel gloves."

"And why is that?"

"She was an attendant at one of the area hospitals. A scrub girl."

That seemed a poor excuse. "And Belgian scrub girls aren't capable of saving their money, Chief Inspector? I find that hard to believe."

"Well, not for gloves, no. And especially not for these gloves, Inspector."

"And no well-off boyfriends?" said Hoffner.

"Not this girl," said van Acker. "There's something of a stigma attached to—" He stopped. "Look, to be honest, it's more of an asylum than a hospital. These are girls who can't get work elsewhere. They also don't usually spend much time away from home, for rather obvious reasons. And this girl had no family. You understand."

Sadly, Hoffner did. Insanity as infection, he thought, with its equally despicable maxim: that only the most pitiful, vile, and unprepossessing would be willing to risk contamination by cleaning up the filth produced by a group of lunatics. Berlin's own Herzberge Asylum was proof that such idiocy was still thriving well beyond the narrow minds of the provinces. Hoffner had often walked along its dingy halls not sure which of the two groups—the patients or the menial staff—deserved to be under lock and key, although with the latter, he did recognize that malice, and not madness, was more often the dominant pathology.

"I see," said Hoffner. "Then perhaps this isn't the girl."

"Not to be blunt, but did she have the look of a—" At least van Acker was trying to be delicate. "—well, of one of these types."

"Hard to tell, Chief Inspector. The face was . . . gnawed away at."

"Of course," said van Acker. "To be expected, I suppose. Any other distinguishing features?" He was doing his best to go through the motions, making sure to touch on everything. "Your wire didn't specify anything beyond height, weight, coloring. We do have a description of a marking on the left leg and another on the back. Anything there?"

The mention of the leg gave Hoffner a moment's hope. "Where on the leg?" he said.

"Mid-shin, according to her application file. A scar from childhood."

Somehow, Hoffner had known it would be too low. "There wasn't enough of it left to check."

"Naturally," said van Acker, moving on. "And nothing on the upper back? There's supposed to be a very recognizable birthmark there. A strawberry-colored splatter, as if someone threw a bit of paint at her. You'd have seen it immediately."

Van Acker was picking all the most interesting spots. "The back is more problematic," said Hoffner. "It's been"—he did his best to find the least troubling word—"disfigured. The entire area between the shoulder blades. It's impossible to tell what would have been there."

Hoffner expected to hear a summary "oh well" and then an equally quick wrap-up to the conversation, but the line remained strangely quiet. When van Acker did speak, his tone was far more pointed: "Disfigured?" he said. "What kind of disfigurement?"

The change in tone momentarily threw Hoffner: for the first time in the conversation, van Acker sounded as if he was actually investigating something. Hoffner chose his words carefully. "Just some knife work, Chief Inspector. We're dealing with something of an artist here."

Van Acker continued to press. "How do you mean?"

Hoffner remained cautious. "We didn't find a birthmark."

When van Acker next spoke, the hesitation in his voice was undeniable: "It's—not a pattern, is it?"

The word jumped at Hoffner. He took his time in answering. "Yes," he said. "A pattern."

Van Acker was now fully committed. "Could you describe it, Inspector?"

Again Hoffner waited. He gazed over at Fichte. These were rare moments: the possibility of a piece falling into place, no matter how disturbing its implications. And, as always, Hoffner forced himself not to look beyond it. He also knew not to give anything away. The information had to come to him. "A few lines, Chief Inspector," he said. "Not much more."

When the line remained quiet, Hoffner continued, "Suffice it to say someone decided to make a pretty nice mess of it."

"I see." Van Acker's voice was strangely cold; what he said next was no less chilling. "These wouldn't be ruts, would they, Inspector, with a central strip running down the middle? That's not the pattern you're describing, is it?"

Fichte moved closer in when he saw the sudden reaction on Hoffner's face. Hoffner shook his head as he put up a hand to stop him. With great reserve, Hoffner said, "And why do you ask that, Chief Inspector?"

There was a long silence before van Acker answered: "You wouldn't need to ask if you'd seen them."

Fichte was having trouble keeping up as the two men mounted the stairs back to Hoffner's office: he had yet to hear a word about the conversation with the man from Bruges. Instead he had been told to stand by the door for nearly ten minutes while Hoffner had sat at the switchboard taking notes and asking questions.

Once inside his office, Hoffner told Fichte to shut the door and take a seat. Hoffner began flipping through the pages he had just written, matching them against a second notebook that he now took from inside his desk drawer. Still scanning, Hoffner said, "According to van Acker, the man we've been looking for is a Paul Wouters."

Fichte tried to minimize his reaction. "This Wouters left the same trail in Bruges?"

"He did," said Hoffner as he jotted down a few words in the first notebook.

"He won't be easy to trace."

"Oh, I think he will." Hoffner looked up from the pages. "He's been in the Sint-Walburga Insane Asylum, just outside of Bruges, for the past two years."

Fichte needed a moment. "When did he escape?"

"He didn't. He's still there."

Once again, Fichte was at a loss. "I don't understand."

Hoffner nodded and went back to the pages. He began to cross-reference every detail van Acker had been able to give him, most of it from memory: texture of the ruts, quality of the blade, intervals between the killings. As it turned out, van Acker had been the lead inspector on the case, and his recall was remarkable. It was why he had taken such an interest in the girl's case, and why he had been eager to follow up even the most obscure requests from as far away as Berlin.

The girl had been one of Wouters's night attendants. There had been rumors of something more than mopping up and scrubbing between them, but nothing had ever been found. In fact, the doctors who had petitioned and won to keep Wouters from the gallows—a lab rat for them to study—had insisted that such intimacy might be an indication of a positive response to the treatment. The intimacy, they reasoned, would have amounted to little more than adolescent groping—about right for the mental age of both—and so they saw no harm in it: as long as offspring could be avoided, or terminated prior to development, the doctors felt it would be beneficial to Wouters's eventual recovery. Van Acker, of course, had been the sole voice of reason—he had wanted Wouters dead from the moment they had taken him—but science had prevailed. The fact that Wouters had been brutally killing women prior to having received this extraordinary treatment seemed an inconsequential detail to everyone but van Acker. The doctors reminded him that those women— Wouters's victims—had been older. "Much older, Monsieur **Le Chef Inspecteur.** That was his purpose in the killings. His desire. The age. Because of his history. This girl poses no such threat." Somehow, van Acker had been unable to locate pimping in the Hippocratic oath. Having done nothing to stop them, however, he alone now felt responsible for her fate.

The one aspect of the case about which van Acker had been hazy was the placement of the bodies. The Bruges police had caught Wouters in mid-etching, kneeling over his third victim; they had failed to look for a pattern in the discoveries because there had never been enough of a body count to create one.

"At least now we have a name for the girl," said Hoffner as he continued to flip through the pages. "She was called Mary Koop. She worked at Sint-Walburga. She disappeared about two months ago."

Fichte said, "So, if Wouters is still in the asylum, what are we dealing with here?"

Hoffner nodded as he scanned his scrawl. "That was the first question I asked myself."

Fichte decided to take a stab. "Maybe it was someone who read about the case? Someone who was imitating him? Like that fellow who took up where Chertonski left off."

Hoffner looked up. "Chertonski?" he said in mild disbelief. "You can't be serious. That was knocking over old women's flats, Hans, not killing them, and certainly not leaving them with pieces of artwork chiseled into their backs."

Fichte seemed to shrink ever so slightly into his coat. "No—of course not. You're right, Herr **Kriminal—**"

Hoffner put up a hand to stop him. "Whatever it is, Hans, I was trying to say it's the wrong question." Hoffner was about to explain, when he stopped. His hand became a single finger as he listened intently; he glanced over at the door and then motioned Fichte over. Fichte stood and, with a nod from Hoffner, quickly opened the door.

There, poised in a knocking position, stood Detective Sergeant Ludwig Groener.

"Herr **Kriminal-Bezirkssekretär,**" said Hoffner. "Can we help you with something?" On instinct, Fichte took a step back.

Groener stood motionless. He held a stack of papers in his hand as he peered at Fichte, then Hoffner.

He remained outside the office. "Herr **Kriminal-Kommissar**," he said. "You received a telephone call from abroad. There was no entry in the log."

Hoffner nodded in agreement. "If there was no entry, how do you know I received it?"

Groener had no answer. Instead he took aim at Fichte. "As his **Assistent,** Herr Fichte, it's your job to fill in all appropriate logs. You know this, of course."

"Of course, Herr **Kriminal-Bezirkssekretär,**" said Fichte. "When the Herr **Kriminal-Kommissar** receives a call. Absolutely. I'll make a note of that."

The two men stared at each other for several seconds. Realizing that Fichte was going to be of no help, Groener again turned to Hoffner. "It's my job to know when calls come in, and the like, Herr **Kriminal-Kommissar.**"

"And to listen at the doors of detective inspectors' offices?" said Hoffner. "Do you find that equally exciting?"

For an instant Groener looked as if he had gotten a whiff of his own breath. Then, just as quickly, he resumed the taut stare of bureaucratic efficiency. "The telephone call from Belgium, Herr **Kriminal-Kommissar.** Have your man make a note of it in the log at the switchboard." Groener turned and started to go.

Hoffner stopped him by saying, "Would you like me to give him a detailed account of what was said, Herr Groener? Or is the notation of information you already have sufficient?"

Groener kept his back to Hoffner. He turned his head slightly and said, "What was discussed is your business, Herr **Kriminal-Kommissar.** It's your case."

"Yes, Herr **Kriminal-Bezirkssekretär,**" Hoffner said coldly. "It is."

Groener offered a clipped nod and then retreated down the hall.

Fichte waited until Groener had moved out of sight before turning back to Hoffner. "God, he makes the place stink."

"Close the door, Hans." With a plaintive look from Fichte, Hoffner said, "All right, wave it out a few times." Fichte opened and closed the door with gusto, and then shut it before returning to his seat. Hoffner said, "So, who else knew about the wire?"

"It was on your desk when I got back from Missing Persons. I assume just one of the boys and the wire operator. That's it."

"Evidently not." Hoffner sat, thinking to himself: Why would anyone else have been looking for it in the first place?

"Why the wrong question?" said Fichte, resuming their previous conversation.

It took Hoffner a moment to refocus; he looked over at Fichte. "Because right now it doesn't matter who's doing the killing, or why. What matters is how he got to Berlin."

Fichte's all-too-predictable "I don't understand" was out before Hoffner could explain.

"Look at what we have." Hoffner settled back in his

chair as he spoke: "You'd think the piece out of place would be Wouters—everything in the Bruges case is the same, everything points to him, except he's locked away in an asylum seven hundred kilometers from here, a fact that is both frightening and astounding—but it's not. That's not the piece that doesn't fit. Imitator or not—it doesn't matter which—the killings are taking place here by someone who knows the Bruges case. By someone who must have been in Bruges. But not because he can make a few markings on a woman's back. No, the reason he must have been in Bruges is that, unless he was there, how else would he have been able to bring the girl from Bruges to Berlin? Given her mental state, she clearly couldn't have made it on her own. So how did anyone get from Bruges to Berlin over two months ago? The only transports would have been military. No one else could have crossed the lines, even after the armistice. How? And how does he bring a girl with him?"

Fichte needed a moment to absorb the information. "So the fact that it's not Wouters doesn't trouble you."

"Of course it troubles me, Hans." Hoffner's tone was thick with frustration. "It horrifies me. But right now, it's not the most inconsistent piece of information we have."

"It's a shame Kroll didn't have anything for us on the grease. That might have been helpful."

Hoffner nodded slowly. He had decided to keep

this recent discovery from Fichte: until he knew what it all meant—and now, with the information from Bruges, he had no idea when that might be—Hoffner needed to keep everything as focused as possible. As much as he wanted to trust Fichte with it, he knew that would be unwise: the appearance of the Polpo had made that abundantly clear, not to mention the leak. The less Fichte knew, the safer it would be for everyone involved. "Yes," said Hoffner. "We'll have to wait on that."

Fichte tried another tack: "Was the Wouters case well reported in Belgium? I mean, during the war, would they have spent a lot of time with it in the newspapers? That could be of use."

Hoffner had been thinking the same thing. "Excellent question, Hans. You'll have to ask the Chief Inspector when you see him."

Fichte's confusion returned, and Hoffner explained: "We need to know what they have in Bruges, and we need it quickly. More than that, we need to hear what Mr. Wouters has to say, and whom he might have said it to." Fichte remained silent. Hoffner tried to lead him. "There is another way to get from Bruges to Berlin, Hans, also controlled by the military, although a bit quicker than a train." When Fichte continued to stare back at him, Hoffner said, "You've never been in an aeroplane, have you, Hans?" Hoffner watched as the blood drained from Fichte's face. "Not so bad, really. Just remember to turn your head away from the wind." Hoffner smiled

at Fichte's blank stare. "Trust me," he said. "You'll
know when."

⊨ THE PACT ⊨

Victor König, Hoffner's onetime partner, had spent
the last hour of his life circling over a vast stretch of
lake hidden beneath fog in the autumn of 1915.
König had not realized it, but had he flown just another twenty kilometers east, he would have seen the
lights of a village and been able to land his Fokker E-I
in any number of open fields. At the time, the
"Eindecker" had been a relatively new aeroplane,
renowned for its synchronous Spandau machine
gun—that clever little gear which allowed it to stop
firing when the propeller blade was moving directly
in front of it—but König had been flying in empty
sky: what he had needed was light, not a miracle gun.
With his fuel dangerously low, and the sun dipping
out of the horizon, König had chanced a drop dive
into the cloud cover. Thinking he was coasting just
above the water, and only a few hundred meters from
open land, he had hit the lake head-on at full speed.
The impact had left nothing of the aeroplane to recover, let alone any traces of Captain Victor König of
the German Second Aircraft Battalion.

It was an odd mistake for so experienced a flyer to
have made. König had been flying since 1909, and
had placed third in the **Rundflug** in both 1912 and
1913. It was why the Air Corps had overlooked his

rather advanced age of thirty-eight on the application: a sky pilot with five years of flying under his belt
was prime material. It was for those reasons that his
squadron had assumed he had been hit somewhere
over France. None of them had even considered the
possibility of those final tormenting minutes that
König had had to endure. Far from enemy fire, alone
and blind, he had been done in by nothing more
than the dark. It was probably better that no one had
known. Victor had been a terribly proud man.

Next to Hoffner, Tobias Mueller had been struck
hardest by König's death. Mueller had been a brash
twenty-four-year-old with a genius for flight, and
König's closest comrade in the squadron. Hoffner
had met him once during one of their leaves: they
had liked each other instantly.

Mueller had been something of a celebrity during
the war. He had brought down eighteen French fight-
ers in just over two years before being sent home in
1917: it had not been his decision. He had lost part
of his right foot, along with a few fingers, in a crash
landing, and now walked with a considerable limp.
He had insisted he could still fight; the Air Corps,
however, had seen it otherwise. Even so, Mueller had
been too good with a stick to let go: he had been flying supplies in and out of Berlin for the past two
years. True to form, it had taken Mueller no time to
discover that a good deal of money could be made by
a pilot willing to fly any number of other items in
and out of Germany. He had been caught only once,

luckily by the civilian police, and since the black market was Kripo jurisdiction, his case had landed on the third floor at the Alex. Hoffner had been the one to make it all go away, and Mueller had never forgotten him for that. The monthly supply of cigars and cigarettes was a particularly welcome treat.

For now, Mueller was favoring the aerodrome at Tempelhof as his base of operations. It was little more than four or five buildings scattered across a stretch of wide-open grassland, and was still considered second-rate when compared to the airfields at Johannisthal—the site from which the **Rundflug** fliers had set off and returned during those wild, prewar days of summer—but it did have the advantage of being closer in to town. It was the preferred stop of the supply runners for that reason, more so because no one really paid it much attention. Planes could come and go as they pleased. On occasion, a little something for the station guard was advised, but aside from that, sky pilots had the run of the place. It also meant that Tempelhof was always in need of a good overhaul.

Hoffner and Fichte were finding that out for themselves firsthand as they slogged their way across a field that was more like a mass of dense pudding than a runway. It was clear why boots were a staple of the aviator outfit.

Hoffner was the first into the hangar. It would have been difficult to call the domed tent a building, as it was nothing more than a tarp hung over several very long poles. Ten or so aeroplanes of every color and design stood in a row along the side wall, half of them stripped for parts in aid of the other five. Mueller was pilfering something from one of the stray engines when he looked around at the sound of footsteps. He was wearing a pair of coveralls, streaked in oil and grease from collar to foot. His boots, however, were immaculate. He started toward them.

Still far enough away not to be heard, Fichte said quietly, "I'm getting into an aeroplane with a cripple? Wonderful."

Under his breath, Hoffner answered, "I won't tell him about your lungs, and you don't mention the limp. Fair enough?"

Mueller drew up to them, and, wiping the grease onto a cloth from his remaining fingers, he extended his hand. Without hesitation, Hoffner took it. "Hello, Toby," he said.

"Nikolai," said Mueller. "Nice to see you."

"This is Hans Fichte. Your passenger."

Mueller extended his hand to Fichte, who tried a smile and took Mueller's hand. Fichte squeezed gently and felt the gaps in the grip. "It's an odd sensation," said Mueller, "but you get used to it." Fichte nodded awkwardly. Mueller smiled. "I was talking about flying. You never get used to the hand." Mueller laughed. Again Fichte nodded, as he pulled his hand away.

"How soon until you can go?" said Hoffner.

"The sky's clear enough, for now. Up to you. Everything's ready on my end." Mueller nodded over to a biplane along the row, one with a tapered undercarriage and a high skid under the back fin. From the little Hoffner recalled, it could have been anything from a Siemens-Schuckert D-IV to an English Sopwith Snipe. Hoffner was putting nothing past Mueller, these days. Mueller had been talking about getting his hands on a Bentley engine for weeks: the 230-horsepower B.R.2, if memory served. It was a bit tougher to handle, but the power was unmatched, over 300 kph in a dive, according to Mueller. Hoffner had trouble even conceiving of those speeds. The chances, however, of one having "fallen" into Mueller's lap during his travels was just too good. Hoffner knew Georgi would have been able to spot it instantly.

Mueller turned to Fichte. "We can fly above the rain, but you'll need something warmer than what you've got on. There are some things back in the office you can try." Fichte nodded.

"So I can leave him with you, Toby?" said Hoffner. "I need you there for a day, two at the most. You can work that?"

Mueller said, "Bruges is as good a place as any to find castor oil."

Seeing Fichte's expression, Hoffner said, "To grease the cylinders, Hans. An old sky pilot's trick."

Mueller headed for the office as Hoffner lagged behind with Fichte so as to give the boy some last-minute instructions. "Get what you can and wire me, Hans." Not that Hoffner was thrilled to be sending Fichte off like this—there had been only time enough for Fichte to throw an extra pair of socks and some shaving equipment into a satchel—but given the leak, Hoffner had no interest in having the Bruges story come out before getting the information firsthand. Fichte would have to make do. "And mark the wire 'restricted.' I'll have a boy waiting at the desk, day and night. Send it whenever you can."

Fichte said, "You don't think it would be better for both of us to go?"

Hoffner had explained this twice on the ride over. He tried to be encouraging. "Of course it would, Hans, but then who's going to find that leak?" Hoffner paused. "You're from the big city. Use it to your advantage."

Mueller had reached the office. He turned back. "All right, boys, we've got about three and a half hours of light left. We need to be in the air in ten minutes if we're going to get as far as Köln by tonight, and I want to get as far as Köln by tonight." He stepped into the office and headed for a locker. "Now," he said to himself in a loud voice, "let's see if we've got anything big enough for Herr Kripo in here."

Hoffner patted Fichte on the shoulder and started for the field. "Safe trip, Hans." Almost at the opening flap, he added, "And try not to fall out." Hoffner was gone by the time Fichte turned around to answer.

The Ullstein Building is the site from which most of Berlin's popular news is processed and packaged for daily consumption. Having stood its ground for the past forty years, the building had survived relatively unscathed during the weeks of revolution. In the distant past, its editors had made it through Bismarck's right-wing barrages, and later the left's equally vicious attacks for the paper's support of the war. The men of Ullstein had even found ways to defuse the ever-recurring anti-Semitic assaults. Leopold Ullstein, the publisher and founder—along with his five sons—had done a remarkable thing for Berlin by giving her workingmen newspapers written just for them; Ullstein senior had even sat on the city council in thanks for his services. But Jews were Jews, and there was always something so threatening in that, and so, whenever things got a bit slow, the Ullstein papers were the inevitable target. According to the current editors, however, if they had managed to weather those storms, a few shots from some disgruntled soldiers weren't going to stall the presses.

Since November the real intrigue had been taking place elsewhere—at the offices of the Social Democrats' **Vorwärts** a few blocks away, and at the ever-relocating rooms of **Die Rote Fahne,** Luxemburg's "authentic" rag of the people. Ullstein's **Die Berliner Zeitung am Mittag** (the **BZ**) and its **Morgenpost,** on the other hand, had chugged along quite nicely, and had left the rabble-rousing, and all its attendant mayhem, to the less stable publications. The **Morgenpost** had continued to report on the life of Berlin in full detail; the **BZ** had offered her up in little vignettes.

For fifteen years now, the **BZ** had been the city's boulevard paper—to be picked up, read, and discarded—with stories that had just enough meat on them to keep the reader hooked for a tram ride or a morning coffee. It gave a snapshot of the city: eclectic, pulsating, and immediate. The only in-depth reporting the **BZ** ever did was the Monday sports section—horse races, motorcycle rallies, sailing, boxing, football, handball: the pages were always thick with the sweat of the middle class. It also liked to titillate and shock—murder was its biggest seller—which was why most of the men of the Kripo were familiar with its offices.

Hoffner pushed his way through the swinging doors and into the **BZ**'s editorial department. The sound of typewriter keys striking metal cylinders, and the constant clatter of the newswire machines, gave the impression that the fourth floor was under attack from a legion of angry, pellet-throwing elves. Even the ringing of the telephones took on a sirenlike wail, as if a miniature ambulance corps were shuttling unseen from one side of the room to the other. The **BZ** staff seemed oblivious to the noise; they remained focused on the news. The one or two who did look over as Hoffner made his way through knew exactly where he was heading. When the Kripo came, they came looking for Gottlob Kvatsch. It was probably why Kvatsch insisted that his desk remain on the back wall: he liked the view it presented. He also liked to keep his distance. Ullstein was beginning to hire too many of its own kind. Kvatsch might not have been able to avoid working **for** Jews; he just had no desire to work side by side **with** them. He had moved his desk three times during the last year. None of his co-workers had shown the least concern.

Kvatsch saw Hoffner long before Hoffner had made his way past the "cooking tips" and "affordable fashions" desks. Kvatsch quickly began to fold up the few notebooks that were spread out in front of him, and was placing the last of them inside a drawer when Hoffner pulled up. Keeping his gaze on the desk, Kvatsch found something to busy himself with: he began to rearrange the pens on his blotter. Hoffner stood quietly for a few moments and enjoyed the performance.

Kvatsch was wearing a weathered suit, the kind found on any of those Saturday wagons in the Rosenthaler Platz or near the Hackescher-Markt. The tie was also secondhand. The shirt, however, was crisp and white: Kvatsch chose his creature comforts carefully. To the men of the Kripo, he had always reminded them of a slightly bedraggled detective sergeant, one whose time had never come, yet who continued to wear the once-impressive suit in the hopes of being noticed. There was the story that Kvatsch had actually applied to the Kripo and been dismissed years ago, but Hoffner guessed it was more of a cautionary tale for young recruits than the reason for Kvatsch's persistent choice in attire. Even so, they all knew what Kvatsch liked to be called around the

BZ: he was "the Detective." Maybe, then, the clothes were a deliberate choice, thought Hoffner, even as the word "pathetic" ran through his mind.

"Hello, Kvatsch." Hoffner spoke with just the right tinge of contempt.

"Herr Detective Inspector." Kvatsch was still intent on his pens. "What a surprise."

"'Sources in the Kripo.' That's very impressive. I'd like to know which ones."

Kvatsch looked up. His face always had a nice sheen to it, as if his wide pores were the source of the oil used to comb back his hair. And he was always pursing his thick lips, afraid, perhaps, that his teeth might slip out without constant supervision. Kvatsch reached into his jacket pocket and produced a pack of very expensive cigarettes: he was making clear his own connections. He took one and laid the pack on the desk. "I'd offer you one, Herr Inspector, but I know you don't smoke." Kvatsch lit up and settled back comfortably into his chair. His lips continued to purse around the butt of the cigarette.

"Let's save ourselves some time, Kvatsch. Just tell me where you got it."

"Please, Inspector. Have a seat." He indicated a space in front of his desk, then took in a long drag. There was no chair in front of his desk. "Are you confirming the story?"

Hoffner smiled. "I'm just trying to find out who's been passing false information on to our friends in the press."

"False information?" echoed Kvatsch. "Is that why you're here? It worries you that much that someone might be misleading me?"

Hoffner kept his smile. "The name, Kvatsch. I'd hate to have to bring you down to the Alex."

Kvatsch nodded slowly, as if he were about to submit. His eyes, however, had the look of a little boy's with a secret. "Haven't you heard, Inspector? The socialists have introduced something quite wonderful. It's called "freedom of the press." The Americans have been doing it for years."

"Really?" Hoffner gently moved the pens out of the way so that he could take a seat on the lip of the desk. His proximity seemed to straighten Kvatsch up in his chair. "They also have libel laws. Little things like that. We don't, so we get to use other methods." Without the least bit of threat, Hoffner reached over and pulled a cigarette from Kvatsch's pack. He took Kvatsch's cigarette and lit his own.

Kvatsch showed no reaction. "Would you like a cigarette, Detective Inspector?"

"No thanks." Hoffner took a drag on his own, and then crushed out Kvatsch's in the ashtray. "You know, Kvatsch, I don't think the socialists had you in mind when they started parading out all of these freedoms."

"Must be up to four or five by now, if you're this keen for my source, Inspector. And here I thought it was just your run-of-the-mill little murder. Not even front-page material. Tell me, is it true about the knife markings? I think that's the part that's going to sell the most papers."

"We both know it's going to take me no time to find this out. You can either do yourself a favor, or you can do what you always do. End up a few steps behind, kicking yourself for having been so stupid." Hoffner enjoyed the momentary flash in Kvatsch's eyes. "These socialists are an unpredictable bunch. It's another week before the Assembly votes get tabulated. Who knows where we might be then? Between you and me, Kvatsch, I don't think this is the time not to have a friend in the Kripo, do you?" Hoffner stood. He crushed out his cigarette. "Just something to think about."

"I'll do that," Kvatsch said icily.

"Good." Hoffner reached over and took the pack from the desk. He was turning to go when he stopped and said, "Oh, by the way. Nice suit. Just your style, Detective." Hoffner pocketed the cigarettes and headed for the door.

Fichte had vomited twice, once during a barrel roll, the other just after they had touched down in a field on the outskirts of Köln. To be fair, that last one had been due more to relief than to motion; still, it had brought Fichte in under the limit. Mueller had been banking on at least three such episodes, but Fichte had survived the nosedive and the spinout without so much as a burp. Mueller had been duly impressed. Tonight the drinks were on him.

"You see," said Mueller as he watched Fichte dry-heave a last string of saliva onto the ground. "I told you you'd get used to it." He rapped him on the back. "We just need to get you something to settle that stomach."

Fichte nodded as he stared, hunched over, into his own spew. He pulled out his handkerchief and wiped his mouth. Oddly enough, he had never felt more exhilarated. He spat, stood, and peered up into the dusking sky.

It was all so unreal, he thought. Thirty kilometers out of Berlin, and the clouds had lifted; the sky had opened, and Fichte had known what it was to be in flight. Mueller had tried explaining it to him over the din of the engine and wind, but Fichte had heard only pieces—nondimensional coefficients, lift-drag ratios—none of which had made even the slightest bit of sense to him. For Fichte, flight was a matter of faith, and with it had come a feeling of such profound solitude—stripped of any hint of loneliness—as to make it completely serene. He could still feel the wind slapping at his face, his hand as he had held it out, its enormity stretching out over houses and fields and rivers, all of them cradled in the thickness of his fingers and palm. There was a vastness to the world at those speeds and at that height, a totality that could easily have provoked a feeling of utter insignificance, but Fichte had felt no less vast. Up there, he had known why Mueller had continued to take to the sky: not for the thrill or for the ego, but for the connection with that totality, a sensation of perfect wholeness only imagined from the ground looking up. At two thousand feet—in an open box made of metal and wood—it was forever in his grasp.

Fichte spat again and placed the handkerchief in his pocket. "A couple of shots of whiskey should do it," he said.

Mueller laughed. "Oh, I think that can be arranged."

Mueller knew most of the best spots in and around Köln. In fact, Mueller knew most of the best spots anywhere west of Berlin. He was also not averse to using his disabilities to his advantage. The girls in Köln were known to drop their prices, and various other bits, for a cripple, now and then. Mueller told Fichte he would see what they could do for a cripple's friend. Fichte thought about mentioning his lungs, but he reckoned the trade-off wasn't worth the few marks he would save: better to have Mueller thinking him a robust young detective than the jackass who had sucked in on the gas at the wrong time. Of course, it never occurred to Fichte that Mueller might already be wondering why his passenger had managed to miss out on all the fun at the trenches. Mueller was praying that Fichte's quick departure from the Kaiser's service had had nothing to do with a certain very delicate area: that was a wound no one liked to talk about. Fichte's hesitation over the girls had gotten Mueller thinking that maybe the prices were not going to be the real problem tonight.

All such concerns, however, were quickly put to rest five hours later, when Mueller, Fichte, and two willing young ladies stepped into the attic loft that Mueller had found for them over one of the seedier bars in town. It was one room, but Fichte hardly seemed to mind. He had been sustaining a very nice drunk since his third beer, and immediately pulled down his pants the moment the four of them were alone. Mueller laughed at the sudden appearance of Fichte's shortish but exceptionally thick erection. Mueller tossed his own girl onto the room's one bed and dove in after her. He then turned to Fichte as the bedded girl began to pull off his clothes.

"What is it with you cops and instant nudity?" said Mueller, slapping at the girl's hands as she tried to undress him. "Pants down. Service, please. Where's the romance?" Mueller howled with laughter as the girl found what she had been searching for.

Fichte stood there, chortling quietly to himself as his girl took hold of her prize.

Mueller said, "Nikolai's the same way, you know. No shame, no patience."

Hoffner's name seemed to slap some life into Fichte. He turned to Mueller as he pushed the girl's face from his crotch. "The **Kriminal-Kommissar?**" said Fichte, tripping over the last few syllables. He immediately snapped his head back at the girl, who was trying to reacquire her target. "Hey there!" he said. "Hold on a bit." She laughed and continued to probe. Fichte shrugged and looked back at Mueller. "Herr Hoffner?"

Mueller was having his own trouble concentrating on the conversation. "I could tell you stories," he said in a throaty tone.

"Really?" said Fichte, teetering as he spoke. "Like what?"

The girl had mounted Mueller and was now riding him with vigor. When he spoke, his words issued in a tom-tom cadence. "Ask him about the pact."

"About the what?" said Fichte. Fichte's girl pushed him down onto a chair. She took his hands and strapped them onto her thighs. She, too, began to drive down onto him.

"The pact," said Mueller, becoming winded. "Just ask."

The girl on top of Fichte grabbed his face, focused it on her own, and said, "You want to talk, or you want to fuck?"

It took Fichte a moment to find her eyes. She was really quite pretty, he thought. And she had nice big tits. Bigger than Lina's.

"Fuck, please," he said.

She grabbed his head and thrust it into her chest. She then began to ride him with even greater abandon. Fichte was glad he had brought his inhaler. He would need a few good sucks before round two.

⚜ CHUCHYA ⚜

Hoffner had lain awake for most of the night. He was a periodic insomniac, and, except for the fact that he actually enjoyed the long hours of intense thought, he might have attributed it to some sort of cosmic payback for a waking life of chosen isolation. For some reason, though, dead-of-night focus on a case always left him feeling refreshed in the morning. It was dreaming that exhausted him.

He had come to the conclusion—sometime around 4:00 a.m.—that the note from K might be the only piece of recent information that could lead him forward. Everything else seemed to be generating lateral movement: the grease had introduced the possibility of a military connection; the gloves had raised a whole series of problems—the girl's transport, the girl herself, and the fact that Wouters was in a different country. Hoffner had considered the "second carver" theory—the smooth versus the jagged and angular strokes—but that hardly explained who the first carver might be, what with Wouters safely locked away in Sint-Walburga. And, of course, there was Luxemburg, which had brought in the Polpo and which, to Hoffner's way of thinking, was somehow linked to the leak.

That left him with the note from K, which, on the surface, seemed equally cloudy. The small hours, however, did more than just concentrate Hoffner's mind; they allowed his instincts to come to the fore:

by the time Martha had begun to show signs of life at five-thirty, Hoffner knew with absolute certainty that the note was unrelated to everything else. He just had no notion why.

Finding out, however, would have to wait. He slipped out of bed, dressed, and grabbed a quick breakfast—yesterday's cold potatoes and coffee—and was out the door before the rest of the house knew he had been home. At this hour, cabs were easy pickings and Hoffner was at the Alex by half past six.

Little Franz was standing over a washbasin in one of the attic alcoves when Hoffner pulled up next to him. It was now a quarter to seven, and the light had just begun to creep through the porthole window directly above them. Hoffner had ducked his way under the beams and past the three beds—two of which were still occupied—all without drawing attention. He now waited for Franz to turn off the tap.

"Up nice and early," said Hoffner when the splashing finally stopped.

The boy nearly jumped. He stood there as water dripped down his cheeks and onto the floor. He had that same concave, pale little chest that Georgi had, but his biceps were already beginning to show genuine muscle: this was a boy who had learned to survive. Hoffner knew that any comparison with his own son was strictly of his own making. Hoffner reached over for the paper-thin towel hanging from a hook, and held it out to him.

Franz took the towel. "Yes. Good morning, Herr

Kriminal-Kommissar." He continued to stare at Hoffner.

"Don't let yourself catch cold, Franz." Immediately the boy went to work on his hair and face. "I've a favor to ask you." Franz nodded from under the towel and continued with the fury that was a ten-year-old boy drying himself. "You might want to leave a little skin on your face," said Hoffner.

Franz looked up. His hair was shooting off in all directions, but his face had that lovely pink-and-white hue. "Yes, Herr **Kriminal-Kommissar.**"

Hoffner placed the towel on its hook as Franz began to do what he could with a hairbrush. "You remember Herr Kvatsch? At the **BZ**?" The boy had tailed Kvatsch during a case last year; he had proved himself exceptionally good at getting the names of the people Kvatsch saw during the day.

Franz nodded. "The one with the teeth," he said. "Yes, Herr **Kriminal-Kommissar.**" Franz had managed something of a part; he placed the brush by the basin.

"Good. I'm going to need you to find out who he's been talking to." Hoffner knew Kvatsch was lazy: the man would eventually contact his source. Hoffner only hoped it would be quicker than the last time: then, Franz had spent the better part of a week in Kvatsch's shadows. "It's five pfennigs a name," said Hoffner. The boy's eyes lit up: it had been two, the last go-round. As then, Hoffner had no reason to worry that Franz might pad the list in order to make a few extra coins; the boy took too much pride in his work. It was why Hoffner had known Franz would be at his washbasin at a quarter to seven in the morning.

Franz reached over for his shirt. He slipped his arms through and began to button it. "Today, Herr **Kriminal-Kommissar**?"

"Today." Hoffner watched as Franz crammed his shirttail into his pants. Once again Hoffner had to remind himself that this was no ordinary ten-year-old, the boy's gawkiness notwithstanding: no doubt Franz was already proficient with a blackjack, maybe even a knife. "One other thing," said Hoffner. He nodded back over his shoulder to the two sleeping boys. "Which one of them do you trust?"

Franz peered past Hoffner and pointed toward the boy in the far bed. "Sascha. He's all right."

Hoffner turned to the sleeping boy. From this angle, he might have been his own Sascha, a few years removed. Again, it was best not to think about it. "I need him by the wire room, all day and all night, if necessary. Anything comes in for me, he's to hold it and find me. Can he do that?" Franz nodded. "Good. Tell him I'll telephone the switchboard at eleven to see if anything's come in." Hoffner waited for another nod; he then headed for the door. He was figuring that Fichte and Toby would be landing in Bruges sometime around ten if they could manage to get themselves out of bed in the next hour. Then again, Hoffner had spent his own weekend with Victor and Toby, that trip to the Tyrol, most of which he now recalled as a smoke-filled, boozy blur. Hoffner stopped and turned back to Franz. "Better make it noon."

The morning commuters were long gone by the time Hoffner arrived in the South End: Linden-strasse was virtually empty. Even so, he stood on the corner for perhaps ten minutes, gazing from his newspaper to the few passersby, none of whom seemed the least interested in Luxemburg's building. Satisfied, Hoffner tossed the paper into a trash bin and headed for Number 2.

This time the landlady let him in without so much as a question. Breakfast was in the offing, but Hoffner politely refused and asked if anyone else had come to the flat since his own visit: the woman recalled no one.

Luxemburg's rooms were untouched, except for a few very subtle changes: the teacup had been rinsed and returned to its shelf; several of the pictures had been straightened on the wall; and the smell of dried wood had been aired out, although the windows were once again shut tight. K, as it turned out, was more than just a secretive man; he was a neat one. Hoffner found that in keeping with the tone of the note.

The purpose for the return visit, however, was a bit more difficult to pinpoint. In fact, it took Hoffner nearly twenty minutes to find what K had sent him back for. When Hoffner did find it, he realized it was in the most obvious, and therefore least likely, place to have been searched. Sitting atop her desk—and side by side with the unread speeches—was a stack of books and papers held together by a rough piece of cord. K had been clever: the stack had been placed in such a way as to seem a part of the speeches. Hoffner now saw it otherwise. He stepped over, sat in Rosa's chair, and began to loosen the knot.

Within half a minute he was flipping through one of her private diaries, February through May 1914. The other volumes chronicled her life in equally short and arbitrary installments: July 1911 through January 1912; November 1915 through July 1916; and an entire book devoted to August 1914. The beginning of the war had marked the end of the International; with German workers voting to fight against their French and English brothers, Luxemburg's dream of a Universal Socialism had come crashing down. It had been the great disaster of her life—"workers of the world" choosing country over one another—and had thus inspired pages and pages of grief-stricken prose, all with the requisite hair-pulling of a Greek tragedy. Hoffner quickly moved through them.

The more startling discovery was the collection of loose letters slotted into each of the books. Hoffner estimated several hundred from a first glance-through: it was clear that they had been hastily included, the addressees and dates even more haphazard. There were more than thirty names, with dates reaching as far back as 1894, the most recent from only a few months ago. The one constant was the writer. They were all from Rosa.

How, then, thought Hoffner, had K amassed nearly two hundred of Rosa's private letters in just over a week? The answer—and K's identity—obviously lay with the recipients, but Hoffner knew any attempt to contact Luxemburg's coterie would elicit only blank stares and denials: the remaining Spartacists—her band of left left-wingers—would never give up one of their own to the Kripo.

He also knew there would be nothing in the stack to tell him who K was; even so, Hoffner needed to make sure. He went to work on the names.

Of those who had received letters, only three had a **K** in either initial. The first was Karl Liebknecht, and unless he had risen from the dead, it was highly unlikely that he had been the one to show up at the Alex last week. Hoffner eliminated Liebknecht.

The second was a Konstantin Zetkin—Kostia, in the letters—a boy fifteen years her junior, the son of Luxemburg's good friend Clara, and, from what Hoffner could make out, Rosa's lover for a short period of time. That, however, hardly distinguished him from any number of the other correspondents: Paul Levi, her lawyer; Leo Jogiches, her mentor; and Hans Diefenbach, her doctor—who had actually married Rosa during her last stint in prison, but who had died at the Russian front before reaping the benefits—had all kept in contact with her both before and after the affairs; all, of course, except for Diefenbach, although there were a few diary entries in which Luxemburg had carried on some lively conversations with him postmortem.

What made it clear that she would never have allowed Zetkin to compile her letters was the fact that the boy simply didn't have the smarts to do it. Zetkin was a classic **Luftmensch,** all air and no substance, and although Rosa had tried to mold him into something artistic, the journals made it clear that he had been a lost cause. Hoffner quickly recognized that Kostia Zetkin was not his K.

That left Karl Kautsky. Most of the letters were addressed to his wife, Luise, but even Hoffner had heard of the very public falling-out between Luxemburg and her onetime comrade. It was generally agreed that squabbles among socialists made for the most entertaining reading in town: vitriol and sarcasm never had quite the same shrillness elsewhere, and the newspapers knew it, even if most of their readers never understood the finer points. In fact, no one understood the finer points; they were meaningless, anyway. The comedy was in the personal swipes, and Luxemburg had given Berlin a **tour de théâtre** with her dismantling of Kautsky. Suffice it to say Kautsky had not been the one to lead Hoffner to the flat.

K had left nothing in the letters that could be tied to himself; he was too clever for that. He had signed the note for a reason, but for now, his identity would have to wait.

Hoffner sat back. He noticed a decanter of brandy on a nearby shelf, and, reaching over, brought it to the desk. There was a glass among the papers, and he poured himself a drink. He imagined that K had brought him here to see the real Luxemburg—stripped of the caricature of fanaticism—and while the pages did paint a more flesh-and-blood picture, Rosa remained distant. There were moments of raw emotion, but they came across too self-consciously: pain was never simply pain—it was acute, or frantic, or unbearable—beauty never less than triumphant. There was a morality to socialism that seeped into everything. It was as if she had been unable to separate herself from the woman who shouted down to the crowds, even when writing for herself. A few lines would hint at more, but then, just as quickly, the exclamation points would return—the heightened sense of purpose—and the other Rosa would slip quietly away.

Hoffner refilled his glass and realized that the room had been cast in much the same way. During his first visit he had seen it as a place for gatherings, warmth: now that seemed contrived, as well. The pillows and photographs were placed too perfectly to be inviting. There was an earnestness to the intimacy, which made it all the more suspect.

Glass in hand, Hoffner stood and moved across to one of the bookshelves. He scanned the titles and pulled out a volume of Pushkin: maybe he would find more of her in how she read than in how she wrote? But here, too, her marginalia lived in the extremes: Pushkin was either a genius or a fool. The same held true for Marx and Korolenko, a special diatribe reserved for a collection of essays by a man named Plekhanov. No matter where, her words, like herself, were intended for display. There seemed to be no private Rosa in any of it.

Hoffner finished his drink and began to squeeze the book back into place. He was having trouble getting it in when he heard the sound of something falling behind the row. He peered in through the gap, but it was too dark. Pulling a handful of books from the shelf, he found a thin volume lying flat on its back: it was little more than a pamphlet. He placed the stack on the desk and retrieved the book.

At first he thought his eyes were playing tricks on him. It had been years since he had seen it, a standard edition of Mörike's poetry. Not that it was so momentous a find: every first-year university student could recite a few passages from memory. But it seemed odd to find it here, in and among the weighty tomes. Then again, it really hadn't been with them, tucked safely behind. Hoffner pulled over a chair and opened the leather cover.

The pages were almost clean—a mark here and there, or a word—but nothing like the constant commentary he had seen elsewhere. And yet it was clear from the ragged corners that Rosa had spent a good deal of time with the book. Hoffner leafed through, allowing the pages to lead him. They came to a stop

on a poem called "Seclusion." He needed to read
only the first line to understand why:

Oh, world, let me be.

The rest was equally telling:

Tempt me not with gifts of love.
Let this solitary heart have
Your delight, your pain.

What I grieve, I know not.
It is an unknown ache;
Forever through tears shall I see
The sun's love-light.

Often, I am barely conscious
And the bright pleasures break
Through the depths, thus pressing
Blissfully into my breast.

Oh, world, let me be.
Tempt me not with gifts of love.
Let this solitary heart have
Your delight, your pain.

The one place where she had made a mark was next
to the word "conscious"—no exclamation point,
nothing to explain, just a simple dash to draw her eye
each time she turned to the page. She had been fully

aware of her own isolation and had kept it hidden away. Evidently, even K had not been privy to it.

There was something powerfully real about this single page. It gave no greater insight to the source of her solitude, but it made her far more human. Perhaps better than most, Hoffner understood her plea.

He caught sight of his watch, and nearly blanched when he saw the time. It was quarter to two. He had been with her for over five hours and had let the time slip by. K had brought him back for her theories and ramblings, but it was only here at the end that Hoffner had found something he could understand. This Rosa was far more compelling than he had imagined.

Nonetheless, she would have to wait: he needed to get in touch with the wire room. Looking around for something to hold the papers, Hoffner spotted a bag that was tucked in between the chair and desk. Evidently K had thought of everything. Hoffner shuffled the diaries and papers into a single stack and slid them in. He repositioned the chair and picked up the Mörike. He was about to place it back behind the row when he stopped. He stared at the weathered cover.

Oh, world, let me be, he thought.

He slipped the book into his pocket and headed for the door.

Downstairs, a strident "Yes" greeted his knocking. Hoffner spoke up and the door opened instantly: the woman's smile seemed to grow broader with each subsequent unveiling.

"Madame," said Hoffner. "I was hoping I might use your telephone."

At once, she stepped back. "Of course, Herr **Kriminal-Kommissar.** Please."

The woman brought him into her sitting room, which was the same layout as upstairs, although Rosa had shown better taste when it had come to the furnishings. This was a mishmash of styles. Hoffner wondered how many departing tenants had arrived at their new homes only to discover a missing chair or table. No doubt a few of Rosa's things would soon be relocating a few flights south.

Hoffner put in the call; the woman retreated through a swinging door to give him his privacy.

The wire room had received nothing. According to the new boy, little Franz had not been back since this morning. Herr **Kriminal-Bezirkssekretär** Groener, on the other hand, had passed by several times to ask Sascha what he was waiting for. Hoffner told the boy to ignore Groener and to remain by his post.

Hoffner hung up just as the woman was returning with a tray of food. Hoffner said, "Very kind of you, Madame, but I really must . . ." The look of disappointment on her face bordered on the tragic. "Well, maybe just a sausage."

She brightened up at once and placed the tray on a nearby table. She then sat and waited for Hoffner to join her: evidently, this was going to be a formal sitting. Hoffner obliged, and she started to spoon out three short, wrinkled pieces of meat from a can and onto a plate for him. When she was done, she poured out a glass of something pale yellow. Hoffner thought it better not to ask.

He took a spoonful and slid the first of the pieces into his mouth. It was army surplus, probably two months old, and had a leathery texture that tasted liked dried tobacco. Hoffner smiled and swallowed. The woman beamed. She was very proud of her husband's scavenging, and probably had no idea that she was feeding contraband to a police officer. "You knew Frau Luxemburg well?" he said.

The woman watched him with a mother's joy as he ate. "As well as any of the tenants."

"You knew her friends?"

Her lips puckered at the thought of them. "No. I didn't know any of those people." The word "those" carried a particularly sneering tone.

"Gentleman friends?" He shoveled a second piece of the meat into his mouth, and did his best to swallow it whole. "One reads the papers, hears things."

The woman gave a tight smile. "I don't interest myself in such things."

Really, thought Hoffner. He had noticed several of the more notorious papers—the popular rags—in a rack by the sofa when he had been on the phone. He now looked over again and scanned them for their dates: all late December. It had been about that time that most of the papers had begun to chronicle the seedier side of Rosa's life, all of it, no doubt, with lies meant to discredit her: "Judah is reaching out for the crown!" "We are ruled by Levi and the devil Luxemburg!" had been the most popular slogans around town. Hoffner knew there was only one reason his hostess would have saved them.

The woman saw where he was looking. For a moment she looked as if she had been caught. Then, just as quickly, the tight smile returned. "I don't read them. They're—my husband's. As I said, I don't look at such trash."

Hoffner smiled with her. "Even if you might have been the one to give them the information for their stories."

The woman's face went white. "Herr **Kriminal-Kommissar**! I would never—"

Hoffner raised a pacifying hand. "I don't really care, Madame. I hope they paid you well. But I would hate to flip through one of those rags and find the mention of one of Frau Luxemburg's special friends. Say, a bearded man who might have had keys to the flat?" The woman's eyes went wide as she listened. Her entire body stiffened as she tried to find a response. "So there was someone?" said Hoffner. He turned his attention to the last piece of meat; he was trying to scoop it up, but was having trouble getting it onto his spoon. The woman's eyes darted nervously as she followed his progress. When Hoffner finally landed it, he looked back at her. "There was someone?" he repeated. She stared at him; she nodded once. "Did he have a name?" said Hoffner. He popped the meat into his mouth.

The woman's hand seemed eager for her neck, but she managed to keep it in her lap. "Most of them had beards." A light desperation had crept into her voice. "They always had beards. Filthy people. They would stream in and out. I never knew which was which." She suddenly remembered something. "There was an umbrella," she said. "Yes. An umbrella. The man— her special one—he always carried an umbrella with him."

An umbrella, thought Hoffner. Very helpful. That simply meant K was no idiot; after all, he was living in Berlin in the winter. "But no name." She tried to find it, but shook her head. Hoffner nodded and stood. "Well, if you think of it."

As before, she suddenly brightened up. "He was a Jew," she said, as if she had just recalled the crucial piece in the puzzle.

The comment should not have surprised Hoffner, but it did. Nonetheless, he showed no reaction. "A Jew," he said.

"Oh yes." She was so pleased for remembering. "You can always tell Jews. This man was definitely one of them."

"I see." There were any number of things Hoffner thought to say, but he said none of them. Instead he stood quietly until he knew he had no choice but to speak: "Well. I have work to get back to. Thank you for the luncheon, Madame."

She stood. "Not at all, Herr **Kriminal-Kommissar.** If I can be of any further help."

Hoffner tried to match her smile. He didn't really try all that hard.

At first sight, Sint-Walburga was not nearly as chilling as Fichte had thought it would be. Van Acker had taken the scenic route, which, on a clear, sunlit day, gave the asylum the look of a country villa, if only through half-squinting, hungover eyes: Fichte had yet to put anything solid in his stomach—Mueller, of course, had had a full breakfast before taking off—and, except for several tall glasses of water, Fichte had done his best not to stir things up. For some reason, this morning's flight from Köln had helped to relieve his anguish. The ups and downs and turns of the road out to the asylum, however, were beginning to take their toll: there was a distinct sloshing feeling. Fichte kept his head facing out the window.

Walburga was three stories high, set atop a small hill, and with enough surrounding woods to make it seem almost cozy. Closer in, however, the illusion vanished. The iron bars across each window and doorway came into view as the automobile made its final turn out of the trees. Chips pockmarked the thick walls, and water damage veined the stones in thin green streaks, as if a spider, infected by the disease within, had let loose with its own demented weaving.

Van Acker pulled the car up to the main gate. He beeped his horn once and waited for a guard to

saunter across the gravel courtyard. The man fit perfectly into his surroundings: his face was scarred, and
his uniform had the same weathered look as the
walls. The sight of the gun in his belt was little comfort. He reached the gate and spoke to van Acker
through the bars. "No one said you'd be coming up
today, Chief Inspector." His voice was a perfect
monotone.

Van Acker nodded dismissively. "No one's been answering your telephone. I've been trying since noon."

It was difficult to know whether the guard had understood; his expression and posture remained unchanged. Had the eyes not been open, Fichte might
have thought the man asleep on his feet.

With a sudden jerk, the guard reached for the lock
on the gate. "Yuh," he said in the same lifeless tone.
"Telephone's out." He released the chain and slowly
walked the gate open. Fichte expected van Acker to
pull up by the main door, but he continued around
to a small archway off to the right. At some point it
might have been the delivery entrance; now it was
Walburga's only access. Fichte noticed several automobiles parked behind the building.

"How's your French, Detective?" said van Acker in
German as the two men stepped up to the doorway.
He pulled the cord for the bell.

Hoffner had omitted Fichte's "in training" status
when he told the Belgian who was coming. In fact, he
had even given Fichte a promotion, figuring Fichte
could use all the help he could get. Back in Bruges,

van Acker had been duly impressed by so young a detective inspector. Per Hoffner's instructions—and given his head this morning—Fichte had kept as quiet as possible during the ride up from town. "It's all right," said Fichte without much conviction.

They heard footsteps through the door. Van Acker said, "I'll translate. Make sure there's no confusion."

A second guard opened the door and ushered them into a tiny vestibule. It was lit by a single bulb and was in no better state of repair than the outside walls. A large iron door waited directly across from them. Van Acker was forced to suffer through a repeat performance of the conversation at the gate before being permitted to sign the registry. "Everyone who comes in or goes out," he said as he handed the pen to Fichte. "Staff and visitors alike." Fichte finished signing just as the guard was unlocking the iron door that led into the asylum proper. "Don't be fooled by the surroundings," said van Acker. "They take this all very seriously."

The scrape of the bolt in the lock behind them was enough to tell Fichte how seriously Sint-Walburga took its inmates. Van Acker led them down a narrow corridor and into an open hall. It might have been any country house entrance hall—vaulted ceiling, fireplace, chairs and sofas—except that its windows had all been bricked over, leaving it devoid of any natural light. What light there was came from a collection of overworked lamps, placed at odd intervals along the walls, that did little more than create a stark, yellow pall within the space. That, however, was not the hall's most disconcerting feature. The grand staircase, which still sported remnants of a once-magnificent carpet, was encased in a cage of thick bars that ran along the banisters and up to the second floor. There was barely enough room to squeeze an arm through; even so, they had taken every precaution: a second iron door stood at the bottom of the steps where the banisters met. Shadows from the bars spilled out into the hall and seemed to trap the single guard on duty in his own phantom cage. He gave a perfunctory nod to the two men; he knew they were not heading up.

For Fichte, however, the sounds coming from above made the rest seem almost inviting. At first he thought it was the mewling of dogs; he quickly realized, however, that these were human voices. Some murmured in whispers, others in incoherent wails. The one constant was an unrelenting desperation. One voice suddenly broke through, its anguish enough to prompt Fichte's own sense of despair. Almost at once, a door bolted shut, and the voice again retreated into the amorphous mass of sound.

"The patients are on the top two floors," said van Acker, as if relegating them to the upper reaches could in any way mitigate their presence throughout the building. Fichte did his best to nod. "The Superintendent keeps himself down here."

All but one of the doors off the hall had been barred over. Van Acker led them over to it and knocked once before letting himself in. He told

Fichte to wait outside. Fichte agreed, glad to have put some distance between himself and the stairs. He watched as van Acker made his way across the office and began to speak quickly in French to the man seated behind the far desk.

Fichte had lied. He barely understood a word. He could pick out the mannerisms of a greeting, or small talk, but he was completely at sea until he heard van Acker mention the name Wouters. Fichte did, however, recognize the look of confusion on van Acker's face the moment the Superintendent began to reply. Confusion turned to shock. Fichte needed no French to know that something was wrong.

When the man finished speaking, van Acker slowly turned back to the door. He hesitated and then motioned for Fichte to join them. "Herr **Kriminal-Kommissar,**" he said. "Could you join us?"

It took Fichte a moment to remember his "promotion." He stepped into the office. It was clear that van Acker was on edge: the introductions were brief.

The room fell silent as van Acker seemed unsure what he wanted to say. Finally he turned to Fichte and, almost under his breath, said, "Wouters is dead." He did nothing to hide his own disbelief and regret. "It seems he hung himself two nights ago."

Fichte remained surprisingly calm; he let the information settle. He then said, "I'll need to send a wire."

Hoffner got lucky. At this hour, most of the city's cabs were already back in central Berlin, picking their spots for the rush hour. The sky had opened up, and, had it not been for the sudden appearance of a black Tonneau Mercedes dropping off a fare—and his own quick sprint to flag it down—Hoffner would have been left to slog his way through the downpour to the nearest bus stop. Even so, he received a nice dousing of his pants for his efforts. It was an acceptable trade-off: his shoes would have gotten soaked through, anyway. Once safely inside, he thought about a nap, but that was not to be. He was having trouble shaking Luxemburg.

On the edge of downtown, he told the driver to head up toward Friedrichstrasse. The man disagreed. "You want to avoid **die Mitte** this time of day, **mein Herr.** Faster if we hook over south of the Hallesches Gate."

"Just try Friedrichstrasse," Hoffner said. "All right?"

The man shrugged. "Your time, your money."

As promised, the traffic slowed once they hit the middle of town. The spray from the wheels of the cars rapped mercilessly at the cab's windows and repeatedly dissolved the outside world into a swirl of melting pictures. Hoffner rolled down his window when they hit Friedrichstrasse, so as to minimize the distortion. He checked his watch; it was about time for tea. Positioning himself back on the seat so as to avoid the splatter, he peered out.

He spotted her at Schuckert's, just beyond Leipziger Strasse. She had ducked in under the awning, and was waiting for the worst of it to pass.

Her coat was too thin for the weather, and she held her arms across her chest for added warmth.

"Pull over!" shouted Hoffner over the patter of the rain.

The driver turned abruptly for the curb. Several horn squawks accompanied the maneuver. "I told you it would be bad."

Hoffner paid and hopped out. He placed the papers under his coat and darted over to the restaurant. It was not until he had removed his hat that Lina recognized him. She tried to hide her pleasure in a look of surprise, but her face was not yet sophisticated enough to carry it off. Hoffner shook out his hat as he approached. "I thought it might be you," he said, deciding to play out the charade.

"Herr **Kriminal-Kommissar,**" said Lina. "What a nice surprise."

"You look absolutely frozen, Fräulein Lina. Let me buy you a coffee."

She hesitated before answering: "I can't bring them inside unless I'm selling." She glanced down at her basket of flowers, then back at Hoffner. "And the tea hour is my best time, Herr **Kriminal-Kommissar.**"

"Not in this weather, it isn't," he said, before she could find another excuse. He looked over and saw the lone waiter who had been stationed for the outside seating. The man was holding his tray across his chest and staring out at the rain. Heated lamps or not, no one would be stupid enough to sit out today. "Herr **Ober,**" said Hoffner, calling the man over.

Hoffner reached into his pocket and pulled out his badge. Well trained, the man showed no reaction as Hoffner continued: "This young lady is going to leave her basket out here while we go inside for a coffee. You'll be good enough to see that nothing happens to it, yes?"

The man gave a swift nod. "Of course, **mein Herr.**"

"Good." Hoffner turned to Lina, and motioned her to the door. "Shall we, Fräulein?"

Schuckert's was known for its sweets. The place smelled of raisins and honey, and everything was immaculately white: napkins, tablecloths, even the waiters' coats. In a lovely old-world touch, the tea silverware was marvelously ornate and heavy, and seemed to overwhelm the small marble tables, each of which was surrounded by a quartet of straight-backed wrought-iron chairs. From the far corner, a violinist played something soothing. Hoffner thought it might have been Mozart, but he could have been wrong.

A plump maître d' was chatting up one of his customers when he saw Hoffner and Lina come through the door. The man gave an overly gracious bow to the table, and then headed over. It was clear that he recognized Lina; he was kind enough, though, not to mention it. He smiled and extended his hand to the room. **"Mein Herr,"** he said. "A table for two?"

Hoffner knew that he and Lina were not Schuckert's usual clientele. Grandmothers and granddaughters sat over hot chocolates and scones; elderly bankers shared a plate of figs—Schuckert's had just the right sort of connections to keep its pantries full, no matter what the rest of Berlin might be suffering through; and young women, whose husbands would one day be eating those figs, sat with each other and their packages from KaDeWe or Tietz, or wherever else they had spent the day. One or two were tactless enough to stare at Lina as she passed by, but the rest took no notice. It had never occurred to Hoffner: people could think what they liked. But if Lina was bothered by their looks, she showed none of it. She walked past them with an air of seamless ease. Hoffner felt mildly foolish for having put her through it.

They reached the table and sat. Hoffner helped her out of her coat, and she let the collar fall back across the chair. He noticed that the rain had gotten through to her dress. The wet fabric clung tightly to her thighs. They were long and wonderfully slim, and the cloth was nestling deep within the perfect triangle between them. Without acknowledging his stare, Lina aired out the skirt of her dress and then placed her napkin on her lap. Hoffner looked up to see her peering over at him with a knowing smile. He liked the feeling of having been caught. "Let's find a waiter," he said, and turned to the room.

A man approached from the other direction; Hoffner failed to see him.

"**Et voilà,**" said Lina. Hoffner turned to see a waiter holding out two menus. Lina was not one to wait. She said ecstatically, "I'm going to have a hot chocolate."

Hoffner declined his menu, as well. "Coffee for me."

The man was gone as quickly as he had appeared.

Lina leaned in closer and spoke in a soft, low whisper. "He's asked me to the cinema twice. Must be strange to take my order, don't you think?"

Hoffner felt the excitement in her breath, as if telling him had somehow made her more attractive: it had, of course. He reached into his coat pocket and pulled out his cigarettes. "Must be." It was Kvatsch's pack, a nice impressive brand. Hoffner lit one up. "Well, this was lucky," he said.

"Yes. It was." She continued to stare at him.

There was something thrilling in not knowing if he was being overmatched. Hoffner said, "I was meaning to send you a note about Hans, but I didn't have your address."

"No. You wouldn't have."

"Just in case you were wondering where he might have gotten to."

"Just in case."

Hoffner looked at the girl. He liked the way her eyes widened almost imperceptibly each time she spoke. He liked the slenderness of her shoulders, and the smallness of her breasts. Most of all, he liked how she continued to bait him. "He's out of the country for a day or two," he said. "On an investigation."

"How very exciting for him."

Hoffner took a drag on his cigarette; he was enjoying this more than she knew, or, perhaps, as much as she was permitting. He had yet to figure out which.

"In Bruges," she said. "Yes. Hans managed to get a note to my flat before he left. But thank you for thinking of me, Herr **Kriminal-Kommissar.**"

"Not at all, Fräulein." The drinks arrived.

Lina spooned up a dollop of the cream with her little finger and slipped it into her mouth. There was nothing sexual in it; she was simply too impatient to reach for her spoon. Her eyes slowly closed. "Heaven," she said with delight. The waiter was gone by the time she opened them, and she peered over at Hoffner. He marveled at how her smile gave nothing away. She slid the cup toward him. "Have some. Please."

Hoffner took his spoon and sampled the cream. He nodded. "Very nice."

She took her own spoon and, leaning toward the cup, delicately dug through for some of the chocolate. Hoffner watched as she deftly tried to bring the liquid up along the side of the cup so as not to disturb the cream. She seemed so intent on the task. It was then that he noticed the half-blackened nail on her right hand; she had bruised it somehow, most likely from a slamming door, or a fall on the ice. She had done nothing to hide it. Hoffner kept his eyes on the nail as she raised the spoon to her lips. She blew gently, then sipped it down. Wincing a moment at the heat, she quickly recovered and went in for a second spoonful.

Hoffner said, "It's best if you mix it with the cream. Less bitter."

Lina kept her eyes on the spoon and cup. "I like it this way," she said. "At least at the start." Hoffner took a sip of the coffee. It was the first good cup he had had in weeks. Lina looked over at him and said, "Would you like my address?"

It was rare for Hoffner to be caught out like this, but here it was. He felt something sharp run through his chest. It moved up to his throat and made his mouth suddenly dry. He hadn't felt it in years. It was anticipation. He slowly placed his coffee back on the table. Out of necessity, he said, "Is that such a good idea, Fräulein?"

She spoke with certainty: "You came to find me. Didn't you?"

When he had no choice but to answer, Hoffner said, "I've been wondering if you make enough to survive, selling flowers and matches."

For the first time, he saw the smallest slip in her otherwise perfect stare. Just as quickly, she recovered. "Have you?" She placed the spoon in the cup and began to fold the cream into the chocolate. "I do all right. I've started modeling. For an artist."

Hoffner watched as the liquid became silky brown. Lina was merciless with even the smallest floating fleck of cream. She seemed to take a wicked pleasure in drowning each of them to oblivion.

"How very exciting for you," he said. He retrieved his cigarette, took a few puffs, and crushed it out. Digging the last of the butt into the ashtray, he said, "Yes." He let go of the cigarette and looked at her. "I did."

Again, her cheeks flushed, although she was too good to let it take hold. She stopped mixing and placed the spoon to the side. "I'm glad." Taking her cup in both hands, she brought it up to her lips. She was about to take a sip, when she stopped and peered over at him. "I wouldn't want anything to change with me and Hans," she said. "A chance to leave my basket behind. You understand that." She took the sip.

Hoffner suddenly remembered how young she really was. He doubted Lina realized it, but in that moment she had shown herself at her most vulnerable. She might just as well have said, "I'm not expecting anything, so don't feel you have to give anything." Or, perhaps, it was just what he had wanted to hear.

Hoffner watched as she placed the cup on the table. He slowly reached over for her hand. It might have been an awkward movement, but the two came together too easily, and he ran his thumb gently over her palm. Just as easily, he let go. "Thank you for the lovely time, Fräulein Lina." He picked up the pack of cigarettes and placed them in his pocket.

"Yes," she said warmly. She then said, "Kremmener Strasse. Number five."

Hoffner waited a moment. He nodded and, somewhere, he thought he heard Victor König laughing. He found a few coins in his pocket and placed them on the table. He then took his hat and stood. "A pleasure, Fräulein."

"As always, Herr **Kriminal-Kommissar.**"

Hoffner tipped his brow and headed for the door.

Back at the Alex, the security desk was under frontal assault from a group of irate **Hausfrauen** when Hoffner walked in: something to do with a pickpocket, from what he could make out. Hoffner decided to avoid the commotion and instead started for the wire room, when the duty officer put up a hand and shouted over:

"**Kriminal-Kommissar.**" Hoffner stopped. "Your Sascha's been looking for you."

Hoffner was momentarily confused. Why would his son have come to the Alex? "Sascha's been by?" he said. Hoffner immediately thought of Georgi.

The man had no time for games. "Yes. Sascha. He's asked for you twice." Before Hoffner could answer, the women were once again on the attack.

Only then did Hoffner realize which Sascha the man had been referring to: "Sascha the runner," Hoffner said aloud to no one in particular. He shook his head. He needed to concentrate, no matter what might, or might not, be happening later tonight: König's laughter seemed to be growing louder by the minute. Hoffner stepped through to the courtyard.

Kripo Sascha was sitting on the ground, reading outside the wire room, when Hoffner pushed through and into the corridor. At once the boy stood. He took a folded sheet from inside the book and held it out to Hoffner.

Hoffner took the note and said, "So, when did it come in?"

"Just over an hour ago, Herr **Kriminal-Kommissar.**" The boy spoke with great precision.

"And no one else has seen it?"

Sascha looked almost hurt by the question. "No, Herr **Kriminal-Kommissar.** No one."

"Good." Hoffner crooked his head to the side so as to take a look at the book in the boy's hand. **The Count of Monte Cristo.** Hoffner was liking this boy more and more. "Planning an escape," Hoffner said with a smile.

For the first time, Sascha let his shoulders drop. He smiled, and shook his head. "No, Herr **Kriminal-Kommissar.**"

Hoffner pulled a coin from his pocket and, taking Sascha's hand, placed it in the boy's open palm. "Our secret." Before Sascha could say a word, Hoffner was nodding him down the corridor.

Hoffner's mood changed the moment he started reading:

WOUTERS DEAD STOP HANGED
HIMSELF TWO DAYS AGO STOP
STRANGE BEHAVIOR AS OF FIVE
MONTHS AGO STOP NO BATHING
CUTTING HAIR STOP PUT IN
ISOLATION THREE MONTHS AGO STOP
AWAIT INSTRUCTIONS STOP

Hoffner read the note several times to make sure he had missed nothing. "No bathing, cutting hair." He stepped into the wire room.

The man behind the desk was just finishing off a wire. "Yes, Herr **Kriminal-Kommissar,**" he said without looking up. "You've something for me to send?"

"A reply," said Hoffner; he handed the original to the man.

The man examined it. "To Bruges?"

"Yes."

The man took out a pen and paper. "Go ahead."

"Two words," said Hoffner. "'Shave him.'"

THREE

⊱ SIX ⊰

Paul Wouters had been destined for Sint-Walburga as early as 1898. His mother, having no way to support or handle the already troubling three-year-old, had given him over to her dead husband's mother, Anne, to raise. It was, perhaps, not the wisest choice given that the recently deceased Jacob Wouters had committed suicide after a short life in which he had been unable to reach beyond the traumas of his own childhood with Anne. That his bride decided to take her own life three weeks after Jacob's death pretty well set the table for young Paul.

Anne Wouters was a woman of uncommon cruelty. Whatever love she might have felt for her son, Jacob—and there really was none to speak of—had long since dried up by the time her grandson, Paul, was thrust into her life. By then, she had come to believe that the wretchedness of her existence granted her the right to compound that of the boy. Not that she was aware of her malevolence—the most accomplished never are—but she could never have denied the singular pleasure she took at seeing him, hour after hour, slouched over a bobbin and thread. To her mind, it was justice at its most pure.

Before he was five, Paul was taught the art of lace-making; it was the only skill Anne knew, and would have made for an ideal living, filled with camaraderie and pride, had Anne not given birth to Jacob out of wedlock. At the time, there had been rumors of rape—even Anne had let herself believe them for a while—but the truth was that she had simply been foolish. And so went her life: her sin kept her forever from the inner circles; her skill kept her alive. For, whatever else she might have been, Anne Wouters was, without question, a virtuoso with lace. Everyone in Bruges knew it, and it was why the most intricate patterns always found their way to her tiny attic room at the Meckel Godshuizen, one of the more decrepit almshouses in town. At night, and on the sly, women—unable to match her artistry at the mills—would bring their pieces to her and pay her a tenth of what she deserved, all the while telling her that she was damned lucky to be getting any work at all. She would keep her eyes lowered, her head bowed, as they described the meshes they themselves could never achieve, and her teeth would grow sharp from the silent grinding.

When Paul was old enough to handle the pins himself, she put him to work, and for fifteen hours a day they sat in silence, manipulating the thread. He was unusually small, and though his fingers were nimble, they were often overmatched by the tools. Each missed stroke earned him a deep scraping of those tiny hands with a sharp bristle: there were mornings when the blood would still be tacky on his knuckles as he got back to work. Worse was when she fell short of her quota; then she would tie him to a chair and beat him with a strop. She liked the upper back. It was where the bone was closest to the skin.

Paul's future life could easily have been attributed to the torture of his eight years with Anne. His choice that one night, when he had grown just tall enough to wrest the bristle from her hand and strike it repeatedly into her throat until her neck snapped and the blood spilled out in a pulsating streamlet, would have seemed the reasonable response to an unbearable situation were it not for the fact that Paul Wouters was not a victim of his circumstances. No doctor was needed to explain his horrifying condition. No, the real reason for his behavior was that Paul had been psychotic from his very inception: he had simply needed time to grow into it. Some are born evil, and Paul Wouters was one of the lucky few whose madness was no by-product of his setting. His father, Jacob, had learned to embrace his self-loathing; his mother had eventually succumbed to her self-pity; even his grandmother Anne could look to the world's viciousness for her own. But Paul needed none of that. He felt no vindication, no joy in his killing. He killed because he could.

He was not, however, the man now lying naked on a slab at Sint-Walburga. In all fairness to the attendants, they had shaved part of the body yesterday afternoon: the top bit of his skull, so that the doctors could cut through and retrieve the brain. The doctors had been certain that the cause of Wouters's mania would appear to them in the guise of some malformed lobe or conduit. The brain, however—now in a jar of formaldehyde on the shelf—had proved to be in perfect condition. The chief neurologist's only response had been to utter the words "How very odd," over and over again.

Yesterday's disappointment, however, paled in comparison with this evening's shock. Van Acker stared in disbelief as the thick locks of hair fell to the floor and revealed a face not at all similar to that of Paul Wouters. The shape and coloring of the narrow little body, on the other hand, were close enough to the contours van Acker remembered.

"You're sure?" said Fichte, keeping his handkerchief over his nose as the attendants continued to scissor through the hair.

Van Acker shot him a frustrated, if tired, glance. "Yes, Herr **Kriminal-Kommissar.** I'm sure."

Wisely, Fichte chose not to answer.

Van Acker turned to the gathering of officials who had accompanied the two policemen to the asylum's laboratory; he knew he was dealing with idiots. He spoke in French: "You mean to tell me that none of you saw an iota of difference in the man's appearance, his attitude, his behavior?" Fichte might not have understood a word, but he knew that van Acker was taking his frustrations out on the people who could least help him. Worse, the doctors actually seemed to be pleased to have discovered that they had been dealing with the wrong brain: still hope for the lobe theory, after all. "That seems almost impossible to me," van Acker continued. "Who were the morons who were supposed to be looking after him?"

The Superintendent spoke up: "There's no need for that sort of language, Inspector. Clearly, a mistake has been made—"

"A mistake?" said van Acker, amazed at the man's audacity. "What you have here, Monsieur, is nothing less than criminal. Men don't simply trade places, and, I might be wrong here"—his words were laced with ridicule—"but who do you imagine would have volunteered for that role? I don't think Mr. Wouters knew anyone who was eager to step in for a few weeks while he took the air. Do you?"

Everyone in the room remained silent. For a moment, van Acker looked at Fichte; he then turned away and began to shake his head. It was clear that he was more than a little embarrassed to have had a Berlin detective inspector witnessing this scene. Had

Fichte been a bit more poised in his newfound position, he might have known what to say; instead, he stood there like everyone else.

Van Acker switched gears. For Fichte's benefit—though probably more out of spite—he spoke in German: "I want a photograph taken of this man; I want every entry log you have for the past five months—who came, who went; I want guard rotations, doctor rotations—any rotation that had to do with our friend Wouters. And anything that might have happened out of the ordinary. The smallest thing. A misconnected telephone call. You have the records. I want to know about them."

No one moved. Van Acker glanced sharply at the Superintendent, and the man realized he had no choice. He nodded to his colleagues, and the other men started for the door.

Fichte waited until most of the men were out in the hall before turning to van Acker. "The **Kriminal-Kommissar** would have done the exact same thing," said Fichte. Realizing he might just have given the game away, Fichte quickly added, "Nikolai, I mean. Hoffner. You work the same way."

For the first time in nearly three hours, van Acker's jaw slackened. There might even have been the hint of a grin in his eyes. "You're not a detective inspector, are you, Herr Fichte?"

Surprisingly, Fichte's answer was no less forthright. "Not yet, Monsieur **Le Chef Inspecteur.** No."

Van Acker's grin grew. "Well, at least you've put me in good company."

Hoffner reached across the desk for his cup, and checked the clock. He had corralled little Sascha for a second posting to the wire room almost three hours ago, but there was still no word from Fichte. Hoffner took a sip of the coffee, careful not to drip any of it onto the pages that were spread out in front of him.

He had stopped on this particular letter about an hour ago, when the word "relationship" had jumped out at him. The language was as dramatic as ever, but it was a different Luxemburg that Hoffner heard, now having discovered her secret within the shelves.

> **. . . I know you don't get much pleasure out of our relationship, what with my scenes that wreck your nerves, my tears, with all these trivia, even my doubts about your love. . . . It's too painful to think that I invaded your pure, proud, lonely life with my female whims, my unevenness, my helplessness. And what for, damn it, what for? My God, why do I keep harping on it? It is over. . . .**

Her despair was not so much for the solitude to come, as for her own fallibility: she felt no remorse, only a relief in the affair's dissolution. Once again, Hoffner felt a certain kinship with this Rosa, and that, he knew, was dangerous. Victims needed to remain victims. The only mind Hoffner wanted to find his way into was that of the man who had wielded the knife.

Focusing on the page itself, Hoffner traced the imprints of the razorlike creases. The letter—sent to Leo Jogiches in the summer of 1897—had been read over and over, folded and unfolded a hundred times since then, and with an almost pious precision. Rosa's fear that Jogiches might have laughed at its absurdity, or at its woman's insecurity, had been completely unfounded. Not only had Jogiches held on to it, he had kept it with him at all times: in a billfold, from what Hoffner could tell. There was an unrefined, crushed leather residue on the sheets—the kind found only on the inside pockets of a man's wallet—from years of safekeeping. K was evidently well-enough connected to have pried the letter loose from Jogiches's grip.

Half an hour ago, Hoffner had discovered its companion piece—a second letter to Jogiches with identical creases and residue—written three years earlier, also kept in the billfold, and equally desperate. This time, however, a different kind of frustration dominated:

. . . Totally exhausted by the never-ending Cause, I sat down to catch my breath, I looked back and realized I don't have a home anywhere. I neither exist nor live as myself. . . . It's boring, draining. Why should everyone pester me when I give it all I can? It's a burden—

**every letter, from you or anyone else, always
the same—this issue, that pamphlet, this
article or that. Even that I wouldn't mind if besides, despite it, there was a human being behind it, a soul, an individual. . . . Have you no
ideas? No books? No impressions? Nothing to
share with me?! . . . Unlike you, I have impressions and ideas all the time, the "Cause"
notwithstanding. . . . Now I'd like to ask you
the following questions: 1. Is it right to say
that in 1848 the French people fought mainly
for general elections? 2. Did the Chicago
demonstration take place in 1886 or 1887? 3.
How many rubles to a dollar? 4. Did the
strikes of the gas workers and longshoremen
in England break out in 1889 and was it for an
eight-hour day? . . . Read my letter carefully,
and answer all questions.**

Hoffner wondered if Jogiches had kept the letter as
a reminder to himself to be diligent in his humanity,
or simply because he had enjoyed the adorable shift
in tone at its end. Hoffner was guessing it had been a
bit of both.

And yet, however charming Rosa's caprice might
have been, it was the care that Jogiches had taken
with the letters that told Hoffner the most about his
victim. From what he could gather, the romance between the two had come to a bitter end sometime in
1907: there had been accusations of infidelity and

threats of violence from him; Luxemburg had purchased a revolver, and had been forced to produce
it during one of their more heated arguments. And
through it all, Jogiches had continued to subsidize
her—her rent, her paper, her ink. Hoffner was not
sure which of the two lovers had been the moth
and which the flame—he doubted they had known
themselves—but it was clear that this had been a
relationship incapable of permanent fracture. In
fact, Hoffner was learning just how crucial a figure
Jogiches had been during the revolution, even if
his name had never once appeared alongside Luxemburg's, Liebknecht's, or Levi's. Jogiches had always been the man behind the scenes, the silent
partner.

Hoffner stopped scanning the page. Was he missing the obvious? Had he just uncovered his K, he
wondered.

The telephone rang and he picked it up as he jotted down a note to look into Herr Jogiches's past a bit
more closely. "Yes," he said.

"You're in for a busy night, Herr **Kriminal-
Kommissar.**" It was the duty sergeant from the
front desk.

"And why is that?" Hoffner continued to write.

"A Schutzi corporal just found another one of your
bodies. Markings and all." Everyone, evidently, was
now aware of the case.

Hoffner was on his feet and reaching for his coat
when he asked, "Where?"

"Senefelderplatz," said the man. "In the subway excavations."

Only once in the courtyard did Hoffner remember Sascha and the wire room. He quickly stopped by the duty desk and asked the Sergeant to get a note to the boy: should anything come in, he was to bring it up to the site. The man understood. Hoffner also told him to telephone the porter at his own building in Kreuzberg; a direct call to Martha at this hour would only frighten her. Still, she liked to know when he would be late. No reason. Just that he would be late.

Hoffner decided to walk. It took him less than twenty minutes to make his way to the square; this time, however, Wouters's pattern eluded him. These were not the wide avenues around the Unter den Linden; here the streets and alleys were too narrow, and the turns too clipped and sporadic, to give Hoffner the precision and line that he needed to enter the design. Even the people and cabs were too few to bring the buildings to life. Hoffner knew better than to expect anything from this part of town. He was skirting the edge of Prenzlauer Berg, Berlin's underbelly, a place of stifled quiet after dark. If nothing else, the pattern demanded movement, and there was none to be found here.

More than that, Wouters and his pattern were no longer abstractions. Hoffner had no need to conjure them, and that made them somehow less his own.

He turned in to the empty square and followed the echo of a barking dog across the cobblestones and over to the site. A glowing red ember, perhaps two meters wide, stared like an angry sun from a poster painted onto the brick of one of the building walls. It was an advertisement for men's shirts. The cigarette drooped from a mouth that was beyond the reach of the lamplight. A sharp chin in profile balanced the dark blue of the starched collar, and yet, even cut off at the lips, the **Henzeiger Mann** remained the picture of elegance. According to the print, he was also now stain-resistant.

A lone Schutzi patrolman had leashed the dog to a lamppost and was doing all he could to calm the animal with his boot. The mutt was big, and his white teeth glistened in the light each time he chopped his head forward in another snarl. The patrolman was young and having his fun as he slapped at the dog's head before each quick kick to the gut. The dog, however, seemed undeterred by the taunting: his eyes peered menacingly at the darkened entry to the excavations as ribbons of hot steam poured from his nostrils. Hoffner approached and pulled out his badge.

"Enjoying yourself, patrolman?" he said, the reprimand clear enough in his tone.

At once the boy stood upright. The sight of Hoffner's badge produced a wonderful blend of confusion and embarrassment. "Herr Detective," he said. "No. I'm just—" He offered the only excuse he had. "He's got to be put down. He's had the taste of blood." The patrolman actually seemed to believe his own justification. "It's in his eyes, Herr Detective," he added.

"Nothing we can do. Just waiting for the wagon, that's all." The growling continued unabated.

Hoffner might have conceded the point: the dog's eyes had, in fact, glazed over. That, however, did not make this patrolman any less contemptible. Hoffner said, "The dog found the body?"

The question caused a moment's confusion. Evidently the boy had never been included on an investigation. Hoffner guessed that he was the halfwit who was always told to stand outside, or wait downstairs, or sit in the hall so as to keep any interested passersby at bay. Tonight he had been given the dog. Even that had overtaxed his resources.

"Yes, Herr Detective," he finally said. "About an hour ago. Someone heard the howling. They called my sergeant. He's—"

Hoffner cut him off. "And they're down in the site?" The patrolman nodded. Hoffner waited for more, then pressed, "Is there a ladder, a ramp?"

Instantly the patrolman understood. "Oh yes," he said eagerly. "This way, Herr Detective." He led Hoffner across a series of wooden planks and through the entryway. Lamps along the scaffolding lit their way down and into the pit. At the base of the ramp, the patrolman pointed to the top of a ladder another ten meters on, which disappeared into the depths of the excavation.

"So, a ramp and a ladder," said Hoffner with mock enthusiasm. The patrolman stared for a moment and then nodded slowly. "Never mind," said Hoffner. He was about to head for the opening when he said,

"And no more business with the dog. We're clear on that?" The patrolman nodded sheepishly. "Good. Now get back to your post."

The patrolman was already up the ramp and gone by the time Hoffner reached the ladder. Bending over for the first rung, Hoffner heard a movement off to his side, and immediately spun toward it, as a figure emerged from the darkness.

It took him a moment to recognize little Franz. The boy had been leaning up against a mound of cleared earth. "I thought it was you, Herr **Kriminal-Kommissar,**" Franz said as he approached.

Hoffner stood there, waiting for his heart to slow. He stepped away from the ladder. "You startled me, Franz."

The boy looked genuinely surprised. "Did I? Then I wish I'd brought a towel for you."

Hoffner remembered this morning's episode at the washbasin. "Fair enough." He noticed how threadbare the boy's coat had become, and how exposed his little neck was without a scarf. Franz, however, was showing no signs of the cold. Tough little man, thought Hoffner. "What are you doing here, Franz?"

"What you told me, Herr **Kriminal-Kommissar.** Following Herr Kvatsch."

Hoffner understood at once. He peered over at the ladder, then back at the boy. "When did he get here?"

"About fifteen minutes ago."

"He received a telephone call?"

Franz had grown accustomed to the accuracy of Hoffner's guesses. "Yes, Herr **Kriminal-Kommissar.**"

"Where?"

"Reese's Restaurant."

"With anyone?"

"No, Herr **Kriminal-Kommissar.**"

Hoffner nodded. Kvatsch's star was rising: he was being permitted a firsthand account this time round. Someone wanted the story on the front page, not the fourth. That, however, was not the boy's concern. "So," said Hoffner, switching gears as he pulled out his cigarettes. "Any interesting names on the list?" He lit one up and watched as Franz stared eagerly at the ember. The boy continued to gaze as Hoffner exhaled a wide plume of smoke. "All right," said Hoffner reluctantly. He reached into his pocket and offered one to Franz. The boy took two. "You'd do better to get yourself a scarf, Franz," said Hoffner as he watched the boy slip the extra one into his pocket. Franz nodded curtly, then placed the cigarette in his mouth. He waited while Hoffner lit it.

"**Kriminal-Bezirkssekretär** Groener," said Franz. "Over lunch." Smoke streamed from his small nose. "They were together maybe five minutes. I couldn't get close enough to hear what they were saying."

A little obvious, thought Hoffner, but why not? The question remained, Was Groener clever enough to have had a reason to leak the story? Spite hardly seemed a sufficient motive. Hoffner said, "The next time they meet, you come and get me. All right?"

The boy nodded. "Good. Now get yourself back to the Alex. You can leave the list on my desk." Hoffner would have liked to have had Franz wait around and trail after Kvatsch for the rest of the night, but the boy had been out in the cold long enough for one day. Then again, from the way Franz was working the cigarette, Hoffner might just have been underestimating him; Fichte could have taken lessons. "And stay at the Alex," Hoffner added with a bit more grit. "No slipping out tonight, all right?" For a moment Franz looked as if he might play the innocent; instead, he nodded.

Hoffner walked back with him until they were halfway up the ramp. He had a sudden impulse to pat the boy on the shoulder, but the gesture seemed wrong. Luckily, Franz gave him no time to consider it; with a strangely knowing nod, the boy darted up the remaining few meters and out through the entryway.

Hoffner watched him go. The patrolman was busy elsewhere and took no notice; the dog kept his gaze on the site. Its barking, however, had become hoarser. Hoffner could almost hear a desperation in its throaty growls, as if the dog knew that the measure of its time was spent the moment its last salvo came to an end: it was holding on for as long as it could. Hoffner continued to watch as Franz—once more a ten-year-old boy—crept up to within a few meters of the dog and let go with a howl of his own. The dog responded with a sudden and renewed vigor; Franz howled again and raced off. The patrolman spun around and shouted after Franz, but the boy was already lost to the shadows. The dog, however, had regained full pitch. Franz had given him new life. Hoffner turned and headed back into the pit.

The climb down was shorter than he expected. The Rosenthaler Platz site had been a good twenty meters deep; here it was, at best, ten to twelve, which made the air less thick, though the smell of decaying flesh was no less present. It was also a less complex layout than before. There were no spokes or distant caverns to navigate, just a long tunnel, dimly lit by a series of string lights hung from above. Various air pumps with ventilation hoses sat silent along the dirt floor, but it was clear that this station was still under construction: the wood slats along the walls were freshly cut, the steel beams still had a shine to them, and the piles of shovels and picks were placed for easy retrieval. From the cigarette butts strewn about, Hoffner was guessing that a crew had been here as recently as yesterday afternoon, maybe even this morning. The supply lines were back up and running.

A sudden flash of light drew his attention to the far end of the tunnel. He began to make his way toward it as the din of conversation grew more distinct.

". . . completely in the buff," came a voice. "I'm telling you. And she wasn't shy, either."

The men laughed. One of them caught sight of Hoffner and his expression hardened at once.

"Gentlemen," said Hoffner as he drew up with his badge held at eye level. "Quite a little gathering."

There were four of them: a Schutzi sergeant, his patrolman lackey, a man with a camera, and, of course,
Herr "Detective" Kvatsch. They were standing to the
side of a woman's dead body. Hoffner returned the
badge to his coat pocket. "I see we've already started
in on the group photos."

There was a stiffness to the quartet now that Hoffner
had arrived. The sergeant was unsure how to respond.
He went with what he knew best. "We found her about
an hour ago, Herr **Kriminal-Kommissar**—"

"Yes," Hoffner cut in. "Your man upstairs filled me
in on the details." It was clear from the sergeant's expression that the man upstairs had been told to give
more than just the details when the Kripo arrived: a
little warning would have been nice. Another botched
job from the halfwit, Hoffner imagined. "How fortu-
nate that our friends from the **BZ** arrived so quickly
to keep you company."

Kvatsch said, "As always, one step ahead of the
Kripo, Herr Detective."

"Or one phone call," said Hoffner. He waited a
moment, then added, "I hear the bean soup was particularly nice at Reese's tonight." Hoffner watched as
Kvatsch's lips shifted into double time. Hoffner then
turned to the sergeant. "I'm assuming you've got my
cut, Herr **Wachtmeister.**" The sergeant looked almost relieved. He began to reach into his tunic;
Hoffner's gaze soured instantly. "Greedy **and** stupid,
eh, Sergeant?" Again, the man was at a loss. "That's a
dangerous combination, don't you think?" Without

waiting for an answer, Hoffner reached over and took the camera from the fourth member of the party. He opened the back cover and removed the film.

"Excuse me, Detective," said Kvatsch, now with an edge to his voice, "but I paid for that," as if anything he said mattered down here.

Hoffner said, "Well, then, that was a bad investment, wasn't it, Herr Kvatsch?" Hoffner crumpled the film in his fist and handed the camera back to the man. The photographer seemed wholly indifferent; Kvatsch had evidently already paid him for his services. "Who made the call?" said Hoffner.

Kvatsch said, "I thought you'd have that figured out by now, Detective. Wasn't that the promise?"

Hoffner smiled stiffly. "Someone's leading you around by the nose, and you don't even realize it, do you?"

"We'll see who's leading whom."

Hoffner nodded. "I thought newspapermen were supposed to track down stories, Kvatsch, not have them spoon-fed to them."

Kvatsch was not biting. He answered coolly, "You want a name. I need a photograph. That seems a fair trade."

"Does it?" said Hoffner.

Kvatsch actually thought he was gaining the upper hand. "You know, it's so much nicer dealing with you than with your old partner. König never understood the art of negotiation. Always too quick with the rough stuff."

Hoffner started to laugh to himself until, without warning, he grabbed the scruff of Kvatsch's coat and shoved him against the planks on the near wall. The other men immediately stepped off. Slowly, Hoffner brought his face to within a few centimeters of Kvatsch's. He held him there and spoke in an inviting tone: "That's just what this city needs, isn't it, Kvatsch? Something else to set it off in a panic." Kvatsch was doing his best to maintain some semblance of calm. He swallowed loudly. Hoffner continued: "Revolution, war, starvation—they're not enough for you, are they? You know, if you had half a brain, you'd realize that that's exactly what your 'Kripo sources' want." Hoffner smiled quizzically. "Why is it that you always have to be such an obvious rube?"

The sheen on Kvatsch's face had begun to glisten in the low light; nonetheless, he remained defiant. "Glad to see you've picked up where König left off, Detective. By the way, " he said more insistently, "how is the widow? I never got to pass on my condolences."

Hoffner continued to stare into the callous little eyes. With a sudden surge, he pulled Kvatsch from the boards and slammed him into a bare patch of muddied rock. Kvatsch winced as he let out a blast of tobaccoed breath. He was clearly in pain, but said nothing. Hoffner held him there for several seconds longer, then let go and stepped away. He turned his attention to the dead body. "We're done here." Hoffner crouched down and began to scan the dead woman's clothes: the dog had gotten to them; her blouse was in tatters. "Make nice with the good sergeant, Kvatsch, and get out."

Kvatsch needed a moment to pull himself together. The sergeant—perhaps out of a twisted sense of loyalty—tried to help, but Kvatsch quickly pushed him aside. With a forced ease, Kvatsch straightened his coat and smoothed back the loose strands of his hair. He then spoke, undeterred by the back of Hoffner's head: "What you've never understood, Detective, is how little it matters what you do, or how you do it. What matters is how it's perceived." Kvatsch knew there would be no response; even so, he waited. "And all for a little photo." He nodded to the cameraman to start back for the ladder. Kvatsch was about to follow, when he added, "How much easier your life could have been, Detective." He let the words settle. "Shame." He then followed the cameraman out.

Hoffner waited until the sound of footsteps had receded completely. Without looking up, he said, "You two can wait upstairs, as well."

The sergeant bristled at being lumped in with his subordinate. He offered a clipped bow to Hoffner's back, then motioned officiously to the patrolman. The two men started off.

"Oh," said Hoffner, still with his back to them. "And we'll need a Kripo photographer down here. Tell him he can catch a ride in the ambulance." Hoffner paused a moment. "And my guess is he won't be paying, Sergeant."

This time there was no bow. "Yes, Herr **Kriminal-Kommissar.**"

Finally alone, Hoffner stared down at the chiseled back through the strips of cloth: the ruts were again smooth, and the little bumps from the flawed blade appeared again at perfect intervals. She had been killed like the others, strangled and etched elsewhere—two, maybe three days ago, from the smell and look of the skin—then brought here to be put on display: the drag lines in the dirt—from some sort of crate or trunk—made that clear enough. Hoffner glanced at the side of her face. This woman had been in her late fifties. Her hands told of work in a mill: there were countless wisps of threaded cloth trapped beneath the fingernails, all of which had come to resemble little calluses on her skin. These were the by-product of years on the line, not souvenirs from any recent struggle. Not that she could have put up much of a fight. Like all of the victims, she was small, even delicate, if one put aside the gnarled texture of her hands. That, too, was a common trait: hands that had known a life of labor.

Unlike the others, however, her neck was horribly distended. Hoffner jabbed the end of his pen into the swollen flesh. That was more of the dog's handiwork. Its teeth marks were still fresh in the fleshy skin just below the chin, yet the back had gone untouched. Instinct, thought Hoffner. Even the animal had sensed the depravity there and had kept clear.

He looked up and scanned the surrounding area.

He knew he would find nothing: Wouters, or Wouters's surrogate—Fichte would have to clear that up—was always far too careful to leave anything behind. Luxemburg and Mary Koop had been diversions: the killer was now back on form.

Hoffner placed a finger on her skin. It was cold and tough and greaseless. He ran his hand along the diameter-cut. The ridges of hardened flesh bent back easily against the pressure of his thumb. There was something oddly consoling in its familiarity, in the shape and texture of a pattern that he had known so well up until a week ago. Now there was far more to it than that: jagged ruts, and gloves, and grease, and a name, and a revolutionary, and on and on and on. It was all supposed to bring him closer to a solution, and yet, with each new "discovery," Hoffner felt himself being drawn toward something that had little to do with the deaths of his five unremarkable and unconnected Berlin women. He was beginning to wonder where the diversion really lay.

Ten minutes later, Hoffner stepped back out into the raw air of Senefelderplatz. The chill settled on his face and, for an instant, let him forget all of the pieces that were flying through his head. Sadly, the first image that made its way back in was of Kvatsch. Hoffner knew that the first explosion of articles would appear in tomorrow's papers. A lovely sense of panic would sweep over the city as the story jumped from the **BZ** to the **Morgenpost,** and up and down the Ull-

stein line, until, like a brush fire, it would leap across
the avenue to the Mosse and Scherl presses, and blaze
across the headlines of all of their high- and low-end
papers. Kvatsch had probably come up with some
clever name for the murders already. It was irrelevant
what he had seen: he would invent what he needed.
And a million eyes would now be peering over Hoffner's shoulder, waiting and wondering.

The ambulance was still nowhere in sight. Hoffner
knew there was no reason to wait; there was nothing
else he could do here tonight. He had started across
the square when he heard the sound of the sergeant
running up from behind him. Hoffner dug his hands
into his coat pockets and continued in the other direction. He spoke over his shoulder: "The ambulance," he said. "Make sure she gets back to the
Alex." A mumbled, "Yes, Herr **Krim . . .**" faded into
the distance as Hoffner picked up his pace.

It was only then that he realized how quiet the
square had become. Hoffner glanced over at the
lamppost. He noticed that a small, horse-drawn
wagon had pulled up under the light; a rifle was
propped up against its back wheel. The horse stood
content with a bag of oats, while the driver struggled
to untie the leash from the post. Hoffner stopped.

The leash was now heavy from the weight of the
dog's lifeless body. The man had shot it once, in the
throat. Save for an occasional bob of the head from
each yank on the line, the dog lay quiet in a pool of
its own blood. This time there had been no Franz to

save it. Hoffner waited until the man had freed the dog. He then slowly headed off.

Van Acker checked the bottle before pouring out three more shots of whiskey.

The Bruges **Stationsplein** bar was not perhaps best known for its quality of stock, but it always kept enough of it flowing freely to satisfy the detectives of the city **Politie.** The rest of the station clientele had to be content with a Tarwebier or Chimay, tasty beers to be sure, but neither with enough of a kick to smooth over a ride out of town. Whiskey, on the other hand, always let you sleep. Mueller took his glass and raised it in a toast. Fichte was having trouble finding his.

"To your left, Detective," said van Acker; he brought his own up to meet Mueller's. Fichte eventually got hold of his and, spilling most of it on his pants, reached up to join them. "That's very good, Detective," said van Acker. He finished with the toast: "To finding one's glass."

Mueller and van Acker tossed theirs back. Fichte thought for a moment, let out a long breath, then placed his untasted back on the bar.

Mueller said, "Well, at least you tried."

The last train to Berlin was set to leave Bruges in the next twenty minutes; it promised an eleven-o'clock arrival in Berlin tomorrow morning, and, with any luck, would get there by two. Still, it was quicker than waiting for first light; at best, Mueller could get Fichte to Berlin by early evening, and that was not accounting for weather or stops for fuel and oil. No, the train was the best bet. Van Acker had insisted. He had also used his pull with a certain transportation minister—a man whose wife had yet to learn about a young lady he was keeping in a lovely gabled house near the Begijnhof—to make sure that Fichte would have no trouble with any military delays at the German border.

Van Acker had come to this decision just after he and Fichte had stripped the asylum clean of every piece of paper having to do with Wouters: correspondence logs, visitor logs, psychiatric reports, staff interviews, medical files, the last of which had included details of Wouters's eating and digestive habits—Fichte had been amazed to discover just how many varieties shit came in—all dating from the beginning of September. Plus, van Acker had taken them back via his office so as to pick up his personal case files on Wouters.

The train, though, was another matter. Fichte had wanted to send a wire to Berlin, just in case Hoffner had any other instructions. Van Acker had convinced him otherwise: better to bring all the necessary documents to Berlin by tomorrow morning than to lose valuable time to the drawn-out exchange of cables. "Don't you agree, Detective?" Fichte had nodded quietly. The more he drank, however, the less he was looking forward to having to ask that question of Hoffner in person.

They had rounded up Mueller about an hour ago.

Mueller, of course, had been disappointed to hear that he would be making the return flight solo, but once the invitation had been extended to join them for a few farewell drinks, all was forgiven.

"I still don't see why you don't come along," said Fichte to van Acker. "Your case. You know the man better than anyone." It was the first coherent thing Fichte had said in the last half-hour.

"I appreciate the offer," van Acker said, "but not my jurisdiction. I had my chance." He stared down at his glass. "I'm also guessing Herr Hoffner wouldn't be that keen on the company." Fichte tried to disagree, but van Acker continued: "I don't want our friend back in Belgium," he said with a sudden resolve. "And I don't think you'll want him in Germany, either."

Fichte understood. Van Acker had failed to kill Wouters; he was telling Hoffner not to make the same mistake.

An amplified voice announced the train's final boarding. Mueller tossed back Fichte's untouched whiskey, and the three men headed out to the platform.

"They won't wake you at the border," van Acker said to Fichte as they walked. "I've seen to that."

Fichte nodded his thanks.

Van Acker continued. "Tell Herr Hoffner—" He tried to find the words. "Tell him I would have loved the chance."

The men stopped at the steps up to Fichte's car, and, placing his valise on the platform, Fichte said,

"My guess is, so would he, Monsieur **Le Chef Inspecteur.**" Van Acker appreciated the gesture. He said nothing.

"All right," said Mueller impatiently. "If he's going to be sleeping the whole way there, you and I'll need to make up for his lack of commitment."

Van Acker had known Mueller for less than an hour and was already a devotee. "One of us has a wife, Mueller," said van Acker with a grin.

Mueller said, "Well, don't look at me."

The whistle blew, and Fichte gathered up his things. "I leave you in good hands, Chief Inspector," he said. He shot a glance at Mueller. "Well, at least a few good fingers."

Mueller laughed. He then turned to van Acker. "You do keep your pants on until the second course, don't you, Inspector? Not like the Berlin boys?"

Fichte mounted the steps and van Acker said, "I'll expect cables." Fichte turned back and nodded. "Safe journey," said van Acker. Another nod from Fichte. Van Acker then slapped Mueller on the back and started off. "Come on, Toby. I'll introduce you to my wife."

Fichte was out cold by the time the train had reached the outskirts of town.

At ten-thirty, Hoffner stopped by the wire room to send Sascha up to the attic for the night. It was too late for a cable now, not that he needed one to tell him what they had found. Anything other than Wouters would have caused a minor panic. Fichte, no doubt, had his hands full. Still, Hoffner would have liked to make sure that Fichte was loading them down with the right material. That, however, would have to wait for tomorrow.

It was nearly eleven, then, when Hoffner finally turned onto Kremmener Strasse.

He had long ago dispensed with the empty distinctions between character and weakness, at least when it came to decisions like these. To his mind, only men who claimed to have no choice struggled with those labels: to them, lack of choice granted a kind of freedom from consequence, or at least a softening of responsibility. Their angst, their wailing, their mea culpas of self-betrayal, all stemmed from that initial claim of powerlessness. Hoffner had never been that stupid or that impotent. He knew there was nothing inevitable about his seeing Lina. He was making the choice to venture back into the familiar of the unknown, and she was willingly inviting him in. Of course, had he seen Lina as anything more than that, he might have persuaded himself to hope for more, and that would have been dangerous. Hope fostered despair, and Hoffner had no desire for either.

The moon had broken through, and the houses melded into one another like a wide sheet of chalky gray stone. Lina's building stood in the middle of the row, six wide steps leading up to its stoop, which boasted two flower boxes, each with a clump of frozen mud and a few gnarled twigs as reminders of some distant strains of life. Like the street itself, the boxes lay barren. Kremmener was one of the last outposts of the city's Mitte district, a single street removed from the criminal haunts of Prenzlauer Berg. Ten years ago the gulf between the two would have been immeasurable; now it was a distinction only in name.

Lina had found a room on the top floor of Number 5, and although a woman living alone was far less of a shock these days—especially in this part of town—she had taken a roommate. Elise worked the coat-check room at the White Mouse. She was someone to know, according to Lina, a girl who was moving up. She was also rarely home before 2:00 a.m., and was infamous for forgetting her keys. A ring of the bell and the sound of scurrying feet up the stairs no longer drew the watchful eye of the landlord. He had grown fond of Elise and equally accustomed to her late-night, keyless returns.

Hoffner, with no inkling of a roommate, rang the bell anyway. He suspected that Lina had taken care of any possible awkwardness, and he was right. Two minutes into his wait, she appeared through the glass and opened the door. She was wearing a long lilac dressing gown that pretended to be silk, with tatty little ruffles at the sleeves and collar. On anyone else, they might have seemed vulgar; on her, they looked playful. She had kept her hair up, the tight ringlets along her forehead holding firm in a little row of Os that, from a certain angle, seemed to be **ooh**ing at

him. She was wearing a bit more rouge than he remembered from this afternoon. Hoffner liked that.

She quickly put a finger to her lips. In a loud voice she
said, "Nice and early tonight, Elise. That's a lucky
break." Lina stifled a laugh and motioned for Hoffner to
head up the stairs. He did as he was told; she followed.

The room was more cluttered than he had imagined. The slant of the roof left little space for windows. Two small ones, recessed into narrow alcoves,
peered up more than out, and gave a cropped view of
the starless sky. Everything else also came in twos—
bed, dresser, chair—except for the small stove and
washstand. Those the girls shared. Hoffner noticed a
large rectangular gap on one of the walls. A picture
had clearly hung there for years. He wondered what
could have been so offensive as to merit its removal.

"A bare-bosomed slave girl," said Lina, having followed his gaze. "Horrible. She was being sold to some
old letch, or something like that. We hated it." Lina
closed the door. She saw Hoffner reaching for his cigarettes. "Not in the room, please," she said. Hoffner
found the request charming. Or perhaps Lina was
more concerned with Fichte's highly developed sense
of smell. Hoffner returned the pack to his pocket.

She moved past him and over to an icebox that he
had failed to see until now. She opened it and pulled
out a plate of various goodies: crackers and pastes and
cheeses, and something that looked like chocolate.
Hoffner knew otherwise; Lina could never have afforded the real thing. She placed the plate on a small

side table by the bed. Two glasses and a bottle of kümmel already stood at the ready.

Hoffner said, "I wasn't expecting all of this."

Lina continued to organize the treats. "So you were thinking it would be off with your pants and into bed," she said with a smile as she pulled open a drawer and retrieved a few more crackers. She placed them along the rim of the plate. "I thought you'd be hungry." She licked at a bit of paste that had grazed one of her fingers. "I also thought you'd be here a bit earlier. The paste's too cold now. Oh, well." She smoothed out the blanket on her bed and sat. She motioned for Hoffner to join her.

Hoffner took off his coat.

"Just there on the chair," she said, pointing across the room.

Hoffner laid his coat across the chair and then joined her on the bed. He sat with his hands on his thighs. He said nothing. Lina reached over and poured out two glasses of the liqueur. A bit dripped on her hand, and again she quickly lapped it up. She handed Hoffner his, and they toasted. Lina then placed hers back on the table before bringing the plate to the bed and setting it between them.

"The other bed," he said. "I'm assuming that one belongs to Fräulein Elise."

Lina handed him a cracker with a thin slice of cheese. "She knows not to come home before two. We've plenty of time."

Hoffner was unsure how to react to the precision of

the night's planning. He took a bite; the cheese had no taste, at all. He said, "She's used to this sort of thing, your Elise? Does it on a regular basis?"

Lina looked up. The implication was obvious. She smiled disingenuously. "She's at the White Mouse most nights." She took a cracker for herself. "And she does it only for Hans. There haven't been any others."

"I didn't imagine there were," he said.

Lina chewed as she stared at him. Her smile softened. "So," she said. "Do you like my little place?"

Hoffner took another quick scan. "Very nice." He reached for a piece of the faux chocolate. To his amazement, it was real.

"Not expecting that, either, were you?"

"No," he said. "Not that, either."

He was enjoying the chocolate's sweetness when, very gently, she reached over and started to undo his tie. No less gently, Hoffner reached up and took hold of her arm. He held it there. Lina peered at him, unsure why he had stopped her. For a moment she looked almost fragile.

"Why?" he said calmly. There was nothing uncertain in his question, no need for affirmation. He simply wanted to know. "Why me?"

She brought her hand back to her lap. It was something she had never considered. It took her a moment to answer. "Does it matter?" she said.

Hoffner held her gaze. "Yes. It does. Why?"

Again she waited. "Don't look at me that way," she said. Hoffner said nothing; he continued to stare.

"With your eyes like that." Her smile grew uncomfortable. "It's too much . . . looking."

Hoffner waited, then dropped his eyes to the plate. He took another wedge of cheese. "Better?"

"Much."

He brought the cracker to his mouth. "So . . . how much do you pay for this place, you and your Elise?"

Lina once again had her glass. "Are you planning on helping out?" she said with a coy smile. She took a sip.

Hoffner laughed quietly. "I don't imagine that's the way this is going to work."

"The way what's going to work?" she said with mock innocence. "Oh, this. No, I don't imagine it will."

"You split it?"

Lina said, "You're awfully concerned with how I'm getting on. At tea today, wondering whether the flowers were enough, now my rent."

"Sorry," said Hoffner. "I won't ask anymore."

"No. It's nice."

"Good." Hoffner finished off his cracker. "You still haven't answered my question."

She casually placed her glass back on the table. "Forty. Yes. We split it. Twenty each."

Hoffner watched as her neck twisted with the movement. It was almost a perfect neck. "That's not the question I meant."

She turned back. "I know. I haven't come up with an answer for that one, yet." Without waiting for him, she reached over and took his glass. She set it on the table, then did the same with the plate. Hoffner knew exactly what was coming, yet he did nothing. He sat there as she moved closer, as she untied her dressing gown and let it drop off her shoulders. It spilled into a pool of silk by her thighs. She was wearing a nightgown beneath, pale white and thin, with two ribbon straps over her shoulders. Her small breasts were almost lost, save for the deep crimson of her nipples that puckered at the cloth.

Hoffner could smell the tangy sweetness of the rosewater in her hair. Her neck arced slightly, and he could see a thin ridge of powder that had gone unsmoothed by her chin. He felt a distant weakness in his arms and legs.

She slowly took his hand and placed it on her waist. "How many do I make, Nikolai?" she said. Hoffner felt a heat below the gown, the suppleness of her skin. "Girls like me," she said. "The ones that mattered. How many?"

Hoffner followed the moisture of her lips. Without warning, he pulled her into him. He saw her eyes widen as she let out a sudden breath. She showed no vulnerability, no guile. He could taste the saltiness of her breath.

"How many?" she said.

"Six," he answered without having to consider the number for even a moment.

Lina's smile returned. The total was irrelevant. All

she had wanted was an answer. She placed her hand on his cheek and brought him into her.

Twenty minutes later, Hoffner was asleep, his naked backside still glistening from the exertion. Lina pulled the blanket over him. She liked the weight of his arms and chest on her, the thick flesh of his back as his breathing grew heavier. He had taken her without reserve, and had left her spent. She had never felt such hunger in a partner. She could still feel him inside her, a deep vacancy where he had been. She imagined what it would be like to be loved by this man. She felt no less empty.

At one o'clock she woke him. Hoffner roused himself slowly. He had been dreaming, something to do with wild dogs and Georgi. He felt as if he had been running for hours. He dressed quietly and finished off his glass. Lina sat and watched him from the bed; she was relieved that there would be no need for a repeat performance. She held the blanket around her naked shoulders as she brought him to the door.

"You don't ask any questions about Hans," she said.

Hoffner half smiled and shook his head. "No."

She ran her hand along his chest. "That's good." She kissed him.

An hour later, Hoffner dropped his pants and shirt at the foot of his bed and crawled in next to Martha; she hardly seemed to breathe. With the scent of Lina still fresh on him, Hoffner placed his arm around Martha's back and was asleep within minutes. No

dreams. Instead, for the first time in weeks, he slept
through the night.

⟞ POINT ETUDE ⟝

On his third time through the notes, Hoffner wrote:
"No pleasure or purpose in it; no imperative; kills because he can." Fichte was on his knees at the foot of
the desk, busy with one more stack of papers that he
had just pulled from his valise. He had come directly
from the train and had been pleasantly surprised to
find Hoffner in an almost buoyant mood. There was
nothing to apologize for; van Acker had been right:
best to get it all here as quickly as possible. Fichte had
decided not to question his good fortune. For Hoffner, though, the clear evidence of van Acker's hand in
the choice of documents had been far more important than the speed. As far as he could tell, the Belgian had sent along everything they might need.
Unfortunately, it would be another hour before
Fichte would have the papers in any kind of present-
able order, but at least they were here.

Unwilling to wait, Hoffner had started in on what
looked to be the most self-contained and thus coherent of the packets. It was the transcript of van Acker's
first interview with Wouters, dated October 7, 1916,
two days after Wouters had been taken into custody.
Not surprisingly, it was making for some rather interesting, if disturbing, reading:

Hoffner reread the last line, then sat back and

REPORT CASE #: 00935
SUSPECT: WOUTERS
INTERROGATOR: ACKERS

7 OCTOBER 1916

CI van Acker: So you killed your grandmother. Anne Wouters.

M. Wouters: Yes.

CI van Acker: Because of the way she treated you.

M. Wouters: Because I had the bristle.

CI van Acker: So you deserved the beatings?

M. Wouters: (Pause) I don't know. I don't think so.

CI van Acker: And you were pleased to kill her. As you said, to "watch the blood flow down her neck."

M. Wouters: (Pause) I don't think I understand.

CI van Acker: You liked watching her die.

M. Wouters: No. Why should I like watching her die?

CI van Acker: Because she had been beating you. Because of the scars on your back.

M. Wouters: I don't think so. I don't know. (Pause) Would it be better if that was why?

CI van Acker: If what was why, Mr. Wouters?

M. Wouters: Would it be better if it was
                 because of the scars on my
                 back? Would that be right?

CI van Acker: (Pause) Are you sorry your
                 grandmother is dead?

M. Wouters: You're asking the same
                 question again.

CI van Acker: No, I haven't asked that
                 question.

M. Wouters: Yes. Yes, you did.

CI van Acker: I can assure you, I didn't.

M. Wouters: Yes. You asked if I was
                 pleased to kill her. "To
                 watch the blood flow down
                 her neck." You see.

CI van Acker: (Pause) And you buried her
                 outside the city.

M. Wouters: Yes.

CI van Acker: "In the soft earth near the
                 Shripte factory."

M. Wouters: Yes. The dirt smelled like
                 coal, there.

CI van Acker: Like coal. I see. (Pause) So
                 if there was nothing wrong
                 with what you did, Mr.
                 Wouters, why not tell the
                 police when they asked you
                 about her disappearance?

M. Wouters: Tell them? (Pause) They
                 didn't find the blood. I
                 cleaned that. With a brush.

CI van Acker: And, after that, you lived
                 on the streets and in the
                 almshouses.

M. Wouters: Yes. I moved about.

CI van Acker: Until the day you decided to
                 kill another woman.

M. Wouters: Yes.

CI van Acker: You waited nine years, and
                 then just went out to kill
                 another woman.

M. Wouters: Yes. Nine. If you say it
                 was nine.

CI van Acker: Nine years, and then three
                 more women.

M. Wouters: Yes. Three more. One, two,
                 three.

CI van Acker: And you decided to carve out
                 these designs on their
                 backs.

M. Wouters: Yes.

CI van Acker: I see. (Pause) Why so long,
                 Mr. Wouters? And why so many
                 at once?

M. Wouters: (Pause) It took time to find
                 the ideal.

CI van Acker: To find the what?

M. Wouters: (Pause) It seemed the right
                 thing to do.

peered across at the map. He continued to think. "Kills because he can." It was the same conclusion van Acker had drawn two years ago; Hoffner saw no reason to question it now. For Wouters, brutality carried no moral weight, no meaning beyond the act itself. His answers made that abundantly clear: there was no remorse, no pride, no delight in the killing. And yet, strangely enough, Wouters was neither cold nor detached in his responses. Van Acker's notes said as much. It was as if Wouters had been genuinely confused by van Acker's horror and disbelief.

It was that last answer the Belgian doctors had fallen in love with. To them, it had made everything crystal clear. Here was the created madman.

Hoffner was not so convinced. He had never cottoned to the theory that every beaten boy was destined for violence, or that every act of violence was traceable back to a beaten boy. People did what they did because they chose to. The motivations were ultimately irrelevant, inevitability merely an excuse. And yet, even in Berlin, the proceedings at the Reichstadt Court were beginning to sound more like medical seminars than legal prosecutions. In the hands of a clever attorney, the predilections for stealing, maiming, and raping were no longer criminally inspired; instead, they were all symptoms of some hidden disease. That disease, as far as Hoffner could make out, was called childhood. Luckily, most of the judges were, as yet, unwilling to accept the sins of the father as a legitimate defense: they still believed in the culpability of the individual.

Except, of course, when it came to a deeper depravity, that special brand of horror that tore at the very cloth of humane society. Then the judges, whether German or Belgian, were told to step aside so that the doctors could explain away the birth of psychosis. Hoffner imagined that it made them all feel so much safer to think that men such as Wouters could not simply be brought into this world; that, instead, they had to be malformed by it. Hoffner was not sure which painted the world in a more feeble light: the fact that it could not defend itself against a pure evil, or that it alone was responsible for every act of corruption.

Either way, it made no difference. The act itself was all that concerned him. That Wouters had killed Mary Koop—a **young** Mary Koop—clearly threw the doctors' theories out the window. Wouters was not reenacting his grandmother's murder. He was simply weak. And as the weak do, he preyed on the weak. There was nothing more profound to it than that. That he had found most of his victims in older, solitary women; that he had chosen to etch his markings onto the area where he himself had been beaten—naturally there was a link, but those elements could in no way mitigate Wouters's decision to embrace his own infamy.

What they did provide, however, was a view into the logic of the killings. Wouters might not have had access to the rational world, but that did not mean that he had not constructed one for himself.

A few points were obvious: the drag marks at each of the murder sites made it clear that the placement of the bodies was essential; otherwise, why go to the trouble of bringing them out into the open? Wouters had buried his grandmother in the "soft earth." He had meant for her to remain hidden. Not so with these women. Hoffner was hoping that van Acker could shed some light on the placement issue with some more information on the three victims he had discovered in Bruges.

More than that, Hoffner was now reasonably certain—ever since the discovery of the gloves—that the diameter-cut design was some kind of lace mesh itself. Wouters's eight years cooped up in an attic room, working a needle and thread, confirmed it. The trouble was, the more Hoffner stared at the design, the less it seemed to jibe with the pins sticking out from his map. He knew there had to be another piece, something that could make sense of the design in the context of the city's layout.

"He's remarkably small," said Fichte. He was still on his knees, staring at a single sheet. "Just over a meter and a half." He looked over. "Weren't some of the women taller than that?"

Hoffner kept his eyes on the map. "All of them." He was fixated on one of the pins; it had begun to sag. "Tell me," said Hoffner. "How does he move them, a man that small? How does he move a healthy-sized woman?"

"A trunk. Something like that. Isn't that what the marks showed?"

Hoffner nodded distractedly as he stood and moved over to the map. "But how does such a little man maneuver a trunk? Up and down stairs? A ramp? A ladder?" Hoffner readjusted the pin. He could still smell the formaldehyde on his fingers from this morning's session with victim number six. She had been of little help. As of now, they still had no name for her. "How does he do that without drawing attention? In fact"—Hoffner was now straightening each of the pins—"how does he do it at all without breaking his own back?"

Fichte thought for a moment. "The second carver." Fichte knew he had gotten it right.

Hoffner looked over at him. His eyes widened as he nodded. "Not the way he worked in Bruges, was it?" Fichte shook his head. "You haven't been at the pins, have you, Hans?" Another shake of the head. Hoffner turned back to the map. "No, I didn't think so."

Still preoccupied with the growing piles of paper, Fichte said, "Mueller knows how to have a good time."

The comment caught Hoffner off-guard. He turned. "Does he?" Fichte's smile was answer enough. "Yes . . . our Toby's not one to let an opportunity slip by."

"I never knew a man who could drink that much and still—" Fichte stopped himself with a little laugh.

Hoffner had felt a mild discomfort at Fichte's arrival this afternoon: another consequence to be considered. Now, hearing of Toby's exploits, he felt a similarly mild dose of relief. "So you had company?" he said. Fichte looked up. He was sporting a fifteen-year-old's grin. Hoffner returned the smile. "Toby never disappoints on that score." For a moment, Hoffner wondered if that was the reason he had sent Fichte off with Mueller in the first place; Hoffner, however, had never considered himself quite that clever, if, in fact, "clever" was the right word.

Fichte began to busy himself with the papers. Trying just too hard at nonchalance, he said, "He was telling me about some of your goings-on."

"Was he?" said Hoffner coolly.

"He mentioned something about Austria. The Tyrol. 'The pact,' he called it." Fichte looked up eagerly. "He said I should ask you."

Hoffner let Fichte sit a moment longer before saying, "Nice big tits on your girl, were there, Hans?" Fichte's face turned a deep crimson. "Toby always likes to give the big-tit girls to his guests. What would your Lina have to say, eh, Hans?"

Hoffner regretted having said it the moment it had passed his lips. Fichte's sudden look of concern hardly helped: not enough to have taken Fichte's girl, Hoffner needed to make the boy feel small for letting himself off the hook. Hoffner had forgotten just how much of himself he kept locked away. Now he was seeing how easily it all came back. "I'm just teasing you, Hans," he said to placate. "You're young. These things happen. She knows that as well as anyone. And if she doesn't, well, then—she doesn't have to."

Fichte nodded. It was clear that he had been trying to convince himself of the same thing since Bruges. Still, hearing it from Hoffner probably helped.

An unfamiliar boy poked his head through the doorway. Hoffner had no idea how long the boy had been standing there. He quickly stepped over and took the boy out into the hall. He had no interest in allowing a set of little eyes to get a glimpse of the files on the floor. "What is it?" said Hoffner.

The boy was particularly small. "The men are waiting in the Press Room, Herr **Kriminal-Kommissar.**"

Hoffner had completely forgotten about the meeting he had promised. In fact, he had blocked out the entire morning of interruptions: every paper in town had wanted to know where Kvatsch had gotten his story on the "chisel murders." Clever little title. Just right for Kvatsch. The telephone had started ringing at nine o'clock and had continued unabated until nearly ten-thirty. Hoffner had told them four o'clock. He checked his watch. For newsmen, they were remarkably prompt.

"I'll be right down," he said. The boy headed off, and Hoffner stepped back into the office. "Pack it up, Hans." He angled his head toward the bit of mirror that was visible through the bookcase. "We'll need to lock everything in the filing cabinet." Hoffner ran a hand over his face. His beard was a bit rough. Made him look diligent, he thought. That was all right.

"Pack it up?" said Fichte. "Why? What did the boy want?"

Hoffner checked his teeth. "This should take about twenty minutes." He smoothed back his hair. "That's when they usually run out of questions." He straightened his collar. "Or at least get tired of hearing the same answers."

"Who? Who gets tired?"

Hoffner pointed to piles on the floor. "The papers, Hans."

The Press Room was just off the front atrium. Präger had set it up during the last weeks of the war, when the flow of reporters into the Alex had gone from a trickle to a torrent. It had all started when the General Staff—unwilling to admit just how badly things were going—decided, in its infinite wisdom, to cease any further release of information: the less people knew, the better off they were. Newspapermen, however, never saw it that way: they had turned to the Kripo as their only alternative. Not that any of the detectives had known what was going on outside of Berlin, but there was always something nice and official about quotes that cited "Kripo sources." Naturally, once the revolution kicked in—making for genuine news—the Press Room had become the single most important office in the city. Even the General Staff had been known to send over a junior officer incognito, now and then, for a little information.

It was all very busy and very infuriating, and Präger had reasoned that it was safer to herd the newsmen into a confined space than to have them roaming about the building on their own. The rules were simple: they could come and go as they pleased, as long as they waited patiently in the office for someone to come and get them. More often than not, that wait stretched on for hours. Interest invariably lost out to impatience: the longer they were made to sit, the less frequently they appeared. By all accounts—now that the National Assembly elections had restored a bit of order—the flow had returned to a manageable drip. Then again, the fact that a battle had been waged inside the Alex walls just over a week ago might also have had something to do with it.

Hoffner recognized most of the eleven faces in the room, although the men's clothes were probably a better indication of which papers had sent them. Those still in long woolen overcoats had come from the likes of the **Lokalanzeiger** or the **Morgenpost** or the **Volkszeitung,** men with no time to waste: people were waiting for their copy. Removing a coat could send the wrong message. They paced defiantly at the back of the room. Others had been sent by the **8-Uhr Abendblatt** or the **Nacht-Ausgabe,** Mosse's and Sherl's knockoffs of the **BZ.** For years the two papers had been trying to compete with Ullstein's gold mine, but neither had ever won the kind of following that the **BZ** continued to enjoy. The wrinkled suits and brown socks of these staff writers were proof enough of their second-class status. Sadly, these were men who were always getting scooped by Gottlob Kvatsch. For them, an appearance at the Alex was a kind of humiliation: they had missed it again. They stood off to the side, careful not to make eye contact with anyone else in the room. The final group was made up of men who looked more like stockbrokers than journalists. They were all very well put to-gether—creases and all—and worked for papers such as the **Vossische Zeitung** or the **Berliner Tageblatt.** These were men who reported to the cultural elite, to the Westend highbrows. They sat aloof in the few chairs that were scattered about the room. Chances were, they would see the story for what it was: a bit of tabloid fodder. That, however, would not stop them from publishing it.

"Gentlemen," said Hoffner as he continued to the rostrum at the front of the room. Those who were sit-ting stood. The rest bunched up across from him. "I'm Detective Inspector Hoffner—two effs. I under-stand you have questions about an article that ap-peared in this morning's **BZ.**"

For exactly twenty-two minutes the men asked and Hoffner answered. Fichte stood at the back of the room, marveling at the effortlessness with which Hoffner deflected even the most detailed of ques-tions. It was clear that his **Kriminal-Kommissar** un-derstood the essential rule of the press conference:

that journalists in crowds are never as effective as when alone, probably another reason why Präger had set up the room in the first place. In this game of cat and mouse, each of the men had to be careful not to ask anything too leading lest one of his rivals learn more from the question than from the answer. Hoffner was playing them off each other to perfection. They learned that there were victims—four or five, the number was unclear just yet. That there was knife work—again, there was too little of it to make it a signature piece of the case. And that, thus far, the victims were women—old, young, there was nothing to specify at this point.

Frustrated by the vagueness of the answers, one of the woolen overcoats finally broke down and asked about the locations of the murder sites. He had heard that the women were being killed in one place before being brought to the various sites. Was there any truth to that?

Hoffner had anticipated the question. He was about to answer when a single "Yes" came from the doorway. Everyone, including Hoffner, turned to see **Oberkommissar** Braun enter the room.

"That is, in fact, true," continued Braun as he moved to Hoffner at the rostrum.

Hoffner did everything he could to keep from biting through his tongue. He sensed an immediate shift in the level of interest in the room. Nonetheless, he turned back to the men as if he had been expecting Braun all along. "Gentlemen," he said, "this is Chief Inspector Braun. He is also involved with the case." Hoffner looked at Braun. "So glad you could take the time out for us, Chief Inspector." Out of the corner of his eye, Hoffner noticed that Fichte had been joined by **Kommissar** Walther Hermannsohn.

Braun said, "The Polpo always has time for the truth, Herr Inspector."

A second bombshell landed as the men's interest gave way to tension. None of them had considered the possibility of Polpo involvement. Braun was working his magic.

The frustrated overcoat decided to push his luck: "The Polpo?" he said. "Are we to take it, then, that this is a political case, Herr Chief Inspector?"

Braun offered a cold smile. "In the aftermath of revolution, everything has a political side, **mein Herr.**" To a man, the pens started moving briskly across the pads. Braun continued, "One can never be too careful, especially with a maniac on the loose."

The pens stopped. No one had mentioned the word "maniac." Even Kvatsch had managed to keep it to just this side of lurid.

"You say a maniac," piped in one of the stock-brokers, all traces of indifference now gone. "Can we assume he has designs on the entire city?"

Hoffner cut in quickly: "As of now, everything is lo-calized. Let me say, gentlemen, that there has still been no clear evidence of any transporting of victims, despite any information the Chief Inspector might, or might not, have seen." Hoffner lied, but he needed to do something to muddy Braun's performance.

The stockbroker continued, "But there is at least one occurrence of a victim being moved to a separate site? Is that true, Inspector?"

Hoffner waited for Braun to step in, but Braun said nothing: like the men in the room, he looked to Hoffner. "One case," said Hoffner coolly. The lie was taking on a life of its own. "But there's nothing to indicate a pattern."

"Does that mean that that killing could have taken place anywhere?" the stockbroker pressed.

"As I said," answered Hoffner, "everything is localized." And with just a hint of contempt, he added, "No need to worry, **mein Herr.** Your readers in the west are safe."

The man was not satisfied. "Is that a promise, Herr Inspector?"

Hoffner was getting tired of this. He was also unsure how much longer he could stand next to the conveniently quiet **Oberkommissar** Braun without driving something sharp into the man's chest. "He'll be in our custody long before he figures out what's beyond the Tiergarten."

"And for those of us in the east," cut in one of the brown socks, "it wasn't so pressing?" The man had a point. "A maniac in Charlottenburg is reason to step things up, but a killer in the Mitte district was acceptable? Are our readers less important to the Kripo, Herr Inspector?"

Hoffner sensed how much Braun was enjoying this. "Of course not." Hoffner knew he had to end this, now. "We're in the process of following several very positive leads that should have this man off the streets before he has a chance to do any more harm, in any district of the city."

A man at the back spoke up. Hoffner had not seen him until now. His clothes were out of keeping with the rest of the group. "And is the Polpo as certain as the Kripo about these leads?" the man asked. The question was transparent. It was the surest way to challenge Hoffner's sincerity.

Hoffner gazed at the man. He made sure to remember the face.

"This," said Braun, suddenly eager to chime in, "is a Kripo investigation." It was as if he had been waiting for the question. "I can't comment on any specific leads. But let me say that, while the Polpo has kept itself apprised of all criminal cases since the revolution, it is our policy never to interfere with an ongoing Kripo investigation. The Polpo has the greatest confidence in Inspector Hoffner and the entire Kripo staff to follow whatever leads it may or may not have, so as to bring this unfortunate and unpleasant business to a swift conclusion. Only if it should prove to be more than a criminal case would the Polpo then step in."

Hoffner was impressed. In a matter of two minutes, Braun had managed to disclose crucial and damning elements of the case, foster panic, and undermine

Hoffner's credibility, and all while distancing himself and the Polpo from any kind of connection to the case. It had been masterful, and clearly orchestrated. Hoffner had no choice but to thank him for it.

"Always good to hear, Chief Inspector," said Hoffner. He turned to the room. "And I believe, gentlemen, that's all we have for you at this time." Hoffner motioned for Braun to lead them out; Braun acquiesced. There was a flurry of questions, but Hoffner ignored them. From the back of the room, he saw Hermannsohn follow Fichte to the door.

"Prick" was the first word out of Hoffner's mouth as he and Fichte stepped back into his office.

Hoffner had refused to give Braun the satisfaction of a confrontation. He had thanked him again for his words of confidence, and had then headed upstairs. Fichte had been smart to say nothing.

"And how he enjoys it," Hoffner continued. He moved over to the filing cabinet. He stared at it, his mind elsewhere. "There are things going on here I'm just not seeing." He unlocked and opened the drawer. "I'm getting tired of that, Hans."

Fichte closed the door. "Then I suppose we have no choice but to look at what we do see."

A week ago, Hoffner would have taken Fichte's contribution as little more than a parroting of what he had heard. Now the boy was actually speaking sense: not wanting to impress, Fichte was focusing.

Hoffner had the first of the papers in his hand. "Everything in here deals with what was happening at Sint-Walburga **after** Wouters went missing, yes? Logs, doctors' reports, visitors?"

"Primarily."

"Nothing about his behavior immediately after the arrest, or about his first few months in the asylum?" Fichte shook his head. "Which means reading through them won't help us understand him any better than we already do."

"Well, no," said Fichte, unwilling to concede the point entirely. "We took them because we thought they'd lead us to whoever planned the escape."

"I'm not questioning why you took them, Hans. I'm just making sure I know what we have. Finding the people who helped him only matters once we've got Wouters in hand."

Fichte thought a moment and nodded. He was about to answer, when his eyes lit up. "There was something else," he said as he moved to the cabinet and began to rummage through the papers. "Van Acker mentioned a few things he'd put together himself—interviews, a few last year, two or three the year before, and some drawings." Fichte found the packet. "Here it is."

"Drawings," said Hoffner. He took the packet, placed it on the desk, and began to leaf through as Fichte drew up to his side. "When it's a case that revolves around designs and patterns, Hans, you might want to mention drawings a little earlier on." Hoffner stopped when they came to the sheets with Wouters's scribblings.

There were four pages, each one filled with perhaps twenty lines of intricately drawn lace patterns. The sketches were all the same size, but what was most striking was the patterning of the rows themselves. Each one was made up of seven drawings of exactly the same design; the next row, another design and another set of replicas. Had Hoffner simply been glancing at them, he might have thought that each line was an exercise in perfecting the single designs. He quickly realized, however, that with each subsequent rendering, Wouters was bringing something new to the original drawing. The shapes, the lines, the contours might have been identical, but Hoffner knew there was something different in each one. He stood over the pages and stared, trying to find it, until, almost twenty minutes in, he saw the deviation. It was in the stroke of the pen. Each replica began at a different point of the design and moved through the lines of the pattern on its own distinct course: identical sketches, yet each one uniquely drawn. He had no idea what it meant.

"It's in how he draws it," he said out loud as he began to flip through the pages. He was hoping to find something resembling the diameter-cut. There was nothing.

The sudden break in silence momentarily startled Fichte. "An exercise, you mean?"

"Maybe." Hoffner stared a moment longer. "I don't

know." He then took the pages and grabbed his coat. "Friday night," he said as he slipped his arm through the sleeve. "The only place that handles this kind of lace and that stays open past six is KaDeWe, yes?"

"The shops I tried wouldn't be open this late," said Fichte. "KaDeWe. Maybe Tietz. But KaDeWe definitely."

"Good," said Hoffner as he grabbed his hat. "Then I'm guessing our friend there is going to be able to tell us more about Herr Wouters than you, I, van Acker, or any doctor ever could."

KaDeWe was packed. The revolution was now a distant memory, and capitalism had wasted no time in calling its faithful back to the teat. If any of the store's clientele had seen this morning's **BZ,** they were showing little concern. After all, there was a special on scarves, and someone had heard that a bit of perfume from Paris had finally made its way through. They were in the west, deep in the west. No one killed in the west.

Hoffner and Fichte sidestepped their way through the crowds and over to the glove counter, where, for some reason, things were less frantic. A placard on top of the glass explained:

We regret any inconvenience, however this department will be closing at five-thirty this evening. All inquiries may be taken up at the information desk. Thank you for your patience.

Hoffner checked his watch. It was a quarter to six. He moved across the aisle to lady's handkerchiefs, where a line of three or four women was waiting for the clerk. Hoffner stepped up to the glass. "The gentleman who handles the gloves," he said bluntly. "Herr Taubmann. Where does he change before leaving the store?"

The clerk turned slowly at the interruption as the woman started talking quietly among themselves. **"Mein Herr,"** he said through two stiff lips, "as you can see, there are other customers waiting—"

Hoffner pulled out his badge; he had no time for this tonight. "My apologies. Where can I find him?"

The man's sneer became a weak smile. "Is there something the matter, **mein Herr**?" The man was doing his best not to rattle the ladies. "Surely this is a mistake?"

"Yes, that's what this is," said Hoffner abruptly. "A mistake. Just tell me where he changes."

Three minutes later, Hoffner was leading Fichte through the maze of underground employee corridors in search of Room 17. It was eerily quiet, given the mayhem they had just come from on the main floor.

Herr Taubmann was sitting alone on a long bench, tying his shoe, when Hoffner and Fichte stepped into the cold room; evidently heat was not a necessity for KaDeWe's workers. Hoffner noticed that the walls were in need of a bit of replastering, as well.

Taubmann's suit hung in a locker directly across from him. It was perfectly placed, the creases exact on the hanger. Hoffner saw the open bottle of rosewater placed on a shelf just below the cuffs to keep it fresh: a perfect touch for the man, he thought.

Taubmann looked up, his surprise instantaneous. It was the first time Hoffner had realized how birdlike Taubmann was. "Herr Hoffner," Taubmann said nervously. His head tweaked from side to side as he glanced from Hoffner to Fichte. "This is a restricted area." He seemed unsure what to say next. "Your order has not yet come in." Even Taubmann recognized the absurdity of what he had just said.

"Yes," Hoffner cut in reassuringly. "I'm not here about the gloves, Herr Taubmann." He calmly produced his badge. "It's **Inspector** Hoffner. I just need to ask you some questions about . . . lace designs."

Taubmann was still trying to process the badge. "Inspector?"

"Yes. You've been so helpful in the past. I hope that's all right?"

Taubmann struggled to find an answer. "Questions about lace?"

"Yes." Hoffner needed to move this along. "I know you have an appointment tonight, but this shouldn't take more than a few minutes."

Taubmann's nervousness turned to shock. "How do you know about my appointment?" he said tensely.

Hoffner raised a hand. "I don't," he said in his most pacifying tone. "I merely assumed. There was a note at your counter. You were closing early."

Taubmann's relief was immediate. "Oh, yes. Yes, of

course. The note. I—It's a dinner for my mother. Once a year. We celebrate her birthday. I always leave a few minutes early. Saves an enormous amount of time back here. You can't imagine. Half an hour at least."

It amused Hoffner to see how much information the innocent were willing to volunteer. "Of course," he said. "How nice for you. But could I steal just a few minutes of your time?"

Taubmann was again running through the last half-minute in his head. "You still want the gloves from Bruges, yes?" The salesman was returning.

Hoffner smiled. "Of course."

"Good." Taubmann was recovering beautifully. "That's good. And this is. . . ?"

Hoffner turned to Fichte. "My partner. Detective Fichte. Herr Taubmann."

Fichte offered a quick nod.

"Oh, yes," said Taubmann. "I trust your doctor's visit was a success?"

Naturally, Taubmann would have remembered that. Fichte nodded again, with a forced smile.

"Very good," said Taubmann. He was slightly less efficient out of his perfect suit. He seemed aware of it himself as he motioned for Hoffner to take a seat. Hoffner did so, and pulled out the pages from van Acker's files.

"If you can," said Hoffner, "I'd like to know what these are."

Still not sure what was going on, Taubmann took

the sheets. "All right," he said tentatively. He brought the pages up to his face. As with the gloves, his expression changed instantly. His head began to dart from row to row as he studied the sketches with great intensity. After nearly two minutes he said, "This is marvelous work. Really. Not another aunt, is it, **mein Herr**?"

"Another . . . ?" Hoffner remembered his first lie. "No. Not another aunt."

Taubmann nodded, his eyes still fixed on the sketches. "No, I wouldn't imagine something this unusual as a gift."

"Unusual?" said Hoffner.

Taubmann looked up. "A **point étude.** It's exceptionally rare. It applies to only a handful of meshes."

"I see," said Hoffner.

Gazing at the drawings again, Taubmann said, "Am I right in guessing that you want to know if we can make pieces from them?"

Hoffner found it oddly charming how everything for Herr Taubmann revolved around the sale of lace. A detective had just invaded his changing room, with mysterious sheets of paper, and all Taubmann saw was an order for unusual gloves. The man was perfect. Hoffner could ask him anything without wondering if Taubmann might see beyond the question. It made it all very safe.

"Once again," said Hoffner, "you've guessed correctly."

Taubmann's smile was only slightly self-congratulatory. "Thank you, **mein Herr,** but I'm not quite clear why it's so . . . pressing." He was doing his best to be accommodating. "After all, I will be in tomorrow morning."

"Yes."

"Not that I'm not keen on the sale," Taubmann said eagerly. "But . . . you understand."

"Of course," said Hoffner, easing himself back into character. "It's just that I came across it—this . . . **point étude,** as you say—quite by accident, and I'm simply fascinated by it." Hoffner decided to lead the man. "Much the way you are, I suspect?" He saw Taubmann begin to waver. "Just two minutes, Herr Taubmann. You'll allow me that brief imposition, won't you?"

Taubmann stared uncertainly until, with a long exhalation, he nodded.

"Wonderful," said Hoffner. "Is it some kind of blueprint for different meshes?"

"Some kind of—oh, I see what you mean. Well, yes and no. I suppose one could call them blueprints, but they're more variations on each design."

"Variations?" Hoffner had figured that out for himself back at the Alex. "But each row looks identical. I thought it might be some sort of exercise?"

Taubmann's smile returned. "To the untrained eye, perhaps, **mein Herr.** But a **point étude** is not meant for the untrained eye. It comes from the French. 'Point study.' Of course, the term is inaccurate. A better way to describe it would be 'flow study,' or perhaps 'path study.' Even those don't capture the art one finds in these."

Hoffner had been right. It was the way in which Wouters had drawn them that differentiated each sketch. "I don't understand," he said.

Taubmann invited Hoffner to bend over the page more closely. "Identical in design, yes, but not in the way they are drawn." Taubmann leaned in to illustrate as he spoke. "Each of these drawings begins at a different point on the mesh. The needle, or in this case the pen, then follows the path of the design using very specific directional markers that tell the artist when to loop back, when to bring the thread under or over, so forth and so on. Those shifts in movement occur at the **picots,** or knots, throughout the design." Taubmann sat up. "The point of origin determines the movement of the needle throughout the entire mesh. Change the point of origin, and the design— even though seemingly identical—is nonetheless subtly and significantly altered."

Hoffner nodded. He had been listening with only half an ear since Taubmann had mentioned the words "directional markers." It suddenly struck him how close he had been to unmasking the design, all along. He had always understood it best through movement, in the ebb and flow of the city, and here it was, that very movement reflected in the twists and turns of the needle. It was not enough to take the little pins in his map and search for the pattern. One had to understand the flow of the design. That was the key to the placement.

More than that, the design itself told the "artist" where to go, which meant that the design, in some way, knew where its next crucial change in direction would be. In other words, all Hoffner needed to do was to find the point of origin for the diameter-cut design, and he would be able to follow its flow to Wouters's next dumping site. At least that was the theory.

"So, if you have the point of origin," said Hoffner, "you know which direction the needle will always move, and which major knots along the way it will hit."

"Precisely," said Taubmann. He was now enjoying himself. "But it gets even better. Most lacemakers believe that these kinds of rare designs also have an optimal point of origin—that is, a singular point of entry that will create the ideal mesh." Taubmann once again had Hoffner's full attention. "That's why there are so many versions of the same design in each row. The artist is looking for the ideal mesh. Or, rather, he is waiting for the ideal mesh to reveal itself. In a way, the **point étude** turns a mesh into a living, breathing thing, with the key to its own perfection hidden within it. Remarkable, wouldn't you say? That's why they spend so much time on these **points études.** Or at least why they used to. These days, machines churn out the designs with no care for optimal mesh. Shame, really."

An ideal mesh, thought Hoffner. Living and breathing. Of course. He remembered van Acker's first interview with Wouters: **It took time to find the ideal.** It **was** perfect. In Wouters's twisted mind, the diameter-cut—originated at its optimal point—was actually breathing life into his victims.

Taubmann picked up the pages. "In this particular study, the artist achieves the ideal mesh always on the seventh sketch. That's a bit odd, I suppose, but it does make for a very nice symmetry." He extended one of the pages to Hoffner. "I'm sure you can see the difference in the last ones in each of the rows. They're slightly more—well, perfect."

"Yes," said Hoffner, not really looking. He reached into his coat pocket and pulled out another single sheet. He held it out to Taubmann. It was Hoffner's rendering of the diameter-cut design. "And is this one of these rare designs?"

Taubmann hesitated. It was clear from his expression that he was done with the lesson.

"Please, Herr Taubmann," Hoffner said kindly. "This is the last, I promise."

Taubmann stared a moment longer, then took the page. His brow furrowed as he studied it. "It's very rudimentary. You're sure this is a lace design?"

"That's what I'm asking you, Herr Taubmann."

Taubmann continued to scan the page as he spoke: "It might be." He suddenly looked up. "This isn't about buying lace, is it, Herr Inspector?"

Taubmann's frankness was wholly unexpected. Hoffner had never understood why people asked such questions. Surely they knew there could be no answers. "The drawing, Herr Taubmann. Is it one of these designs?"

Taubmann's discomfort grew. "I'm not really an expert, Herr Inspector."

"You're being modest."

"No," said Taubmann more forcefully. "I'm really not."

Hoffner saw the uneasiness in Taubmann's eyes. This was not something he readily admitted. "Then who is?" asked Hoffner.

The answer came without hesitation. "Emil Kepner. He's the best in the city. In fact, I'm studying with him." Taubmann did his best with a smile. "You see, I hope to have my own shop one day. When I've put enough money away."

"Where can I find this Kepner?"

Fichte answered: "Kleiststrasse." Both men turned to him. Fichte explained: "He owns one of the places I tried last week. Very high-end."

Hoffner turned to Taubmann. "So Herr Kepner would know about my drawing?"

"Absolutely," said Taubmann. "No one in Berlin knows lace like Emil."

"You have the address?"

"He'll be home, by now, **mein Herr.**" Again, Taubmann tried a smile. "You can see why I want my own shop."

Hoffner was growing impatient. "Then his address there. You have that?"

Taubmann's confusion returned. "It's Friday evening, **mein Herr.** It's the man's home."

"I'm aware of that, Herr Taubmann." Hoffner was no longer the genial customer. "I'm also a Kripo detective. Do you have the address?"

Taubmann's face paled. Six minutes later, Hoffner and Fichte were outside, heading for Charlottenburg.

The street names are what give everything away: Goethe, Schiller, Herder, Kant. If the brighter glow from the lampposts, or the whiter shine on the pavements, fails to tip off an errant wanderer that he has strayed too far, then the signs above are a final warning to turn back, now. Charlottenburg had never been satisfied merely to hold tightly to the city's purse strings; it had to stake a claim to her genius, as well. The fact that Goethe and Herder had spent most of their productive years in Weimar, Schiller in Jena and then Weimar, and Kant forever in Königsberg, had never deterred the privileged few from assuming their rightful lineage. Hoffner and Fichte were now in the land of the divine. They were meant to tread carefully.

Among friends, Herr Kepner was always heard to say that he lived in Weimar: after all, his house was on the corner where Schiller and Herder met. Very few ever got the joke, but they laughed anyway. Kepner was that sort of man: always a few steps ahead, but on a road no one else seemed all that eager to follow.

It was a road, however, that had served him well. Kepner's house was three stories high, set off from the street, and with a pleasant garden out front. Aside from the Tiergarten, Hoffner had forgotten the last time he had seen this much grass in one place. He released the latch on the fence and followed the path of stones to the front porch. Fichte followed behind. Hoffner knocked at the door.

After several more attempts, the door finally opened and a man, younger than Hoffner had expected, stepped from the shadows. It was unusually dark inside the house; even so, Hoffner could tell that the man was not in a servant's uniform. The man seemed puzzled by the appearance of someone on his stoop.

"Yes?" he said warily.

"Forgive the intrusion, **mein Herr.** I am Detective Inspector Hoffner, with the Kripo. I'm looking for Herr Emil Kepner."

The man grew more reticent. He looked over at Fichte, then back at Hoffner. "I am Herr Kepner's son-in-law, Herr Brenner. Can I help you?"

"Ah," said Hoffner. "Herr Brenner. Is Herr Kepner available?"

Brenner spoke as if to a child. "It's Friday night, **mein Herr.**"

"Yes. Again, I apologize, but this is Kripo business. Herr Kepner will, I'm sure, understand."

The man seemed to take offense at the suggestion. Hoffner was about to start in again, when a man's voice called out from behind Brenner: "Is something the matter, Josef? Just tell them we are not seeing anyone tonight."

Brenner turned back to the voice. "I have. It's an inspector from the Kripo."

There was a rustling of chairs and a low rumble of voices. Brenner moved out of the way as a man, perhaps in his early sixties, stepped through to the doorway. He was agitated. "Herr Inspector. Has something happened with the shop?" Brenner remained just behind him.

"Herr Kepner?" said Hoffner.

"Yes." Kepner was small, but well fed. "Has something happened?"

"Nothing to do with your shop, **mein Herr,** but if I might have a word with you inside?"

For a moment Kepner seemed torn by the simple request. Hoffner was losing his patience: were the burghers of Charlottenburg beyond the sway of a Kripo badge? Finally Kepner nodded. He extended a hand and welcomed the two men into the house. "This way, gentlemen, please." He led them along a hallway. A few paces on, he turned to his right, through an arch, and into a sitting room. Hoffner was following when he glanced to his left. Directly across the way was a second arch which led into the dining room. A table was set, with perhaps ten people seated around it. Each of the faces stared back blankly at him. Hoffner noticed the two candelabra standing on the sideboard. He saw the skullcaps on each of the men's heads. He turned to Fichte. "Wait here, Hans."

Fichte did as he was told. Brenner remained with him.

Kepner was by the fireplace when Hoffner stepped into the sitting room. "Another apology, **mein Herr,**" said Hoffner. "The Sabbath. I didn't think to ask."

Kepner nodded curtly. "Yes." He motioned to two chairs. "Please." The men sat. "You will understand, then, if I wish to keep this as brief as possible." Hoffner nodded. "So what is it that I can do for the **Kriminalpolizci,** Herr Inspector?"

Hoffner felt foolish now asking about the lace. He had been looking forward to interrupting a nice Charlottenburg dinner party with his request—the rich needed to be kept on their toes—but this was something entirely different. Police and Jews were never a good mix. Jews saw only the threat, never the protection. Sadly, they probably had little reason to see it any other way. The irony of his career choice had never been lost on Hoffner.

He chose candor out of some skewed sense of penance for having reminded the man's family of just how tenuous its position remained. "We're in the midst of an investigation, **mein Herr,**" he began. "We believe you may be able to shed some light on a piece of evidence we've recently uncovered."

"How did you get my name?" Kepner was being cautious.

"A clerk at KaDeWe."

Kepner nodded knowingly. "Taubmann."

"He was explaining the **point étude** when your

name came up." Hoffner saw the slight lift in Kepner's eyes. "I have a rendering of a single design which I'm hoping you'll examine."

"A **point étude.** You know how rare these things are?"

"Yes."

"And I shouldn't ask why this is important, should I?"

"No, **mein Herr.** You shouldn't."

Again, Kepner took a moment. A Jew this old knew to leave it at that. "I can look at this for you, now," he said. "But I can't work on it for you. You understand." Hoffner shook his head. "Not until after sundown tomorrow."

For the second time in the last few minutes, Hoffner felt foolish. He was smarter than that. Of course not until after sundown. He hated appearing the amateur. He said, "I'll need your word that this evidence will remain in your possession at all times. That you will tell no one about it. That you will show it to no one."

Kepner remained stone-faced. "You don't need my word, Herr Inspector. You see how I live."

Hoffner felt another twinge of conscience; this time, however, he was unsure if it was because he should have known better, or because he knew only too well. Did Kepner actually believe that his place was so secured that his life could speak for itself? Could a Jew grow that comfortable in Berlin? Hoffner had no answer. He reached into his coat pocket and produced Wouters's design. Kepner pulled a pair of glasses from his pocket and took the page. He began to examine it. His expression remained unchanged.

"Crude," said Kepner. "But yes. This is a design for a **point étude.**" He removed the glasses. "I can't tell you which specific design it is. I will need more time for that." He folded the page and placed it in his jacket pocket. "But you knew as much before coming to me."

"I was hoping."

"Yes," said Kepner guardedly. "I don't suspect that your hopes are ever that far off, Herr Inspector." Hoffner said nothing as Kepner studied him. "A Kripoman who apologizes for intruding on a Sabbath dinner. Now, that's a rarity, isn't it?" Kepner was not expecting an answer as he began to get to his feet. "I will do what I can for you, Herr Inspector. You will give me a telephone number, and we will talk tomorrow." The two men stood.

A minute later, Hoffner was at the door with Fichte. Brenner had moved them on as quickly as he could. He watched them all the way down the stone path.

Out on the street, Fichte was the first to break the silence. "Bit of a cold fish, don't you think, that Brenner? I suppose Kepner was the same?"

"No," said Hoffner. "He wasn't."

"Oh." Fichte seemed disappointed by the response. "Took me through the whole thing, Brenner did. I'd never heard about a Jewish ritual before."

Hoffner continued to walk. "It's just a meal, Hans."

"The servants turning the lights on and off for them. And all done in Jewish—"

"Hebrew," Hoffner corrected. "They speak in Hebrew."

"Right." Too pleased with himself, Fichte continued, "I'll tell you, he was surprised I had so many questions."

Hoffner said blandly, "Or maybe he was just surprised that you needed to ask them."

The subtlety was lost on Fichte. He asked, "Did the old Jew have what we wanted?"

Hoffner found himself slowing. He stopped and stood there, deciding whether he wanted to take Fichte down this road. Fichte had stopped, as well. Not exactly sure why, Hoffner turned to him and said, "Herr Kepner has offered to bring his expertise to our case, Hans." He spoke with no emotion. "What have you brought to it, so far?"

The sting of the comment took a moment to register. When it did, Fichte's surprise quickly gave way to a look of injured pride. "I don't know," he said icily. "I suppose nothing at all, Herr **Kriminal-Kommissar.**"

Hoffner had no interest in stroking Fichte's ego. He started to walk. "Don't overstate it, Hans."

Fichte was at a complete loss. He had no idea what had just gone so terribly wrong. He caught up and pretended as if nothing had happened; it was the best he could come up with. "Did Herr Kepner think he could help us?"

"We'll know by tomorrow," said Hoffner. They reached a cab stand and stopped. "You want me to drop you somewhere?" It was a hollow offer.

"We're done for the night?"

Hoffner had spent the better part of the morning digging up what he could on Leo Jogiches—his possible K—but it had all been preliminary. He now considered taking another crack at the man, but he was tired. He needed a night away from all of this. "I am," he said. "You're welcome to head back to the Alex, run through the files by yourself, Hans, but that's up to you."

"You're sure?" Fichte was still trying to wrap his mind around the last few minutes.

Hoffner explained. "There's nothing we can do until we hear from Kepner. That's it." And with an unkind finality, he added, "I'm sure you can fill the time with your Lina."

Fichte had reached the limits of his confusion. "Look," he said, trying to make things right, "I'm sorry if I offended you—"

"Offended me?" Hoffner cut in. "You didn't offend me, Hans." Not true, but not the point. "You just have to be smarter than that, that's all." Hoffner decided to make this very simple. "You want to think that way, go right ahead. Not my business. What is, is how you look at a case, and in a case, that kind of thinking only gets in the way. You don't see what you need to see. You see only what you already believe, and that helps no one. In another line of work, it wouldn't matter. But to do what we do—at least to do it well—you can't narrow the scope. Any kind of preconception, no matter how innocent you may think it is, muddies the view. Yes, Kepner is an old Jew, but that's not what he is to us."

Hoffner almost believed what he had said. A detective's cold rationale had always been his best defense for an open mind. He knew it went deeper than that, but neither he nor Fichte could afford to dig that far. Moral indignation had never been Hoffner's strong suit.

Fichte waited before answering. "Yes," he said: something had struck a chord. "I appreciate the advice. And, for what it's worth, I'm sorry."

Hoffner heard the sincerity in the boy's voice. Maybe he had said too much. "Go see your Lina, Hans. Take the day. Be at the Alex by three."

Things were all right again. Fichte nodded and then turned and headed down the street. If he was lucky, he would be on Friedrichstrasse by half past eight: he would have an entire evening with her.

Hoffner called over a cab. He imagined Hans in Lina's arms as he stepped inside. Another act of contrition. Hoffner was becoming quite adept at them.

⸺ THE MASTER DRAFT ⸺

Sascha had been sulking for the last hour. There had been the promise of an outing with friends after school—someone had mentioned horseback riding in the Tiergarten—but Martha had insisted he be home for lunch with her sisters: another Saturday afternoon with the spinsters. Sascha had never understood why he had to be punished for their failures; his father had always wondered the same thing. So, in their last hour of freedom, father and son had snuck out to the kiosk on the corner, Hoffner to assess the damage Herr Braun had wrought, Sascha to check on yesterday's rally results.

The **Tageblatt** had set the tone. Pasted across its front page, alongside a photograph of the American President—triumphant before an adoring Paris crowd—was an artist's rendering of Berlin's latest "chisel murder" victim. At least the editors there had had the decency to keep her relatively well clothed; Mr. Wilson was, after all, a modest man. The **Lokalanzeiger,** on the other hand, had offered her up with a bare back and a bit of thigh showing. Obviously, Ullstein was hedging its bets: if horror failed, then perhaps titillation would move the papers off the stands.

Naturally, the one name that had appeared over and over throughout each of the articles was that of Detective Inspector Nikolai Hoffner. Herr Braun, no surprise, had managed to maintain the elusive title of "Polpo source." Hoffner was glad to see Sascha too busy with his results to take any notice.

A second item—lower down on the page—had also caught Hoffner's eye. They were burying Karl Liebknecht today at the Friedrichsfelde cemetery. An empty coffin for Rosa was to be buried by his side.

Hoffner could only imagine the throngs that would be following behind: the papers were estimating crowds in the thousands. Such was Rosa's continuing hold on Berlin: even absent from her own funeral, she was the day's central attraction.

A week ago, Hoffner would have given the article only a glance. Now there was a human side to it, with poetry and self-doubt and loneliness and a parasol, and somehow Hoffner felt as if these were his alone. Even so, he knew there was something safe in indulging the personal with a woman alive only on paper. He would have to be more careful elsewhere.

Back at the flat, Martha's sisters showed no signs that they had seen any of the articles. The size of their appetites, along with the vacuousness of their conversation, told Hoffner as much.

"Fascinating," he said, as he helped himself to another serving of cold potatoes. Martha had saved up a good bit of the cream from the week; the potatoes stuck to one another like clumps of packed snow. It was his favorite dish.

Gisella, Martha's eldest sister, nodded. She was large and square, and wore wool even in the summer—the result, Hoffner guessed, of sixteen years confined to a secretary's desk in a lawyer's office. "It's going to be a busy time once this new government starts changing the law books," she said. "I can tell you that."

Georgi kept a toy plane by his plate. It was reserved for emergencies only. He picked it up and took it out for a short flight under the tablecloth. His other aunt, Eva, watched him with delight. She was not so large, and very soft. A nurse in a dentist's surgery, she had impeccably white teeth. As a little boy, Georgi had been frightened by her smile.

"Look how graceful he is," said Eva as she beamed.

"Up on the table," said Martha quietly. Georgi brought the plane up for a final approach, and then landed it by his plate. He smiled at Eva.

"I hear this new government might not last," said Sascha, who was seated by his father. The boy was brazen enough to say it, though not yet sure enough of himself to look up from his plate when he did.

"That's quite a statement," said Gisella. Her entire torso shook when she laughed. "Do we have a young politico in the family?"

"Sascha has no taste for the socialists," said Hoffner. He licked at his spoon. "Even the democratic kind."

Gisella tilted her square head at the boy. "You could do a lot worse, Alexander." Like all good aunts, she never forgot what he liked to be called. "It's an exciting time to be young."

Sascha nodded quietly. He felt the starch in his collar grate against his neck.

The conversation might have droned on and on—with a few more test flights before dessert—had the telephone not interrupted: Sascha and Georgi perked up; Martha looked to Nikolai for guidance; Gisella and Eva simply looked confused.

Hoffner stood. "I'm expecting a call," he said.

"About a case." This managed to settle the table. Of course, the call was meant for after sundown—and back at the Alex—but maybe Herr Kepner had grown impatient, so impatient that he had tracked down the telephone number to the flat. **Points études** were rare things, after all. Hoffner excused himself and moved through to the living room.

"Hoffner here," he said when he picked up.

Sadly, Kepner had not been so resourceful: it was the duty sergeant at the Alex. The man apologized for the intrusion. They had found another body, number seven, this one just west of the Tiergarten. Hoffner listened to the details, then hung up.

The zoo, he thought. Over five kilometers from any of the other murder sites. And just a day after Herr Braun's press briefing. How convenient.

Hoffner considered phoning Fichte, but knew that would be pointless. A call to Lina's would be equally ill-advised. He was about to start back to the dining room when he saw Sascha standing in the doorway.

"Yes?" said Hoffner.

"Mother wants to know if everything's all right."

Hoffner could see the total indifference in the boy's eyes. "I need to go out to the Tiergarten," he said. Sascha nodded and started to go. "You can come with me, if you want." Hoffner momentarily allowed himself to forget what it was that he was going to see out at the zoo. The boy turned back. He said nothing. "Unless, of course, you'd prefer locking horns with Auntie Gee all afternoon?" Hoffner thought he saw the hint of a smile. Sascha, however, managed to keep it in check.

"All right," said the boy.

"Good. Get our coats. I'll tell your mother."

The first streetcar took them out west, the second up north. It was a pleasant little ride, the pockmarks of Kreuzberg—those nice thick chips gouged out by stray bullets—giving way to the smooth porcelain-white complexion of affluent Berlin. Even the advertising posters here loomed more gently: docile pinks and yellows infused the tight skirts of the ladies' dresses and men's handkerchiefs. There was a joy in the painted faces that belonged only in the west.

Sascha peered out with contempt. "They got by without so much as a scratch, didn't they?"

Hoffner hardly noticed; he had been watching Sascha for the last half hour. The boy's gaze reminded him of another face, smaller, pressed closer in to the tram window, those distant Sundays when father and son had headed up to Potsdamer or Alexanderplatz to choose a line—a new one each time—before settling in for an afternoon's expedition: twenty pfennigs, and the city had been theirs. He remembered how intently Sascha had listened to all of his stories about the bridges and statues and monuments, Berlin brought to life in a child's gaze; how he had always insisted that they get out—somewhere in the city's remote corners—to sample a chocolate or a cake at some unknown café, only to stash most of it away in a pocket for Martha; and how those remnants had always arrived back at the flat, more lint than chocolate, to Martha's absolute delight.

Hoffner had no reason to blame Sascha for his contempt. Like the boy, that city no longer existed.

"They're going to be governed by socialists now," said Hoffner. "Far worse than any bullets could have done to them." He saw a momentary slip in Sascha's otherwise grim expression. "You like that, do you?" The tram came to a stop, and Sascha gave a shrug. The two stepped off and into the freezing rain. "So do I."

The group outside the Gardens was far larger than Hoffner had expected. He had been anticipating a few shopkeepers, maybe a building porter or two: a body in daylight always brought out the true devotees, no matter what the weather. This, however, was actually a crowd. Moving closer in, Hoffner noticed a small unit of patrolmen. They had set up an improvised barrier and were trying to keep order. Braun's promised hysteria had begun.

With Sascha in tow, Hoffner pushed his way through and up to the nearest of the Schutzi officers. "Who's in charge here?" he asked as he pulled out his badge.

The patrolman recognized the name at once; he, too, had seen this morning's papers. **"Kriminal-Kommissar** Hoffner!" he said in a loud, enthusiastic voice.

Everyone within earshot turned at the mention of

the name: evidently, no one had missed today's news. "The man in charge," Hoffner repeated as he ignored the stares. "Obviously that's not you."

The man snapped to attention. "No, Herr **Kriminal-Kommissar.** Right away, Herr **Kriminal-Kommissar.**" Still keeping the crowd back, the patrolman tried to locate his sergeant.

Hoffner peered past him. Set against the growing herd, the plaza looked desolate. The few who were wandering outside the gate to the zoo had turned up their collars against the wind; fists were pressed deep inside pockets, some in uniform, some not. Hoffner recognized several of the faces from yesterday's briefing: the press had managed to get through. He was about to say something to the patrolman, when he noticed Polpo **Kommissar** Walther Hermannsohn among them. Hoffner wondered if he was meant to be surprised by Hermannsohn's presence. The man was taller than he remembered—no Tamshik, this time, to dwarf him. Truth to tell, Hoffner would have preferred Tamshik. At least there he knew what to expect. Here, even within the small gathering, Hermannsohn seemed to stand alone. "Never mind," said Hoffner as he stepped over the barrier and out into the plaza. "I see who I need."

With a surge of authority, the patrolman reached over and grabbed Sascha by the shoulder. "Not so fast, my young friend."

Hoffner turned back. Again, Sascha's size startled him: the boy was as big as the man clutching him.

"He's with me, Patrolman," said Hoffner. His impatience had little effect. "You've never seen a junior detective, is that it?" The man's conceit gave way to confusion. Hoffner spoke with greater precision. "Any chance I can get my detective back?"

Confusion turned to helplessness. The man suddenly snapped to attention and released Sascha. "Yes, of course, Herr **Kriminal-Kommissar.**"

"Don't let the age fool you, Patrolman. The good ones always start young. At least in the Kripo."

"Of course, Herr **Kriminal-Kommissar.** My apologies." He turned nervously to Sascha. "My apologies, Herr **Kriminal-Assistent.**"

Hoffner was about to answer when Sascha said, "Just don't let it happen again, Patrolman." There was a surprising weight to Sascha's tone. Hoffner bit down on his tongue to keep from smiling.

The man offered an efficient nod. "No, Herr **Kriminal-Assistent.**"

Without acknowledging his father, Sascha pulled up his collar and headed out into the plaza. Hoffner gave the man a reproachful nod, then followed Sascha out. "A little hard on him, weren't you?" he said when they were side by side.

"He'll get over it," said Sascha.

Had **Kommissar** Hermannsohn not turned at that moment, Hoffner might have placed an arm across Sascha's back and taken him out into the city for the day. To hell with all of this, he thought. But Hermannsohn did turn, along with every newspaperman by the gate. As one, they started in toward their prey. Hoffner was about to raise a hand to ward them off when he saw Hermannsohn bark out something to three Schutzi officers who were standing nearby. To Hoffner's complete amazement, the patrolmen moved over and held the pressmen back. Hoffner moved past the buzz of questions and over to Hermannsohn.

"My thanks, Herr **Kommissar,**" said Hoffner.

Hermannsohn nodded quietly. "I imagine that's the sort of thing you can do without, Herr **Kriminal-Kommissar.**" Hoffner realized that this was the first time he had heard the man speak. Hermannsohn's tone was oddly nonthreatening, although there was nothing inviting to it, either. "Ah, and young Hoffner, as well." His familiarity was equally disconcerting. "I hear he's quite the swordsman."

Hoffner now regretted having brought Sascha along. "Yes."

"And this is the source of his resolve on the strip, is it?"

Hoffner had no idea what Hermannsohn was referring to. "Excuse me, **Kommissar?**"

"A boy at a murder site. I imagine we each build character in our own way." When Hoffner said nothing, Hermannsohn added, "A joke, **Kriminal-Kommissar.**"

Hoffner waited, then said, "I imagine it was."

Hermannsohn smiled quietly and then motioned to the gate. "The body is this way."

Hoffner was about to follow when he saw the uncertainty in Sascha's eyes: there had been no mention of a murder or a body during the tram ride out. How could there have been? The complete absurdity of this moment only now came clear to Hoffner. What had he been thinking? "I can't take you inside, Alexander."

Sascha showed an instant of relief before nodding in disappointment. "Well, then, I'll wait here, Father."

The boy acted with such poise, thought Hoffner. "Good man," he said. For just a moment, Hoffner placed a hand on Sascha's arm. Somehow, neither seemed to mind it. He then reached into his coat pocket and pulled out a small flask. He opened it and handed it to Sascha. "Should keep you warm for a while." Sascha hesitated. "Go on. She doesn't have to know." Sascha took a quick sip, and coughed as he handed it back. Hoffner smiled. Just a boy, he thought. What had been so frightening in that? Hoffner then held the flask out to Hermannsohn. **"Kommissar?"** Hermannsohn politely refused. "No, I didn't think so." Without taking a drink, Hoffner pocketed the flask and followed Hermannsohn out into the Gardens.

There was something so depressing about the zoo in rain. The little buildings—some Frenchman's notion of international kinship—were each designed in the style of the countries from which the animals had come. Laden with ice and damp, they looked less like invitations to foreign climes than sodden gingerbread houses. A merry skip past them became a somber slog: not much fun in knowing what dreary looked like in China or India or darkest Africa.

Hoffner said, "Nice when the Polpo puts in an appearance on a criminal case. Or did I miss the **Oberkommissar**'s point yesterday?"

Hermannsohn ignored the question; he seemed the type to ignore anything he found unpleasant. He took them past the elephant house—Hoffner wondered how many elephants actually roamed the Taj Mahal—and into the more remote regions of the Gardens. "You were planning on bringing the boy to the site," said Hermannsohn. "I find that most interesting."

"Do you?" Hoffner could change the subject just as easily. "As interesting as I find having the **Tageblatt** and the **Morgenpost** on hand?"

"Ah, yes," said Hermannsohn. "You really never can trust these Schutzi patrolmen, can you?" He led Hoffner away from the animal houses and down a path that wound its way past a public toilet and beyond a small utility shed. The trees grew thicker as they walked.

They came to a link chain that hung across the path. A small sign dangled from it that read, DURCHGANG VERBOTEN. Two exclamation points hammered home the message: **Passage Forbidden!!** Hoffner knew his Berliners. This would have been enough to keep a small band of revolutionaries at bay. Hermannsohn stepped over the chain. Hoffner did the same. Half a minute later, they came to a clearing.

Hoffner was genuinely surprised by what they

found: at the clearing's center was the all-too-familiar
fencing, scaffolding, and power engine that had come
to define Berlin under construction. Two Schutzi patrolmen stood at either end of the small opening to the
pit. Beyond them was a wider gap in the trees, an avenue for a single wagon to make its way through with
supplies. More interesting were the three black Daimler convertible saloons that were parked at its edge;
their chauffeurs were each enjoying a nice smoke.

"At least your man is consistent," said Hermannsohn, as he led Hoffner toward the ladder.

Hoffner kept his eyes on the automobiles. The
chauffeurs' coats were not yet soaked through: they
had not been here long. "I had no idea they were
building this far out," he said.

"They're not," said Hermannsohn. He reached the
ladder and started down. Hoffner followed.

Had Hoffner been looking for consistency, the excavation site would have served perfectly. The climb
down brought him into a cavern that seemed almost
identical to the one he had seen two nights ago in
Senefelderplatz, police lamps and all. Even the group
of four men standing at the far end of the tunnel felt
eerily familiar. That, however, was where the similarities ended.

It was clear from their clothes which of the four belonged to the Daimlers above. Like their automobiles, three of the men were long and sleek: Russian
fur lined their coat collars; English wool creased the
cuffs of their trousers; and their boots had the shine

of Italian leather. War had done nothing to compromise their politically impudent tastes. For Hoffner, though, it was the fingernails—even at this distance and in this light—that made plain the stratum from which these men had descended: flat and pink, and never once having been cut by the men themselves. Hoffner knew exactly who they were: Prussian businessmen, and a far more dangerous breed than their military counterparts. War never thinned their numbers; inflexibility never stifled their success. They spoke to one another in hushed tones, a language that required fewer words, though greater subtlety of gesture, than the patter that flowed from the jaws of common Berlin. These were men who survived—and survived well—no matter who might be wielding the reins of government.

The fourth among them was Polpo **Direktor** Gerhard Weigland, in all his roundness. He looked completely out of place, nodding continuously while the others spoke. When he caught sight of Hoffner, he clumsily cleared his throat. The others turned.

"At last," said Weigland with no small amount of relief. "Gentlemen, this is the Kripo detective I've been telling you about." Hermannsohn remained in the shadows as Hoffner drew closer. "**Kommissar** Nikolai Hoffner, may I present the Directors of **Firma** Ganz-Neurath. Herren Träger, Schumpert, and Biberkopf"—Weigland motioned with his arm—"**Kommissar** Hoffner."

Hoffner had never been the recipient of three such

crisp bows of the head. **"Meine Herren,"** he said, with a lazy nod of his own.

"Herr **Kommissar.**" Träger spoke for all three.

Hoffner cut right to it. "I'm guessing this would be one of your sites, Herr **Direktor**?"

"Along with those in the Senefelder and Rosenthaler Platz, yes, Herr **Kommissar.** I believe you're familiar with them?"

"The projected U-Bahn stations," said Hoffner. "And dead women keep cropping up inside of them."

Träger appreciated Hoffner's bluntness. "Yes. They do."

"You're aware, **mein Herr**"—Hoffner spoke as if neither Polpo man was present—"that Herr **Direktor** Weigland and Herr **Kommissar** Hermannsohn are not with the Kripo?" He was enjoying seeing Weigland stand silently by.

"I am."

"So you consider this a political case?"

Träger took a moment. He was gauging Hoffner, not the case. "The Herr **Direktor** and I are old friends, **Kommissar.** He has been kind enough to extend the services of his department."

Hoffner had no reason to believe that fealty was the sole reason for the Polpo's continuing interest in his case. Weigland might have convinced Träger and his fellow Directors of that, but Hoffner knew otherwise. "I see."

"I'm not sure you do, **Kommissar.**" There was nothing combative in the tone: it was a simple statement of fact. Träger continued: "What I'm about to tell you cannot leave this site. Are we clear on that?" Hoffner nodded. "Good, because where we are standing doesn't actually exist." Träger saw the surprise in Hoffner's eyes. "Yes. We first moved ground here just over five years ago. December of 1913. This was going to be the grand terminus for a line leading all the way back into the heart of the city. By the end of the decade. That was the aim, **Kommissar.** That was what the Kaiser wanted."

"Forgive me, Herr **Direktor,**" said Hoffner, "but I don't recall reading anything about a proposed line this far out."

"Of course you don't. No one does. The Kaiser was afraid that if news got out that an underground train—not a tram, mind you, or an omnibus, not something in the daylight, **Kommissar**—but something like this was being designed to connect Berlin West to the scum of Kreuzberg and Prenzlauer— well then, a great many people might have had good reason to make the Kaiser's life as uncomfortable as possible. Safety, insulation—that sort of thing. What the Kaiser knew was that his Charlottenburg faithful simply needed time to see how wonderful his new underground trains were going to be. He knew they would eventually come begging for their own, so why not have the trains at the ready when they did?"

"But only as far as the zoo," said Hoffner.

"Yes."

"No reason for the Kaiser to press his luck by taking the trains into the heart of the West."

Träger was enjoying this more than he was letting on. "Something like that, **Kommissar.**"

"And then the war came."

"Exactly. We all discovered that the Kaiser was more interested in the world beyond Berlin than in her trains. Everything came to a stop, and the Number Two U-Bahn line happily drifted into oblivion. That is, of course, until last week. I can't say we enjoyed hearing that women were being killed and then moved to our sites, but until this morning, **Kommissar,** no one knew about that. Luckily, they still have no idea about the Rosenthaler station. That, I have no doubt, will come out soon enough. When it does, our firm will have to answer some rather unpleasant questions. That, however, does not concern us. Embarrassment fades. The sites in the middle of town threaten no one." He paused. "This one, however, does—especially given recent events. You understand what I am saying now, **Kommissar?**"

Hoffner did. The revolution had made an underground site this far west far more troubling. The image of a ten-thousand-strong mass moving down the Siegesallee in early January was still fresh in everyone's minds: how much more frightening would the prospect be of an endless stream of such filth making its way out from beneath the streets in the dead of night? At any moment, they could emerge like rats to run rampant. Herr **Direktor** Träger and his cohorts might be willing to stomach the hysteria produced by a maniac on the loose; they would not, however, tempt the kind of panic that could tear Berlin apart at the seams. "And you've managed to keep it hidden all this time?" said Hoffner.

"They think we've been building a holding pool for some enormous fish," said Träger. "Tell me, Herr **Kommissar,** does this look like a holding pool to you?"

Hoffner said, "May I see the body, Herr **Direktor?**"

"You understand our concern, **Kommissar.**"

Hoffner spoke candidly: "That the Polpo knows how to keep the press at bay, and that we in the Kripo—especially those of us who live in Kreuzberg—have never been quite as useful? Yes, Herr **Direktor.** I understand that quite well. May I see the body now?" Hoffner enjoyed the sudden tension that was radiating from Weigland.

Träger, on the other hand, seemed amused by the jab. "Then we're clear, **Kommissar?**"

"Absolutely, Herr **Direktor.**"

"Naturally, my colleagues and I are eager to assist you in any way we can."

"I'll keep that in mind, Herr **Direktor.**"

Träger waited. He continued to gaze at Hoffner as he spoke to Weigland. "You shouldn't have let this one get away to the Kripo, Gerhard. That's not like you."

Weigland tried a smile. "No, Herr **Direktor.**"

"**Any** help at all, **Kommissar.**"

Hoffner nodded.

Weigland waited to make sure that Träger was finished before motioning Hoffner in the direction of the body. "It's this way," he said as he led Hoffner to the end of the tunnel; the three directors started back for the ladder.

"Always have to be clever, don't you?" said Weigland under his breath.

Hoffner said dryly, "You have some very impressive friends, Herr **Direktor.** I'm very impressed."

"Just finish the case, Nikolai. Make all our lives easier."

The woman was lying facedown in the dirt, at most a day since she had been killed. Hoffner crouched down next to her and saw the drag marks leading up to the spot; he saw the ripped bodice of her dress, the age in her face, the diameter-cut design etched across her back, and he knew, with absolute certainty, that this was not the work of Paul Wouters.

Hoffner might have been guessing had he come to the conclusion from her clothes alone. The dress and shoes were too young for a woman her age, and there was nothing of the solitary nurse or seamstress in them. Hoffner drew out his pen and lifted up the back hem of her dress. There, as he had expected, he found the telltale sign just above her knee: a little purse was tied on tightly to her thigh. He weighed it in his hand. It was still filled with coins. This woman had been a prostitute, and far more than Wouters could ever have handled.

The clothes and occupation, however, were only

confirmation for what Hoffner saw in the design. He ran his thumb along the ruts. He pressed down onto the cold flaps of skin. They were jagged, their angle wrong. These had come at the hands of the second carver.

Hoffner glanced down the tunnel and felt Weigland's gaze over his shoulder. Someone had gone to great lengths to create the perfect setting. Everything was laid out exactly as it had been in Senefelderplatz two days ago, as it had been over the last month and a half at each of the other sites: the Münz Strasse roadwork, the sewer entrance at Oranienburger Strasse, the Prenzlauer underpass, the grotto off Bülowplatz. Everything perfect, thought Hoffner, and just a day after Herr Braun's revelations.

He was about to turn back to the body when something else stopped him. Hoffner continued to stare down the tunnel. He saw it in the lights hanging from above, in the placement and dimension of the wooden boards along the dirt walls. It was in the layout of the planks, in the steel beams, in the height of the ceiling, its contours—everything about the tunnel. He had been distracted, first by Träger, then by the victim. Now it was infinitely clear.

Hoffner jumped up and started toward the directors, who were almost to the ladder. He quickened his pace. "Herr **Direktor.**" He began to run as he yelled out, "One moment, please."

Träger stopped. He turned around. "Herr **Kommissar?**"

Hoffner drew up to him. He could hear Weigland trying to catch up from behind. "Herr **Direktor.**" Hoffner spoke with intensity. "This site. These sites. How are they designed?"

Träger seemed unsure of the question: "You mean how is the tunnel built, Herr **Kommissar?**"

"No, the designs, Herr **Direktor.** How are they configured?"

Träger glanced momentarily at his colleagues. "We have a model. What's called a Master Draft. It acts as a central plan. Why, **Kommissar?**"

"Each site, Herr **Direktor**? Each one is designed in the same way?" Hoffner felt the pieces falling into place.

"In theory, yes." Träger was still not sure what he was explaining. "One basic tunnel design. One basic track design. It makes for much more cost-effective production of materials, instruction to foremen, so forth and so on." Träger was finished answering questions. "Why is this of any importance?"

"So the Senefelder site would be almost identical to this one?"

"More or less, yes." Träger was growing impatient. "Why are you asking this?"

"Even something as involved as the Rosenthaler Platz station. An arcade. That, as well?"

Träger answered abruptly. "With a few modifications, yes. The same construction. **Kommissar,** what has this to do with your case?"

Images were flying through Hoffner's head. He saw

the frustration in Träger's eyes. "Thank you, Herr **Direktor.**" And without another word, Hoffner took hold of the ladder and headed up.

Out on the plaza, Sascha was holding court among a group of Schutzi patrolmen. Hoffner caught his breath as he made his way across.

"Excuse me, gentlemen," he said, still winded. The men moved off. "I need a favor, Sascha."

The boy's eyes widened, and not for the misuse of his name. This was the first time he had ever heard his father ask for help. "A favor?" Sascha said uncertainly.

"I need you to go back to the Alex. To my office."

"Now?" he said more eagerly.

"Yes, now. There might be a telephone call. If Herr Fichte shows up, you tell him I'll be there as soon as I can."

Sascha nodded through the instructions. "And if the telephone call does come in?"

Hoffner had not thought that far ahead. "Good point. You tell the gentleman that I'll call him back. A Herr Kepner. Take his number. He's to say nothing else on the line. You're to make sure of that. Nothing else. Do you understand?"

"Yes, Father."

"Excellent." Hoffner reached into his pocket and pulled out some coins. "You're doing me a tremendous good turn, Sascha." He handed the coins to the boy. "Whatever you don't use on the trams, you keep for yourself, all right?" He squeezed a hand on the boy's arm. "Thank you." He then headed off.

"You're welcome, Father." But Hoffner was already out of earshot.

Five and a half kilometers across town, a sign had replaced the Schutzi patrolman: ENTRY STRICTLY FORBIDDEN. Evidently it had worked just as well. The Rosenthaler site was completely deserted. Hoffner took hold of the ladder and headed down.

Fifteen rungs in, the cavern became pitch black. He reached the bottom, struck a match, and gently wedged it between two wooden slats.

From the little he could see, Hoffner managed to locate a stray pick lying on the ground. He took it and began to wrap his handkerchief around its wooden end. He then pulled out his flask and doused the cloth in liquor. Holding the pick by its chisel edge, he struck a second match and lit the improvised torch. At once the underbelly of the station opened up in wild shadows in front of him. The odor of feces was long gone, as was any indication that a family had been living down here until ten days ago. Even the boards for the feather beds had been restored to their rightful places.

Träger had been right: the space was virtually identical to the other designs Hoffner had seen in the past three days. The spokes that led out into the arcade were simply other single-line tunnels, those "modifications" Träger had mentioned. They, however, were not the reason Hoffner had come.

He set off down the central spoke and back toward the cavern in which they had first found the body. He deliberately kept his head down, his eyes on the dirt path. He needed to see it from Wouters's perspective—from the proper angle—and that was possible only from inside Mary Koop's cavern.

Hoffner made his way through various entryways and along several tunnels before he reached the opening and headed for the far wall. He found Koop's indented outline in the dirt: six weeks of occupation had kept it fresh. The little ridges of mud seemed to ripple in the torchlight. Even now, her frame looked as if it had been a part of the flooring, all along. Hoffner took in a deep breath and turned around.

"My God," he whispered.

The design was everywhere. Hoffner could have closed his eyes and traced its path without ever once taking a false step. He moved back to the cavern's opening and felt himself being pulled into the pattern, not in the way he had felt on the streets of Berlin—not in some conjured reimagining of the ruts and curves of a woman's back—but in the actual carvings themselves: he turned, and the tunnels turned with him; he reached out for a crossing line, and the wall gave way to an opening that cut across his path; he ran his hands along the walls and felt the cold ridges of human flesh. He had missed it before, too many distractions, too much to get in his way. Now he was a part of the diameter-cut.

The edge of the design ended abruptly at the entryway to a tunnel that led back to the central cavern. Beyond the entryway, two steel support beams were rooted into the walls directly across from each other. Hoffner stepped through the entryway and continued down the tunnel and away from the design, back toward the ladder. He found another set of steel beams perhaps twenty meters on. A third pair appeared, again at the same interval.

Here the construction was almost identical to those in the Senefelderplatz and the Tiergarten. Hoffner turned around and quickly headed back to where the Wouters design began.

He started in through the entryway: twenty meters, forty, sixty. There were no steel beams. The tunnels here were not a part of the Master Draft design. They had been added on, and quickly: too quickly to afford the arrival of the steel beams.

Someone had given Wouters a home, the only one capable of making him feel safe: sculpted in the perfect image of his own twisted mind.

Hoffner was suddenly struck by the word. This **was** perfect. This was Wouters's ideal. **Of course.** Another piece of the puzzle flashed into focus.

Hoffner found himself running back to the cavern, back through the opening, back to the outline of Mary Koop's body. He stepped inside the small ridges and drove the pick into a wooden beam above his head. The torch glowed freely as he pulled his note-book and pen from his coat pocket and began to sketch the diameter-cut, one last time. The lines danced on the page from the light, but it was there. He drew an **X** for the spot in which he was now standing, and stared down at the page.

The "optimal point of origin." He had found it. Mary Koop was his starting point. All he needed, now, was to understand the design's flow, and he would have Paul Wouters.

Hoffner missed the call by five minutes.

"He told you nothing?" he said as he pulled Wouters's original sketches from the filing cabinet. He was moving quickly. He needed to see Kepner.

"Nothing," said Sascha.

Fichte said, "The boy was remarkably convincing." They were both caught up in Hoffner's impatience.

"Good." Hoffner placed the sheets in his coat pocket and pointed to Fichte. "You and I have a man to see." He then pointed to Sascha. "And you need to get home." He saw the disappointment in Sascha's eyes. "I know, but even I can't stretch the rules that far." It was all he needed to say.

Out on the Alex, they found a taxi for Sascha, then one for themselves. Hoffner ran through an abbreviated version of the afternoon's events on the ride out. Any theories he might have come up with about the directors from Ganz-Neurath, or the reappearance of the second carver, or even the design of the Rosenthaler station, he kept to himself. Hoffner knew that Fichte would have had trouble processing the information. He was having trouble with it himself. Best, then, to concentrate on Wouters, for both of them.

Kepner showed no surprise when the two Kripomen appeared at his door: the brevity of the telephone conversation had told him to expect visitors. He brought them into his sitting room, where Herr Brenner was already waiting. Hoffner noticed several pages of sketches laid out across the coffee table. Kepner had worked quickly.

"The three on the far left," said Kepner. Hoffner was already scanning the sheets. Kepner told the men to sit. "I believe those are what you are looking for."

Fichte spoke up as Hoffner reached for the pages: "Perhaps Herr Brenner would care to wait in another room?"

Hoffner had to stifle the urge to upbraid Fichte in front of the two men. He took the sheets. "My apologies for my **Assistent,** Herr Kepner. He is—overly cautious."

Kepner waved Hoffner off. "Better that than the other, Herr **Kommissar.**"

Out of nowhere, Fichte rose to his feet. He snapped his head in a bow. "My apologies, Herr Brenner."

Hoffner thought the gesture a bit extravagant, but he knew it would keep Fichte quiet for the rest of the interview. Brenner nodded quietly.

"It's a Bruges design," said Kepner. "I have yet to

determine an optimal point of origin—" He stopped himself. "You understand what I mean by this?"

"Yes, **mein Herr.** The starting point."

"Exactly. These are only rough sketches. Anything more detailed will take more time."

It was odd, seeing the design drawn with such precision: a woman's flesh created its own imperfections; Hoffner's rendering had been "crude" by Kepner's estimation. This, however, showed the true artistry and intricacy of the pattern. Lines and turns Hoffner had never imagined filled the little sketches. He wondered if, perhaps in his haste, he had missed the design in one of Wouters's pages. It hardly mattered now; he was about to show Kepner where to find his optimal point of origin.

"What if you were to start here, **mein Herr**?" Hoffner placed the sheet on the table and pointed to the spot that approximated the point where Mary Koop's body had been found.

Kepner pulled out his glasses and leaned forward. He had not been anticipating suggestions from the Kripo. Fichte seemed equally surprised. "From where?" said Kepner. Hoffner kept his finger on the sheet as he turned it toward Kepner. Kepner gazed down with an uncertain stare until his eyes began to move through the sketch. "All right," he said absently. Without looking up, he pulled a short pencil from his pocket and, very slowly, began to create another replica, another possible route for the design. He continued to glance back at the other drawings he

had made, along with a list of calculations he had
written out on a separate page. "Is this a guess, Herr
Inspector?" he said as he continued to draw.

"An educated one, **mein Herr.**"

"Yes, I imagine it would be." Kepner hummed in a
monotone as he went back and forth between drawings and figures.

Progress was slow going—Kepner kept at it for
nearly twenty minutes—as Hoffner began to see
what he needed. If Mary Koop had been the optimal
point of origin in the station design, then the Rosenthaler Platz—Wouters's home—had to be the origin
in the city design. What else could it be? It was the
one site that Wouters had meant to keep pure, or at
least beyond the reach of death. The preserving
grease had said as much. That was why it was the deviation; and that was why it held the key.

Hoffner tried to reconstruct the path of Wouters's
victims in his head, taking Rosenthaler Platz as his
starting point: southeast to Münz Strasse, due west
to Oranienburger, northeast to Prenzlauer, west to
Bülowplatz, and finally north to Senefelderplatz. All
the while, he continued to watch Kepner. With each
turn of the pencil, Kepner was following the identical
shifts in direction. Hoffner rarely let himself give in to
moments like these. Now his heart began to accelerate
as Kepner drew closer and closer to the sixth knot.

"There," said Hoffner.

Kepner looked up, unsure why he was being asked
to stop. "It's hardly finished, Herr Inspector."

"That was your sixth knot?"

Kepner went back and counted. "The sixth that required a direction change. Yes."

Hoffner stared across at the design. "Southeast," he said to himself.

"Excuse me, Herr Inspector?"

Hoffner refocused. "Nothing, **mein Herr.**"

"'Nothing,'" Kepner echoed cautiously. "And this is what you needed?"

Hoffner thought for a moment. If Wouters—and not the second carver—was consistent, he would be depositing his next victim sometime in the next three or four days. There was little chance that a body was already waiting for them at that sixth knot. Even so, Hoffner had no intention of making a return trip to Charlottenburg. He told Kepner to continue.

When Kepner began to make the turn away from the eighth knot, Hoffner stopped him again. "There. That's fine, **mein Herr.**"

Kepner glanced up. "You're sure this time?" Hoffner nodded. "Good." Kepner dropped the pencil and sat back. He removed his glasses and rubbed two fingers on the bridge of his nose.

Hoffner picked up the pencil. "May I?" he said. Kepner looked over; he was still blinking the strain from his eyes. He nodded indifferently.

Hoffner took a clean sheet and began to sketch Kepner's design, but on a much larger scale: large enough to conform to the map that was hanging back on his office wall. Hoffner finished and slid the drawing across the table. Kepner had been watching him. He now leaned in to take a closer look.

"The dimensions are still accurate?" said Hoffner.

Kepner continued to examine the sheet: "As I said, Inspector, these drawings are rough. I would need other tools to make a perfectly accurate rendering, but this, I suspect, is as close as any I've constructed." He slid the sheet back to Hoffner. "I doubt this mesh would ever be configured on such a large scale, but then again, I doubt many Kripo officers would be as consumed by lace as you are." Kepner raised a hand to stop Hoffner from answering. "I don't want to know the details, Herr Inspector. I'm tired, that's all."

Herr Brenner stood. "You have everything you need?" Brenner might have been a cold fish, but he was a cold fish devoted to his father-in-law.

"Yes, **mein Herr.**" Hoffner began to shuffle the papers together. "May I take these?" He continued to stack them.

"You **are** taking them, Inspector," said Kepner with the hint of a smile. He had sunk back comfortably into his chair. "What would I do with them, anyway? Just make sure you catch him before he comes too far west, that's all." Hoffner stopped in mid-shuffle. Kepner enjoyed Hoffner's momentary surprise. "There's no stricture about **reading** before sundown, Inspector."

Kepner had known exactly what he was doing, all along. He had simply managed to feel safer not knowing the details.

"I'll try, **mein Herr.**"

"Good," said Kepner. "There is one favor I have to ask of you."

Hoffner finished stacking. "Of course, **mein Herr.**"

"This aspect of your case. The lace. I'm hoping it can remain out of your reports. Lace, you see, is primarily . . ." Kepner hesitated. "That is to say, the quality of this particular lace—"

"Lace is a Jewish concern, Inspector," Brenner cut in bluntly. "In Berlin, trade and production of this type are run primarily by Jews."

"I see," said Hoffner.

Kepner deferred to his son-in-law. Brenner continued: "If it should get out, if the newspapers should decide to print that we were in any way associated with this case—that this man was using our designs as some kind of inspiration for his madness—you understand our concern."

Fichte piped in, "A loss of business, **mein Herr?**"

The room fell silent. Brenner had long ago learned to swallow his rage. When he answered, he spoke quietly, deliberately. "No, Herr Detective. Another excuse to blame the Jews. Not that the revolution hasn't delivered on that front."

Before Fichte could open his mouth again, Hoffner said, "Of course, **mein Herr.**" He stood, the pages in hand. "None of this needs to come out. The reading public never goes in much for the details, anyway. You have my word."

Brenner remained silent. He glanced at Kepner.

The older man nodded. Brenner then turned back to Hoffner. "I'll show you out."

Forty minutes later, Hoffner stood in his office, slowly penciling the last lines of the design onto the map. He made sure that the lengths of each of the segments conformed to the basic proportions of Kepner's original, but it was clear even before he had made it halfway to the sixth knot where Wouters would be bringing his next victim. Hoffner stared at the spot. Somehow he had known all along.

The **Ochsenhof.**

What could be better, he thought. Two city blocks filled with the worst human refuse that Berlin had to offer. Murder was routine in the "cattle yard," not that Wouters could have known that. The man was simply following his design. That it was now leading him to a place that, in essence, lay beyond the reach of the Kripo was simply his good fortune.

Hoffner stared a moment longer, then began to remove the pins.

Fichte said, "How did you know where to tell Kepner to start?"

Hoffner continued with the pins. "That's an excellent question, Hans." Hoffner went to work on the tacks that were holding the map to the wall. "Give me a hand here." Fichte stepped over and the two brought the map to the desk. Very delicately, Hoffner began to fold it.

Fichte said, "We don't need the map anymore?"

Hoffner concentrated on the folds. "We don't need anyone else seeing what's been written on it."

Fichte understood. "So how did you know?" he said.

Hoffner made the final crease. "The cavern inside the Rosenthaler station," he said. He felt strange placing the map inside the filing cabinet rather than in a folder for the archive clerk. Maps came down only when cases were complete. This case, however, was changing the rules as it went.

"What about it?" said Fichte.

Hoffner locked the drawer. "We'll have plenty of time to discuss it. Right now, I need ten minutes. Then meet me downstairs, and bring whatever's going to keep you the driest."

A LAST STROKE OF THE KNIFE

Wouters was making them wait.

Three days camped outside the **Ochsenhof** had taken its toll. Fichte complained of everything—cramp, filth, exhaustion; Hoffner was feeling it in his lower back and legs. He said nothing. He knew that Mulackstrasse was never kind. At best, it only goaded the rain. Tonight the wind was whipping up. Even the most secure nooks and alleyways had fallen prey to the biting damp and chill.

Three a.m., and they were holed up in a recessed stairwell directly across from the tenement. Six or so of its entrances were in clear sight. Hoffner had found a bit of a muslin tarp that, along with a flask of brandy, was helping to keep them warm. It was a relative term. And, of course, there was the price to pay for the added heat: three minutes each morning at a nearby washbasin and toilet were doing little to dull the stink. Fichte was a large man. He was giving off as good as he got.

Stench and cold aside, Hoffner was grateful to be out on the streets: it meant that he was away from the Alex. The last few days had brought the "chisel murders" to a fever pitch. Any reason to avoid those unending requests for interviews and the like suited him just fine: Sunday, the Tiergarten body had graced the front pages, although Weigland's pull had managed to keep any mention of Ganz-Neurath, or U-Bahn 2, from the public; Monday, Berlin had met the Rosenthaler Platz victim, though she remained unidentified, as Hoffner and Fichte were the only ones, thus far, to have given Mary Koop a name; and today, the list of the remaining victims—dating all the way back to the very first, in Münz Strasse—had appeared in Kvatsch's **BZ** afternoon article.

The Kripo leak had been working double time to make sure that any momentum lost to the revolution was now being paid back, and with interest. Anxiety over a pair of murders that had occurred in the last ten days was gaining a kind of retrospective boost of panic: the murders stretched back over months, and Berliners felt compelled to make up for lost time. The first accusations of Kripo incompetence were beginning to surface.

Hoffner stretched his neck. "I'm going to check on the boys."

Hoffner had known from the start that the tenement was too large to manage from one lookout point, and so he had turned to little Franz. There was no one else at the Alex he could trust: word would get out, and Wouters would slip through their hands. Hoffner had told Präger that he was getting close; Präger might have been feeling the pressure himself, but he was smart enough to know that Hoffner worked best on his own terms.

Franz had recruited a group of teenaged **Schlägers,** street thugs who blended in perfectly with their surroundings: probably one full set of teeth among them. They needed the money; Hoffner needed the manpower. He had shown each of them the photograph of Wouters—the one he had pulled from van Acker's file—although a description of Wouters's diminutive size, and the fact that he would be dragging a trunk, had been far more helpful.

The nights had been easiest for Hoffner. Fichte preferred the days, what with the chance to stretch his legs, move through the crowds, get something hot to eat. All that changed after dark. In the silence, Fichte would drift off and leave Hoffner alone to piece together the strands that lay beyond Wouters: the second carver, the military connection to the Ascomycete 4, the "additions" to the Rosenthaler station, even the choice of the Tiergarten site as a threat to the city's tenuous social order. They all led him back to one name: Luxemburg. Naturally, the **why** still eluded him. In a strange way, it was Wouters who now seemed more and more out of place. Rosa, however, remained suspended above it all, the world unwilling to "let her be," even in death. Hoffner had kept the little book with him. He had read through it from time to time as Fichte slept. It held no answers, but there was something quieting in it.

He pulled back the tarp. "I'll be back in ten minutes," he said. The sudden slap of chilled air forced a muted grunt from Fichte. Hoffner stood. "Try to stay awake this time."

Cramp in his leg forced Hoffner to take the steps one at a time. Keeping to the shadows, he peered out in both directions. The street was empty; even the prostitutes were staying in. Hoffner pulled down the brim of his hat and headed out into the lamplight.

He played the drunk during his rounds. The shuffling feet, the bobbing head, the single hand held out along the shop fronts for balance, were not an uncommon sight this time of night on Mulackstrasse. In fact, on his last circuit, Hoffner had nearly bumped into the genuine article: a weaving body had appeared from a side street, doing its best against the rain and wind and its own inebriation. One of the boys had actually mistaken him for Hoffner and popped out. The boy had been too late to see his mistake. Caught, he had done what any boy in his position would have done: he had tossed the man for everything he was worth. Hoffner had pretended to retch during the performance. The man, to his credit, had suffered it all with a drunk's affability. He had even managed a pat on Hoffner's back—"It'll pass, my friend, it'll pass"—as he continued down the street. This time, Hoffner walked alone.

Halfway down the block, he propped himself up against a wall as if he were catching his breath. "Anything?" he said quietly.

The boy had learned his lesson; he remained within the shadows. "Not a peep, Eminence."

This one had a sense of humor. "No one to clean out this time?"

"Not my cock-up."

"No choice, was it?"

"That's right."

Hoffner bent over as if he were about to retch. "But you'll be splitting the proceeds with your mates, yes?"

"Splitting the what?"

"Just make sure Franz gets his cut."

There was a silence. "Yeah. All right."

Hoffner spat a few times, then moved off. He turned the corner.

The western side of the building was no less desolate. Another six or so entrances waited silently under the lamplight. Hoffner knew that they had been lucky thus far. Lamps had a tendency to burn out at the oddest of times in this part of town. Mulackstrasse in shadow was one thing; in total darkness it was suicide.

He checked in with the other boys, two more lookouts with nothing to report. He dropped a pack of cigarettes in the shadows at each of the posts: something to keep the boys awake. He then headed back, the sound of his own footfalls a solitary echo on the street. He was tired and wet. Maybe he could take a nap, let Hans earn his pay? Not much chance of that.

It was only when he reached the stairwell that Hoffner heard the scurrying of feet from behind him. He turned to see little Franz running up. The boy's expression told him everything.

With newfound energy, Hoffner whispered into the shadows. "We've got him, Hans." He waited to hear the tarp being pulled back before running out to meet the boy. Hoffner no longer felt the damp.

"Where?" he said as the two met in the middle of the street.

Franz spoke through gasps. "Just now." He motioned back to the corner. "The fourth entryway."

"Alone?"

The boy nodded.

"With a trunk?"

Again, the boy nodded.

Hoffner had heard nothing, no scraping of metal on cobblestone. How had Wouters maneuvered the trunk? There was no time to worry about that now. Without another word, Hoffner raced off. He was at the corner—Fichte and Franz chasing after him— when he saw five or six of the boys gathered at one of the far entryways, each of them pressed up against the door. Hoffner ran up to them.

"He's gone down to the pit rooms," whispered one of the boys. "Heard him go down. We can take him, if you want."

Hoffner pulled his Mauser one-four-eight from his belt and tried to catch his breath. The pistol had been with him since 1912. He had fired it twice in the last seven years, once to test the action on the trigger, the other to salute König in a drunken farewell on some Tyrolean hillside. The lettering on the gripstrap marking—**KripoDZ. 148**—still shone like new.

At the sight of the gun, the boys edged back. Even Fichte was momentarily unnerved. Hoffner said, "No one takes him." His breathing was still heavy. "You see him leave the building, you start shouting. You don't go near him, you keep him in sight. Understood?" Fichte nodded along with the boys. "Get out your pistol, Hans." Fichte did as he was told. Hoffner then pulled open the door and headed in.

The short corridor was lit like an interrogation room: stark light bounced off cracked walls and tile, and the smell of cabbage filled the air, a sourness seasoned with urine. At the stairs, Hoffner stopped. Somewhere above, someone was taking a nice beating; higher still, an old woman laughed or cried: even at this hour, the sounds of muted desperation trickled down. Hoffner put up a hand. Fichte stayed where he was, and Hoffner took two steps down to listen.

He heard it almost at once, its incongruity drawing him farther down the steps: a faint if high-pitched squeal was repeating in perfect intervals as it grew more distant. It was too even, too precise, and therefore completely out of place inside these walls. Hoffner suddenly realized what it was. He was following the rotation of a rusted wheel. An image popped into his head. The trunk was being moved on a porter's wheel, the sort to be found at any train station. The marks at the sites had not been formed by the dragging of a trunk, but by a wheel pressing down into the mud. The weight of the bodies had simply flattened and thus widened its imprint.

Hoffner continued to listen. This was the sound of Wouters transporting his final victim. With a quick wave for Fichte, Hoffner started down.

The lower reaches of the tenement spread out in a warren of narrow corridors, bare bulbs dotting the walls, only here they were placed too far apart to create continuous light. Checkerboard patches led off in all directions. The infamous pit rooms—where pipes and coal stoves bristled with heat, and where only the most wretched took refuge—appeared at equally disjointed intervals. Half of the doors had gone missing for firewood. The rest clung to rotting hinges, or leaned out menacingly into the corridors, but they did nothing to keep the swelter from infiltrating. The air here was oppressive. Hoffner felt the perspiration forming in the creases of his neck as he heard Fichte begin to labor for breath.

The squeal called to them from one of the corridors, and Hoffner, his pistol held chest-high, moved toward it at an even pace, following the twists and turns, just fast enough to draw them closer to their man. He could feel Wouters's presence, the sound of his footsteps slowly growing more distinct. Wouters was moving rhythmically, easily, uninterrupted—no idea that he was being followed. For the second time in a matter of days, Hoffner felt the sharp pull of anticipation.

And then, without warning, Fichte let go with a choked gasp. Dumbstruck, Hoffner turned to silence him, but it was too late. Fichte was doing all he could to stifle the seizing in his lungs. It was as if his throat had collapsed in on itself.

Hoffner turned back to the empty corridor. The squeal had stopped. Silence, and then a sudden crash and the sound of darting feet. Hoffner looked back at Fichte. The boy was on his knee, sucking desperately on his inhaler.

Hoffner ran, forcing himself to move faster, his hand sliding along the chipped walls as he propelled himself forward. Wouters's steps were faint, but they were there. Taking a turn, Hoffner nearly fell over the abandoned trunk. It lay on its side and was blocking most of the corridor. For an instant he imagined what lay inside; putting it from his mind, he clambered over the wood and metal—still slick from the rain—and continued after Wouters.

Whether it was the nights out in the cold, or the sudden heat, or simply his own incapacity, Hoffner felt himself giving way. He strained for breath. He felt the stress in his legs and chest, his throat ready to explode, and still he pushed himself on. Wouters was disappearing into the endless corridors. He was slipping out of Hoffner's hands, and all Hoffner felt was his own desperate failure. All of this would start again. **All of it.** And there would be nothing he could do to stop it.

A single shot rang out, and Hoffner froze. He planted his hand against the wall for support, and tried to quiet his breathing long enough to locate its origin. A second shot was fired, and Hoffner began to move. The echo hung in the air and led him first left, then along a corridor until he saw a shadow move beyond the open door of one of the pit rooms. He tightened his grip on his pistol, drew up to the door and, bracing himself, shouldered his way in.

What he saw was mind-numbing. A small body lay perfectly still in the half-light. Hoffner recognized it at once. It was Wouters. He was dead. A single bullet had entered his left thigh. Another had cut deep into his chest. He looked remarkably peaceful.

A board moved from across the room and, no less dazed, Hoffner looked over to see **Kommissar** Ernst Tamshik crouched down, rummaging through scrap wood.

"No body," said Tamshik as he got to his feet.

Hoffner was still catching his breath as he tried to make sense of what he was seeing. "What are you doing here?" he said in a near whisper.

"He's not much to look at, is he?" This was a different Tamshik, one intent on police work. The bullying and sneers were nowhere in sight. "All this trouble for so little a man. Remarkable."

Hoffner finally caught his breath. "What are you doing here?" he repeated.

Tamshik continued to scan the room. "Looking for a body, **Kommissar.**"

Hoffner tried to focus. Instinctively he pointed back to the corridor, toward the trunk, but stopped himself. "How did you know he would be coming down here?"

Tamshik peered over at Hoffner. "You didn't think you'd be the only one to find a way inside his head, did you **Kommissar?**" The smirk returned. "Typical Kripo arrogance."

Hoffner's mind was spinning. A minute ago, he had thought he had lost Wouters. Now he had the man's carcass in front of him, compliments of the Polpo. Hoffner was hard-pressed to say which was making him feel worse.

"You shot him?" said Hoffner, still trying to clear his mind.

"Yes."

"Why?"

Tamshik holstered his gun. "Because I thought he would get away, **Kommissar.**"

Again, Hoffner glanced out at the corridor. That made no sense. He thought out loud. "I was behind him. You must have been directly in his path. There was nowhere else for him to go. Except in here." Hoffner again looked across at Tamshik. It suddenly struck him that Tamshik had shown no surprise at his own appearance. It was as if Tamshik had been waiting for him. Things suddenly began to come clearer. Hoffner's mind slowed. "Unless you thought he'd overpower you, **Kommissar**?" Hoffner's tone sharpened. "A man of his tremendous size. Is that it?"

Tamshik stared blankly. "He was a maniac. I didn't know what to expect."

Hoffner returned the stare. "And the shot to his thigh wasn't enough to stop him?"

"No. It wasn't."

"I find that hard to believe."

"Believe what you like."

"You were waiting for him, weren't you?"

For just an instant, Tamshik's eyes narrowed. "The man's dead, **Kommissar.** You have a strange way of thanking someone for doing your job."

Hoffner felt a sudden urge to step over and crack a fist across Tamshik's face. Luckily, Fichte poked his head through the doorway at that moment. Hoffner could hear the wheezing in his breath.

"I heard shots," said Fichte, catching his breath. He noticed Wouters. "Oh, God." Fichte laughed nervously through his gasps. "You got him. Good Christ. We got him."

"Yes, Herr **Assistent,**" said Tamshik from the far corner. "You got him."

It was only then that Fichte saw Tamshik. He nearly jumped. "**Kommissar** Tamshik? What . . . ?" Fichte looked to Hoffner for an answer.

"Your **Kriminal-Kommissar** has gotten his man," said Tamshik with mock admiration.

This only seemed to rattle Fichte further. "Yes," he said uneasily.

Hoffner kept his eyes on Tamshik. "I shot no one, Hans."

Tamshik said, "It's a proud day for the Kripo, gentlemen."

"'A proud. . . ?'" murmured Fichte. Again, he looked to Hoffner. "I don't understand."

Tamshik spoke to Hoffner: "Think of all the money and time saved, **Kommissar.** No need for a trial. No reason to parade out your madman. And all because of your heroics. Well done."

Hoffner had no idea what game Tamshik was playing. "Who were you pulling the trigger for, Tamshik? You're not this clever. Who sent you down here?"

"Don't worry, **Kommissar,**" said Tamshik with his accustomed venom. "This one's all yours. No one needs to know about all the help you've gotten from the Polpo."

Hoffner had heard enough. He started for Tamshik, but Fichte, still not knowing what was going on, had the good sense to hold him back. "He's not worth the trouble, Nikolai," he said in a whisper.

Slowly, Tamshik drew up to them. "Your case is closed, Herr **Kommissar.** Congratulations." Hoffner managed to pull his arm free. "I wouldn't do that," said Tamshik coldly. He stared a moment longer, then nodded to Fichte. **"Assistent."** Tamshik then stepped over Wouters's body and headed out into the corridor.

When the footsteps had faded, Fichte released

Hoffner's arm. "What the hell just happened in here?" he said.

Hoffner remained motionless. He stared down at the body. Wouters had nothing to tell them, not now. Tamshik had made certain of that. Slowly Hoffner walked to the back of the room and slammed his hand into the wall.

"It is a bit odd."

Kriminaldirektor Präger sat uncomfortably behind his desk. His skin was still pasty from sleep. Polpo **Direktor** Weigland sat across from him. It had been nearly twenty years since either of them had seen the Alex this early in the morning.

"I don't know what he's so upset about," said Weigland. He turned to Hoffner, who was standing at the window. "Nikolai. The case is finished. Tomorrow the papers will call you a hero."

Hoffner continued to stare out. The dull gray of pre-dawn hung over the square like an unwashed towel: it only reminded him of how tired he was. "I'll ask one more time, Herr **Direktor,**" said Hoffner as he turned to the two men at the desk. "What was **Kommissar** Tamshik doing in the pit rooms of the **Ochsenhof?**"

Weigland threw up his hands as he looked across at Präger. "There's no convincing him, Edmund. This is a gift horse. I don't see what the problem is."

"I understand," said Präger: for the first time he was actually holding his own with the Polpo. "**Kommissar**

Tamshik obviously had his reasons. We're not interested in Polpo business. But you can understand the **Kriminal-Kommissar**'s concern." Präger glanced over at Tamshik. The man stood unnervingly still. Fichte, by comparison, looked almost pitiful by his side. "That said," Präger continued, "I think we can all take satisfaction in having eliminated this problem."

Hoffner started in. "That's not the point, Herr **Kriminaldirektor**—"

Präger put up a hand. "The bodies are here. They'll be here tomorrow. Whatever else can wait until then."

Hoffner disagreed. "I'm not sure that's true."

"You're tired, **Kriminal-Kommissar.**" Präger was telling him, not consoling him. "You should take tomorrow at home. With your family. Take two days. The rest can wait."

Hoffner stared across at Präger. There were any number of things he thought to say, but his mind was a jumble. Exhaustion was getting the better of him. More than that, he knew Präger was right. This wasn't the time, nor the audience to press things any further. "Fine, Herr **Kriminaldirektor.**"

"Good," said Weigland, his relief all too apparent.

Hoffner said, "Just so long as no one touches anything. Nothing happens until I see the bodies."

"Of course," Weigland said eagerly. "Naturally." He wanted this done. "Everything stays exactly as it is tonight. No question."

Hoffner ignored Weigland. He kept his eyes on Präger.

Präger said, "It's still your case, **Kriminal-Kommissar.** Nothing gets touched."

Hoffner nodded. He then looked over at Tamshik. "And I want that man nowhere near my evidence."

Tamshik stared straight ahead as if he had heard nothing. Weigland spun back to Präger.

"Edmund, really!" Weigland's exasperation had returned. "That tone was completely uncalled for."

Hoffner said, "I think we're beyond protocol, Herr **Direktor.**"

"We're done here, Nikolai," said Präger, ending any further discussion. Hoffner had overstepped the line. "You did well with this. Take your two days." He glanced over at Fichte. "You as well, Herr **Kriminal-Assistent.**"

Fichte perked up. He blinked quickly several times. "Thank you, Herr **Kriminaldirektor.**"

There was nothing else to be said. The room became uncomfortably still. Finally, Hoffner picked up his hat and started toward the door. Fichte moved to join him, but Hoffner continued past him. "You get home safe, Hans, all right?" Fichte had hoped for more. Hoffner, however, was not in the mood.

Out on the Alex, Hoffner pulled up his coat collar. The air felt somehow kinder; it was of little comfort. Wouters's eyes were still with him, their silence like a last stroke of the knife.

Hoffner peered up into the first light. Small specks of snow were swirling overhead. Odd, he thought. By nightfall, Berlin would be under a blanket of white.

PART TWO

FOUR

≈ K ≈

They made them into heroes.

The announcement came on Friday, the day of Hoffner's scheduled return. Rumors had been circulating, but nothing had been confirmed. "You don't rush these things, Nikolai." Präger was famous for his timing. "You have to let the city set the tone." Evidently the city wanted Friday. And so, with the hysteria at just the right pitch, Präger presented Berlin with her new saviors.

From that moment on, Hoffner and Fichte lived on the front pages of every daily in town. Photographs of Wouters's body—his chest laid bare, the tiny charred hole where the bullet had entered—sat side by side with images of a beaming Fichte and a less than enthusiastic Hoffner. Präger insisted: Hoffner would be a good little soldier. The last of the interviews dragged on into Saturday.

What was worse was how the papers were harping on the fact that Wouters was a Belgian: still more reason to cheer. Some speculated that he might have been an agent sent in during the last days of the war to create mayhem in the capital. Others took it as a sign that German savvy—if not for the incompetence of the generals—would surely have gained the ultimate victory in the war. Even Kvatsch managed to write something mildly favorable. To a paper, though, all agreed on one incontrovertible truth: that Hoffner and Fichte now stood for all that was right with Germany.

Naturally, the directors of Ganz-Neurath invited them to a special luncheon on the following Monday to thank them for their outstanding work. Chancellor Ebert himself put in an appearance to express his faith in the fine men of the Kripo. Ebert, too, needed to align himself with what was right with Germany.

But the crowning moment came on the Tuesday— one week after all the excitement at the **Ochsenhof**— when the Kripo whipped together an elaborate promotion ceremony outside the old Royal Palace: Fichte to detective sergeant, Hoffner to chief inspector. The Alex was still a shambles and hardly the image that Präger wanted to convey. More photographs, more beaming from Fichte, and all the while, the Polpo remained curiously silent.

Martha, on the other hand, was enjoying it all immensely. The neighbors down the hall had sent over a small bottle of kirsch—dreadful stuff, and not even a premium brand—in congratulations. All that business about the flat had been a misunderstanding. No reason to let it spoil things. An invitation to tea was extended. "Certainly," Martha said. "When my husband can find time in his very important schedule, Frau Rimmler. We should be delighted."

Sascha, too, was reaping the benefits. Herr Zessner, his physics teacher, had cited Sascha as "a model for us all" in front of the entire class. Herr Zessner lived alone with his mother, and had been hearing the poor woman's torments over the "chisel murders" ever since the news had broken: she was the same age as the rest; she spent time outside the flat. "You know the boy's father, Heinrich. Have him do something!" Detective Hoffner had saved Herr Zessner from an early mental breakdown. Young Hoffner would therefore be finishing the year at the top of his class. Good feelings all around, Sascha even managed to put in an appearance at the air show at Johannisthal: a few cold moments, to be sure, but, all in all, the thaw was progressing quite nicely.

And Georgi—the dailies spread out on the kitchen floor—was making a habit of pointing out his own last name in the papers every morning. "Hoffner. Like Georgi Hoffner." He cut out each one—not the articles, just the names—and kept them in a cigar box under his bed. If Hoffner was being kept from the office, at least Kreuzberg was radiating a very comforting mood.

When Hoffner did finally get back to the Alex in that first week of February, Präger was prepared for him. Cases Fichte would have handled on his own as a detective sergeant suddenly required Hoffner's expertise. Pimps and whores, bar-front brawls, low-lifes ending up dead, and Hoffner would be called in to clean up the obvious mess. It was a week into it before he began to wonder whether Präger's intention was to keep him in the papers or out of the office.

Through it all, the snow returned—again and again—as if it knew that Berlin had something to hide. A hint of grime would peek up through the streets, and a new dusting of white would quickly settle from above. Better not to know what lay beneath. It was a popular attitude.

All that began to change on the twelfth when Leo Jogiches—from somewhere in hiding—printed his account of Rosa's death. The article had appeared in the communist **Die Rote Fahne** almost a week ago. The rest of the city's papers had failed to pick up on it. Hoffner had seen it for the first time only this morning.

It was a startling tale of Liebknecht and Luxemburg on the run. Hunted down by members of the Cavalry Guards Rifle Division—those charming soldiers who had taken such joy in beating students to death in the last days of the revolution—Karl and Rosa had been snatched from an apartment on the outskirts of town and then brought to the Hotel Eden near the zoo, where a Captain Pabst and a rifleman named Runge had seen to the killings. Jogiches had even included a photograph of the drinking bout at which the murderers had celebrated the deaths. It was all very dramatic, very shocking, and, as Hoffner well knew, not even half the story.

Not surprisingly, the government was showing little interest. They preferred the original reports from mid-January: that an angry mob had ambushed the Reds and killed them in a wild frenzy, a tragedy of the revolution, to be sure, but not all that much of a tragedy. "The proper expiation for the bloodbath that they unleashed," the **Tägliche Rundschau** had written at the time. "The day of judgment on Luxemburg and Liebknecht is over." Ebert and his cronies were more than willing to agree. They had no intention of dredging it all up again. There was mention of a possible trial, but no one was all that keen to pursue it, especially as the accusations were coming from the people who had started all the trouble in the first place.

Meanwhile, the Polpo—still silent, and still with Rosa's body somewhere up on the fourth floor—continued to say nothing. They seemed happy enough to let it all fall at the feet of Pabst and Runge. The Wouters case was closed. Weigland even made a special trip down to the third floor to remind Präger of proper jurisdiction. Luxemburg was a Polpo matter. The men of IA would handle it as they saw fit.

Präger had nodded. He liked a victory—along with

the good press—as much as anyone else. However, he also liked his victories clean. Two minutes after Weigland had scuttled back upstairs, Präger called Hoffner into his office.

The photograph that Jogiches had printed now stared up at Hoffner from his desk. It was a dreary affair, twenty or so men in gray uniform, another few in black, one little barmaid in white standing at the center with a tray in her hands. Hoffner had been studying the faces for almost an hour. It was the first such block of time he had been able to devote to the case in almost three weeks.

They had let him see the bodies on that first Friday after he returned to work: the woman inside the trunk had been no different from the others, another lonely seamstress with no family to claim her; Wouters had not been much of a surprise, either, except for his hands. Even lifeless, they had shown remarkable strength, especially on so small a man.

More than that, however, was no longer available. The bodies were in the ground; Weigland had made sure of that during Hoffner's extended absence. It seemed only appropriate given the speed with which the case had resolved itself: Tamshik's single shot, all discussion closed. Why bother with the evidence?

Hoffner's eyes continued to drift to the girl in the photo. It was clear that she had been persuaded to pose with the men: she seemed uncomfortable in their presence. The soldiers, however, needed a symbol for what they had been fighting to protect. The entire group stared grimly into the lens, except for one fellow who was seated at the front. He was sporting a tight smirk, with one hand in his coat pocket, the other around a thick cigar. His had been a job well done.

Rifleman Otto Runge and his cohorts looked to be the perfect dupes, posed over a few buckets of beer, and without a spark of intelligence among them. Runge himself had the air of a halfwit, with his drooping moustache and narrow eyes: not difficult to see that the best these men could have managed was a quick crack on the head, or a bullet to the ribs. Hoffner had no doubt that they had killed Liebknecht and Luxemburg, but the etchings on Rosa's back—and her connection to Wouters and beyond— were clearly far too involved for their simple minds. Like Tamshik in the pit rooms, someone had set them on their task. The question remained: Who?

And yet, the more Hoffner studied the photo, the more he realized that Jogiches was trying to tell him something with it. There was a certain arrogance in the assumption, but Hoffner had not been wasting all of his time in recent weeks. Stealing a few minutes here and there, he had begun to dig deeper into Herr Jogiches's past. Last Thursday, while rummaging through it, Hoffner had stumbled upon his K.

Naturally, it was Rosa who had led the way: her 1912 journal had held the key. Several of the entries detailed a period during which Jogiches had been living under an assumed name somewhere in the city. Rosa, of course, had never given up the name—Hoffner had admired her discretion—but she had let slip the address of a hotel in two of the passages. Hoffner had paid a visit to the hotel: what he had unearthed was a story worthy of a Rossini libretto.

Years ago—long before her move to Berlin—Rosa had told her family that she and Jogiches had been married in Switzerland. It wasn't true, and by 1911, when the two were no longer together, it had become something of an embarrassment whenever members of Rosa's family came to visit. While she had been willing to concoct a sham marriage so as to save face, she was not so eager to present her family with a sham divorce. To maintain the fiction, Jogiches had agreed to leave his name on the lease and to rent a room at the Hotel Schlosspark under an assumed name. Unfortunately, Jogiches's tailor had never been fully apprised of the arrangement. Hoffner had discovered a receipt—still in the hotel files—for a pair of trousers that had been delivered to the room of a K. Kryzysztalowicz, on the fourteenth of March, 1912. The name on the receipt, Leo Jogiches.

Further proof of the alias came from a much earlier entry devoted to Leo's brother, Osip, that dated from 1901. According to that journal, Osip had been dying of tuberculosis since the early nineties and, in the last weeks of his life, was advised by his doctors to take a trip to Algiers for his health; naturally, Leo had insisted that he join him. Hoffner had checked the ship's manifest and, once again, had found meticulous German paperwork up to the task. Osip had indeed sailed for Algiers. Oddly enough, Leo had not accompanied him. A Dr. Krystalowicz, however, had.

Spelling variations aside, Jogiches was his K.

More than just the name, though, Hoffner's digging had begun to lay bare the man himself, one obsessed with hidden meanings and ciphers. Jogiches inhabited a world built on secrecy and intrigue, and, more often than not, used them as tools to test those closest to him. Not surprisingly, Rosa had been his favorite target over the years. Resilient as she was, however, his incessant goading had ultimately torn them apart.

Why, then, thought Hoffner, would Jogiches treat the recent article and photograph any differently? They were simply the latest pieces in his puzzle: the note to return to her flat; the papers waiting there; the creased letters that had led Hoffner to Jogiches in the first place? Presumptuous as it might sound, Hoffner believed that Jogiches was now testing him, that he had been testing him all along. Jogiches's inclusion of the photograph—hardly a damning piece of evidence on its own—could only mean that he knew far more than he was willing to print, or that he thought safe to expose. He was simply waiting for Hoffner to contact him. At least that was the theory.

Unfortunately, Hoffner was now alone in his speculations, for while he had been busy unpacking Jogiches, Fichte had been occupied elsewhere.

Most nights, Fichte could be found at the White

Mouse, drinking too much and allowing himself to be photographed with any number of popular faces. Last week, the **BZ** had included the young detective sergeant in a candid photo with three of the Haller Revue girls, lots of thighs and teeth, along with a leering grin from Fichte. Fichte had become the new image of the Kripo, vibrant and charming—it was a Fichte whom Hoffner had never known—and Präger seemed only too happy to encourage it. Fichte was now irresistible to the night-crawl crowd. In fact, Fichte could hardly resist himself. Even his knock on Hoffner's door had grown in stature. Where before, several light taps had signaled his approach, now two rapid-fire raps announced his presence.

Hoffner looked up from behind his desk. Fichte had been given an office of his own down the hall, but the files remained here.

"We're done with this one, yes?" said Fichte. He placed the pages on Hoffner's desk: a drunk had stabbed his wife and then confessed; it was hardly a case. Fichte already had his hat in hand.

"New suit?" said Hoffner.

Fichte glanced down at the jacket. One of the shops along Tauentzienstrasse had given it to him as a gift, the least they could do for a hero of the Kripo. Fichte smiled. He had been working on this particular smile for a week now. "Sure. You should get one for yourself. They want to know when you're coming in."

Hoffner took the sheets and moved over to the filing cabinet. "You don't think about it anymore, do you?"

Fichte had trained himself to look mildly amused whenever his old confusion reared its head. A furrowed brow was hardly in keeping with his new image. "Think about what?" he said.

"I sent a wire to van Acker." Hoffner flipped through the files. "See if they've come up with anything on that body. Wouters's replacement."

Fichte stayed with amusement. "The man's dead, Nikolai. That usually means a case is closed."

Hoffner replaced the file and closed the drawer. "I'll keep that in mind."

"Präger's satisfied. Why shouldn't I be?"

Hoffner nodded indifferently. He found something else on his desk. "Off to Maxim's?"

"White Mouse," said Fichte as he watched Hoffner shuffle through more pages.

"With your Lina?"

Fichte hesitated before answering. "She doesn't like the crowds."

Hoffner was still focused on the papers. "And you're a magnet for them, are you?"

There was a momentary crack in Fichte's otherwise effortless stare. Just as quickly the lazy smile returned. "Can't help it if they want to meet me."

Hoffner looked up. There was no point in prodding at him; Fichte was too far gone. Hoffner only hoped that the boy would survive the road back. Not that Hoffner was encouraging him to find it any time soon. There was still the pull of Kremmener Strasse, and Hoffner had been taking full advantage of

Fichte's inattention. Lina had become something of a regular indulgence, high times in Kreuzberg notwithstanding. She had even started allowing him to smoke in her flat. It was an intimacy Hoffner had yet to give much thought to. "No, I'm sure you can't," he said. "You tell that shop of yours I'll be coming in for my suit, all right?"

Fichte's eyes widened. "Naturally." He spoke with the enthusiasm of a first infatuation. "They'll be very pleased, Nikolai."

Hoffner bobbed his head once.

It was all Fichte could have hoped for. "You have a good night, Nikolai." He placed his hat on his head.

Hoffner kept busy with whatever it was that was on his desk. "Good night, Hans."

She was a "word city."

Hoffner had heard it, or read it, somewhere. Not just in her newspapers, but in her advertisements, her signs, her schedules, and most important, in her **Litfassäulen**—those pillars that appeared on almost every corner of every neighborhood—Berlin breathed as a metropolis of language. It was the pillars, however, that stood apart. They were the modern town criers, filled with the chaos of endless messages: sell a bed, post at the corner; workers' meeting tonight, post at the corner; find a girl, post at the corner. Capped by their crowns of green wrought iron, the pillars rose two meters higher than anything else on the street, and thus demanded attention. Even the figures in their posters were more garish than anything to be found in a window or on a billboard. Couples decked out in glaring reds and greens screamed out in aggressive poses to passersby: everything angular, sharp, and desperate for recognition. The pillars indulged their own disorder and thus mirrored the life of the streets even as they catered to it.

Find K, post at the corner.

Hoffner had used the Alex's hectograph to make copies of a single sheet of paper, which he had plastered throughout the Mitte district over the last few days. His two index fingers were still stained with the aniline dye from the ink. It was always something of an adventure using the machine, pressing the sheet to the gelatin pad, waiting the few minutes for the page to absorb the ink, and then hoping not to smear anything in the removal. Hoffner could stomach only forty or so such tries. His patience and the dye usually gave out at about the same time. He was trusting that the simplicity of his note, and not its beauty, would make it stand out among all the more elaborate postings:

Krystalowicz. Café Dalles. 10 o'clock. I'll bring the brandy this time.

Hoffner had been at the café for the past two nights. Jogiches had yet to make an appearance.

In the meantime, Hoffner had decided to track down the one living link he still had to the diameter-cut: the engineer from the Rosenthaler station, the man who had helped to design the site under the tutelage of the great Grenander himself. In the last week, Hoffner had stopped in at three of the city-run shelters for the homeless. So far, no Herr Tüben or his wife and two boys. Hoffner scanned the new map he had hung on his wall. He had been making his way east. Tonight it was Fröbelstrasse, and the heart of Prenzlauer Berg.

Durable and cold was how the red brick of state institutions always announced themselves to Hoffner. Situated next to a bit of open ground, with a few trees planted about—not by nature, but by a bureaucrat's pen—the shelter and its adjacent hospital showed little in the way of life. Even the long line of huddled bodies waiting for admission gave off nothing that might have been construed as flesh and blood. They were cracked faces, etched by hunger and resentment, and buried beneath the dust of decades. The snow seemed a starker white in their presence. Hoffner moved past them and up to the main door.

Several desks were laid out inside to process the line of applicants. Hoffner showed his badge, and a man motioned him over to one of the far desks. The chief administrator, a Herr Mitleid, was tending to one of his charges.

"You've come at our busiest time, Chief Inspector," said Mitleid when Hoffner had introduced himself. The place reeked of sterility, with the tangy odor of

ammonia emanating from every corner. It mixed uneasily with the smells of cooking and drying clothes
and digestion. "You see us at our best and at our
worst."

This was not the typical administrator, at least not
from Hoffner's recent experience. Unlike the other directors, Mitleid seemed in tune with his own humanity. It was as if the man knew what it was to carry his
life in a small sack on his back, or to feel the weight
of a refugee's thousand-kilometer walk in his legs, or
to sense what gives a man a look of both fear and confrontation in his every gaze. Mitleid was a man of
pure compassion. Hoffner wondered where they had
found him within the ranks of officialdom.

"We open the doors at four, close them at nine.
Takes about two hours to fill each of the dormitories.
You find us in mid-filling, Herr Inspector."

Hoffner explained what he was looking for: the
name, two sons, a former engineer, sometime in the
last month and a half. Mitleid thought for a moment.
He seemed to recall something, and then brought
Hoffner into his office. The two men sat, and Mitleid
began to run through a roll of filing cards on his desk.

Hoffner noticed a stack of empty application documents. He took one and was astounded to see how
bad things had gotten:

Case No. —— P.B.
Was heard by the court in Berlin, on —
—— 1919.

Mr. —— was instructed to find
himself alternative accommodation
within five days, failing which,
notwithstanding the most strenuous
efforts on his behalf to do so, he would
be punished for making himself
homeless. The appellant was further
warned that in accordance with #361,
subsection 8, of the Criminal Law of the
German Empire, such punishment will
consist of up to six weeks in prison,
and in accordance with #362 ibid.,
transferred to the police authorities, for
placement in a workhouse.
　Approved and signed.
　Signature of the homeless man in
question ——
　Signature of the police case
worker ——

"Dreadful, isn't it?" Mitleid was still searching.
"Five days to find housing. Can you imagine?"

Hoffner replaced the sheet. "You show me someone
who can find a flat that quickly in Berlin these days,
I'll show you your criminal."

Mitleid tried a smile, but the topic was too close to
home. He pulled out a card and said, "Here it is." He
read through it quickly. "I knew it sounded familiar."
His brow furrowed. "You're sure about the name?"

"Tüben," Hoffner repeated.

Mitleid continued to look puzzled. "This is a Teplitz. A Willem Teplitz. Wife, two boys. I thought for sure." He shook his head and began to replace the card; Hoffner stopped him and took the card. He read as Mitleid spoke. "Clever man, Teplitz. Helped us rework the placement of the beds. Gave us room for four more each night. Never said he was an engineer, but you could tell."

According to the card, Herr "Teplitz" had arrived on the night of January 16, the night Hoffner and Fichte had come across Mary Koop.

"Who fills out this card?" said Hoffner.

"I do."

"Do you have anything Herr Teplitz might have signed?"

Mitleid stood and moved across to a large filing cabinet. He returned with a small folder and handed a sheet to Hoffner. It was a form to request that the family be kept together while inside the shelter. "Another abomination," said Mitleid. "But the Reichs Ministry insists we have it."

Hoffner scanned down to the signature, where the lettering was deliberate and uneven. Teplitz had labored with his own name. Hoffner had seen the same hesitation many times before. This was Tüben. He had been scared enough to take a false name, and Hoffner was guessing that his fears had had nothing to do with the body his son had discovered at the site. "How long did they stay with you?" he asked.

Mitleid took the card again and flipped it over.

"Their last day was the twelfth," he read. "Last Wednesday." He looked across at Hoffner. "You believe this is your Herr Tüben?"

Hoffner was thinking about the date. February 12: the day Jogiches's article had appeared. Frau Tüben and her boys were five days gone from Berlin: they could be anywhere now. "Was there anyone here that he was particularly friendly with?"

Mitleid again studied the card. "Dormitory three." He thought for a moment, and his eyes lit up. "Oh, yes. Of course." He began to get up. "The Colonel." Mitleid started for the door and then motioned Hoffner through. "Marvelous fellow. A Russian. Fought for the Tsar. You'll like him at once."

Dormitory 3 was like all the others, long and narrow, and with two rows of beds jutting out from the walls, barracks-style. There were also a few stray cots that had been placed down the center aisle, the extras Herr Tüben had managed to reconfigure. More than half of the beds were filled with men, flat on their backs, here and there a cocked elbow drawn across the eyes. The few who did look up did so with vacant stares. Hoffner knew they were looking directly at him; he just couldn't feel their gaze.

Beyond a partition was another hall: here, instead of beds, small wooden cubicles—large enough to accommodate four or five people—appeared at intervals along the walls. These were for families. A gas burner and range stood in each of the corners of the hall, places for the women to do their cooking. Washing hung where it could, the cleverest of the women having placed their lines over the gas burners so as to help with the drying. The clothes might have picked up the sour smell of cabbage broth, but better dry and pungent than damp and fresh.

At the end of the row, Mitleid came to a stop. Unlike the other cubicles, this one had managed to keep its clutter in check. It was also far roomier, with only one bed inside and a little chair: evidently, rank had its privileges. A few photos hung on the inside walls, along with an officer's cap. Below, a stack of books and papers rose to nearly a meter high, while on the bed, a large man, somewhere in his late sixties, lay stiffly on the tissue-thin linens with his eyes closed. His boots pointed to the ceiling, while his pant legs disappeared into the cracked leather just below the knees. Even in sleep, the Colonel looked as if he were on parade.

Mitleid seemed reluctant to disturb him. "Colonel Stankevich?" he said quietly.

At once, Stankevich's eyes opened. He peered over, and just as quickly, offered a gracious smile. "Ah, Herr Mitleid." Stankevich was sitting upright, his feet firm on the ground, before Mitleid could make the introductions. Years of interrupted sleep had prepared the Colonel well.

"May I present Herr **Kriminal-Oberkommissar** Nikolai Hoffner of the **Kriminalpolizei?**"

Stankevich peered straight ahead for another moment. All signs to the contrary, he was still in the last grasp of sleep. With a sudden clearing of his throat, he stood and offered a bow. Hoffner bowed as well, and then insisted that the Colonel retake his seat. Mitleid waited until the two men were seated across from each other before taking his leave.

"Very German, our Herr Mitleid," said Stankevich with a wry smile as he watched Mitleid go. "Very perfect." He turned to Hoffner. "Are you also so perfect in your Kripo, Herr Inspector?" His German was flawless, but Hoffner recognized the accent.

"No worries on that front, Herr Colonel," said Hoffner. "Kiev?" he added.

Stankevich showed a moment's surprise. He then spoke in Russian. "You know Ukraine?"

"Once, to visit, as a boy," said Hoffner. His Russian was not quite as fluid as he remembered.

"Odessa, actually. But close enough."

Hoffner nodded.

"Your mother?"

Another nod.

"Always the mothers who ran off," said Stankevich. "Find a nice German boy, give him nice German babies."

Hoffner's mother's story was not quite as charming as Stankevich imagined, but Hoffner had no interest in muddying the illusion with mention of Cossacks and rifles and burning villages. Instead, he continued in Russian: "You're a long way from Odessa, Colonel."

"Yes." The word seemed to carry the weight of the man's history with it. "Someone decided to turn the world on its head, Inspector."

Hoffner knew it would be a mistake to go down this road. "I'm told you knew Herr Teplitz, the engineer."

Stankevich looked as if he might answer. Instead he reached across and pulled the cap from its hook. He held it in his hands like a boy caressing a new toy train, a tender blend of pride and reverence. "They let me keep this, you know," he said as he gazed at the cap, its crimson band all but faded. "Ripped the epaulettes from my shoulders, the citations from my chest, but this—this they thought would be humorous to leave me with." He paused. "A corporal. A boy in my company. Tired of taking orders." Stankevich looked up. "Laziness. That's what made him a revolutionary, Inspector. And here I sit in a shelter in Berlin." He placed the cap back on its hook. "Yes, I knew Teplitz."

Hoffner did his best to console. "The world will find its way back, Colonel."

"Yes, but not while I'm here to see it." Stankevich stood. He needed to distance himself from the cap. "Always better to walk, Inspector. Frees the mind. Shall we?"

Stankevich strode as if he were on inspection, his left leg hitching every third or fourth step from some hidden ailment. He nodded to the families as he passed by. Everyone knew the Colonel. A moment's recognition from him was enough to spark some life into the line of tired eyes: his gift to them, Hoffner imagined.

"They have no past," Stankevich said quietly. "So they have no hope."

Hoffner nodded even though he had no idea what the Colonel meant.

"You think it's the other way round, don't you?" said Stankevich. "No future, no hope. But the future is fable, air. How can you draw faith from that?"

"It's an interesting way of looking at things, Colonel."

"It's a very Russian way of looking at things, Inspector. Only the past gives you something to stand on. Without it, how do you know where your feet are when you're looking to the heavens?" Stankevich's leg buckled momentarily. "They are without hope because their past has been taken from them. It's been rendered meaningless, and so, like me, they have nothing to build their hope on."

Hoffner waited before answering. "And Herr Teplitz? Was he also without a past?"

Everything about Stankevich moved stiffly, which made the ease of his smile all the more surprising. "I'm passing on great wisdom, and all you want to know about is Teplitz."

Hoffner smiled with him. "Unfortunately, yes."

Stankevich let go with a throaty, quiet laugh. "It's nice to hear Russian again. Yours is quite good, but it's the eyes that give you away. Too dark. That's your past, Inspector. Germans don't have such depth. And how can you trust that?" He waited, then continued. "A war in China, another in Japan, the Great War, and a boy of nineteen tells me that my country is no longer mine. And you want to hear about a little German engineer." Stankevich shook his head slowly. "Seems a bit frivolous, don't you think?" They moved through to the next hall. "My corporal had weak eyes. I remember that."

An attendant was mopping up something in one of the corners. A boy, in stocking feet and short pants, stood staring at the swirling motion of the mop. Hoffner noticed that Stankevich was gazing over, as well. Stankevich showed no pity for the boy, only a stifled despair. This was what his life had come to, thought Hoffner, watching a boy fascinated by a mop.

"So you chose Berlin," said Hoffner.

Stankevich stayed a moment longer with the boy, then fixed his gaze straight ahead as he walked. "So I became a burden on your city? Is that what you mean? Yes. They don't employ old men here, Inspector."

"They're having trouble with the young ones as well, Colonel."

"Little consolation." A pot of something brown was boiling over on a nearby range. No one seemed to be taking any notice. Stankevich stepped over and removed the pot from the burner. "I came to Berlin seven months ago. There was a woman. A friend from before the war. She took me in. Brest-Litovsk.

We were no longer enemies, after all." The water in the pot settled. Someone had been boiling socks. "She died from the influenza a little over three months ago. Herr Mitleid was kind enough to house me without the usual paperwork. A generous man." Stankevich peered down at the floating wool. "You know, of course, that Teplitz's real name was Tüben." Hoffner said nothing. "Quite popular, as well. A colleague of yours was here asking for him."

Hoffner showed no reaction. "Another policeman?"

Stankevich began to walk. "If you try to sound so uninterested, Inspector, it gives the game away." Stankevich swung his arm as if he were remembering what it was to have a crop in his hand. "This other policeman, this man wasn't like you."

"The eyes not as deep?"

Stankevich allowed himself a smile. "That, too, but no. He wasn't the kind to hunt down little Belgians who kill old women."

Hoffner was impressed. "So you actually read those newspapers?"

"Nothing to do but read in here, Inspector."

"The political police?"

Stankevich nodded.

"Herr Mitleid didn't mention it," said Hoffner.

Stankevich had anticipated the response. "This man didn't waste his time with Herr Mitleid, Inspector. He simply appeared at my bed."

"And you told him what you knew about Herr Tüben?"

Again, Stankevich stopped and turned to Hoffner. "Now, why would I have done that?"

Stankevich liked his Russians, even his half-Russians. The man from the Polpo—**Kommissar** Hermannsohn, from the description—had merited no such consideration. Hoffner and his dark eyes, on the other hand, were another matter entirely.

According to Stankevich, Tüben had left the shelter nearly a month ago, alone and with no explanation. His only request had been that Stankevich act as his conduit: Tüben had thought it unsafe to address his letters directly to his wife, who had remained behind with the boys. Two letters had arrived prior to the twelfth, both postmarked from Zurich, which Frau Tüben had read and then destroyed. Stankevich knew nothing of their contents. A third had come after the twelfth, but by then, the entire family had gone.

Back at his cubicle, Stankevich produced the letter. Hoffner read:

MY DEAREST ONE,

All sinks deeper into despair. Access to the account remains an impossibility if we are to keep our whereabouts a secret from our friends in Munich. I have no concern for my own well-being, but I fear that they would not be satisfied with my life alone. It seems that the monies promised for my designs were never intended as payment, but

more as a lure should circumstances require my silencing. I will not play the mouse to their cheese. It is something of a miracle that we have managed to elude them for this long.

You, of course, had the good sense from the start. These were not men to be trusted and, if not for my naïveté, you should not be in such distress now. I have failed in the most fundamental of my obligations—the security of my family—and have only my constant remorse and loneliness to show for my efforts.

I will wait until the 23rd as agreed, and hope that by some good fortune you are able to accompany me. If not, then I hope you can forgive me for the destruction of our lives. Choose your friends wisely, and may they deliver you to me.

IN CONSTANT ADORATION, P.

Hoffner asked Stankevich for the envelope. The postmark was also from Zurich, dated the fourth of February. Hoffner examined the envelope's flap, then brought it up to his nose and sniffed. There was no residue of talc, nor were the edges crimped by steam: the letter had not been opened and then resealed. Whatever Hoffner might have thought of the Polpo—and whoever else those "friends" might be in Munich—he could at least rest easy that neither had been so thorough as to intercept the letter before it arrived at the shelter. Hermannsohn might have tracked down Stankevich, but he was not monitoring the Colonel's mail.

Hoffner continued to scan the letter as he spoke: "How much money did you give her, Colonel?"

Stankevich pretended not to have heard. "Pardon?"

"Frau Tüben," Hoffner said, "or whatever her real name is. My guess would be something a bit more Russian. Where did you send them, Colonel?"

Stankevich did his best to sound convincing. "I don't know what you mean, Inspector."

Hoffner nodded to himself as he continued to look down at the letter. "We both know German isn't his first language. 'The destruction of our lives.' 'You are able to accompany me.'" He looked up. "He means 'join me.' The syntax and language are wrong throughout. It's also much too formal. He gives himself away, as you knew he would when you let me read it. So now that I've passed your test, Colonel, where did you send them?"

Stankevich looked as if he might try another dodge; instead he simply smiled. "They made you out to be quite brilliant in the newspapers," he said. "I thought it was all something of a joke."

"It was."

"No, I think, in spite of themselves, they managed to get that right."

Hoffner spoke deliberately: "Where is Tüben, Herr Colonel?"

Again, Stankevich waited. It was now a matter of

trust. "Sazonov," he said. "His name is Pavel Sazonov. The wife's maiden name was Tüben."

Hoffner had guessed as much. "So sometimes it was the fathers who ran off and wanted nice German babies?"

"What do you want with them, Inspector?"

"The same as you. To help them."

Stankevich was not yet convinced. "Your colleague said the same thing."

"Yes," said Hoffner more pointedly, "but you didn't show him the letter, did you?" Hoffner held the single sheet out to Stankevich.

It was an obvious point. Still, Stankevich hesitated. "No," he said. "I didn't." He peered down at the letter. Then, as if a weight had been lifted from his shoulders, he said, "Better for you to keep it, don't you think?"

Hoffner pocketed the letter.

Stankevich now spoke as if to a longtime confidant. "I don't think he knew what he was doing, Sazonov. Not that he explained any of it to me. He did mention once that he had been clever, something about hiding in the last place they would look, but more than that he never said."

Clever until his son had discovered Mary Koop's body, thought Hoffner. "And his wife?"

"She knew less than I did. She simply wanted a roof over their heads. I don't think she'd slept in weeks."

"And he never mentioned his 'friends' in Munich?"

Stankevich shook his head. "The letter was the first I heard of them. Or of an account. Or a rendezvous.

The man was terrified, Inspector. I did what I could. I had a few marks. It was enough to get him wherever he was going. Evidently that was Zurich. He said he would send more for his wife and the two boys, but the money never came. And then, last week, Frau Sazonov informed me that it was no longer safe for her to stay in Berlin. I don't know why. I didn't ask." Stankevich paused. "I don't care how long he had been in this country, Inspector, he was still a Russian. This was a good man."

"And one, no doubt, with a past worth saving?" said Hoffner.

For the first time in minutes, a warmth returned to Stankevich's eyes. "Yes."

Hoffner nodded slowly. There was nothing else to be learned here. He stood and pulled his wallet from his jacket pocket.

The Colonel's reaction was instantaneous. His hand shot up. "Really, Inspector, there's no need—"

"My card, Colonel," said Hoffner. He had no intention of embarrassing the man. "Nothing else." Hoffner held it out. "Over the years, my wife has learned to make a very nice walnut dumpling—Kiev style, I'm sorry to say—but close enough. An expert's opinion would please her to no end."

Stankevich cleared his throat; he was not particularly fond of his emotions. He took the card.

The stink of ammonia was still with Hoffner as he drew up to the Café Dalles's front doors: two steps down, and a bit of sawdust to keep the ice at bay.

It was always tough going, getting the weight of a place like Fröbelstrasse out of one's system. Hopelessness, whether informed by a past or a future, was all the more stark when projected against a backdrop of cold white tile and yellow light, more acute when seen through the faded red of an officer's cap: Hoffner doubted the Colonel would be joining them for dumplings in Kreuzberg any time soon. At least the desperation inside the café had a nice jaunty feel to it, small tables and dim lights, with a prostitute or two catching up with her pimp. These were always pleasant reunions, money handed over, a few drinks into her system as she sat like a queen atop his lap. New stockings invariably demanded attention.

The band—a violin and piano—plunked out something that blended easily into the haphazard spray of conversation, nothing to take focus, though the air would have grown stale without it. Hoffner began to navigate his way across to the far corner and what had become his usual table. Like a distant shore under mist, it was obscured by clouds of smoke. He checked his watch and saw that it was a quarter to ten. The place was just revving up as he passed by a waiter and told the man to bring over a bottle of Mampe's, no doubt the watered-down stock, but why should tonight be any different, he thought.

Hoffner loosened his tie, settled in, and pulled a cigarette from his pack. He knew he could have sat like this for hours, a full glass, watching the little dramas play themselves out at the nearby tables: parry, thrust, parry, thrust, and always at a safe distance.

He was taking in one such performance—the muffled pleadings of a heavyset girl to her indifferent lover—when the bottle arrived. Still intent on the scene, Hoffner pulled a few coins from his pocket.

"Very kind, Herr Inspector."

Hoffner looked up to see Leo Jogiches pouring out the second of two glasses. For an instant, Hoffner thought he recognized Jogiches, not from Rosa's photographs, but from somewhere else, something more immediate. The sensation passed, and Hoffner returned the coins to his pocket.

Jogiches was no longer a handsome man. His beard, a silky brown in the photos, had grown gray and knotted, as if a cat had been grooming him. Worse was the hairline that rose just too high on one side and made everything seem to droop to the left. His skin sagged as well, especially under the eyes, where sleeplessness and beatings collided in an array of dark blotches and fading bruises. Only the eyes themselves recalled the past: they showed that same deep calculation and fierceness that Rosa had known. This was a man who had lived his life on the run, and the uncertainty of his world—the inherent danger in his very presence—was like an intoxicant to him. Ancient photographs aside, Jogiches was exactly what Hoffner had expected.

"But again, my treat," said Jogiches. He capped the

bottle and took a seat. "To your health, Inspector."
He tossed back the brandy and settled in.

Any sense of validation Hoffner might have felt at
seeing the man—the theoretical K, now flesh and
blood—quickly fell away. Jogiches's presence confirmed far more than just good detective work.

Hoffner held up his pack. "Cigarette?" Jogiches
took one and Hoffner continued: "I didn't see you
when I came in."

"You weren't meant to," said Jogiches. He lit up
and explained, "Two nights. By the bar. To make sure
you were as determined as you seemed."

"And tonight you got your answer?

Jogiches took a deep pull. "We'll see, won't we?" The
smoke trailed slowly from his mouth as he gazed out
into the crowd: "The man there is a thief," he said
with certainty. "The woman there doesn't want us to
know she's a whore, but she's a whore just the same.
And the couple there"—the indifferent lovers Hoffner
had been tracking—"that boy will kill someday. Look
at how he crushes his cigarette into the pile of ash,
over and over. There's no satisfaction in it. The wonderful tension in his hand. He wants to crack the girl
across the face, but he keeps digging the little butt
into the ashtray." Jogiches's gaze seemed to intensify.
"One day he'll have the courage." He watched a moment longer, and then turned to Hoffner. "And then,
Herr Inspector, you'll have to hunt him down."

"Quick to judge, aren't you?"

Jogiches's smile was unlike any Hoffner had ever

seen: the mouth conveyed the requisite joy, but the eyes remained cold. It was as if even his face was keeping secrets from itself. "No judge, Herr Inspector, just the accuser. I'll leave the judging to someone else."

Hoffner flicked a bit of ash onto the floor. "I enjoyed your article."

Jogiches poured out a second glass for himself. "Not nearly the entire story, but then someone had to prod your case into life again."

"And what is my case?"

"Rosa." He spoke the name as if it were part of some incantation, hushed and filled with meaning. Then, too casually, he added, "You've heard, of course, that tomorrow's **Lokalanzeiger** will say she's in Russia, plotting with Herr Lenin to overthrow the Ebert government." Jogiches was too busy reordering the ashtray, table lamp, and salt shaker to allow a response. "'Where's the body, Berlin?' they'll ask. 'Rosa dead? Nonsense. Watch yourselves. For she'll sweep in and rip your hearts out when she brings her revolution back again.'" No less intent on his task, he added, "But then, we both know she's dead, lying on a slab on the fourth floor of the Alexanderplatz. Still, it'll make for a good bit of press."

Hoffner had his glass to his lips when Jogiches let go with this little tidbit; Hoffner wondered how many other items Jogiches might be holding in reserve. He tossed back the brandy and set his glass on the table. "No reason for me to play coy, is there?" said Hoffner.

"No."

"You have someone inside the Alex."

"Yes." Jogiches seemed satisfied with his redecorations: order had been achieved. He sat back.

Hoffner said, "So who's been working for you?"

For the first time, Hoffner was aware that Jogiches was studying him. He wondered which crime Jogiches might be imagining for his own future. Hoffner was about to ask when Jogiches's eyes suddenly seemed to lose themselves, as if they were looking directly through him.

"You know," Jogiches said vacantly, "she was much cleverer than all of us." It was as if he were admitting to some long-held secret. His gaze remained distant.

Hoffner had spent enough time with Rosa now to come to her defense. "Shame you never told her," he said.

"Yes," said Jogiches. His gaze refocused and he looked directly into Hoffner's eyes. "I suppose it was."

Guilt, thought Hoffner, had an uncanny way of exposing itself. Jogiches, however, had spent too many years denying his own faults to allow any instinct for atonement to take hold for more than a few seconds.

Jogiches said, "You've never read any of her work, have you? Her real work, I mean." Hoffner shook his head. "I didn't think so. No, no, I don't mean it that way. I'm sure you could have understood it. She was quite superb in that way. Theories only the geniuses could master, and she made them simple. Marx's **Capital**—a morass, completely impenetrable, and then Rosa writes her **Accumulation** and suddenly Marxist economics has a place in the twentieth century. She even improved on the old man, with a little help, of course."

"Of course," said Hoffner.

Jogiches liked the challenge. "You think she could have done it without me?"

Hoffner had neither the inclination nor the ammunition to take on Jogiches. "That story about the gun," he said. "Did she really pull it on you?"

Jogiches seemed surprised by the question. His answer came with a bit more bite. "She wrote about that?"

"In great detail," said Hoffner. "I would have thought that you'd have been the first to read through the journals, cover to cover."

"Evidently you have."

"But not you?"

Jogiches tapped out his cigarette. "And slog through an endless tirade of revisionist history, Inspector? I'll take a pass."

Hoffner heard the self-rationalization in his tone. "So she never pulled the gun?"

"Of course she pulled it. Why not? She couldn't understand why I wouldn't permit her to continue seeing that idiot Zetkin."

Hoffner could feel Jogiches rising to the bait. "You wouldn't permit her?" he said.

"Something like that." Jogiches took a last pull, then crushed out his cigarette; he continued to play with the stub. "She thought she could make him into a novelist or a painter, or something equally ludicrous. You've read through it. I forget which. Waste of time." He let go of the stub and brushed off his hands. "She couldn't accept the man for what he was, and when she tried to make me into something that was her fantasy—" Jogiches caught himself. It was only a momentary hitch, but it was enough to sour his tone. "Zetkin. When she insisted **Zetkin** could be all of her marvelous romantic ideals—it was pathetic. A woman her age. I told her so. She became very dramatic. Rosa loved the drama. And so out came the little revolver." He shrugged it off with too much indifference. "She said she never wanted to see me again, which made it even more ridiculous."

Even now, Jogiches had no idea what the drama had been masking. Hoffner poured himself a second glass and said, "The journals said you promised to kill her if she stayed with Zetkin."

Jogiches tried an unsuccessful laugh. "That again. The woman was obsessed."

"She seemed to think it was the other way round."

"Did she?" Jogiches was now fully engaged. "I'll tell you something about obsession, Inspector. A nine-year sentence in Mokotów—and we both know what goes on inside those walls—and she thinks **I'm** having an affair with some woman halfway across the country? I don't see daylight for five months, and I'm the one carrying on. Guilt is a remarkable thing, don't you think? She should have shot me when she had the chance. Would have served her right."

Crushing out his cigarette, Hoffner said blandly, "So who's in Munich?"

For just an instant, Jogiches winced. It was hardly a movement, the recovery as immediate, but it was enough to tell Hoffner that he had hit a nerve. In that moment, Jogiches knew that he had been outmaneuvered. His eyes grew cold. Hoffner said nothing.

"I see," said Jogiches icily. "You let me ramble on like a fool, and I give you Munich. Well done, Inspector."

Hoffner had known to hook Jogiches by his pride—Rosa had told him as much in the journals— but he had never expected this level of self-reproach. "I'm not sure I'd have used the word 'fool,' **mein Herr,**" said Hoffner, "but I think we're at the point where you can volunteer a little something."

Jogiches answered cagily, "Am I so easily manipulated?"

"I don't imagine anything of the kind."

Jogiches was still cold: "And you think I'm eventually going to trust you, don't you, Inspector?"

Hoffner pulled a second cigarette from his pack. "I wouldn't want to set a precedent, **mein Herr.**"

"No," said Jogiches, eyeing him more closely. "That would be dangerous, wouldn't it?"

A clarinet had joined the band. There was hardly space between the tables, yet someone had decided that that meant dancing. Luckily, all the bouncing was keeping itself to the other side of the room.

Jogiches said, "It's when the smoke clears that the trouble begins, Inspector." He was on his fourth glass of brandy, though as sober as when he had first sat down. "Berlin wants to dictate to the rest of Germany, but the rest of Germany isn't all that keen to listen. Communists in Bremen, Social Democrats in Hamburg, royalists in Stuttgart, God knows what else in Berlin, and on and on and on. The revolution isn't over. It's simply waiting to see who has the will to see it through."

"And Munich?" said Hoffner.

Jogiches spoke with absolute certainty. "Munich will make all the difference, even if Berlin doesn't know that, just yet."

"But you do."

Jogiches had a habit of staring at the ember of his cigarette as he held it by his glass. "Did you ever ask yourself **why** they're keeping Rosa's body on a slab of ice in Alexanderplatz?"

"Every day."

"Yes, but you've been asking for the wrong reasons." He looked across at Hoffner. "You think it's something to do with your little Belgian."

"No, I think it extends far beyond that, but I have nothing to tell me why. Isn't that the reason we're having this little chat?"

Jogiches conceded the point. He took a pull on the cigarette. "There's the obvious answer."

"Which is?"

"She makes your murder case political."

Hoffner disagreed. "That's not enough. She'll be forgotten the moment these idiots they're rounding up get a slap on the wrist. You don't actually think anyone's going to pay for her death?"

Hoffner was expecting a bit of fire in the answer, but Jogiches was no longer biting. "That would be something, wouldn't it?" said Jogiches, his eyes drifting for a moment. "Justice for a socialist." He again stared across at Hoffner. "They're keeping her so as to use her. This is about taking the reins, Inspector, and the when and the how are what matter. The why is far too obvious."

It made Hoffner uneasy to see how much pleasure Jogiches took in the prospect of something so far-reaching. Men like him saw conspiracies and revolutions at every turn, but the more Hoffner sifted through the pieces he himself had brought together, the less implausible those possibilities seemed. "Munich," he said, still unsure why.

Jogiches smiled elusively. "Precisely."

There was nothing remotely satisfying in the answer. Whatever Jogiches thought he had been making clear was as impenetrable as that insufferable smile. "You know I have no idea what you're talking about," said Hoffner.

"I imagine you have more than you realize, Inspector."

Impatience was seeping into Hoffner's tone: "Then tell me what makes Munich so important."

For the first time, Jogiches hesitated. "I don't know," he said with frustration. "In the same way I don't know why a Prussian business interest, or a discontinued military ointment, or a substitute madman who was willing to kill himself so as to protect your little Belgian, are involved. But I do know they all revolve around Rosa. The when and the how, Inspector. That's what you need to find out."

Hoffner was impressed; Jogiches had mentioned virtually everything except, of course, the design of the Rosenthaler station, but then how could he have known about that? Hoffner was the only one to have put it together. It made the link to Munich even more startling: Stankevich's letter had come from the engineer; the engineer was the only link to the station. Now Jogiches was mentioning Munich without any knowledge of the engineer.

Hoffner measured out two more glasses. "You seem to be doing fine on your own."

"That has its limitations," said Jogiches. "A revolutionary crying foul doesn't exactly provoke a response, especially when the powers that be already consider him dead."

"Your article."

"The final nail, as they say. And dead men don't have much luck catching trains out of Berlin."

Jogiches was right. There was nowhere he could turn: the Social Democrats would do nothing to protect him; the right-wing troops would stop at nothing to eliminate him; and the police . . . well, not really their jurisdiction. His only option had been the truth, and that was something Jogiches had never managed terribly well on his own. "Your source is very thorough," said Hoffner.

"He has to be. There's a great deal at stake now."

And there it was, thought Hoffner. The catch-phrase. There was always "a great deal at stake" for men like Jogiches: grand causes tended to subordinate every motivation to a singular truth. Only action mattered, which, as Hoffner now thought about it, made Jogiches's approach not all that different from his own. The one distinction was in how each of them saw the confluence of events. For Jogiches, the details came together like pieces in a boundless jigsaw whose cover had gone missing, so that the final picture, though dimly imagined, remained forever a mystery: completion was always just another few days off, which made the eternal search all the more compelling. For Hoffner, the pieces produced a finite picture, smaller, of course, and without a sense of the greater totality, but no less coherent: the final product might have been only a tiny segment of the larger puzzle, but it brought resolution, and that, in the end, was all that mattered. There was either truth and causes and sacrifice, or there was practicality and cases and death. Hoffner had never questioned which took precedence.

He said, "So I have an ally inside the Alex?"

From his expression, Jogiches had never thought of it that way. Truth to tell—until this moment—neither had Hoffner. "I suppose you do," said Jogiches.

Hoffner waited as a lifetime of mistrust stared back at him. Luckily, the dead are quick to realize that they have nothing to lose.

"Groener," Jogiches finally said. "Detective Sergeant Ludwig Groener."

Jogiches enjoyed the moment immensely. "Oh, don't look so surprised, Inspector. Why do you think he never won promotion? Bit of an embarrassment to his uncle the General, I suspect, but then maybe that's the reason he became one of us in the first place. I never asked. Groener's far more than you ever imagined."

In fact, Hoffner had never even conceived of it, not that he had heard much beyond the name. It had come at him like a wave of gibberish, a word in a child's game with syllables and cadence but no meaning. **Groener?** The name was, at this moment, completely incomprehensible.

It was the perfect lead-in to the garbled singing that suddenly erupted from one of the tables by the front door. A drunk had taken to his feet and was already at full throttle:

"When lovely eyes begin to wink, when full glasses gleam and clink, there comes once more the call to drink, to drink, to drink, to drink!"

Everyone at the table laughed. It was loud enough

to draw half the café's attention, Hoffner with them. When he turned back, Jogiches was on his feet. "We'll do this again, Inspector," he said as he reached for his hat. "There's another door through the kitchen. They won't have anyone there."

"You still haven't told me how you know about Munich."

Jogiches placed his hat on his head. "And you, Herr Inspector, have to leave me some secrets." Jogiches grabbed his umbrella and, without another word, headed for the back of the café.

It was only then that Hoffner remembered where he had seen Jogiches before. Rücker's bar, the day they had found Mary Koop, the professor with the umbrella. It was a startling image. Hoffner wondered: Had Jogiches been watching him even then?

The front doors opened and a Polpo detective appeared; the man was too obvious to be anything else. Hoffner watched as the singing drunk suddenly maneuvered himself out into the aisle and clumsily blocked the detective's path. Jogiches had picked his lookout well: the man showed a tremendous dedication to his task.

Taking advantage of the commotion, Hoffner stood and quietly made his way back toward the kitchen.

Martha was asleep by the time he stumbled in. As always, she had left a light on for him.

Hoffner was still mulling over his first encounter

with Jogiches as he tossed his clothes in a pile and turned out the light: had Munich been a consideration back in January? Had Jogiches stayed in the shadows and allowed three more women to be killed rather than expose what he knew? Had Groener done worse? Hoffner quietly slipped into bed. His head was still thick from the brandy as he lay back, closed his eyes, and tried to piece it all together.

"Late night." Martha's voice filled the darkness.

It had been a long time since she had waited up for him. "You're awake, then," he said. He listened for movement; when none came, he added, "Not that late. Go back to sleep."

There was the hope that she would give in, but they both knew better. She spoke quietly and without any hint of judgment. "Nothing you want to tell me, is there, Nicki?" She kept her back to him.

It always came here, he thought, with no distractions, nothing to run to for a moment of relief: a newspaper lying about, a package recently delivered, a boy passing by the door. Only darkness and conversation and the unbearable weight of the two.

"Tell you what?"

"That's up to you, isn't it?"

She had always had the good sense to wait until things had sputtered out before posing the question. It was safe by then, each of them aware of what he had done and how he had chosen not to let it drag on. There was a kind of victory in that for them both. Now, however, it was four years on since his last slip, and her timing had gone off.

"The Wouters case," he said. "Loose ends." He did his best to wrap it in the truth, which, of course, only made it more cruel: anything other than his confession signaled her miscalculation.

"Oh," she said vaguely. She was trying not to sound betrayed.

"Yes. I might have to take a few days in Munich."

"Munich?" she repeated with false blandness.

The stupidity of what he had just said struck him at once. A few days in Munich? Could anything have been more obvious? The truth had snuck in and was now lashing away. He said, "Two days, at the most. I'm not even sure how the trains are running." He would have given anything for an outburst of anger or despair or loathing, but Martha always let her strength work its magic.

She said, "Sascha's friend is coming up at the weekend." Hoffner had no idea what she was talking about. "Kroll's niece. The girl from Frankfurt. It's all planned. So I'm sure the trains are running fine."

Hoffner wondered if, perhaps, they had moved past the worst of it. Unpleasantness loomed somewhere, but he chose to ignore it. "Geli," he said: the name came to him like an unexpected gift. Sascha had met the girl on his last summer holiday: she was bright and pretty and thirteen and equally taken with the boy. Hoffner recalled something being said around the table last week. It was all very hazy.

"He's in such a nice mood about it," said Martha. She rolled toward him. "And you've been very good, Nicki. A boy needs that sort of thing."

The air was clearing. They were well beyond it now. "He's a good boy," said Hoffner. Not that he knew his son well enough to say it, but he knew Martha needed to hear it.

"I saw the Mörike," she said. It took Hoffner a moment to follow. "I found it in your jacket. You haven't read him in years."

Again, he needed a moment. "No. I—just came across it."

"You were always so fond of him."

"Yes."

She continued to stare up at him. "You don't love her, do you?"

And there it was, the banality of the question so much more painful than its answer. It might have been comical had Martha known the book's source, but then again, he had chosen to keep it. Perhaps the question wasn't as absurd as he thought. "No," he said with quiet certainty. "I don't." Hoffner waited, wondering if she might drag them back into it; instead, she rolled away and onto her side.

She said, "I saw the gloves. They're lovely. Thank you, Nicki."

He had left them for her this morning with a little note on her pillow. "With warm affection," or some

such thing. It would have been too much on poor
Herr Taubmann to return them now.

"Does everyone have a partner!"
Tamako—he might have been Japanese, but it was
anybody's guess—called out from high above on his
catwalk to the throng of dancers below. As always, he
was immaculately togged in silk tuxedo and vest, and
stood shouting into his now-infamous white megaphone, which he had named "Trubo." Tonight,
Tamako was keeping his dyed ginger-blond hair
greased back to show his inordinately high forehead,
which, for some reason, was powdered in white.
"You!" he said, leaning over the railing and pointing an accusatory finger at no one in particular.
"Higher knees! Herr Trrrrubo wants higher knees!"
A woman at the edge of the floor began to lift her
legs with greater abandon. Her dress flew up and she
laughed as the men around her helped to hike it up
farther each time she kicked.
"I see knickers!" shouted Tamako. "Black and gold
knickers! Oh, those lovely knickers! Three cheers for
the lady in blue!"
The dance floor erupted, and the orchestra took it
as its cue to raise the decibel level. Everything grew
more feverish, while Fichte, seated at the bar with a
vodka and orange, watched in delight.
He enjoyed the view from the bar. More than that,
he enjoyed how he could be viewed from the bar.
Hardly a quarter-hour passed without a handshake or

a drink for the young detective. The girls had grown less attractive over the weeks—after all, who could keep a Haller Girl interested for more than a few days?—but some of the middling ones were still coming by. Tonight a buxom counter girl from one of the stores along the Kurfürstendamm was on his arm: she had a flat of her own; she had made that very clear early on in the evening. She was drinking champagne, but Fichte was figuring it would be worth the extras.

She pulled away from him and showed a bit of thigh as she flapped her skirt. "I want to dance, Hans. Let's dance."

Fichte imagined the treats in store for him. He placed his drink on the bar and followed her out as a photographer flashed a shot. It was a slow night. Who knew? Fichte might even make it back into the morning papers.

The girl was all thrusts and kicks, and she liked it when Fichte kept his hand clamped around her buttocks. He bent closer in and placed his cheek on hers, and little beads of sweat started where their skin touched. She smelled of talc and matted hair as Fichte reached up and stole a squeeze of her breast. She slapped at him playfully, and the cloth clung momentarily to his palm as he pulled it away.

Back at the bar he bought her another champagne. He was handing it over when a familiar voice from behind broke through the crowd.

"Something of a madhouse tonight, isn't it?" said the voice.

Fichte turned to see Polpo **Oberkommissar** Gustav Braun reaching out for two glasses of his own. Fichte took a moment to process the image. Smiling, and with his hair mussed at the front, Braun looked almost human.

Fichte's girl was growing impatient. "Hans—my drink?"

Fichte recovered and handed her the champagne. Braun, however, remained no less perplexing. With a false camaraderie, Fichte said, "Herr **Oberkommissar.** What a surprise."

Braun was handing one of the drinks to a lady friend of his own. "We're not at the Alex now. It's Gustav, please. Allow me to present Fräulein Tilde Raubal. Fräulein Raubal, Herr Fichte. This is the young detective I've been telling you so much about." The woman extended her hand.

Fichte took it and brought it to his lips. "A pleasure," he said. "This is—" He had forgotten the girl's name. There were several moments of uncomfortable silence before the girl said with an unflattering tartness, "Fräulein Dimp. Vicki Dimp." She extended her hand, though not with quite the same grace as her counterpart.

Suffering through the girl's sweaty little hand, Braun said, "You must come and join us. Wouldn't want to drag you away from the cameras, but we do have a table away from the noise, unless you prefer the bar."

Fichte answered instantly. "Wonderful." He motioned for Braun to lead the way. Fräulein Dimp, though less than enthusiastic, followed Fräulein Raubal into the crowd.

The air was slightly less steamy away from the bar, which made squeezing into the half-moon booth more pleasant than it might have been. Even so, the women were forced to sit shoulder to shoulder, while Fichte kept most of his heft teetering on the edge of the banquette: he placed a hand on the side of the table for balance. He smiled awkwardly at Frau Raubal, who seemed expertly bored.

"He might be a she," said Braun, gazing up at the catwalk and a strutting Tamako. "There are rumors." Fichte peered up with him. "Then again," said Braun, "he might just be a diseased homosexual."

Fichte found Braun's chumminess thrilling. If only for a few moments, he was being invited into the inner circle. Fichte had guessed at Tamako's darker secrets. Now here was a man who could more than merely speculate. Fichte said eagerly, "If only Herr Trubo could speak."

Braun was momentarily confused by the response—seeing that Herr Trubo was, in fact, a megaphone whose sole purpose **was** to speak—but he nodded anyway and raised his glass. "To the times ahead," he said.

The four toasted, and Fichte turned to his girl. "Herr Braun"—he corrected himself—"Gustav is very high up with the Polpo. They handle the more complex cases at the Alex."

Fräulein Dimp needed no coaching "I know what the Polpo does, Hans. I read the papers, too."

Braun said genially, "We don't spend a lot of time in the papers, Fräulein." He was becoming more human by the minute. "We leave that to heroes like Hans, here."

Fichte would have blushed, but his face was too busy sweating.

"What we do," continued Braun, "is always less interesting to the public."

Fichte perked up. "Not true at all. You manage what's most interesting to them without their even knowing it. The Polpo keeps a different kind of peace."

Braun said, "You've been talking with Walther Hermannsohn, from the sound of it. Good man, Hermannsohn. Knows his business."

Fichte had in fact spent more than a little time chatting with the young **Kommissar** over the last few weeks: a few chance meetings at a lunch spot around the corner from the Alex. Hermannsohn was, as Braun said, quite a good fellow. Fichte said, "Yes, not what one expects, really."

Braun gave him no time to backtrack: "And what did you expect?"

Fichte was suddenly on the spot. "Well, you know," he said, trying to buy some time. "What people imagine goes on inside the Polpo."

"**Un**informed people," said Braun.

"Yes. Exactly," said Fichte, trying not to show his relief. "The common misconceptions."

Braun raised his glass and with a knowing look—one that only confused Fichte—downed his whiskey in one swallow. He then reached into his jacket pocket and pulled out his wallet. "Why don't you two girls have a spin at the roulette wheel? Give Herr Fichte—"

"Hans," corrected Fichte enthusiastically.

"—Hans and me a chance to talk." Braun pulled a five-mark bill from his wallet.

Fräulein Raubal looked relieved, as if she had been waiting for the suggestion all along; Fräulein Dimp simply marveled at the amount of money.

Braun was on his feet. The women slid over, and Frau Raubal placed a nice kiss on Braun's cheek as she took the bill.

"You talk as long as you want," said Fräulein Dimp as she reached across the table for her drink. She made sure to give Fichte a nice view of her cleavage. "We'll be just fine, Hans, darling. Don't you worry about us."

And like that, the girls were gone. Braun settled back into his seat and managed to wave down a passing waiter. He ordered two whiskeys. He said, "Nice-looking girl, Hans. Very enthusiastic."

Fichte tried his best to keep up. "I certainly hope so." He laughed a bit too loudly, but Braun let it pass.

"I imagine you've been on quite a tear since the Wouters case broke."

"I can't complain."

Braun offered him a cigarette. "You enjoy that kind of work, do you? Murders and the like." The two men lit up.

"I don't know if I'd say 'enjoy,' but it is interesting."

"Of course. Interesting in a limited sort of way." He saw Fichte's confusion. "I only mean that the cases have fixed parameters." This didn't seem to help. Braun spoke more slowly. "You catch the killer and the case is closed. That sort of thing. They don't really lead anywhere else."

"Oh, I see what you mean. Well . . . yes and no. There are some cases that lead elsewhere."

"And you like those?"

Fichte tried to find the right words. "Well, I haven't had the chance yet to work on one that's led beyond the . . . you know, beyond the case. But I've certainly read about the ones that have."

Braun nodded amiably. "Of course." He took a drag. "Pretty much all we do in the Polpo. Nothing ever seems to find an end up on the fourth floor. Always leading from one thing to the next to the next." He picked at a piece of stray tobacco on his tongue. He examined it as he said, "From what I've seen, you look like you might have a talent for that sort of thing." He flicked the tobacco away and looked across at Fichte warmly. "We were all very impressed with your work on the Wouters case."

Fichte tried an awkward pull on his cigarette and began to nod his head quickly. "No. Of course. That's the sort of thing I do best."

"Have you ever considered the Polpo?"

The suggestion caught Fichte completely by surprise. "Considered the Polpo?"

Braun was still unnervingly relaxed. "It's just something I wonder about when I see work of that caliber, that's all. A bit of healthy competition, you understand. Wanting the best that the Kripo has to offer." He waved a dismissive hand. "Don't listen to me, Hans. I'm just a jealous detective who'd like to filch from the boys on the third floor. You'll be getting quite a bit of that in your career, I imagine." The waiter arrived. Braun said, "Shall I order two more while we have him here?"

Fichte fumbled with a nod.

Braun waited until they were alone before continuing: "I've made you uncomfortable. Forgive me. You're a Kripo man, through and through." He raised his glass. "To fine work on whichever floor it happens to be coming from." The two men drank.

Fichte sat with his glass in hand. He was feeling a bit light-headed, although he was doing his best to keep himself under control. Not that he had ever thought of the Polpo. They were safe in deep water, shoals closer in, or something like that: he could never remember the exact words Hoffner had used. But that seemed so far from the truth, given tonight, more so given his recent encounters with Hermann-sohn. Still, Fichte knew to be wary. "I need a bit more under my belt before I start thinking about any of that." He took a sip.

Braun nodded. "That's your **Kommissar** Hoffner speaking now." Braun corrected himself. "Your
Oberkommissar. Pardon me. How can we forget the
great promotion ceremony at the Royal Palace? Quite
a show they put on."

The word "show" pricked at Fichte. It reminded
him who was sitting across the table. "Yes," he said.
"The Kripo spares no expense."

Braun seemed surprised by the answer. He smiled.
"I've offended you again. My apologies." He took a
slow pull on his cigarette. "I'd like to say it's the
whiskey, but we both know it's that jealousy rearing
its ugly head. Ignore it, Hans. I do."

This time Braun's mea culpa seemed more contrived. Fichte returned a bland smile and took another sip.

Braun said, "You're quite devoted to your Herr
Hoffner, aren't you?"

The tone of the conversation had shifted, and
Fichte was strangely aware of it. He knew that Braun
was hinting at something. Even so, Fichte took his
time. He placed his glass on the table and said, "He
was my **Kriminal-Kommissar,** and he remains my
partner. I've learned a great deal working with him."
He looked across at Braun. "He also happens to be a
brilliant detective."

"Your loyalty is admirable."

"Thank you."

"If a bit naïve."

This time the word more than pricked. Fichte was

not terribly good at hiding his resentment, especially with a few drinks in him. "I'm not sure what you mean by that, Herr **Oberkommissar.**"

Braun was more direct. "We don't like letting the good ones get away, Hans. And we're very persistent."

Fichte waited. "Why naïve?"

"Herr Hoffner is an excellent detective. No question about that."

"And yet you don't let the good ones get away."

"We don't. But you have to understand that it's more than just detective work up on the fourth floor. It's a man's character, his past. Herr Hoffner . . . well, he comes up a bit short on both counts."

Fichte was amazed at Braun's candor. "We're talking about my partner, Herr Braun."

"Yes," said Braun unapologetically. "I know."

Fichte felt suddenly ashamed for having let it get this far. There was something decidedly petty in Braun's style. Fichte reached for his glass and downed the whiskey. It was a mistake. He instantly felt the effects. "It's been a pleasure, Herr Braun. Thank you for the drinks." He started to get up.

Braun said calmly, "He's fucking your girl, Hans. Not much character in that."

Fichte stared across the table. He was certain he had misheard. "Excuse me?"

"Your girl," said Braun no less directly. "Lina. Herr Hoffner's been screwing her ever since your little trip to Belgium, or didn't you know that? There's your Kripo, Hans. There's your loyalty."

Fichte felt his legs begin to slip out from under
him; luckily, he was still only a few centimeters above
the banquette. It did nothing to help the sudden
throbbing in the back of his head. Fichte wanted to
answer, make a joke, but he was swimming in booze,
drowning under the image of Hoffner with Lina. He
felt his neck constrict, his lungs tighten, and he began to gasp for breath. He thought Braun was saying
something, reaching out a hand, but he could hardly
see him. Fichte fumbled in his pocket for his inhaler.
He took in a long, deep suck and his lungs began to
open; he could breathe again. He felt himself standing. Not sure what was coming out, he said, "Thank
you for the drinks, Herr **Oberkommissar.**" He tried
to regain his focus. "You'll excuse me."

Without waiting for a response, Fichte made his
way for the front doors. His head was clearing, but
his face felt as if it were on fire. He needed cold air,
anything to be away from this noise and the crush of
bodies. He began to push his way through the crowd,
when he saw little Elise, Lina's roommate, standing
alone inside the coat-check room. The sight of her
was like another crack to his skull. Fichte barreled his
way over.

Her expression soured the instant she saw him.
"Ticket, sir," she said sharply,

Fichte steadied himself on the counter. "Is she fucking someone?" he said loudly.

Elise looked past him, afraid that someone might
have heard. "Keep your voice down, Hans."

Fichte was no less insistent in a whisper. "Is she fucking my partner?"

It was clear that Elise had been waiting weeks to hear the question. She now took her time in answering. "What do you care?" she said in a hushed, nasty tone. "You've been screwing everything that walks through that door in the last month. Serves you right."

Fichte held himself rigidly at the counter. He wanted to reach over and slap her to the ground. With a sudden jab, he thrust his hand into his pocket. He saw her flinch, and he laughed sloppily. He then pulled out his ticket and tossed it on the counter. His words were growing more slurred. "My coat, you fucking bitch."

Elise had shown all the fight she had. She backed away slowly and turned to the rack. She laid the coat on the counter and again stepped away.

Fichte teetered momentarily. He tasted a dry sourness in his throat. "Bitch," he said. He then grabbed his coat and headed for the doors.

AS BRITTLE AS PAPER

Sometimes you need a bit of good fortune, and today it was Hoffner's turn.

A cable had arrived in the morning from Belgium: van Acker had come up with a name for the substitute Wouters. He was a Konrad Urlicher, a German from Bonn. Strangely enough, it was Urlicher's anatomy that had been the key to his identity. During the autopsy of the body, the doctors had discovered that Urlicher had suffered from a rare bone disease. This discovery might have meant nothing had there not also been indications that Urlicher had been treated for the disease using somewhat innovative if experimental techniques: something to do with marrow extracts. The upshot was that only a handful of clinics in Europe had been using the new techniques. Photographs of the man had been sent out to each of them. Within a week, Urlicher's name had come back.

What was more startling was that Urlicher had not been insane. He had simply been dying. Who better, then, thought Hoffner, to take the place of a madman? Van Acker had sent along as much information as he could on Urlicher—and his stay at Bonn's Fritsch Clinic—including background, family, and recent past. He had also included the names of those who had visited Urlicher while he had been hospitalized, and it was there that Hoffner had turned up gold.

Two names appeared on both the Sint-Walburga and clinic sheets: a Joachim Manstein and an Erich Oster. Both men had visited Urlicher one week before his disappearance from the Bonn clinic in October of 1918, and again two days before he had killed himself at Sint-Walburga in January of 1919. Hoffner had also discovered that Manstein had made a solo trip to the asylum in June of 1918, some six months before the suicide, and it was the tracking of that first visit that had brought the picture into focus.

Whatever these men had had in mind, their plan had been initiated as of June 1918. It was at that time, according to the doctors at Sint-Walburga, that the real Wouters had begun to let himself go: no bathing, no cutting of the hair. It was clear now that the purpose of Manstein's first visit in June had been to prepare Wouters for the switch to come in October. By then Wouters would be unrecognizable, allowing for a reasonable facsimile—long hair, etc.—to take his place. The visit to the Bonn clinic in October had been to alert Urlicher that the switch was coming. And the last visit to Sint-Walburga in January had been to give Urlicher his final orders. That he had wrapped a rope around his neck was proof enough that Urlicher had been willing to follow them to the letter.

The precision of the operation—and it was an operation, in Hoffner's mind—led him to conclude that the military connection extended beyond the Ascomycete 4. That Manstein and Oster had been able to cross into Belgium on two separate occasions during the war—one to prepare Wouters, the other to make the switch—could have been possible only with military credentials. A single man without papers might have been able to slip across the border. Three men—one of them looking like a raving lunatic—would not.

With the names in hand, Hoffner now knew where to start digging: the Office of the General Staff.

Fichte, of course, had yet to appear this morning. These late arrivals were becoming irritatingly commonplace. Hoffner was about to write him a note when there was a knock at the door. He looked up to see Polpo **Direktor** Gerhard Weigland standing in the hall.

"Busy, Nikolai?" Hoffner's mistrust must have registered on his face. "Just to talk," said Weigland. "If you have a minute?"

Hoffner placed the pages in a drawer and motioned Weigland to take a seat. "Of course, Herr **Direktor.**"

Weigland glanced around the office and then sat. "As organized as ever." Hoffner remained silent. "A chief inspector should have a bigger place, don't you think?"

"This suits me fine, Herr **Direktor.**"

"Yes," said Weigland. "I imagine it does." He shifted tone. "Nice bit of press for you and young Fichte. Quite the heroes, these days."

"The press believes what it wants to believe, Herr **Direktor.**"

"Does it?" Weigland nodded knowingly. "So, no heroes, then?"

"You'd do better to ask Fichte about that, Herr **Direktor.** I'm sure you see more of him than I do."

Weigland ignored the jab. "The boy has ambition. Not such a bad thing."

Hoffner cut to it. "What is it that I can do for you, Herr **Direktor?**"

Weigland nodded knowingly. "No time for

chitchat. Of course. All those murders to get to." He reached into his pocket and pulled out a silver medallion that hung on a ribbon. He placed it on the desk. "I've had this for a good many years. It was your father's."

Hoffner barely moved as he glanced down at the small pendant. He looked across at Weigland and said coldly, "It's very nice. Was there anything else, Herr **Direktor**?"

"It's meant for you, Nikolai."

Hoffner nodded to himself. "And is there a reason it's coming to me now?"

Weigland reached for the pendant and flipped it over. "There's an inscription." He read: "'Third Highest Marks, Political Police Entrance Examination, Martin Hoffner, 1877.' Your father gave it to me." Weigland stared a moment longer at the silver finish. "He didn't want it after all that business." Weigland set it down and looked across at Hoffner. "It was a long time ago. I thought you might want it."

There was never any subtlety with Weigland: no doubt someone had been standing by the wire room, Weigland now aware that the lines between Berlin and Bruges were still very much open. It was a further reminder for Hoffner not to step where he wasn't welcome. "You've been waiting for the right moment, is that it, Herr **Direktor**?"

Weigland looked as if he might reply with equal callousness; instead he said, "I just thought you might want it. A medal for a hero. Silly, I suppose.

But then one can't always be a hero. Best to make the most of it while you can." Subtlety, thought Hoffner. Always subtlety. Weigland stood. "Well . . . please pass on my congratulations to **Kriminal-Bezirkssekretär** Fichte. When you see him."

Hoffner stood. The two men exchanged a nod and Weigland moved to the corridor. He was at the door when he turned back and said, "I imagine it's time for a new map, Nikolai. Keep to what you do best." Weigland waited a moment and then headed out.

Hoffner listened for the footfalls to recede before he sat and reached across the desk for the medal. It was a cheap little thing, silver plate, something to be won at any school outing. Hoffner read the inscription: the lettering had blackened over the years.

He found himself staring at the date. His father had been a young man then, and ambitious. Hoffner could hardly imagine it. It was not the man he had ever known: Weigland had seen to that. For a moment Hoffner felt his father's bitterness as his own. He tossed the thing onto the papers and slammed the drawer shut.

Regimental Affairs was a relatively small office on the third floor of the General Staff building. None of its occupants looked up as Hoffner stepped inside: a distinguished-looking major sat at the far end—beyond a waist-high partition that ran the width of the room—his desk piled high with thick volumes; four lieutenants, also at desks and just this side of the partition, were leafing through mysterious reams of paper; and a young clerk—his coat off, his rank another mystery—sat closest to the door and was typing up the pages as they came down the line. The walls were nothing but floor-to-ceiling bookshelves, each filled with tall brown volumes with dates and regiment numbers etched across their spines. It might have been a university reading room—the air had that musty, academic smell to it—if not for the ramrod-straight backs of the men: these were soldiers, not scholars.

Hoffner pulled out his badge and said to the clerk, "I need a word with your Herr Major."

The boy looked up. "May I ask what business the Herr Chief Inspector has with the Herr Major?"

"Personnel."

The boy stood and moved briskly through the swinging half-door to the other side of the partition. Hoffner watched as the boy waited for the Herr Major to acknowledge him. The two exchanged a few words, and the clerk returned. "The Herr Major wishes to inform the Herr Chief Inspector that the Personnel Office is located—"

"On the third floor," Hoffner cut in. "Yes. I've just had the pleasure of your Captain Strasser's assistance. I'm not interested in the personnel of the General Staff. I'm looking for specific regimental members."

Again the clerk made his way back. This time the Herr Major looked up and gazed out at Hoffner. Half a minute later, Hoffner was seated in front of his desk.

"This is a criminal investigation, yes, Herr Inspector?"

"I'm afraid I can't say."

The man showed no reaction. "All investigations of personnel, criminal or not, are handled internally, Herr Inspector. I don't think we can be of any help to you."

Hoffner wondered if men like this ever got tired of giving the same answer. "We're interested in this man after his service, Herr Major. When he was a civilian. We're simply trying to track him down. We don't consider this a military affair."

The Herr Major answered coolly. "Then I fail to see why you are troubling us with your investigation."

"He's not your responsibility, Herr Major. This happened after he was discharged."

"So, again, I fail to see why you are troubling us."

This, thought Hoffner, was why the war had been lost. "Our dossier is incomplete, Herr Major. Any information would be most helpful. However, I wouldn't want to tax the General Staff beyond its limits. Perhaps the Polpo might be a better place for me to begin?" Hoffner began to get up. "Thank you for your time, Herr Major."

This was not the first time the man had played at this game. He said calmly, "Have a seat, Herr Inspector." He waited until he had Hoffner's full attention. "The General Staff is, of course, eager to do what it can in the aid of a political case."

It was remarkable to see the effects of one little word, thought Hoffner. Even the high walls of army insularity buckled at the prospect of the political police. "I didn't say it was a political case, Herr Major."

"No, of course not," the man answered. "You have a regiment number, Herr Inspector?"

"No." Somewhere behind the eyes, Hoffner saw a look of mild surprise.

"Of course you know a name will be of no help," said the Herr Major. "We file everything according to regiment number. It would be impossible to wade through over a thousand volumes in search of a particular name."

Hoffner—of course—did not know this. He nodded anyway and, thinking as he spoke, opted for the only other detail he had. "But you do list discharges by date, isn't that right, Herr Major?"

"Those volumes are kept in a separate office, yes."

Again Hoffner nodded, so as to give himself time to calculate. Van Acker had placed Urlicher's arrival at the Bonn clinic in the third week of March 1918. Figuring on time for dismissal, transportation . . . "March seventh, 1918." Hoffner spoke as if he were reading the date from a file. "The name is Urlicher. Konrad Urlicher."

The information was written down and the clerk called over. The Herr Major then went back to his books, and fifteen minutes later the clerk returned with two large volumes. Hoffner had been spending his time alternating between counting the number of books on various shelves and the number of times the Herr Major blinked in any given minute. The books had won out eight to one.

The clerk handed the first of the volumes to the Herr Major and said, "It was the fifth of March, Herr Major. I checked four days in either direction."

The boy had marked a page two-thirds of the way through. The Herr Major scanned it as he answered indifferently, "Well done, Corporal." He found the name, flipped the book around to Hoffner, and pointed to a line on the page. It read:

Urlicher, Konrad. First Lieutenant. Anemia and Osteitis Deformans. Unsuitable for service.

Hoffner, however, was more interested in the further annotation:

14th Bavarian, Liebregiment.

Keeping his eye on the page, Hoffner said, "The Fourteenth Bavarian is recruited out of Munich, yes, Herr Major?" It was a reasonable-enough guess. Hoffner was still recovering from the gambit with the discharge date.

The Herr Major turned to the clerk, but the boy was one step ahead of him. The boy produced the second volume, his finger wedged between two pages. He opened it and handed the book to the Herr Major.

Once again the Herr Major glanced down the page. "Yes, Herr Inspector," he said without so much as a nod for his clerk. "Munich recruits." With a twitch of his fingers, he dismissed the boy.

Hoffner said, "May I, Herr Major?"

It was the Division Lists, broken down into regiments, battalions, and units, the last of which were alphabetized. Urlicher had been a member of the **Liebregiment,** Second Battalion, First Unit. Several lines above his name was an entry for a Second Lieutenant Erich Oster. Joachim Manstein, however, was not to be found. Hoffner casually flipped through to see if Manstein might appear in another unit or even battalion, but a quick scan turned up nothing. He knew anything more than a perfunctory glance would have caught the Herr Major's attention. Hoffner brought out his pen and wrote down the names in Urlicher's unit. He then closed the book and handed it back.

"The names you've written," said the Herr Major. "Some of these men remain active members of the regiment, Herr Inspector. I'm correct in thinking that they will not be a part of your investigation?"

Hoffner pocketed his pen. "Of course, Herr Major."

With a nod, the two men stood. The Herr Major said, "The man is dead by now, Herr Inspector. The disease is crippling and ultimately fatal. The bones become as brittle as paper. As you said, he is no longer our responsibility."

Hoffner understood. The work of Regimental Affairs was now devoted to toting up the dead like so much excess inventory. Urlicher's discharge had saved them valuable space; they were not intent on finding a spot for him now. "Then we won't need to see each other again, will we, Herr Major?"

At the door, Hoffner tipped his hat to the clerk. The boy almost forgot himself with a smile.

Back at his office, Hoffner wrote out a short list of names: Urlicher, Oster, and Manstein, Träger, Schumpert, and Biberkopf—Jogiches had mentioned "Prussian business concerns," so why not include them?—and for good measure, Braun, Tamshik, and Hermannsohn; Weigland, he knew, was not clever enough to merit inclusion. At the bottom of the page, he wrote the words "Rosa" and "Wouters." He also jotted down dates next to each of the men's names, indicating when they might have become involved, or at least when they had shown some connection to Rosa and Wouters. How far back that went was impossible to say.

The first three had conspired to set Wouters loose on Berlin starting in June of last year, but to what end? To get rid of Rosa without a trace of political involvement, by having it appear that she was just one more victim of Wouters's madness? Why not simply do the killings themselves, if it was all a ploy? Why dredge up Wouters? If Urlicher, Oster, and Manstein had in fact been working in conjunction with any of the last three on the list, why was the Polpo holding on to her body? Why set up Wouters, unleash him, and then keep Rosa hidden? Jogiches's "obvious" answer made sense only in hindsight. Worse, Hoffner had nothing to say about the three names in the middle. The design of the Rosenthaler station and the missing engineer—Herr Tüben/Sazonov—pointed to the construction company of Ganz-Neurath, but Berlin money linked to a Munich regiment not only seemed a stretch, it was completely out of character: there were no heights steep enough from which a Prussian could look down his nose at a Bavarian. The timing there was also troubling: when had Herr Tüben/Sazonov made his alterations so as to give Wouters his ideal surroundings?

The only recourse Hoffner had was to track down Oster and Manstein, which only confirmed everything Jogiches had been saying: Munich.

Hoffner reached over to telephone the duty desk for a train schedule and saw little Franz standing in the doorway. It was unclear how long the boy had been there. "Something I can do for you, Franz?"

The boy was oddly hesitant. "A note's come in for you, Herr **Oberkommissar.** To the duty desk."

"Well, give it here." Franz produced the small, familiar-looking envelope. "Same man with the beard?" Hoffner sliced open the top as Franz nodded.

Odd, thought Hoffner. Jogiches was hardly a man to repeat himself. "Anything on Herr Kvatsch?" He pulled out the card. He had given up hope at this point: Kvatsch was playing it far better than he had anticipated. Still, it was good to ask; keep the boy on his toes.

"A few more times with Herr **Kriminal-Bezirkssekretär** Groener," said Franz, "but nothing more, Herr **Oberkommissar.**"

Groener, thought Hoffner. More dirty work for Jogiches. He made a mental note to sit down with the detective sergeant. Over a whiskey. It was the only substance he could think of strong enough to counteract the stench.

The card was the same quality as before, except this time Jogiches had chosen a typewriter. There was an address, the word "Urgent," and the signature "K."

Hoffner looked up. Franz was peering across at him with surprising interest. "Yes?" said Hoffner.

For just a moment the boy looked as if he had been caught out. "Well . . ." he said, "I've been following Herr Kvatsch around for you, Herr **Oberkommissar,** and for a couple of weeks now." Franz let the words linger.

Hoffner understood. He reached into his jacket pocket and pulled out a few pfennigs. He placed the coins on the far side of the desk and said, "Never be afraid to ask for what you're owed, Franz."

The boy walked over and took the money. "Yes, Herr **Oberkommissar.**"

Hoffner knew there was no point in keeping after Kvatsch now. Even so, he said, "Ten pfennigs a week for more information, all right?"

This seemed fair. Franz nodded. He pocketed his wages and headed out the door.

Forty-five minutes later, Hoffner stepped out of a cab and into the overwhelming stench of hacked flesh. Fichte was still nowhere to be found, but the note had been clear: urgent. Hoffner would manage Fichte later.

The address from Jogiches was out in the slaughter-yard district, about as far east as one could go: killing of this kind was too much even for the folks in Prenz-lauer Berg; they wanted it out of their backyards, as well. The whole area was little more than a series of slick cobblestone alleys and dirty gray walls topped by barbed wire, although the cows and hogs and whatnot were hardly there long enough to merit the precaution. Someone had once joked that the wires had been set in place to keep the rest of Berlin from sneaking up and stealing a few pieces of meat. Given the state of things now, no one was laughing.

Oddly enough, it was the one place in town that re-minded Hoffner of his father's Berlin, where the smell of manure outpaced the stink of automobile petrol, and where the lazy hoof-fall of an overworked nag replaced the coiled snap of a tram wire from above. This was a world of wagons and pushcarts, the red and yellow spokes of the slaughterhouse two-wheelers as common a sight as a Daimler in the Westend. No amount of snow could cover the grit that was here; a constant plume of locomotive smoke

rose from the Belt Line Railway yards—livestock
rolling in from East Prussia and Pomerania and Brandenburg—soaking the flakes in soot before they had
a chance to make it to the ground. It hardly mattered,
though: there was nothing to hide out here. It was
killing, pure and simple.

Hoffner found the building, a worn sign for MECK
UND SONNE above the door. The shortages had
forced some of the smaller houses to consolidate, a
nice word for shutting down the works and letting go
fifty men. The surrounding buildings had fallen victim, as well. Hard to imagine something more depressing than a row of slaughterhouses, but here it
was, a row of abandoned ones.

The lock on the door had been jimmied. Hoffner
wondered if Jogiches had recognized the irony in his
choice of lodging; then again, maybe a man as good
as dead could tempt the fates?

Hoffner stepped inside and was struck at once by
the taste of raw meat in the air. The building was ice
cold, but the chill had done nothing to minimize the
rancid remnants of Herr Meck's once thriving business. Hoffner realized he was standing inside an enormous hall, brick wall rising to a ceiling some twenty
meters above. A grim light poured in from a series of
windows that stretched around the uppermost
reaches of the walls, but it did little more than cast
odd shadows: at ground level, the space was a collection of amorphous shapes in black and gray. One of
them began to move toward him, and Hoffner

stepped over to meet it. "Herr Jogiches," he said. The next thing he knew, Hoffner was feeling the ripping pain of a well-placed boot to his ribs.

He doubled over instantly, his nausea only slightly more acute than his surprise. Hoffner had no time to react to either as a second blow landed on the back of his neck, a gloved hand from somewhere behind making its presence known. Hoffner's face slammed to the floor, the echo of his own stifled breath ringing in the hall. He tried to reach for his gun, but he had never been terribly good at any of this. The blows came more rapidly now, fists and boots with excruciating precision. Hoffner was doing all he could to curl into himself, but it was all too vicious and determined to permit any kind of retreat. A first taste of blood dripped to his lips as a thick set of fingers ripped into his hair and jerked his head up. Hoffner choked out a cough, only to smell the breath of an unwashed mouth a few centimeters from him.

"No more questions," whispered the voice. "No more late-night meetings. No more visits to the file rooms at the GS. You understand? Step off, Herr Inspector."

Hoffner did everything he could to answer: he twitched his head once.

"Good." The man held him there for several more seconds before releasing. Hoffner's head fell to the cobblestone with a compressed smack even as the smell of foul breath continued to linger over him.

The man was hovering. Hoffner tried to open his eyes, but there was no point.

"No more," said the voice.

There was a last kick to his kidneys, but Hoffner was too far gone to feel it. He heard the sound of receding steps, sensed a sudden shock of light, but he was out cold by the time the door slammed shut.

Half an hour later, his eyes opened.

The pain was a constant throbbing, though the stiffness in his chest was far more of a problem. He tried not to breathe too deeply: every intake was like a cracking of bone. Swallowing, too, had become impossible, no saliva to be had. It was several minutes before he found the strength to push himself up to his knees, and, at no better than a crawl, he made his way over to the near wall and began to prop himself up. At least they had left him his legs. Hunched over and holding to the wall, Hoffner forced himself to the door and out into the light.

The sudden brightness brought his hand up to his face, the reflex a mistake, and his entire back arched in pain. Stifling a groan, Hoffner spotted a series of water taps sticking out from the wall of the building, and making his way over, tried his luck with the first in line: miraculously, a stream of cold water began to flow. He gingerly placed his lips under the tap and drank. Almost at once the ache in his head lifted; it was clear that the real damage had gone on below his neck. Stretching his arm to the ground, he grabbed

for a ball of sooted snow and placed it on the back of
his neck. The sense of relief was instantaneous even
as a pool of soiled water collected at his collar. Slowly
he stood upright. The uncoiling sent a rush of pain
through his ribs and lower back while he tried to assess the damage. They had broken nothing; better
still, they had left no marks for anyone to see. Save
for the small bump just above his temple, where his
head had smacked against the stone, the bruising lay
hidden below his shirt; his face had gone unscathed.
Hoffner had to appreciate the professional quality of
the work.

Step off, Herr Inspector. And so polite, he
thought. He dropped the snow and reached into his
jacket pocket for his flask. The whiskey was wonderfully warm and immediately went to work. Four or
five long pulls, and he felt fit enough to push himself
up from the wall. It was only then, with his head
clearing, that he began to consider the note. Someone had played him, someone who had known about
K. More astounding, someone who had seen him at
the Office of the General Staff this morning. **No
more visits to the file rooms . . .**

He was getting close, and he was still alive. There
had to be something in that.

Hoffner found a taxi and told the man to
drive. In his condition, he was not that uncommon a
fare for this part of town, although four o'clock
might have been a bit early for it. Even so, the man

showed no surprise when Hoffner went back to the whiskey—his neck had begun to tighten—and by the time they arrived in Kreuzberg, Hoffner could move through the courtyard without drawing too much attention to himself.

Mercifully, the flat was empty. Wednesdays Martha spent with Eva: Herr **Doktor** Keubel taught at some dental college and gave his staff the afternoon off. Hoffner slowly got undressed and ran a bath. He noticed some nice discoloring under his right arm, which extended to his lower back, where it looked as if a thousand tiny veins had exploded below the skin. He had had worse—always in the company of König—but never as a threat. Hoffner recalled the early days when König's quick thinking had helped them run down some of the city's more unsavory types; or, rather, when König had relied on his own unsavoriness to expedite matters. The two had always given as good as they got, or at least König had. Hoffner still had trouble with his wrist from one of those encounters. Sitting back in the steaming water, he laughed at the thought of it, and his entire left side cramped.

It was a foolishness he had long since left behind. Why, then, he thought, was he now no less intent on following the case to Munich? Why invite the chance for another beating, or worse? It wasn't ego. He knew he had nothing to prove to men like Braun; more important, he had nothing to prove to himself on their behalf. Crime had never been a game of one-upmanship for Hoffner. It was why he had never sent in that application to the fourth floor, and why his father had never forgiven him for it. No, there was nothing to prove to those living or dead.

Nor was there anything particularly noble in it. Hoffner readily admitted that he had never gone in for abstractions such as justice. It was simpler than that: action-reaction, choice-consequence. He left the moral scales to men like Jogiches. The only deeper meaning he sought was in seeing something through to its end, and the satisfaction he found when he had moved beyond it: fresh start, new map. The rest of his world had never been as clear-cut or as accommodating, and it was for that reason, and that reason alone, that Munich remained worth pursuing.

A draft of cold air blew in from the corridor, and Hoffner heard the front door closing. The water had grown tepid and he waited for Martha's voice. "Nicki?" she shouted. "Are you home?" He had left his clothes in a line along the corridor: a direct path. The bathroom door squeaked open and she appeared. "What a lovely life you lead," she said as she stayed by the door. She noticed the bruising on his chest, and her expression hardened. "What happened?"

Hoffner did his best to prop himself up. "Nothing," he said. The water had done wonders, but not enough to make the movement less than strained. "I fell on some ice."

She caught sight of his lower rib cage. "You didn't fall, Nicki."

"No," he said. "I didn't."

There was a sudden sadness in her eyes, and Hoffner knew instantly where her mind had gone to: an angry husband or lover and just retribution. It was unclear, however, whether her pity was meant for him or for herself.

She let it go. "I've got some ointment," she said as she started down the corridor. "Dry yourself off. We'll put you back together."

She was remarkably deft with the bandages, knowing exactly where to place them, how to press them up and around his ribs for support, and, except for the smell, the ointment was equally soothing. He had forgotten just how good she was with all of this.

"You and Victor gave me lots of practice," she said as she tied off the last of the cloth. "How's the wrist?"

He extended his hand to test it and, for just an instant, saw her tense as if she thought he might be reaching for her. He slowly brought his hand back and said vaguely, "Good. It's good."

She placed the kit in the drawer. "Are you here for dinner?"

"You were right," he said. "I shouldn't have gotten myself involved with them. They're the kind who like to use their boots."

Whatever else she was feeling, Martha could never hide her concern. "Weigland's men did this?"

"Best guess. They'd prefer it if I let the case go."

She became more insistent. "And you're going to do what they say, yes, Nicki?"

Hoffner marveled at her capacity to care for him, not for her own sake or for the boys', but for him alone. He had never understood it. He imagined it made her feel weak, but he knew it was anything but that. Her only weakness was that she lacked the courage to ask him if he loved her, and that was a shame. He had never told her, and that perhaps was worse.

"It's my case," he said. "It ends when it ends."

He saw the tautness in her jaw. "You do what you like," she said, and then moved out into the hall.

He had promised to be there by eight; it was ten to when the cab dropped him outside the address. Hoffner rarely traveled to this part of the city—Steglitz—which, over time, had become the haven for Berlin's bohemians. These were the leftists who knew nothing of workers' marches or revolutionary tactics. They were the artists and writers and foreigners and Jews and homosexuals who had sliced out a sanctuary for themselves, off in the southwestern section of town. Of course, half of Charlottenburg could always be found slumming it at a reading or an opening, or simply at a café, watching the cultural animals at play. For the rich, art and intellect were always best observed from behind a glass partition, or at least from the safety of a nearby table. That way they could laugh at the absurdity of the lives around them without stepping in too close and chancing infection. An hour or so inside the menagerie, and then it was back to their grand houses, or perhaps a dice game up north with an even seedier crowd: that was always delicious.

Unlike the rich, Hoffner drew stares. He lit a cigarette and checked the address again. The shabby little building didn't seem quite right. It was wedged in among far more serious structures, storefronts and the like with well-kept glass windows and high-quality stenciling on the doors. This one boasted none of that, and looked dark all the way up. Still, it was the number she had given him. Hoffner pressed at the bell and waited. It was too late, now, to turn and go.

He noticed that someone had done a halfhearted job of clearing out the snow: a frozen slab of speckled white rose to knee level just to the side of the door. Hoffner put it to use and sat. Three minutes on, he began to think that maybe the choice was being made for him—the cold was seeping through to the seat of his pants—when a figure appeared on the other side of the glass, coming down a set of stairs. The man was dressed in a neat suit and a bow tie, and had a drink in one hand. He opened the door.

Hoffner stood and said, "Good evening, I'm looking for—"

"You must be the policeman," the man said jovially, too pleased with himself at his discovery. "You can't be anything else." He ushered Hoffner in and started up the stairs. "We're up on the third floor. Not too crowded just yet. I'll be very interested to hear what you think."

The man talked nonstop the rest of the way up, confiding in Hoffner that he was less than thrilled with the current showing, but then, she was working in a new medium, and that always took time. Hoffner continued to nod as they came to a small door on the third floor and stepped through into a large studio that was humming with conversation. "Get yourself a drink," said the man. "Take a look around. Very casual. Enjoy." And with that, he pressed on into the crowd, having spotted someone far more interesting than Hoffner.

If Hoffner had been out of place on the street, he was now an eyesore up among the artistes. They were all postures and attitudes, geometric shapes in the guise of bodies, long sharp necks peering down at canvases, pencil-thin arms at angles in the service of a cigarette or a drink. There was a distinctly chiseled feel to everything: Hoffner chalked it up to a lack of food. He noticed Lina by one of the sculptures. She, too, was managing a triangular effect of her own, legs apart, arms straight at her sides, standing on the edge of a group intent on a man who was yammering away about one of the pieces. Hoffner quietly drew up to her side and pretended to be listening. It was several seconds before she realized he was standing next to her. Her reaction was not what he had expected.

"Nikolai?" she said uncomfortably. "You came."

Hoffner saw the welt under her eye. It was fresh, and her powder was doing little to conceal it. "Yes," he said, trying not to look too closely.

"You didn't get my note."

Evidently the day had been filled with notes. "No," he said. He wanted to ask about the eye, but knew it would be a mistake. "Was it important?"

She answered distractedly, "No. Not really."

"I can go if you like."

"No," she said quickly. "You don't have to do that." She seemed to be convincing herself. "I don't want you to go."

He tried to lighten things up. "Just wanted to see what your painter has done with you, that's all."

Lina did her best with a weak smile; she could always appreciate the attempt. "It's etchings, Nikolai. Lithographs. She's not painting now."

"Oh," he said, the distinction meaningless.

She moved him over to a less crowded area. There were still bodies everywhere, but she managed to carve out a small circle for them.

Hoffner kept close. He said, "So, which one are you, then?"

She motioned carelessly to the far wall. He expected her to lead him over; instead, she looked directly at him and said, "You didn't say anything to Hans, did you?" There was almost a hope in her tone, as if knowing it had come from him would have made things all right. Naturally, she knew better. "No, of course you didn't."

"Did he do that?"

"Does it matter?"

She was right, of course. He wasn't likely to teach Fichte a lesson. By the look of things, Fichte had already mastered the tools by himself.

"Lina!" a voice shouted out over the din. Both looked over to see a wide orb of a man heading toward them. A second, smaller ball rested atop his neck, and this was his head.

"Oh God," said Lina under her breath. She perked up and produced an engaging smile. "Herr Lamprecht," she said. "What a pleasure."

Lamprecht plowed on. "There are people who want to gawk at the model, over by the drawings." He managed to step out of himself for a moment. "Good God, what's happened there?" He pointed tactlessly at her eye. "Has someone been slapping you about?"

Hoffner cut in. "I'm Nikolai Hoffner." He extended his hand. It was enough to distract Lamprecht.

"Yes, hello there," said Lamprecht; he took Hoffner's hand. "Are you with our Lina?"

"She asked me to come, yes."

Lamprecht refocused. "So look, dear. They're the money, and they're just over by the—"

"By the drawings," Hoffner cut in again.

Lamprecht seemed confused by the interruption. "Yes," he said. He was searching for something else to say; when nothing came, he settled for, "Well, all right, then." He then forced a smile and—clearly outmatched—headed back into the crowd.

Hoffner said, "Is he as unpleasant as he seems?"

"Not always." And with surprising energy, she added, "All right, I'll take you for a look. But from a distance. I'm not that keen to be on display tonight."

The drawings were off on a side wall in a group of three, all of which seemed to be of the same subject in different stages of completion: mourners peering over the body of a dead man. There were variations in the facial details, in the number of mourners, in the angle of a torso or a hand, but the one constant was that of a mother and child gazing down into the dead man's lifeless face. Hoffner quickly realized that the mother was the only woman in any of the drawings; more fascinating, she and the child were the only ones staring directly into the face. The rest of the gathering either gazed out or looked down into nothingness. It made it impossible not to stare with her.

Hoffner knew the gaze. He had woken to it several times himself, but had said nothing. He never knew why Lina stared at him as he slept. He had never thought to ask.

He said, "You're right there in the middle in each of them. That must be good. She must like you to put you there."

Lina was less enthusiastic. "It looks like I haven't eaten anything in weeks," she said. "It's not very flattering."

Hoffner knew that wasn't the point. "You look fine. And it's not supposed to be you."

Lina seemed ready for a nice sulk, when a voice just behind them said, "He's right, you know, so stop your complaining."

They turned. A woman had appeared from behind a small door: by the sounds of the gurgling water beyond, Hoffner was guessing the toilet.

It was a sad face with thin lips and well-manicured eyebrows. Hoffner would have said somewhere in her fifties, but the gray hair might have made her older.

"Don't move," said the woman. "If we stay like this, no one can see me here, and then you'll have made me very happy."

Hoffner said, "And if someone wants to use the toilet?"

The woman liked the question. "There's always the window, Herr Inspector." Before Hoffner could respond, she said to Lina, "I'm assuming this is the older one, because if it's the younger one"—she raised a perfectly groomed eyebrow—"my God, then you're in trouble."

Lina made the unnecessary introductions: even a Kripo detective could visit a museum now and then. Hoffner had recognized Käthe Kollwitz the moment he saw her. Funny how Lina had never mentioned it: "A woman; two marks an hour." That was all she had said.

"You know who that is, of course," said Kollwitz, peering past him at her drawings. "You're probably the only one in here who does."

Hoffner looked over. He had been so focused on

Lina's figure that he had failed to pay any attention to the dead man. Even so, the face remained unfamiliar.

"They let me see him the morning after he was shot," Kollwitz continued. "At the morgue. The family brought me in, as if I could add anything more to their tragedy. It's all rather nauseating, isn't it?"

Hoffner now recognized him, albeit without his customary beard and spectacles. "Liebknecht," he said.

"I saw him speak," said Kollwitz. "Very passionate, very rousing. I didn't much go in for the violence, but they did." She nodded at the figures in the drawings. "The workers. So I gave him to them. I imagine they'll be the ones to miss him most." Her gaze deepened. "It's all very rough, but I think some of it's right."

Hoffner had never put much stock in fate. Lina, on the other hand, saw signs in everything. A girl selling flowers along Friedrichstrasse had no other choice: how else could she imagine a life beyond it? The coin placed in her basket from the year of her birth, the piece of newspaper blowing into her hand with a phrase that she had dreamt of the night before, the color of the coat on a man dashing over to buy a few roses for his wife: these were the markers along the way that told her that she was following the right course, that life had more in store for her than she could possibly know at present. All she needed was a bit of patience to see it through. She had mentioned one or two of her "sightings" to Hoffner and had laughed at them, admitting to their silliness, but with just enough hope in her voice to betray what she needed to be true.

A drawing of Karl Liebknecht inspired nothing so fanciful in Hoffner. Not that he saw it as a random occurrence within a universe lost to chaos: that idea, now all the rage, was equally absurd. Coincidence was born of proximity. Kollwitz was simply the perfect candidate for Liebknecht's memorial; her drawings and posters of browbeaten Berlin had made her the willing, or unwilling, voice of the working class. That one of their own—a lean, less than beautiful girl with a striking gaze—had drawn Kollwitz's eye was hardly beyond possibility. It had drawn Hoffner's as well, albeit for different reasons. Who was to say, then, that artists and detectives were not the ones most likely to see something beyond a stare? It was as much whimsy as Hoffner would concede. Of course, had Kollwitz produced something on Rosa, now that might have been less easy for him to dismiss.

"I wanted to do something on Luxemburg," said Kollwitz, "but that's not as clear-cut, is it?" She looked up at Hoffner. "So what do you think, Inspector? Is she off in Russia, or have we seen the last of Red Rosa?"

At least the cosmos had a sense of humor, thought Hoffner. He said, "Are you that keen to have her back?"

It was clear Kollwitz was enjoying this. "It's not for me that she'd be coming back, now is it, Inspector?"

More than you realize, Fräulein, he thought. "Did you know her?" he said.

"Should I have?" she said quizzically. "Yes. We met once, at a concert, two old women enjoying some music. We told each other how much we enjoyed each other's work. It was very polite."

He said, "I would have thought the two of you would have been kindred spirits."

"You would, wouldn't you?" said Kollwitz dryly. "I'm sure history will have it that way. And Emma Goldman, too. Lump all of us in together. In fact, we might just be the same person. Wouldn't that be something?" She smiled. "I thought she was a devotee of feminism. I asked her, and she took it as an absurd question. Women, Jews, it didn't matter to her. Socialism didn't care about those distinctions, so why should she? Everything would be made right after the great event. I thought it was very . . . honest . . . though not terribly helpful. But she did do profound things, and for that I'm infinitely jealous. You don't have a drink, Inspector. Let's go get you one."

Hoffner gazed over at Lina and was reminded that, yes, he really was the old one. For all that was behind her stare, Lina looked as if she had just spent the last few minutes lost in a foreign country.

They made it halfway to the drinks before Kollwitz was torn from them. Hoffner's last image of her was of a small gray rabbit being sucked into a bottomless pit of groping hands. She went bravely and even managed a little smile back to them before she was gone. Hoffner took a whiskey and wondered how much longer they would need to be here.

The answer came far more quickly than he could have imagined. There was a loud conversation outside the door, and a moment later Hans Fichte—a drunken Hans Fichte—stepped into the studio. Hoffner had had his chances not to be here: the look of the building, the ice in the seat of his pants, Lina's first hesitation; he had taken none of them. This was now his reward for those missed opportunities.

Fichte's face was red from the climb, his eyes marginally focused, though he spotted Lina at once. A man in front of him tried to ask what he was doing here, but Hans already had Hoffner in his sights: nothing was going to keep him from the drinks table. He pushed through.

Fichte stood there breathing heavily and saying nothing. He took no notice of Lina; his gaze was fixed on Hoffner.

"Hello, Hans." Hoffner spoke with no emotion. "You've had a bit to drink." Fichte continued to stare in silence. "This isn't the place for this."

There was a rage behind the eyes; Fichte was doing all he could to keep it in check. "And where would that place be, Herr **Kriminal-Kommissar**?" Fichte suddenly spoke in a loud voice. "Where you could throw her over a chair and fuck her?"

Everyone in earshot looked over. Hoffner could feel Lina's embarrassment, though he felt none for himself. He waited for the conversations to pick up again before saying, "Why don't we go downstairs?"

Fichte was having none of it. He reached out for Hoffner. "And why don't you—"

Hoffner caught him by the wrist and twisted. Had Fichte not been drunk, it would have made no difference, but Fichte was drunk, and his reaction was slow. Hoffner twisted tighter and saw the pain run across Fichte's face, the shoulder now on fire, even as Hoffner felt his own rib cage wrenching at the exertion. Fichte teetered, and Hoffner put out a hand to steady him. They now had a captive audience, and within seconds Hoffner was maneuvering Fichte to the door, then to the staircase, forcing him up against the wall for balance as they sped down. Two floors on, their momentum drove Fichte into the front door, which seemed to stun him for a moment. It was enough time for Hoffner to move him back, pull open the door, and take them both out into the cold air. With what little strength he had left, Hoffner dropped Fichte onto the snow pile and then bent over and gasped for breath. His ribs were in agony as he staggered back to the wall and continued to suck in for air, all the while keeping his eyes on the lump that was Fichte.

It was nearly a minute before either of them could say a word. Hoffner spat. "You all right?" he said, still breathing heavily.

Fichte was having trouble focusing. The door had done more damage than Hoffner had imagined.

Fichte was trying to rub his shoulder when Lina raced out onto the street. She was holding her coat, and stood there motionless as the door clicked shut behind her.

Hoffner got himself upright. The bandaging was now useless and only making things worse. "Put on your coat," he said. "You'll freeze."

Without thinking, Lina did as she was told.

Fichte had recovered enough to lift his head. "You always do what he tells you?"

Hoffner said, "Watch yourself, Hans."

Fichte let go with a cruel laugh. "That's rich. And what do you need to watch?"

Hoffner's head was buzzing; he thought he might be sick, and he bent over. Lina was still by the door. She had pulled her coat tight around herself, her arms crossed, her hands tucked up under her chin. She was doing all she could not to cry.

"Feeling sorry for yourself?" said Fichte. "That's a laugh."

"Shut up, Hans." Her face became laced with anger. "Don't tell me anything. Not a thing. You think I don't know what's been going on with you? You think I didn't know all along? Did you hear anything I said last night?"

Fichte shook his head sloppily. "Since Belgium," he said. "Since before any of this, which makes you a whore." He looked over at Hoffner. "Congratulations. You made her a whore."

Hoffner saw Lina raise her hand to strike Fichte,

and he quickly reached over. Her arm was shaking
when he caught it; Hoffner tried to pull her into him,
but she threw him off, barking out in frustration as
she stepped away. Hoffner could feel her loathing as
he leaned back against the wall. Fichte had slouched
over his open knees, his arms resting on his legs. Lina
kept her back to both of them.

Staring down at the ground, Fichte said aimlessly,
"You're a son of a bitch, you know."

Not much question in that, thought Hoffner.
"Yes," he said. "I know."

There was a long silence. "I thought I was in love
with her," said Fichte. "I did."

Lina turned toward him, the rage now in her eyes.
She stared at Fichte's hulking shoulders and his
blotchy skin, at his enormous fingers clenched together in one giant fist. "Shut up, Hans," she said
bitterly.

Fichte bobbed his head once. "'Shut up, Hans,'" he
echoed.

Hoffner said quietly, "Maybe he did."

Lina shot him an icy glance and again turned away.

Hoffner felt a strange sense of relief, not in the discovery or the accusations, but in the simple truth of it
all. No one was blameless, least of all himself, and
there was something comforting in knowing that they
all saw that now. Lina stared away, Hans peered down
at his boots, but it was themselves that they could not
bear to face. Their own betrayals were writ large by
the presence of the other two now here: Hoffner with

Fichte, Hoffner with Lina. Hoffner himself had never denied his role in all of this, and so couldn't share in their shame.

He said to Lina, "We need to get you home."

Both Fichte and Lina looked over. Her powder was streaked. She seemed at the edge of herself, but she managed a nod.

Fichte stared in disbelief. "You must be mad," he said. "You think I'm going to let you take her home?"

"No one's taking her home, Hans," he said. "We'll find her a cab."

"So you can get into the next one and follow her out there? You think I'm stupid?"

Lina cut in furiously, "You think I'd let him come? You think I'd let either of you?"

It was too much for Fichte, who was having trouble following. He searched for something else to say, but instead settled for dropping his head to his chest.

Hoffner stepped over and took Lina's arm; she put up no resistance. "Wait here, Hans."

They found a taxi stand around the corner. They had walked in silence, although Lina had allowed him to keep his arm in hers. He opened the door and they stood there, staring at each other. It was only then that he felt regret, not for their past but for the pain he saw in her eyes.

"He'll be fine," he said, trying to find something to console her.

This only seemed to make things worse. "You think that's what this is?" she said. Hoffner had no answer.

She spoke quietly and without accusation. "He called me a whore and you said nothing." The word slapped at him. "Is that what you think, that I'm a whore?"

Hoffner stood stunned. She was capable of inflicting pain; he had never known that. "No," he said. He wanted to believe that the sudden swimming in his head was from the ribs or the whiskey, but he knew better. "No," he repeated.

It was not nearly enough. Hoffner started to say something else, but she stepped past him and into the cab. Unwilling to look at him, she sat back and stared straight ahead.

Hoffner knew there was nothing to be said now. He watched her a moment longer and then shut the door. He told the driver where to take her and handed the man a few coins, more than enough to get her home.

Fichte was gone by the time he got back. It would be an early night for everyone. Hoffner wondered what Martha would make of that.

⊷ THE THIRD PRISONER ⊷

He had made the reservations for tomorrow, Thursday morning.

Meanwhile, Hoffner had spent the better part of this morning suffering through a series of hot baths and liniment treatments; there had been no way to fight it. He had barely been able to get out of bed, and Martha had lost no time in getting a doctor to the flat. Something had torn, according to the specialist; breathing would be painful for the next few days. Hoffner could thank Fichte's considerable size for that. The doctor had recommended a week in bed. Hoffner had agreed to half a day.

Luckily, it had forced him to see just how useful the telephone could be. Everyone seemed to be far more efficient than when in person. Hoffner was guessing that a request from a disembodied voice conveyed an authority attributable to some higher source: "two tickets for Munich" had never sounded so numinous.

The station envelope was waiting on his desk when he arrived back at the Alex. Hoffner penned a short note and placed it, along with one of the tickets, into a separate envelope. He then called upstairs for one of the boys, and three minutes later, little Sascha arrived at his door.

"How's the Count?" said Hoffner, shuffling through more of van Acker's files. He was still working on Manstein, who remained nothing more than a name. Hoffner glanced over when there was no reply. "Of Monte Cristo," he said. "All's well there?"

Sascha brightened up. "Oh yes, Herr **Kriminal-Oberkommissar.** It's **Treasure Island** now."

Hoffner nodded encouragingly. "Spending your money on books. That's commendable." He held out the envelope. The Kremmener Strasse address was written in thick pen. "You know where this is?"

The boy read and nodded. "I don't buy them, Herr **Kriminal-Oberkommissar,**" he said as he tucked the envelope into his pocket. "Franz gives them to me when he's finished with them." Another bit of surprising news, thought Hoffner. "Do you want me to wait for a response, Herr **Kriminal-Oberkommissar?**"

Hoffner knew the answer would be coming soon enough: 9:13 tomorrow morning if the schedule was correct. "Just make sure it gets there. You don't have to wait."

Sascha was gone by the time Hoffner had dug out a few coins. Odd little fellow, he thought. He would never make it on the streets. Maybe little Franz knew that, as well.

The Hotel Eden remained the temporary headquarters of the Cavalry Guards Rifle Division, the **Schützen-Division.**

Hoffner had made sure to tell the duty sergeant that he was heading over; he wanted anyone taking an interest in his itinerary to know what he was doing this afternoon: a message of his own, as it were, to make it clear that it would take more than a few bruises to derail him. Maybe, then, there was just a hint of ego in all of this.

Unfortunately, Hoffner still had no idea what he intended to do now that he was at the hotel. It was unlikely that Pabst or Runge would have much to say to a Kripo detective; then again, these were not clever men. There was always the chance that they knew more than they should.

Aside from the uniforms, Hoffner was hard-pressed to find anything remotely akin to military precision on the first floor. Soldiers milled about, some armed, others in half-buttoned tunics, most with cigarettes stuck in the corners of their mouths. These, suffice it to say, were not regular troops. What little help Hoffner's badge had been across town at the GS was here the object of sneers and laughter. It was only when he started up for the second floor that a sergeant shouted over from his game of cards.

"And where do you think you're going, Herr Kripo?" The man smiled across at his fellow players.

Hoffner stopped and said easily, "It looks like up these stairs, doesn't it, Herr Sergeant?"

The man was not amused. "No one goes up without our saying so."

Hoffner nodded to himself. "That's good to know." He began to climb again.

The man was up, rifle in hand, before Hoffner had taken two more steps. The sergeant cocked the bolt. Hoffner stopped and the man drew up to the base of the stairs.

"Did you hear me say so, Herr Kripo?" The hall fell silent. Hoffner was now the center of attention.

Hoffner slowly turned around and peered down at the man. He waited and then said, "Are you going to shoot me, Herr Sergeant?"

The man was clearly not used to being challenged; it was wonderful to see a man struggle so publicly with his own arrogance. There were several long moments of indecision before the sergeant said quickly, "Let me see that badge again."

Hoffner was impressed; the man had shown remarkable restraint. Hoffner slowly walked back down the steps, reached into his coat pocket, and pulled out his badge. He held it there, his gaze unwavering.

Without so much as a glance, the sergeant said, "That's all right, then." He nodded his head. "You can go up."

Hoffner remained where he was and slowly placed the badge in his pocket. "Thank you, Herr Sergeant," he said. "You've been very helpful." Hoffner then turned and headed up the stairs. Behind him, he heard the first murmurs of conversation reclaim the hall. Hoffner wondered if it would always be this easy to back these men down.

First Staff Captain Pabst was in his office—a converted hotel room overlooking the Gardens—having a smoke with two of his officers when Hoffner appeared at the door. At least here there was a bit more decorum. A young lieutenant was seated in the hallway. He announced Hoffner and then stepped aside.

Pabst was buttoning his tunic when he invited Hoffner in. He was all cheekbones and charm as he motioned to a chair. "Please, Herr **Oberkommissar.**" He turned to the two other men. "That will be all, gentlemen."

The officers snapped their heads sharply and then moved past Hoffner. Pabst waited behind his desk.

"I hope I'm not interrupting, Herr **Kapitän**?" Hoffner began as he sat.

"Not at all. Cigarette, Herr **Oberkommissar**?" Pabst kept his private cache in a silver holder, which he now pulled from his pocket. Hoffner declined. "A Kripo chief inspector," said Pabst. "What can possibly be of interest to you here?" He placed the cigarette in his mouth and lit up.

"Routine questions, Herr **Kapitän.** A formality, really. About the Liebknecht and Luxemburg killings."

Pabst showed a moment's recognition before the bland smile returned. He nodded knowingly. "Oh yes, of course," he answered as if he were talking about a soldier's missed curfew. "Someone seems to think some of my men were involved, is that right?"

Hoffner found the indifference almost believable. "There was an article, Herr **Kapitän.** Accusations. We simply have to follow them up, that's all."

"Naturally. But, correct me if I'm wrong, Herr **Oberkommissar,** anything untoward would fall under military jurisdiction? That is right, isn't it?"

Hoffner wondered if the phrase was printed in some training manual somewhere. He also saw how Pabst had chosen his words carefully: not "wrongdoing" or "criminal activity," but "anything untoward." Pabst was setting the tone. "These were very public figures, Herr **Kapitän.** It's more about information. How the army deals with its own is not our concern."

Hoffner was pleased with himself for this turn of

phrase, not that he knew what it meant. Luckily, it seemed to be having the same effect on Pabst: mild confusion left him with no real response. "Naturally," said Pabst, his smile less convincing.

Hoffner spoke directly: "Could you then describe the events of January fifteen?"

Pabst lingered with his cigarette. "Of course," he said. He let out a long stream of smoke and began to recount a story that both of them already knew: the arrest in the Wilmersdorf flat, Liebknecht and Luxemburg brought to the hotel, interrogation, identification. Pabst finished by saying, "I then had them sent to the civilian prison at Moabit. We were directed to bring all the captured leaders of the revolt to Moabit."

Hoffner had been writing in his notebook. He looked up and said, "There was some question as to the transport, Herr **Kapitän**."

"I wouldn't know about that, Herr **Oberkommissar**."

"But they were your men?"

"Yes."

"So you would have been given a full report on the unit's activities. That is right, isn't it?"

Hoffner was hoping for more of a crack in the expression, but Pabst was better at this than the men he commanded. "Liebknecht was shot while trying to escape, if that's what you mean."

"And Luxemburg?"

Pabst took his time crushing out his cigarette. "You

seem to need it from the horse's mouth, don't you, Herr **Oberkommissar**?" And without waiting for Hoffner to respond, he lifted the receiver of the telephone. "Send in **Leutnant** Pflugk-Hartung. Thank you." This was not a name Jogiches had mentioned. Pabst looked across the desk as he hung up. "The man who led the unit, Herr **Oberkommissar.**" Jogiches had assigned that role to a Lieutenant Vogel, although he had kept the information out of his article: only Pabst and Runge had made it to press. Before Hoffner could answer, Pabst was raising a hand to the door and ushering the man in. "Come in, **Leutnant.**" It was as if Pflugk-Hartung had been waiting in the wings.

The young lieutenant was the perfect specimen of Teutonic breeding: white-blond hair and piercing blue eyes stood at strict attention by the desk. He was a far cry from the slovenly mess Hoffner had left on the first floor. Looks, however, were deceiving. The moment Pflugk-Hartung opened his mouth, it was clear why he had been relegated to the **Schützen-Division.** This was not a bright man.

"Liebknecht showed himself to be the dog that he was," said Pflugk-Hartung. "It was a pleasure to shoot him when he ran like a coward."

The fact that Pabst had brought him in as his trump card spoke volumes about the Herr **Kapitän,** as well.

"And Frau Luxemburg?" said Hoffner.

Hoffner could see the wheels spinning; he also noticed how Pabst was gazing up at the man, like a tutor waiting to hear the recitation they had just gone over. Evidently, Hoffner's time on the first floor had not been all fun and games; it had given the second floor time to prepare.

Pflugk-Hartung said, "She was taken by a mob. I don't know what happened after that."

Hoffner said, "A mob was able to steal her away from a crack unit of the Cavalry Guards? That must have been quite a mob, Herr **Leutnant**."

Pabst cut in before Pflugk-Hartung could answer. "It was the revolution, Herr **Oberkommissar.** The streets were madness. After all, there were only six of my men."

And there it was, thought Hoffner. The first real detail. Pabst might have been far more self-controlled than his men, but he was no less arrogant, and that arrogance was about to be his undoing. "Six men for two prisoners?" said Hoffner. "That seems a bit sparse, Herr **Kapitän**." He gave Pabst no time to respond; instead, he turned to Pflugk-Hartung and said, "Were you surprised that you were given only five men, Herr **Leutnant,** even for a dog like Liebknecht—and Luxemburg, to boot?" Pabst began to answer, but Hoffner put up a quick hand as he continued to gaze at Pflugk-Hartung. "The horse's mouth, Herr **Kapitän,**" he said. Pabst was smart enough to know that any further objection would only make things worse. Pflugk-Hartung stared straight ahead; he was clearly at a loss. Hoffner said, "Was a **Leutnant** Vogel a member of your unit?"

Pflugk-Hartung looked momentarily surprised; his eyes danced as he struggled to find an answer.

"I ask again," said Hoffner. "Was a **Leutnant** Vogel a member of your unit?"

Pflugk-Hartung answered quickly. "Yes."

"Yes?" said Hoffner with feigned surprise. "Two officers in a unit of six men? Was there a reason for that?" Again Pabst tried to interrupt, and again Hoffner politely held him at bay. "Unless there were **two** units of six men led by **two** different lieutenants? Would that have made more sense?" Pflugk-Hartung was now well out of his depth; he continued to stare ahead. "I'll take that as a yes, Herr **Leutnant.**" Hoffner turned to Pabst and spoke quickly. "You sent Liebknecht and Luxemburg to Moabit separately, didn't you, Herr **Kapitän**? Two prisoners taken from the same flat at the same time, questioned at the same time, identified at the same time, yet transported to the civilian prison one by one. Who gave the orders to separate them?"

Pabst stared coldly across the desk. This was not the way things had been laid out. He was about to answer, when Pflugk-Hartung blurted out, "Herr **Leutnant** Vogel was delayed by the third prisoner." The boy truly believed he was helping his Herr **Kapitän.** "It was therefore decided that my unit should leave at once."

Hoffner gave Pabst no chance to answer. "A **third** prisoner?" said Hoffner.

This time, Pabst cut in quickly. "The Herr **Leutnant** is confusing the informant with a third prisoner. The man was brought in at the same time as Liebknecht and Luxemburg. There was no third prisoner."

Hoffner watched the young lieutenant's eyes. The boy had made a mistake, and he knew it. "I see," said Hoffner. "And what was the delay?"

"What usually happens at those moments," Pabst said coolly. "The informant was demanding more money. Herr **Leutnant** Vogel was resolving the situation." Without looking up, Pabst said, "That will be all, Herr **Leutnant.**" Much relieved, Pflugk-Hartung clicked his heels and headed for the door. Pabst waited until he and Hoffner were alone before saying, "It was one more night in the revolution, Herr **Oberkommissar.**" The affable Pabst had returned. "Guns and mobs. What else do you expect with a Jew radical on the loose? I was lucky not to lose a man. Of course, I take full responsibility for any of the mishaps—the separation of the prisoners, the breakdown in discipline with the informant—but, as you said, that would be for a military tribunal to decide."

Hoffner saw where this was going; there was no reason to press things further. "Of course," he said.

Pabst stood. "Unfortunately, I have given you as much time as I can this afternoon. You'll forgive me, Herr **Oberkommissar.**"

Hoffner stood. "You've been most kind, Herr **Kapitän.**"

Three minutes later, Hoffner was across from the Gardens and stepping up onto a tram. Jogiches had known about the separation of Liebknecht and Luxemburg; he had known about the third prisoner: Hoffner was certain of that. The question was, what was Jogiches protecting?

"**W**hat exactly were you doing at the Hotel Eden, interrogating a Captain Pabst?"

Kriminaldirektor Präger was standing by his window, shaking his head in disbelief. "I've just had a very nice telephone call from the Office of the General Staff, reminding me that Kripo jurisdiction doesn't extend that far." He stared across at Hoffner. "What are you doing, Nikolai?"

It was the most animated Hoffner had seen Präger in months. "Closing out a case, Herr **Kriminaldirektor.**"

Präger nodded skeptically. "Yes, I'm sure that's what this is." He moved back to his desk. "I don't think you realize how tenuous things are right now. You might not care, but no one knows if this government is going to take, so while they're deciding, the GS is being rather stingy with its allegiances. You don't want to get on the wrong end of that, Nikolai."

"You mean I don't want this department to get on the wrong end of that."

"Yes. That's exactly what I mean." Präger was making this very plain. "Whether you want to accept it or not, you're a man with a very high profile at the moment. What you do reflects on all of us. So, next time, think about that before you go poking your nose around where it doesn't belong."

"And if it does belong?" Hoffner said it just so as to see a little gnawing on the inside of the cheek.

"Look, Nikolai"—Präger's tone now far more conciliatory—"I've never told you how to run an investigation. I'm not going to start now. Just be aware of these things. There's more at stake now."

Hoffner wondered if the KD had been talking with Jogiches. He said nothing.

"By the way," Präger added, "there's talk that your young Fichte has been spending his time up on the fourth floor. Anything I should know?"

"I'll keep an eye on it."

It was all Präger wanted to hear. He found a few sheets on his desk and got back to work. Hoffner was left to show himself out.

FIVE

⇥ BARKING SWINE ⇤

The sun off the glass walls was almost blinding at this time of morning. Hoffner pulled down the brim of his hat, but the snow was like a double reflector: the glare had him either way. Like a great hunched bear clad in steel armor, the Friedrichstrasse Bahnhof perched wide on the edge of the river and peered out over the surrounding buildings, all of which seemed to be cowering in its presence. Hoffner showed a bit more grit as he pressed his way through the main doors and over to the platforms.

The station was one of the great wonders of Berlin. Its grand hall rose to an indeterminate height as the haze and smoke from the bellowing locomotive engines lifted into clouds of gray and white and left the roof-skin in virtual darkness. Here and there, odd pockets of sunlight sliced through the glass, only to catch a cloud and infuse it with wild streaks of prismed hues, each droplet bringing wanted color to the drab millings-about underneath. A violet-red rested momentarily on Hoffner's watch face and then was gone. Eight-forty. He had given himself half an hour to see if his note had turned the trick.

At just after nine, she appeared. Hoffner tossed what was left of a roll into a trash bin and headed over. Amid the parade of impatient mothers and men of purpose, Lina seemed to wander in a kind of half-tempo, her small brown case held to one side, her tan coat painfully inadequate for the season. She had spent a few marks on a blue hat that seemed to bob above the sea of endless gray. She caught sight of Hoffner and slowed still further as he drew up to her. An amplified voice barked out a series of platform numbers and departure times; Hoffner and Lina stared at each other as they waited for the tinned echo to fade.

"Shall we get something for the trip?" he said when he could be heard. "Sandwiches, some beer?" He noticed the welt under her eye had all but disappeared.

"That would be nice," she said. They walked toward a small grocer's cart. "Did you think I would come?"

Hoffner took her case. "There was always a hope," he said lightly. "The hat was the great surprise." They reached the cart and he set the bags down. The movement caused a momentary wince.

Lina noticed it at once. "Is that from Hans?" she said.

Hoffner pretended not to have heard, and pointed to two sandwiches. "And two bottles of beer," he said to the man as he pulled a few coins from his pocket.

Lina let it pass. "It was a nice note," she said.

Hoffner pocketed the change. "Just nice enough, I imagine."

It was her first smile.

They found their seats in the second-class compartment, and Hoffner did what he could getting the luggage up onto the rack. Lina offered to keep hers by her feet to save him any further anguish.

They sat side by side, he by the window, she with her head on his shoulder. He had paid extra for the seats. It had been the right gesture. Hoffner could tell she was appreciating it.

A good-looking young man stepped into the compartment and, checking his ticket, picked out the seat across from Hoffner. The man settled his bags and then looked over at his cabin mates. "Would the Fräulein like her luggage up?" he said with an innocuous smile.

Lina hesitated to answer, but Hoffner quickly stepped in. "Most kind of you," he said.

The man tossed it up and sat. He then pulled out a magazine, but chose not to read. He was looking to see if there was any conversation to be had. "Family outing?" he said.

Hoffner gazed across kindly. "My daughter is a deaf mute, **mein Herr,**" he said. "We prefer to travel in silence."

The look on the man's face was priceless. Hoffner
felt the deep pressure on his leg from Lina's hidden
thumb. He was trusting her not to laugh.

"Oh," said the man, trying to recover. "Of course,
mein Herr." Just then the train began to move. The
man smiled awkwardly and opened his magazine.
Hoffner took Lina's hand and gazed out as Berlin
slipped by in an ever-narrowing blur.

Munich came quickly. The handsome young
man had offered his too-loud good-byes less than an
hour into the trip, which had left them six more to
themselves to eat their sandwiches and drink their
beers and while away the time as if the hours were really theirs. Trains had that effect. Now, stepping to
the Central Station platform, Hoffner and Lina returned to a world far more concrete.

He found them a modest hotel by the station and,
with a last nod to whimsy, registered them as man
and wife. They found a small, quiet restaurant—a
recommendation from the concierge—and by seven
o'clock had two plates of what passed for beef and
noodles in front of them. The place had the smell of
frying potatoes, and they sat like a good German
couple, saying nothing as they ate. Hoffner had
splurged on a bottle of wine, and Lina seemed to take
great pleasure whenever the waiter would come by to
refill her glass. It was only when the bill was brought
over that any of the three spoke up.

"Tell me, Herr **Ober,**" said Hoffner as he mopped

the last of the noodles in the broth, "you know of a place to get some drinks? Something a bit lively?"

"Certainly, **mein Herr,**" said the man as he made change. "Depends on what you want. A little dancing?"

Hoffner smiled. "Not for an old soldier." He set his fork and knife on the plate. "Just some drinking. Good company."

The man nodded. "We've plenty of soldiers in town, **mein Herr.** And plenty of beer halls to keep them happy."

The man suggested the Sterneckerbräu beer cellar, not too far a walk, and not so lively that a young woman might not want to venture in. A perfect choice.

Outside on the street, Lina took Hoffner's hand. "I thought maybe we'd just walk for a bit," she said. "Find a café." After all, they were no longer in Berlin; she could state a preference. "A beer cellar sounds so dreary, and it's so much nicer here without the snow and rain."

She was right. Munich was a far cry from Berlin. It had been nearly half a century since the city had watched the best of its artists and writers and architects flee to the new imperial capital with the promise of fast money and prestige: the heady days of the Wittelsbach princes and their patronage were long gone. Now there was something distinctly quaint to Munich, a slower pace, the buildings not quite so high, though the city had recently reasserted itself as the first to try its hand at revolution. Munich had succumbed to the Social Democrats in mid-November, and had been following the Bavarian Prime Minister, Kurt Eisner, ever since. Eisner might have been a displaced Berlin Jew—hence the feeling among Munich's more conservative elements that nothing but evil could come from the Prussian capital—but he was showing the way for men like Ebert and Scheidemann. Munich was once again a political maverick. That its streets were awash with even more military detritus than Berlin's was not, as yet, too pressing a point.

Hoffner squeezed Lina's hand as they walked, and said, "The city's famous for its beer halls. We'd be silly not to try out one or two, don't you think?"

Lina spoke with a knowing ease: "We didn't come just for a day's holiday, did we?"

If he had closed his eyes, Hoffner might have mistaken her for Martha: the same resigned concession. He wondered if he was really that transparent. "Holiday with a purpose," he said. "Not so bad, is it?"

She squeezed his arm a bit tighter. "All right," she said, striking her bargain, "but tomorrow I want a walk in the **Englischer Garten.**"

"Fair enough."

"And a café."

Hoffner brought her hand up to his mouth and kissed it. This far from Berlin, he could allow himself the luxury.

The place was just what he had expected: a wide-open hall with high archways running this way and that, and long wooden tables stretching from wall to wall. Wrought-iron lamps hung from the ceilings and cast a yellow pall over the cavernous space: men and women perched on benches—some of them even up on the tables—with large mugs of beer at the ready. The echo of conversation made it almost impossible to be heard without raising one's voice. Hoffner spotted a collection of young soldiers at one of the central tables and headed Lina in that direction.

They found two places on the bench and settled in as Hoffner flagged down a blowsy waitress and ordered two mugs. He was now in character, staring wide-eyed at the size of the place before turning to Lina with a broad smile. She was equally comfortable playing the country rube. Hoffner had prepared her on the walk over: a bit of make-believe might be in the offing, he had said. After all, she had been playing his wife with apparent ease, how difficult could another role be?

Lina let go with a giddy laugh and swatted playfully at his arm.

"Which regiment are you boys with?" yelled Hoffner to one of the soldiers who was seated on the table, and who was deep in conversation.

The man turned around and looked down. "Pardon?" he said.

"Your regiment," shouted Hoffner. "My son fought with the **Liebregiment.**"

The man leaned over and indicated the markings on his collar. "Sixteenth Bavarian Infantry," he said.

Hoffner raised his eyes wide and nodded. He shouted to Lina, "They're with the Sixteenth Bavarian." Lina nodded up at the man with a smile. Hoffner shouted to her, "Not with Helmut's unit." The man was about to turn away when Hoffner shouted, "My son Helmut was with the **Liebregiment.**"

The man nodded to be kind. "I don't think you'll find any in here tonight, **mein Herr.**" Again, he began to turn away.

Hoffner said, "He was killed at Isonzo, October of '17."

Hoffner had hit upon the unspoken kinship between soldiers. The man now showed a genuine sympathy. "I'm sorry," he said.

Hoffner nodded his thanks. "He won the Iron Cross. For bravery." The man nodded again. "We're here for only a few days, and I was hoping to meet up with some of his comrades, hear about it from them. They said the **Liebregiment** spent its nights here, but perhaps I was mistaken."

The man raised a hand and said, "Hold on a minute." He turned to his friends and called out, "Hey. Hello. **Liebregiment.** Where do they do their drinking?" The others continued to ignore him. He leaned in closer. "Fsst! **Liebregiment,**" he shouted. "This fellow, his son was killed at Isonzo. He wants to look up some of his mates." The man now had their full attention, but unfortunately there were no takers. "Ask down the other end of the table," he said. "Someone's bound to know."

Two minutes later, Hoffner had his answer.

The Alte Rosebad was a much smaller affair, more of a walk, though no less popular. The acoustics, however, were not as ear-shattering: it was actually possible to hold a conversation without popping a vein in one's neck. Hoffner played out the same little drama for a second table of soldiers, this time with a very nice supporting performance from Lina: Helmut was now to have been a butcher and her husband. The men directed them over to a table near the back.

"The roles change," he said to her as they made their way through. "Just follow my lead." He could tell she was enjoying this.

They sat at an opening along one of the long benches. This time Hoffner read through the menu and chatted with Lina before calling over a waiter. He seemed completely uninterested in the soldiers who were an arm's length from them. It was only when he and Lina were halfway through their first mug that he glanced over. "That's not **Liebregiment,** is it?" he said with friendly surprise.

One of the soldiers turned to him. "Pardon?"

"**Liebregiment,** isn't it?"

The man was already well on his way to a very nice night; he smiled. "And who wants to know?"

Hoffner made up a name and said, "That **is Liebregiment.**" He turned to Lina eagerly. "What do you think of that?" She smiled and nodded. Hoffner turned back to the man. "My son had a number of friends back home who went into your regiment."

The man nodded with a bit more interest.

Hoffner said, "Second Battalion."

The man now shook his head with a smile. "No luck, then. It's First Battalion here. Still, I might know a few fellows in the Second."

Hoffner listed three or four of the names he had written down at the GS, making sure to pick the ones that had had the word "deceased" written after them.

The man's face was now more somber. "Yah," he said with a nod. "I knew Schneider. Good man. He was killed in the Italian campaign. Tell your son I'm sorry."

The man began to turn when Hoffner said sadly, "My Helmut was killed at Arras. Sixteenth Bavarian; 1917. But thank you."

There was an awkward silence between them—the man aware that he had no choice but to listen to the story of this man's son—when Hoffner suddenly looked down at the table as if he were trying to recall something important. "What was the name of the boy he said they were always talking about?" He looked to Lina. "The one Helmut met on that leave? You remember the letter?" Lina tried to think, as well. Hoffner popped his head up. "Oster!" he said in triumph. "Erich Oster. Does that sound familiar?"

The man was happy enough to have been given a reprieve. He shook his head, and then turned to his mates, shouting above the din, "Anyone know an Oster? Second Battalion. Friends with Schneider?"

There was a lull, then a shaking of heads, followed by a chorus of noes. The man turned back to give his apologies, when a voice from the far end said, "Erich Oster? Second Lieutenant?" Hoffner leaned in over the table to get a better view of the man.

"Yes," he said eagerly.

"If it's the same fellow, he joined the **Freikorps** a few months back." The man looked to some of his friends. "You know. The fellow who sent out all those leaflets about the Poles." The man laughed, and several others now nodded as they remembered. "Bit of a nutter. I think the battalion was glad to see him go." He laughed again.

Hoffner did his best to look hurt by the accusations. "Oh," he said sadly. Hoffner nodded slowly and sat back.

The first soldier did his best to minimize the damage; he spoke to the far end of the table. "Oster was a friend of this man's son, who died at Arras," he said, emphasizing the word "friend." "I'm sure you remember more than that, don't you?" He prodded with a few nods of his head.

"Oh," said the man, quick to revise his portrayal. "Oh, yes. Of course. He . . . he was a thinker, that Oster. Always reading. And a poet. He wrote those . . . poems." The man suddenly thought of something. "There was that fellow he always talked about." He turned to the man next to him. "You know? He tried to get us to come and hear him. Somewhere up in the artists' quarter."

"That was Oster?" said the friend, who was trying to remember, as well. "You mean up at the Brennessel?"

"Yes. The Brennessel. A poet or something." They had forgotten Hoffner and were now set on figuring out the man's identity.

"Decker or Dieker," said the friend, trying to recall. "Something like that—"

"Eckart!" said the first man. "Dietrich Eckart. Up at the wine cellar."

The friend nodded. "Excellent. That's exactly right." The discovery merited a few quick gulps of beer. The man wiped his mouth and looked back down the table to Hoffner. "You want to know about Oster, you go and see this Eckart fellow." He gave him the name of the bar.

Freikorps and a mentor, thought Hoffner. Oster was becoming more interesting by the minute.

The **Freikorps,** or volunteer corps, had been formed as a direct response to the revolution in late November. Drawn from discharged officers and soldiers, it was initially called on to ward off presumed threats from Polish insurgents. Those threats, of course, had never amounted to much, and by December the **Korps** had taken it upon itself to blot out any

potential communist threats, ostensibly so as to protect the burgeoning German Republic. Recently, units
had begun to sprout up throughout the country—
Hoffner was guessing that the **Schützen-Division**
had provided more than its fair share of recruits—the
most powerful of which were now in Munich and
Berlin. The **Freikorps** made no bones about its politics; they were far to the right, which meant that its
supporters came from a wide range of backgrounds:
monarchists, militarists, thugs, and—as the boy at the
beer hall had said—nutters of every size and shape. As
of now, the **Reichswehr**—the Bavarian Regular
Army—was holding them in check. Anyone with any
sense, though, knew that it would only be a matter of
time before the **Freikorps** could build up enough of a
following to exert a little muscle.

It was nearly eleven when Hoffner and Lina
stepped into the Brennessel wine cellar. The place
was little better than a grotto, run-down and ill-lit,
and seemed to encourage its patrons to stoop, even
though the ceilings were well over two meters high.
Lina had grown tired of the charades, but was being
a good sport. Hoffner explained that it might be a bit
easier this time round: mentors had a tendency to enjoy an audience. All Hoffner needed was to get a few
drinks into Eckart, and the rest would be easy
enough.

As it turned out, Eckart was doing just fine on his
own. He was in the back, holding forth to a half-full
bottle of schnapps and a group of dedicated listeners

when the barkeep pointed him out. Eckart was the obvious choice, all bulging eyes and thick gesticulating hands: the round head—completely hairless—was the final, perfect touch. Eckart might have been a caricature of himself if not for his evident commitment. Hoffner directed Lina over, and the two took seats on the outer rim of a gaggle of soulless eyes and eager ears. They began to listen.

It was several minutes before Eckart noticed the recent additions. He had been going on about the "source of the ancients" and something called the **fama fraternitatis,** when his eye caught Hoffner's. Eckart measured his prey and said, "You're intrigued by what I'm saying, **mein Herr**?"

Hoffner felt every face within the circle turn to him. "It's most interesting, yes," he said with a quiet nod.

"And you just happened upon us?"

"Happened upon you?" Hoffner repeated. "Oh, I see what you mean. Well, no. Not exactly. A friend said I might want to hear what you have to say. I hope that's all right?"

"And who might this friend be?"

Hoffner glanced at the eyes that were staring across at him; he wanted to make sure he was playing the neophyte with just the right degree of hesitation. He looked back at Eckart and said, "Oster. Erich Oster. He was handing out pamphlets. We chatted."

The name produced a knowing nod. "Erich," said Eckart. He waited, then said, "Good man. Welcome." Eckart poured himself another drink and went back to the faithful.

It was remarkable to see a man speak with such energy to so small a group. The hand movements alone were almost athletic, pumping fists and sculpting hands, his pauses equally mesmerizing: the sweat on his cheeks glistened as he lifted the glass to his lips. It hardly mattered what he was saying, not that Hoffner could follow much of it. He had been expecting the usual **Freikorps** claptrap: that the Reds had lost them the war; that the socialists were now denying them their rightful jobs; that the old Germany was being sold off to placate the bloodlust of the French and the English, so forth and so on. This, however, was something entirely different. Eckart spoke about things far more elusive, a German spirit that had been lost to "the struggle with the anti-life." He seemed obsessed with the ancient tales of Fenrir the Wolf and Tyr the Peacemaker, Wotan and Freyer, Asgard and Ragnarok: this was where nobility was to be found, where courage and purpose spoke in a language known only to the "adepts." Hoffner half expected to hear a hushed chorus from **Parsifal** or **Lohengrin** rise up from the men sitting around the table.

It all seemed to be leading somewhere, when Eckart suddenly stopped and began to examine his glass; like the bottle at its side, it was now empty. With practiced ease, he looked to his audience and said, "But the glass is empty. And when the glass is empty, the wise man knows to quiet his mind."

Hoffner was not familiar with this particular apho-
rism, nor was he prepared for the response. Without
a word, the group calmly began to get up. Whatever
Hoffner thought had gone unsaid was evidently not
as pressing to the men now gathering up their coats.
One of the younger ones—a student, judging by his
clothes—rushed over with a few questions, but
Eckart made quick work of him. It was clear, though,
that Eckart was still very much aware of Hoffner.
When the boy had moved off and the table was again
empty, Eckart turned to him. It was only then that
Eckart seemed to notice Lina. He leaned to one side
so as to get a better view and said, "And another
friend, I see." Lina produced a pleasant smile.

Hoffner said, "I hope we haven't been the cause of
an early evening?"

Now Eckart smiled. "There **are** no early evenings,
mein Herr." He waved them over. "Come, sit with
me." Hoffner and Lina joined him. "I'm drinking
schnapps," he added. Instantly, Hoffner turned
around to call over a waiter. Hoffner ordered a bottle.

Eckart said, "You sit patiently. You listen and wait.
So what is it that interests you, Herr . . ."

Hoffner resurrected the name from earlier this
evening. "You speak with great passion, **mein Herr.**"

"And passion is enough for you?"

"When there's something behind it, yes."

Eckart liked the answer. "And what do you imagine
lies behind it?"

Hoffner had several choices. He could follow the

Freikorps trail, although he doubted more than a handful of recruits were finding inspiration in the retelling of childhood fairy tales; the pamphlets, of course, were the most telling feature—where there were pamphlets, there was organization; and where there was organization, there was money—but it was too large a risk to venture into something he knew nothing about, which left him with Eckart's enigmatic stopping point. Hoffner said, "I thought I was about to find out."

The response seemed to surprise Eckart. The pleasant grin became a look of focused appraisal. "Did you?" he said. Hoffner thought the conversation might be heading for a quick close, when the bottle arrived and the waiter began to spill out three glasses. Without hesitation, Eckart downed his and held it out for a refill. The waiter obliged and then set the bottle on the table. Eckart slowly poured out his third as Hoffner pulled out a few coins to pay. This time Eckart let his glass sit. He waited for the man to step off before saying, "The German people lie behind everything, **mein Herr.** Sadly a German people now struggling to find themselves."

Hoffner heard the first tinge of political disenchantment; he took a sip of his schnapps and nodded. "I lost a son in the war," he said, opting for what had been working so well tonight. "The Fräulein a husband. I don't imagine this is the Germany he thought he was giving his life for. It's not the Germany I knew."

Eckart understood. "It's still there, **mein Herr.** It simply needs some guidance." Hoffner now expected the full weight of the **Freikorps** credo to come spilling forth; what came out was therefore far more startling.

According to Eckart, the stories of nobility and strength were not meant to be followed in the abstract: they were meant to be fully realized in the "rituals of rebirth and order." With a few more well-chosen—though equally impenetrable— phrases, Eckart began to show himself for what he was: no ideologue, he was a self-proclaimed mystic. His gift was an understanding of the "core animus" of the German people, a spirit that separated them from all others and thus granted them a greater sense of nobility. He called it the "Thulian Ideal"—a gift from the lost island civilization of Thule—all of it in the pamphlets if one knew how to read between the lines. Hoffner nodded with each subsequent glass that Eckart tossed back. There were other Thulians, he was told, with access to other discrete bits of knowledge, all of whom recognized that the war and the revolution had ripped the soul from the German people, and who now saw it as their duty to rekindle that spirit and order.

Hoffner might have dismissed it all as the harmless, if slightly loonier, cousin of those societies he had so eagerly avoided at university—the image of a naked Eckart running through the Black Forest was dis- turbing to be sure—were it not for the fact that he

had **not** simply happened upon Eckart and his devotees. The line that had led him from Rosa to Wouters
to Oster, and now to this, was too firmly drawn: six
women brutally—and perhaps ritualistically—murdered; the dying Urlicher willing to take his own life
at Sint-Walburga; Hoffner himself still having
trouble breathing from his beating; and the Cavalry
Guard thugs Pabst and Vogel hardly the messengers
of some imagined Teutonic mythos. There was a reality to this that had led him to a Munich wine cellar. What was more frightening was that it clearly led
beyond it.

Hoffner now needed a better sense of that reality.
"And to achieve that order, **mein Herr**?"

Eckart nodded as if he had been anticipating the
question. "Remove the cancer from the body," he
said. "Purge it of the disease." The politician had
returned.

Hoffner stated the obvious. "The socialists,"
he said.

Eckart looked momentarily confused. "The Jews,
mein Herr. The elimination of the Jews, of course."

Hoffner stifled his reaction. It had been said with
such certainty. With no other choice, Hoffner nodded. "Of course."

They begged off at just after midnight. By
then, Eckart had been slurring his words and had
long since drifted from talk of nobility and strength
to his favorite topics of racial superiority and pu-

rity—"Every great conflict has been a war between the races, **mein Herr;** that's the truth that the barking swine Jew doesn't want you to know"—a fitting capper to the evening. He had even explained to Lina why her husband's death had been at the behest of the Jews: "A war for the profiteers to destroy a generation of German youth; your Helmut's blood is on their hands, Fräulein."

Lina and Hoffner were both stone-cold sober when they stepped out into the night. They walked in silence as Hoffner wondered how much of this had been new to her. He, of course, had heard his fair share of Jew-bating over the years, especially in the south, but this was something different even for him, something more fully conceived, and without so much as a trace of restraint. A good anti-Semite usually had the sense to show a little subtlety in his jabs. Eckart's demonization was completely unabashed.

Lina was the first to speak: "So, any more charming drinking partners tonight, or are we through playing?"

Hoffner was glad for her cynicism. She was still so young, and men like Eckart relied on that vulnerability. At least here, Lina was showing none. "Not what I was expecting," he said, matching her tone. "Two cafés tomorrow, then, to make up for it."

The streets were deserted as they walked, Munich after midnight no better than a provincial town, taller buildings, wider streets, but everyone safely tucked away in their fine Bavarian beds. No wonder

Eckart felt so at home here. At the hotel, Hoffner had to ring twice before the concierge came to open the door. The man looked slightly put out. His guests were usually in their rooms by eleven.

Upstairs, she was undressed and in bed before Hoffner had managed his way out of his pants. Not that she was in any great hurry for him; a bed this size was simply new to her: Lina wanted to take as much time in it as she could. She made an effort to reach over and help, but Hoffner seemed to work through his pain better alone.

When they were finally lying naked side by side, she propped herself up on an elbow and said, "You know, you're really quite good at what you do."

He was on his back, staring up at the ceiling, and smiled at her apparent surprise. "Thank you." He had a sudden taste for a cigarette, but the pack was in his jacket across the room: too much of an effort to get up for it now.

"You know what I mean," she said. She took hold of his hand and began to thumb across his open palm. "It was good fun to watch." He stared down at her as she used her nail to pick at a bit of dead skin that was on one of his fingers. "I don't imagine Hans is nearly that clever."

Hoffner had not been expecting Fichte to make an appearance tonight, but here he was, casually tossed onto the bed with them. She seemed easy enough with it; Hoffner was happy to follow suit. "He might surprise you," he said. He could only guess at what the boys on the fourth floor had in mind for young Fichte.

She was busy with his finger as she shook her head. "Not Hans." She brushed away a few flakes of skin and looked up at him. "You think it's strange that I'm talking about him." It was a statement, not a question.

Hoffner did his best with a shrug. "Something we have in common."

Lina drove a nail into the thick part of his hand and said with a rough smile, "Ass. Yes, lying naked in a bed, and that's what we have in common."

Hoffner tried to pull his hand away, but she was too quick. She brought it up to her mouth and kissed the bruised skin and he felt her tongue dabbing at his palm. "You were the one to bring him into the room with us," he said.

"He'll be all right in a few days. Boys like Hans always are." For some reason she had needed to tell him this. "So . . . what's this pact I've heard so much about?"

The question caught Hoffner completely off guard. "The what?" he said.

"The pact," she repeated. "Hans told me. He said he heard about it when he was in Belgium." She stopped, her expression momentarily less animated. She had reminded herself of Fichte's recent cruelties. Evidently her own recovery would take a bit longer than the one she had imagined for him.

"Oh, the pact," Hoffner cut in quickly. Not that he

was all that keen to bring it up, but better that than to allow Fichte's stupidity any greater sway over her. With a careless shrug he said, "Not really that interesting."

He watched as she gazed up at him; without warning, she was on her knees, leaning over his face, her thumbnail hovering menacingly above his cheek. "Really?" she said with an impish grin. "Not that interesting?"

Hoffner lay there calmly. "Not really."

Lina's eyes flashed and, in one fluid movement, she was on him, pressing her hands down onto his shoulders and tightening her thighs around his chest.

All of this would have been quite wonderful, and the prelude to some really exquisite bed time, had Hoffner's ribs not forced him to shout out in intense pain. Lina at once realized what she had done and frantically pulled herself off him. Her knee grazed his abdomen and Hoffner let go with a second, stifled groan.

She was lying perfectly still at his side when he finally managed to say, "We'll try it this way. You promise not to move and I'll tell you about the pact. Fair enough?"

Lina began to nod; she stopped herself and, barely opening her mouth, said, "Fine."

Hoffner kept his eyes on the ceiling as the throbbing in his chest receded to a dull ache.

It had been a long time since he had sought out these memories, three blind-drunk Germans sprawled out under a half-moon on the most perfect Tyrolean hillside he had ever known. He let himself recall the grass under his neck, the taste of the olive trees on his tongue, the sound of König's laughter as it had echoed into the vast nothingness of the valley below. Mueller had been whole then, dancing in the darkness on two good legs, a bottle in each flawless hand, spilling more booze than he could drink. It was life as Hoffner had never known it—before or since—full and vibrant and unbearably real.

"We were in the Tyrol," he said as he continued to gaze up. "A palazzo in the hills. König, Mueller, me. I forget the name. August of '15. I don't remember how we worked it. They flew in, picked me up. Something like that. Anyway, they were on leave, and we found ourselves on this hillside, two, three in the morning. . . ." He turned to her. "You're sure you're interested in this?"

"Yes," she pressed. "I'm sure."

"Fine," he conceded. He adjusted his pillow. "So there we are, two, three in the morning, soused to the gills, and Victor—König—starts in on how much he loves life, how much he understands it now that he's flying over battlefields and seeing bodies and waste and on and on. Until he says that he won't be coming back. That he **knows** he won't be coming back, because he's been given this extraordinary gift to appreciate it all. And Mueller and I just sit there, and listen, and wait until he's finished, and tell him he's an idiot." Hoffner lost himself for a moment. "Of course, he wasn't," he said quietly. Refocusing, he turned to her. "So I say I'm not going to ruin the few days we have together talking about that sort of nonsense. And he says, 'If you're so sure it's nonsense, then make it worth my while.'" Even now Hoffner could hear the arrogance in König's voice. "So I did. If he came home, he came home, nothing else. If he didn't, then I promised to be faithful to my wife. That was it. The agreement. The pact." Hoffner remembered the letter he had received, the typewritten t's that had jumped too high on the line, the word "death" with a little hitch just before the end. He was gazing up at the ceiling again and said, "He was shot down two months later. Mueller and I got very drunk."

Lina lay quiet. She waited until he turned to her before saying, "I thought it was something else. I wouldn't have asked. I'm sorry."

He tried a smile. "No reason to be."

"Do you regret not keeping it?"

"Not keeping what?"

"Your promise."

"Ah." Hoffner nodded slowly to himself. "My promise." He lay with the word a moment longer. "But I did," he said. It was now Lina's turn to look confused. "At least up until a few weeks ago."

Lina brought herself up on an elbow and gazed down at him. He had never seen this look before. There was a caring and a concern that was almost too much to take in. At once, he regretted having told her. She said, "You never told me that."

He kept it light. "Not exactly something you bring up, is it?"

"That's over three years."

"Yes."

"And that was it? You'd spent long enough keeping your word?"

He knew what she wanted him to say—that it had been because of her that he had betrayed König—but that would have been no more true than the other. He said vaguely, "I don't think it works that way."

"Works what way?"

"The way that makes it more than it is." He meant it not to be unkind but to protect, even though he knew it was too late. He could see now how this would all fall apart; it would only be a matter of time. They had been safe as long as questions of intent had remained hidden; his story made that impossible: too much meaning, and they would crumble under the weight; too little, and she would feel a different kind of betrayal. For her, the breaking of the pact had hinged on a choice—imagined or not—which even now Hoffner had to admit might not have been so disengaged, or so consciously made, after all.

For several moments she hovered above him, searching for something more. When it was clear that there was nothing more, she lay back. "You were close with him," she said. "With König."

"Yes."

"And he knew your wife." Again, she was stating, not asking.

Hoffner felt the pull of his cigarettes from across the room. "I suppose. Does it matter?"

"He wanted to help her."

Whether days or weeks from now, he thought, he would always look to this moment as their last. "Do you know where I put my cigarettes?" he said.

"Why did he want to help her?"

Lina was digging with no care for the consequences, and that left him no room to hide. "He didn't," he said. He struggled to get himself upright, then brought his legs over the side and sat with his back to her. "He thought he was helping me, which showed how little he understood." Hoffner got up and moved across to the pile of clothes. "Did I put them in my jacket?"

He was fumbling through his pants when she said, "And what didn't he understand?"

The sting, of course, was in her feigned indifference, but it was hardly fair feeling the least irritation when it had been his own stupidity that had put them here. The past was kept in strongboxes for a reason; he had removed the lid and had been forced to peer in for himself. How could he blame her for making him rummage through to the bottom?

He located the pack and lit one up. "Victor saw things differently at the end," he said. "That's all. I never floated over battlefields and so never gained the same appreciation."

Lina spoke with an honesty that went beyond her years: "That seems unkind."

"Yes, it does, doesn't it?" He suddenly recalled the name. "Terranova. Palazzo Terranova. Victor found it all very meaningful." She looked confused. "New-ground," he explained. "'Terranova' means 'new ground.'"

"You resent him for it."

She had never challenged him like this: endings, he imagined—even at their inception—granted a kind of invincibility. "For what?" he said.

"For seeing things in a way you couldn't."

Hoffner shook his head. "He was creating his own version of nobility, the great sacrifice, and he wanted me to do the same thing."

"So being faithful to your wife was a sacrifice?"

It sounded so hollow, coming from her. At least Victor had done what he had in the name of something vital, a life rediscovered, a gift repaid. But it was a vicious circle: that kind of redemption was only for those who could embrace vitality. Hoffner had survived on an imitation kind, his own fueled by infidelity, which only made his choice to make good on the promise an even greater hypocrisy. He had let himself be fooled—just once—into seeing it for more than it was: some meaningless argument with Martha when he had revealed his self-denial and had staked his claim to nobility, but she had been no more unforgiving than Lina. "What sacrifice?" Martha had said with justified bitterness: his sudden rage, her body sent crashing to the floor. Hoffner now realized that it was the shame of that moment that he had grown tired of; and it was that fatigue, and nothing more, that had led him to Lina.

He took a pull on his cigarette and said, "It's difficult to sacrifice something you never had."

She had watched the sadness in his face, but she showed him no pity. "And you think getting into bed with me makes any difference?"

He looked over at her and he knew: I won't even be a memory to her one day. "No," he said. "It doesn't."

There was something comforting in the truth, even for her. He lay back down and she placed her arm across his chest. Later they made love and they fell asleep and Hoffner dreamed of Rosa.

SHATTERED GLASS

A group of children was playing in the short grass as mothers and nannies looked on from the safety of benches. Hoffner and Lina had settled themselves farther off, under a grove of trees where an enterprising vendor with a coffee cart had set up a few tables and chairs alongside the gravel path. Not yet ten o'clock, and they had already made a full morning of it at the shops and markets, which had been up and running since seven. The Gardens were a welcome relief.

"How did you know about this spot?" Lina asked as

she poured another healthy dose of cream into her cup. Hoffner had never seen a whiter cup of coffee. From her expression, it was still too bitter.

"Pretty, isn't it?" he said. He had made the telephone call this morning and had been told where to find it. "The concierge," Hoffner lied. He checked his watch and took a last sip of coffee before getting up. "I need to find the toilet," he said. "Have a sweet or something while I'm gone." He placed a few coins on the table and headed out through the trees.

Three minutes later he came across his old friend Peter Barens, sitting on a secluded bench. Hoffner drew up and said, "You give excellent directions, Peter." He sat.

"It's good to see you, too, Nikolai."

They had known each other since university, two young law students with an eye to criminology. Barens had made chief inspector almost eight years ago; there was talk of a directorship in his future. Barens said, "I was sorry to hear about König." Hoffner stared out at the park and nodded. "And now a chief inspector," Barens continued. "I imagine even you can't cock up that promotion."

"We'll see, won't we?"

Barens pulled a thin file from his case. "So why the interest in this?" He handed it to Hoffner.

Hoffner opened the file and found ten to twelve pages on the Thule Society, very complete, very organized: Barens really was an excellent detective. "Best not to say," said Hoffner.

"Naturally." He let Hoffner flip through to the next page before saying, "Odd how I get a telephone call asking me if I have anything on a man named Eckart, or anything having to do with—what did you call it?—the 'Thulian Ideal,' when we've been keeping an eye on these people for the past few months." Hoffner nodded distractedly as he continued to scan the pages. "There's a lot of money there, Nikolai. Your friend Eckart has more than he knows what to do with, as do most of the names on that list."

Hoffner continued to read. "And what are they using it for?"

"Besides pamphlets and bad beer ... They've started two organizations. The Workers Political Circle and the German Workers Party. They also recently bought a rag called **The Observer.** Interesting blend of German folklore and race-baiting. They're going after the workers and the nationalists. Not usually Kripo business to monitor the political fringes, but these fellows throw around too much weight not to."

"And they still consider themselves a secret society?"

"In theory. I'm sure that's what they'd like to think. Tough to maintain the image, though, when you go around recruiting as aggressively as they do."

Hoffner came to what he had been looking for: the name Joachim Manstein appeared halfway down the third page. There was a small paragraph on him, but

Hoffner knew he would need more time with it. He closed the file and said, "What about ties to the **Freikorps**?"

"You really have been doing your homework, haven't you?"

"I always did."

For the first time, Barens smiled. "They both hate the communists, but the Thulians save their real venom for the Jews. We've had a few minor incidents, street vandalism, a few punch-ups. Eisner's presence hasn't made it any easier, but it's all pretty local stuff, which makes me wonder why a Berlin **Oberkommissar,** recent hero of the Republic, has come all the way down to Munich to ask about a group of crackpots he should never have heard of."

Hoffner placed the file inside his coat and said, "You're a good friend, Peter."

Barens became more serious. "I'm a good bull, Nikolai. If there's something I should know, you need to tell me. Are they moving beyond pamphlets and bad beer?"

Hoffner waited and then stood. "I should go," he said. "Give my best to Clara and the girls."

Barens remained seated. There was clearly more he wanted to hear. Nonetheless he said, "I'll pass that along." Hoffner turned to go, when Barens added, "And mine to the little chippy by the coffee cart." Barens waited for Hoffner to turn around before saying, "Some things never change, do they, Nikolai?"

Barens had always been impressive, and always in the right way. It was why Hoffner had known to trust him. "I suppose they don't," he said.

Barens stood. "These men aren't far from doing more than simply tossing a store or beating up a few students. I lost a man on this, Nikolai. Why do you think I could get my hands on the material so quickly?"

It was now clear why Barens had agreed to meet, and why he had brought the file: he was as eager for information as Hoffner was. "Lost a man? How?"

Barens had no intention of explaining. "If you do know something, and you're not telling me, I'll be very disappointed." He paused. "And you'll have been very foolish. What do you have, Nikolai?"

Barens had always been known as "the old man," even as a nineteen-year-old at university. It had made him both insufferable and endearing. Hoffner said, "Her name is Lina. And she's the last."

Hoffner could see the frustration in his friend's eyes: favors usually implied a little more give and take. Barens, however, was too good at what he did to let it linger. "I doubt that," he said.

Hoffner grinned. "There's always a chance, isn't there?" He bobbed his head in thanks and said, "Take care of yourself, Peter."

Barens took hold of Hoffner's arm and, like an older brother, said, "Know what you're getting your-self into, Nikolai."

Hoffner nodded. He waited for Barens to release his arm and then headed off.

Lina had settled on a large cup of chocolate for lunch; it was all she had wanted. Hoffner had taken advantage of the beef again, this time with a plate of onions and a few potatoes. More daring, he and Lina were throwing provincial caution to the wind and talking to each other—light fare, nothing from last night—when they heard the first sirens. The klaxons grew louder and curiosity gave way to concern as the sound of shouting began to come from the street. Everyone in the place stopped eating as the waiter stepped over to the door and peered out through the glass. His expression turned to confusion. "There are soldiers in the street," he said to the maître d'.

The man stepped over to verify; his reaction was no more promising: the taste of revolution was still fresh in everyone's throat. At the sound of more sirens, Hoffner got up. He told Lina to wait, then made his way to the door. Against all protestations from the maître d', Hoffner stepped out into the street.

It was almost completely empty. The soldiers were positioned in front of a large domed building at the far end of the street, rifles across their chests, waiting. The few pedestrians who remained on the street were doing all they could to find shelter inside. Hoffner managed to flag one down. "Madame," he said as he tried to keep up with her. "Excuse me, but which is that building up there?"

The woman continued to move quickly as she looked at him: she spoke as if to a halfwit. "That building, **mein Herr**? That's the Landtag." She shook her head in disbelief and hurried off. Hoffner stopped: they're cordoning off Parliament, he thought. Why? He quickly made his way back to the restaurant and over to the maître d'. The man was relieved to see him back.

Hoffner said, "I need to use your telephone, **mein Herr.**" Hoffner pulled out his badge: it might have said Berlin, but the word **"Kriminalpolizei"** was enough to stir the man to action. Hoffner nodded calmly over to Lina as he waited for the operator to connect the call.

"Yes," said Hoffner. "Chief Inspector Barens, please." Hoffner gave his credentials. "I'm aware of that, Fräulein. This **is** of vital importance. Just connect me with the Chief Inspector." Hoffner waited through the static until Barens finally came on the line. Hoffner said, "I'm standing a hundred meters from the Landtag building, Peter. What just happened?"

Hoffner could hear the mayhem in the background. "Hold on," said Barens. There was a round of shouting before Barens came back to the line. "Nikolai, what are you doing near the Landtag?"

It was a meaningless question. Hoffner asked again, "Why are soldiers surrounding the building, Peter?"

There was a pause on the line before Barens said, "Someone's shot Eisner. Half an hour ago. Eisner's dead."

Hoffner tried to stem his reaction. "Who?" he said.

"We don't know yet. A student. That's all we have."

Hoffner asked the more dangerous question: "More than bad beer and pamphlets?"

There was another pause before Barens answered, "I don't know, but I need you to tell me that you knew nothing about this, not even the possibility of this."

"Of course," said Hoffner with more conviction than perhaps was warranted. "What about Ebert?"

"So far, nothing. We're waiting for a wire to confirm. It might already be here. I don't know. Look, Nikolai, get yourself back to Berlin. We'll probably be shutting down the main station in the next hour or so, and if you stay here, you won't be of any use. Trust me. Safe trip."

The line went dead and Hoffner handed the receiver back to the maître d'. Twenty minutes later, Hoffner and Lina were getting their bags from the hotel; forty minutes after that, they were on the last train heading north: Hoffner's badge had seen to that, as well. It would mean that they would have to get out and wait somewhere along the way for the train out of Frankfurt, but at least they would be back in Berlin by tonight. Hoffner now had seven hours to acquaint himself with the men of the Thule Society and Joachim Manstein.

Notes on meetings, December 4, 1918, through January 18, 1919, Thule Society, as recorded by Kriminal-Bezirkssekretär **Stefan Meier:**

December 4: Our first meeting outside the beer hall. We meet at the house of Anton Drexler, a locksmith in the employ of the railroad shops. Drexler is a small, sickly man who talks for over an hour about the "mongrelization" of the German people and the corruption of the socialist regime. He refers to members of the government as "the Jew Eisner and the Jew Scheidemann." There are nine of us. I believe we are only one of several cells of "Initiates" meeting throughout the city tonight. Unlike Eckart, Drexler is a poor speaker. We are instructed to bring documented proof of our Aryan ancestry to the next meeting.

December 9: Again we meet at the house of Drexler. Only four of us are permitted to remain once our papers are examined. Two other members of the Society are present but we are not told their names. One of them is a doctor. He takes a sample of blood from each of us. We are then given copies of two books written by Guido von List (*The Invincible* and *The Secret of Runes*), magazines published by Jorg Lanz

von Liebenfels (*Prana* and *Ostara*), a direc-
tory of pan-German and anti-Semitic
groups by Philipp Stauff (*The German Defense Book*), and the manifesto of the
Armanist Religious Revival from the organization known as The Walvater Teutonic
Order of the Holy Grail, written by Hermann
Pohl. An excerpt from Liebenfel's *Ostara* I,
#69, makes clear the general thinking be-
hind all of these writings: "The holy grail
is an electrical symbol pertaining to the
panpsychic powers of the pure-blooded
Aryan race. The quest of the Templars for
the grail was a metaphor for the strict eu-
genic practices of the Templar Knights designed to breed god-men."

December 13, 18, 24, 29: We meet at the
house of the journalist Karl Harrer (founder
of the Workers Political Circle and chair-
man of the German Workers Party [see be-
low]). He is no better a speaker than Drexler
and, over the four nights, takes us through
the history of the Society (see below), the
rituals of Rebirth and Order (see below),
the Covenant of the pan-Germanic people
(see below), and the hierarchy of the races
(see below). We are each required to recite
long passages from *The Invincible* and to
exhibit physical stamina and strength by

withstanding long periods of heavy objects being placed on our chests.

January 5: We are taken to a house on the outskirts of the city, where we are given our first initiation rites. This includes full disrobement, the cutting of two Runic symbols into the underside of the left upper arm, and the laying on of hands by a man we are instructed to call Tarnhari. We are told that he is the reincarnation of the god-chieftain of the Wölsungen tribe of prehistoric Germany. We are now required to recite from memory passages from *The Invincible* and to pledge a vow to our racial purity.

January 9, 14, 15: The rituals continue at the house of Rudolf Freiherr von Seboottendorf, where we are joined by seven other Initiates from around the city. Seboottendorf is a mystic trained in the art of Sufi meditation. Over the three nights, he leads us in séance-like rituals meant to contact the Ancients from the lost island civilization of Thule. Seboottendorf is the only one of us to make contact.

January 18: We are brought to the lodge on Seitz Strasse and introduced to the mem-

bers of the Thule Society. There are, by
rough estimation, seventy men present. I
am able to learn twenty or so of the names
(see below).

Lina was still asleep when Hoffner turned to the final page. It was written in a different hand and detailed Detective Sergeant Meier's apparent suicide on the twenty-fourth of January: he had hanged himself in his one-room flat. There was no evidence at present to contradict the coroner's findings. Clearly, Barens was not convinced.

Disturbing as Meier's death was, Hoffner was far more interested in the seventeenth name on the list. Reading through the paragraph was like watching the shattering of a glass in reverse, every shard swept up into perfect coherence:

Joachim Manstein, born 1882, Munich, degree in medicine, University of Berlin, 1905, married Elena Marr Schumpert 1907, two children, Magda 1908 and Tómas 1910 . . . Doctor of Neurology and Psychiatric Medicine at Prince-Charles-Theodore Hospital, Lecturer in same at Ludwig Maximilian University . . . Served in 5th Cavalry 1915–1918 as frontline surgeon, received the Knight's Cross of the Military Order of Maximilian-Joseph, and the Order of Merit. The "Blue Max," usually reserved for Prus-

sian officers, was awarded. . . . Signature
member, along with Philipp Stauff and
Guido von List, of the High Armanen-Order
(1911) . . . Published articles include "Refu-
tation of Judeo-Psychritic Origins" (*Prana*,
1912), "The Pathology of the Mob-races"
(*Ostara*, 1913), and "The Specter of Judeo-
Marxism" (*Iron Hammer*, 1916). . . .

The thirty-seven-year-old Manstein had been on the
front lines and had had access to large quantities of Ascomycete 4; his medical background made him the
perfect candidate to seek out Wouters and to orches-
trate his removal from Sint-Walburga. He might even
have had a relationship with the asylum prior to the
war: Hoffner made a note to check in with van Acker.
More than that, the articles made Manstein a devoted
Thulian; and, most important, his wife's maiden name
tied him to the directors of Ganz-Neurath: Hoffner
was guessing she was Herr Director Schumpert's eldest daughter, courted during Manstein's university
days. Hoffner had sent out wires to the registrars of
the Munich universities; he had never thought to look
in Berlin.

And yet the **why** remained unclear. Hoffner had all
the players in line, but he was no closer to understanding what had prompted them to unleash
Wouters on Berlin, or what they hoped to gain by
keeping Rosa in the wings. Eisner's assassination
made far more sense.

The train took a sudden jolt, and Lina opened her eyes. She had been asleep for the last two hours. For a moment she seemed unsure where she was.

"Another twenty minutes," said Hoffner. She stared vacantly at him and then peered out the window as the first lights of Berlin began to appear. She placed her head on his shoulder and went back to sleep.

The news from Munich had brought out a few units of the Guard Fusiliers Regiment, who now patrolled Berlin's Friedrichstrasse station; the soldiers, however, were doing their best not to cause any alarm as they went about their task.

Sascha stood by one of the station kiosks. He peered down at the evening edition of the **Tageblatt** and read with passing interest of the day's events:

Early reports of communist radicals storming the Bavarian Landtag building—followed by equally unreliable stories of a monarchist counterrevolution—had all finally sifted down to one Count Anton Arco-Valley, a young law student with nationalist political leanings who, according to authorities, had acted entirely on his own. Odder still were the rumors that Arco-Valley was of Jewish descent; no one knew what to make of that. Why shoot one of his own? Though rattled, the Social Democrats had reassured everyone that all was well—after all, Eisner had been planning to offer his resignation this very afternoon anyway—and had quickly installed an interim

government without so much as a peep of resistance
from the opposition.

Smoke and shadows, thought Sascha as he read:
some lunatic finds himself a pistol and the entire
country has to hold its breath for a few hours. Shame
they hadn't shot him in the process.

Sascha checked his watch for a third time. He then
smoothed back his hair. He was wearing his school
jacket, this time with the long pants, and had
brought a small bouquet of flowers, which he held
awkwardly in his hand. Kroll had been good enough
to let him meet her on his own. It was meant to be a
surprise. Sascha was hoping Geli would find it as
marvelous as he did.

Hoffner gently nudged Lina awake. Berlin
was slowing all around them, the station just the
other side of the river and strangely less formidable
after dark. He retrieved their bags and headed out
into the corridor. She was behind him, one of her
hands playfully lodged in his coat pocket: they had
left last night behind them. It would find them soon
enough, but Hoffner was guessing that they could
manage another few weeks convincing themselves
that it wouldn't. The train pulled in, and Lina
stepped down to the platform. Ups and downs were
a bit tougher on his ribs, and Hoffner winced as he
joined her. For whatever reason—her sense of invincibility growing by the minute, he thought—she

placed her hand on his cheek and kissed him. Bags in hand, Hoffner had no choice but to submit.

Sascha moved down the platform, trying to pick her out among the stream of passengers. He felt a wonderful burning in his throat and chest, and found it almost impossible not to smile. He thought he saw her among a swarm of hats and gloves, but the girl there was not nearly pretty enough. He continued to move upstream until he caught sight of something familiar though oddly not: he stopped. It took him another moment to fully process what he was seeing. He felt a strange compression in his head, a numbness where the burning had been. He stood there, unable to turn away. Bodies jostled past him, a station announcement crackled above, but all he could do was to stare at his father and this girl and feel the cold rush of an untapped violence.

Hoffner sensed it before he saw it. He opened his eyes and stared back through the flow of bodies. He must have tensed, because Lina instantly turned to follow his gaze.

There was a dreamlike quality to the next few moments, Hoffner placing the bags on the platform, stepping past her, moving toward the boy. He could see himself doing all of it, but he felt none of it. Lina knew to stay where she was.

Hoffner drew up and said, "Alexander." The word

carried no weight at all, the sound of his own voice almost foreign to him. Hoffner tried again, but all he could manage was a long breath out as Sascha stood unnervingly still. Finally Hoffner said, "This is . . ." His words petered out. Is what? he thought. There was no way to see it for anything other than what it was. Hoffner was again struck by his own impotence.

"This is what you are, Father," said Sascha with quiet hatred.

Hoffner heard the certainty in the tone, the betrayal more wrenching given the last few weeks of goodwill between them. Hoffner's crime had now stripped away any boundaries: Sascha could accuse without any thought of reprisal. The boy wanted to hear his hatred justified, and Hoffner had no reason to deny him that. "Yes," said Hoffner. "I suppose it is."

Confirmation only made things worse. The truth brought Sascha to the edge. His breathing grew forced, as if he might strike his father.

Hoffner tried to calm him. "Look, Sascha—"

It was too late. Sascha glanced over at Lina. He felt shamed to be seen by her: she had no right to know him. Uncoiling his rage, Sascha looked back at his father and thrust the flowers into his chest. "Why don't you give them to **her**?" he said. Hoffner tried to answer, but Sascha pushed past him and ran into the crowd. There was a moment when Hoffner thought to go after the boy, but he had no idea what he was supposed to do if and when he caught up with him. This was a consequence that, perhaps for the first time, he had no hope of meeting.

Hoffner looked back for Lina. She was gone as well, along with her case, leaving his off by itself. Hoffner's isolation had never felt so stark.

He stood there for several minutes until a voice broke through. "Herr Hoffner?"

Hoffner turned around and saw a pretty face with bright eyes peering up at him. He needed a moment to recall the girl. It was only then that he even considered why Sascha had been here. Coincidence and proximity, he thought: the cosmos was having a go of it tonight. He did his best with a kind smile. "Fräulein Geli," he said. "What a delight to see you again."

She smiled and said hopefully, "I thought I might have seen Alexander, **mein Herr?**"

"Really?" said Hoffner, thinking as he spoke. "I don't think so," he said lightly. "He asked me to meet you, and to make sure you got these." Hoffner handed her the bruised flowers.

Her eyes lit up. "Oh, really! Will I be seeing him tonight, **mein Herr?**"

Hoffner picked up her case and said, "Fathers never get the full details, Fräulein. I'm simply to bring you to Herr Kroll's, though I imagine they're preparing something quite wonderful for you."

Hoffner had given her hope; it was the least he could do for the boy.

Sascha ran until his lungs gave out. He steadied himself against a wall and hunched over. Only now did he think of Geli waiting for him on the platform, a double anguish to add to his rage. It was too late to go back for her now. He felt queasy and cursed his father: ruined even that, didn't you? He spat with disgust just as a tram was pulling up across the road. Sascha glanced over and read the route heading: **Kreuzberg.** He took it as a sign.

Inside, he drew stares from the other passengers as he paced at the back; he didn't care: he needed to keep himself moving. At Friesen Strasse he leapt out and continued running past the porter and across the courtyard, up the four flights to the flat, only stopping for breath when he had shut the door behind him. He heard his mother in the kitchen, and moved down the hall toward her.

"Nikolai?" she called. "Is that you?"

She was washing something in the sink when he stepped into the room. He realized that his shirt was damp through. Sascha rubbed an arm across his mouth to wipe away the sweat, and Martha turned around.

She looked pleased if a bit confused to see him. "Alexander?" she said. "I thought you were meeting Geli." It took her a moment to recognize the state he was in. "What's the matter?" she asked uneasily.

Sascha was still catching his breath. He took off his coat and threw it on the chair. "You're soaked through. What is it?"

Sascha was working on impulse now: nothing mattered beyond the telling. He said, "Sit down, Mother," as he moved back and forth across the floor. She took a few steps toward him, but he put up a hand. "Please, Mother," he said more insistently. "Just sit down."

She had never seen him like this; Martha did as he asked.

Sascha continued to move as he spoke. "I saw Father," he said. "At the station. Just now."

It was the way Sascha said it, the way his eyes darted about, that told Martha exactly what the boy had seen. She listened, but the details hardly mattered. There was of course the humiliation of hearing it all from her son, but she had long ago refused self-pity: pity of any kind placed the fault with her, and she had no interest in that; it had taken her years to understand it. Sascha's initiation, however, had come less than an hour ago. What pain she felt was for the weight of his new-won burden.

He stopped talking. Instinct told her to go to him, but she knew comfort would only compound his agitation. He needed her to share in his outrage, and she had none to give. With no other recourse, she stood and moved back to the sink. She began to fish through the water for the shirt she had been washing.

For the first time in minutes, Sascha stopped moving. He said, "Have you been listening to what I've been saying, Mother?" Martha heard the stifled rage. She nodded and brought the soap to the cloth. "And you have nothing to say?"

She continued to stare down into the water. "I'm sorry you had to see it."

He stared at her incredulously. "I tell you what he's done, and you go back to cleaning his shirts? Are you that pathetic?"

She turned to him with what anger she had. "You want me to hate him as much as you do, but I can't do that. I know what he is, Sascha, what he does, and why he does it, probably better than he does himself. And I am sorry for all of that, but I won't let you ask me to be pitiable for him. I stay with him because I choose to stay with him no matter what he is. And not out of sacrifice or duty or fear. Hating him would only make me wretched, and that is something I will not do. Not even for you."

For Sascha, hers was a betrayal more devastating than his father's. He had come to even the slate, to find in her a confirmation for his own feelings, but she was letting it all go. It was as if his father were laughing at him. Everything Sascha had wanted at the station now flew back. He stepped over and took her wrists and held them furiously. He didn't see the shock in her eyes as he shouted, "Why do you say that? Why can't you see what he is? Why?" She said nothing and he struck her across the face and she fell to the ground.

Sascha stared at his mother in utter disbelief. His sense of shame was immediate. He went to reach for her, but he saw his brother standing by the door, petrified. Sascha's head and hands began to shake. He had no idea what he was supposed to do. He raced past Georgi and out of the flat.

It was twenty minutes later when Hoffner found them in the kitchen. Georgi was rocking on her lap. Before he could ask, Martha said, "He's been home and gone. He left his coat."

Hoffner saw the bruise on her cheek. "What did he say?"

She gazed up at him; there was no feeling for him in her eyes. "What do you think he said, Nicki?"

"And what did you tell him?"

Martha pulled Georgi closer into her; the boy was oblivious of the conversation. "I told him that we all make choices, some better, some worse. And we live with them."

Hoffner had never heard her speak like this. "You should have told him what he wanted to hear."

"And what was that?" she said coldly. She needed to hear it from him.

Hoffner waited and then said, "That I'm a son of bitch, and that I deserve his hatred."

She continued to stare up at him. "You'll have to do that on your own," she said. She waited, then said, "You need to go, Nicki. Come back when you want, but not now." She stood, lifting Georgi into her arms. She started to go but stopped herself. "He saw him do this," she said. "That's something else you'll have to take care of on your own." She walked past him and into the hall.

Hoffner had nowhere else to go but the Alex. He tried to look over the files again, but his mind was incapable of focus; he found himself wandering the corridors of the third floor. A few lights were on, but it was after eleven and Fichte was long gone, not that finding Fichte was what he was after. Still, he moved toward the boy's office.

In typical fashion, Fichte had left the door open. Hoffner stepped inside, to find a desk, a chair, and a few books scattered about. He wondered how much time Fichte was actually spending down here these days. Hoffner turned on the light and saw a map of Berlin tacked onto the far wall. It was untouched.

He was about to flip through one of the books when he heard something at the far end of the hall. Hoffner stepped out of the office and saw a light spilling from Groener's office. As good a time as any, he thought. Or maybe he just needed the distraction. Hoffner flicked off Fichte's light and made his way down the corridor. He made sure he was alone before knocking.

Groener was at his desk when Hoffner pushed open the door to a look of surprise, then annoyance. "Yes?" Groener said coolly.

Hoffner stepped inside. "Turns out we have a mutual friend, Herr Detective Sergeant."

Groener's face winced as he shot up and passed Hoffner on his way to the door. Groener made a quick scan of the corridor and then shut the door. He took Hoffner by the arm and brought him closer to the desk. "You idiot." Groener spoke in a hushed voice; whispering only seemed to intensify the stench. "Of course we have a mutual friend. You don't leave the door open to talk about him, now do you? How much have you had to drink, anyway?"

It was a fair question, thought Hoffner: one or two at a bar in Kreuzberg, another few in his office. He had hoped to be feeling more of their effect by now, but nothing, it seemed, was going to make tonight any easier. He said, "So how long have you known him?" He took a seat.

Groener was back behind his desk. "Long enough." He was still the sour little man even in the company of a fellow conspirator.

Hoffner searched his pockets for a cigarette. "Who's he protecting?" Groener needed more of an explanation. "The third prisoner," said Hoffner. "At the Eden." Hoffner found a stray and lit up. "The night Liebknecht and Luxemburg were killed."

Groener was still trying to follow. He said hesitantly, "I don't know. He never told me about that."

Jogiches had been careful here: Groener was only a source, not a confidant. The interview continued: "The Ascomycete 4, the directors of Ganz-Neurath,

Wouters's replacement—you managed to track all that down by yourself, did you, Groener?" Groener nodded through each item on the list. "And you know where they're keeping Luxemburg?" This time, Groener remained silent. "Well, we can't have everything, can we?" Hoffner continued. "Still, more to you than meets the eye, isn't there?" Hoffner tapped out his cigarette. "So, why was he having you get in touch with Kvatsch?"

"Who?"

"Kvatsch," Hoffner repeated more clearly. "The reporter from the **BZ.** Why all the clandestine meetings?"

It wasn't the pronunciation that had confused Groener. He continued to stare across the desk before slowly shaking his head. "I know no Kvatsch."

Hoffner knew better. "You've been having lunch with him twice a week for the past—" Hoffner stopped; his mind began to sift through a thousand images. **Idiot,** he suddenly thought. **Of course.**

Groener had never met Kvatsch. There had been no meetings, no list to compile.

Little Franz had been the leak all along.

Hoffner's mind continued to race: the boy's appearance at the Senefelderplatz site; all the wires back and forth to van Acker; the spate of articles detailing the case while he and Fichte had been freezing their asses off outside the **Ochsenhof**—Franz had had time to sort through the files without fear of being spotted; the tip-off to Tamshik to be in the pit rooms; and most recently the trumped-up note from K. At least there Franz had shown a little reluctance. Evidently Tamshik and Braun were paying him more than a few pfennigs for his services.

Hoffner stood and, ignoring Groener, headed for the door. The boy would be upstairs asleep, and Hoffner had questions that needed answering.

He raced down the corridor and nearly collided with one of the interchangeable sergeants from the duty desk. Hoffner tried to sidestep the man, but the sergeant held his ground.

"Herr Chief Inspector," said the young man. Again Hoffner tried to get around him, and again the man held his ground: "I've been trying to find you for the last fifteen minutes. I tried your office—"

"Yes," Hoffner cut in angrily. "What is it that can't wait, Herr Sergeant?"

The man needed a moment to recover. "A body's been found, Herr Chief Inspector. A woman. With the markings."

"What markings?"

"From the Wouters case."

"The what?" Hoffner said in complete disbelief.

"The markings. On the back."

Hoffner tried to clear his head. "You're sure?" The man nodded. "Where?"

"Kremmener Strasse."

Kremmener . . . An image of Lina flashed into Hoffner's head and he began to run.

The cab was still moving as Hoffner opened the door and jumped out. They had cordoned off the street, most of which was eerily quiet. He moved past the barricade and toward a pocket of bright white light that was pouring down from a series of high-wattage arc lamps: it made the milling bodies in the distance look almost ethereal. Hoffner had known which building it would be, the uneven steps, the barren flower boxes. Number 5. The screws in his stomach tightened at the confirmation.

A group of Schutzis was keeping the small crowd at bay. Everyone had seen enough of Hoffner's picture in the newspapers to let him through without so much as a glance at his badge. He stepped through the line and saw the lone sergeant who was standing by a single sheet-covered body that lay at the bottom of the stoop.

Hoffner felt a numbing in his head as he drew closer. He tried to brace himself for what he knew lay beneath, until he saw the shape. The body was too large, the contours wrong. This wasn't her. This wasn't Lina. Hoffner slowed, and the desperate fear he had been carrying with him since the Alex melted away. They had sent him a message: **We know where she is. We know how to find her. Consider yourself lucky this time.** Hoffner knelt down and pulled back the sheet. For several seconds his mind went blank as he stared at the face. Martha's lifeless eyes gazed up at him and Hoffner vomited.

SIX

⇒ HEAVEN ON EARTH ⇐

In the summer of 1903, married less than a year and recently promoted to detective sergeant, Hoffner had taken Martha out to Wannsee for a day at the beach. He had put a little extra money in his pocket and they had rented two chairs and an umbrella and a cabana-tent of their own. She had packed sandwiches and a bottle of Sekt to celebrate, and after lunch they had changed into swimming clothes and waded out to where the water was coolest. Side by side and staring out across the endless lake, he had finally agreed to have a family. Martha had reached down into the water and pulled up a pebble as a keepsake. Hoffner had found it in a box by their bed the day he had buried her.

The following morning he had been relieved of duty. Präger had talked about the strain of it all, that a man couldn't be expected to run a case in his position—any case—but the real impetus for Hoffner's ouster was far more transparent: Präger had been told to clear him out. The order had come from beyond the walls of the Alex. There was nothing either of them could do.

Tonight, Hoffner's refuge was a grotty little bar deep inside the maze that was Prenzlauer Berg, sawdust strewn across its floor for whatever the shadows might be failing to hide. A woman hovered shamelessly by the bartender, the dim light working in her favor: there might just be a warm bed for her tonight. The rest of the clientele showed a little more decorum: chins drooped to chests, aimless fingers clasped at half-filled glasses. Only the sudden shaking of a head and the quick tossing-back of a drink gave any indication that the place was anything more than a repository for propped-up corpses. Hoffner checked the bottle in front of him and saw it was whiskey he had been pouring back tonight.

Time had taken an odd turn in the past few days: it had slipped by with a steady indifference even as it had remained fixed on that moment in Kremmener Strasse. For the first time, Berlin was pushing forward without him: two more bodies had been found in Charlottenburg; the panic had returned. More than that, rekindled accusations of Kripo incompetence now hung over the city like so many added layers of soiled snow. There was even talk of corruption.

The papers, of course, were rewriting the past.

Wouters was no longer the demented madman but the scapegoat for an investigation that had gone terribly wrong: what was the Kripo hiding? The fact that the little Belgian had been shot while wheeling around his final victim had somehow been lost to a collective bout of amnesia. It was even beginning to take its toll on the fledgling government: who was protecting Berlin?

Hoffner read through the articles—coherent moments between bottles—and let everything drift past him. Poor Fichte looked so hapless on all those front pages, no one to buy him a drink this time round.

Hoffner felt a shadow as a figure appeared at the end of his table.

"You've enough for two?" said a voice.

Hoffner looked up to see Leo Jogiches standing with an empty glass in hand; Jogiches placed the glass on the table: it had only been a matter of time, thought Hoffner. He took the glass and filled it.

"Difficult to track you down," said Jogiches as he sat.

"I didn't know anyone was looking."

"I've had a man at your flat."

"Then he must have been very lonely."

Jogiches took a sip of the whiskey. "Keeping yourself busy," he said as he nodded over at the bottle.

Hoffner poured one for himself. "Not as busy as you," he said as he set the bottle down; he tapped at the paper that was on the table. "Can't open one of these without reading about your General Strike.

Workers of the world . . ." Hoffner snorted quietly to himself. "It won't make any difference."

The Party had called the strike three days ago, even though Jogiches had known it was a mistake: still, Eisner's assassination had given everyone hope. Who was he to stamp on that? "Worth a try," said Jogiches. "Someone had to keep them on their toes."

Hoffner took a drink.

Jogiches said, "I was sorry to read about your wife."

"Were you?" Hoffner kept his eyes on his glass. "They send a very clear message."

Jogiches finished off his whiskey and said, "So Munich was a success?"

Hoffner wondered if Jogiches ever saw a human side in all of this. He said plainly, "If by success you mean it was enough to provoke them to kill my wife, then yes." Hoffner refilled his glass.

Compassion made Jogiches uncomfortable. He said awkwardly, "There are children?"

The questions were growing more absurd. Hoffner laughed bitterly to himself. "Yes," he said with surprising sharpness. "There are children." He had spoken to no one about this, and a week's worth of resentments now spilled out. "And since you're so interested, the older boy blames me for her death, while the little one hasn't said a word since. He was asleep when it happened—when they came and took my wife—so you can see how lucky he was, but there's always the chance that he heard something, isn't there?

A few shouts from beyond the bedroom?" Hoffner took his glass and eyed the liquid. "They're living with her sisters now." This carried an added sourness. "Best for everyone, I imagine." He tossed back the whiskey and placed the glass on the table. "You've made the effort. We can move on."

Jogiches might have expected the venom; or if not, at least he understood it. Either way, he was happy enough to leave it behind them. "So you've seen today's papers?"

"Today's, yesterday's, makes no difference."

"Ah, but it does. They've widened their scope." Hoffner didn't follow. "The Kripo isn't all that they're after, Herr Inspector. Word is that the carvings are being inspired by a lace design. A design from a very specific source."

It took Hoffner a moment to sift through the booze. When he did, he recalled Brenner's warning. "They're claiming it's a Jew?"

Jogiches nodded. "A boy was beaten outside a shop in the Kurfürstendamm. There was broken glass and some writing at a synagogue."

For the first time in days, Hoffner stepped outside of himself. The hysteria was taking on a distinct Thulian flavor. Jogiches saw the shift in his expression and said, "And that would be consistent with what you found in Munich?"

Hoffner stared across the table; for several moments he said nothing. He knew he could either pour himself another drink or he could answer. It was as simple as that. Finally he said, "Who was the third prisoner at the Eden?"

Jogiches allowed himself a smile. "You want this as much as I do, don't you, Inspector?"

Hoffner heard the echoes of "cause" and "truth" in the question: how little Jogiches understood. "The third prisoner," he repeated.

"A man named Pieck. One of Rosa's former students. His bad luck to be at the flat the night they were taken."

"And he saw everything?"

"Yes."

"They simply let him go?"

"False papers. Good enough to convince the halfwits of the **Schützen-Division.** They've never been terribly bright over there. Pieck slipped away in the confusion."

"And you trust him?"

"About this, yes."

"So who gave the orders to separate them?"

"Wolfgang Nepp." Jogiches paused for effect. "Former **Wehrmacht** general, and current Deputy Minister of Defense."

This was the last item in Jogiches's private cache, though it hardly made any difference: if the Munich loonies had drummed up disciples in the officer corps and the Polpo, why then not in Ebert's government? Not that Hoffner needed a reason to share what he had with Jogiches: the events of the last week had made discretion somehow passé.

Hoffner traced the line from Wouters through the substitution of the now-dead Urlicher to the beer-hall Eckart, and finally to Herr **Doktor** Manstein and the Thulian Society. He explained the military connections to the Ascomycete 4, and the link between the Rosenthaler station design and the directors of Ganz-Neurath—those Prussian business interests. He ran through the details on the second carver—the jagged versus the smooth lines—then Tamshik's appearance at the **Ochsenhof,** and through it all Jogiches listened intently, never once asking a question.

When Hoffner was finished, he poured himself a glass and said, "All the pieces, **mein Herr.** Nice and neat. You can do with them what you will." Hoffner shot back the whiskey and poured himself another. He expected Jogiches to get up, but the man continued to stare at him from across the table. When it became apparent that Jogiches had no intention of leaving, Hoffner said, "Not enough for you?"

Jogiches waited before answering. "Is it for you?" he said.

Hoffner had answered the question days ago: it was why he was still here. "Let's just say we don't share the same needs, you and I."

"Things have resolved themselves to your satisfaction, then?"

Hoffner did his best to ignore the goading. There

was no point in going down this path. He said, "How much of this did you know in January?" Jogiches showed a moment's surprise. "Rücker's bar," said Hoffner. "The day after she was killed. You were there, keeping an eye on me."

Jogiches recalled their first encounter. "The tired professor. I didn't think you would have remembered that." He nodded his approval. "Groener," he said. "He'd seen Rosa and the carvings when she first came in that morning, and knew the case would go to you. He got in touch with me, told me where I might find you. I suppose I wanted to see the sort of man who would be asked to make sense of it."

"And?"

"You didn't seem a complete idiot."

"No," Hoffner corrected. "And how much did you know?"

Jogiches took the bottle and refilled his glass. "Not enough to have stopped the killings, if that's what you mean. Pieck found me the night before. He told me that Rosa had been taken by Vogel. I knew she was no maniac's victim." He was about to drink, when he said, "Or, rather, I knew she wasn't **your** maniac's victim. Which meant that there was something more to her killing, and more to your killings, than either of us realized at the time." He finished his whiskey.

"And Munich?"

"That came later, after you'd caught the Belgian. There was money flowing into the **Schützen-**

Division. Rifleman Runge wasn't shy about spending his. It took me time to trace it. A Munich doctor. More than that I couldn't find. I assume he was your Herr Manstein. Groener also found telephone logs for calls to and from Munich by a Polpo detective."

"Braun," said Hoffner.

"Yes. He was also meeting with Nepp on a regular basis. The arrogance of these people astounds me."

Hoffner thought about his own trip to Munich: and what had that been, he wondered. He said, "So this Pieck is willing to come forward?"

"If it comes to that."

Hoffner saw something in Jogiches's eyes. "You don't know where he is, do you?"

Jogiches waited: there was nothing apologetic in the tone when he spoke. "No," he said. "Not that it would make any difference. A Red pointing the finger . . . who's going to place much stock in that?"

It was an obvious point, but one that Hoffner would never have thought Jogiches willing to accept, at least not so graciously. And then it struck him, the reason why Jogiches had been with this from the start: the reason he was still at the table. "But a Kripo Detective . . . that's something entirely different, isn't it?" Hoffner waited for a reaction; when none came, he said, "You or your friend Picck put things together and no one has to pay attention. You let the Kripo put it together and suddenly there's a legitimate case."

For several long moments, Jogiches continued to hold Hoffner's stare. He then raised his eyebrows and said, "And there it is." Again he waited. "Tell me, Inspector, would you have trusted anything I might have given you openly? The former lover out for revenge, the mad revolutionary desperate for chaos? Was I wrong? It was all in the aid of truth, so what difference does it make? I certainly wouldn't have trusted you had the positions been reversed."

"You wouldn't have trusted me regardless of the positions."

"Fair enough."

For the first time in a week Hoffner felt a different kind of hostility, one aimed out, not in. It perched at the base of his throat and was oddly comforting. "And now I'm meant to finish what you started, is that it?" he said.

"I started nothing," said Jogiches. "I simply chose the best route to an end."

"Regardless of the consequences."

"You and I aren't all that different in that regard, are we, Inspector?" Jogiches could be equally biting. When Hoffner said nothing, Jogiches said, "You're not the only one to have lost something in this."

Hoffner remained silent: there was nothing he could say to defend himself.

Jogiches shifted tone: "When was the last time you saw a bed?" Hoffner couldn't remember; he shrugged. "You need sleep," Jogiches said as he stood. "I have a place." Hoffner shook his head, but Jogiches already had the bottle. He turned to the bartender. "We'll take this with us." The man nodded distractedly and went back to the woman. Jogiches turned to Hoffner. "You need to get up now."

It was close to eleven when they stepped outside. Hoffner had lost track of the time hours ago—days ago—and was struck by the pitch black of the night sky. Why, he wondered, had he imagined it to be earlier? He breathed in deeply—only a twinge now from his ribs—and let the rawness fill his lungs. He had almost forgotten the taste of crisp air; it cleared his head. He recalled having spent a night at the Hotel Palme in and among the whores and pickpockets, the sight of its tattered awning up ahead now a reminder of muffled voices and thuds coming from somewhere beyond his walls as he had drifted in and out of sleep. He had chosen the Palme for a reason. He now remembered that, as well.

Two streets on, he turned right. Jogiches stopped behind him and said, "Where are you going?"

Hoffner spoke over his shoulder as he continued to walk. "This won't take long." With no other choice, Jogiches caught up and the two walked in silence.

The street might have been any other, a lamp here and there to offer the pretense of civility, but the chipped walls and occasional shattered window of the flats above made plain what kind of life lay within. Even where a strip of light peeked through from the edge of a drawn shade, there was no warmth beyond it. This was a street meant to be forgotten, and it was why Hoffner had chosen it.

He mounted the steps to one of the stoops and pressed his thumb twice, then twice again, against the bell for the third-floor flat. Jogiches had remained down in the street. Hoffner peered up and saw a curtain ripple. Half a minute later he heard footsteps through the door. It opened and a dim light spilled out onto the stoop.

Lina held her arms tightly across her chest, her best defense against the chill in a thin dress. She was without makeup, her skin an ashy white, her eyes smaller and less severe than usual: Hoffner had never noticed the natural beauty in her face. "I'm sorry if I woke you," he said, and she shook her head. "It's all right, then?" he said. "The place?" Hoffner had called in a favor, a black-market meats peddler who kept a spare room. At least Lina was eating well. She nodded. He said, "It shouldn't be more than another few days, just to be safe. You have money?"

"I'm going tomorrow."

Hoffner shook his head. "They might still have someone watching your place."

"Not there," she said. Her eyes dropped as she spoke. "I have an uncle in Oldenburg. In the north. He has a shop."

This was something Hoffner had never considered. He had imagined that he could place her safely away for a time, lose himself, and then return to open the cage: a final act of contrition. Maybe then she would keep him somewhere in her memory, but that, too, seemed not to be. He did his best to sound encouraging. "A flower shop?"

She looked up and tried a smile, but there was too much sadness in her eyes. "I hope not."

"It'll be better there, I imagine." Hoffner had no idea why he had said it.

She nodded unconvincingly. "The boy is all right?"

The boy, he thought. Fifteen-year-old Sascha. What, then, was a girl of nineteen? Hoffner reached into his pocket and pulled out the few bills he had. "You'll want this for the train."

She shook her head and said, "I'm all right. Give it to Elise. She'll need it for the rent." She took in a deep breath and glanced up at the sky as she tightened her arms around her chest. "I'm not running away, you know. It's just too much right now."

Hoffner took her hand and placed the money in her palm. So many things to notice for the first time: the smallness of a wrist, the slenderness of her fingers. He saw her shiver. "You should go in," he said.

Her fingers closed around his hand. "You could come up?"

The warmth of her body and the promise of a bed, he thought: if only it were that simple. He shook his head and took back his hand. Her neck was now a rippling of gooseflesh.

She said, "There really isn't anything here for me, is there?"

Hope and despair, like a wake trailing behind him:

Hoffner could feel himself being pulled in. "You should take a taxi," he said. "As close to the time as possible. No reason to be out on the platform longer than you have to be."

She was reaching for him even as he spoke, her arms wrapped around his shoulders, her cheek pulled tight into his neck. He felt the warmth of her breath, and he placed his arm around her. There was life within her embrace, a sudden strength that was all the more wrenching as she pulled away, her arms folded to her chest. Her face was again a placid gray. "You don't think it will be this way, and then of course it is. Silly, really."

He could tell how much she wanted from him, now with nothing else beyond this single moment. How difficult would it be to give her that? He said, "When this is over—"

"Yes." She cut him off. She didn't want to hear it; it was enough that he had tried. She ran her hand across his chest. She then turned away. A moment later, the door shut behind her.

Jogiches was kind enough not to ask. The two walked in silence, Jogiches directing them with a nod for a street, a building.

The room he had found was no better than what they had just left behind. This one, however, was a step down from the street, recessed behind the stoop and with thick bars across its door and single window. Jogiches rummaged for a key: the door squealed open and he led Hoffner inside. He struck a match and brought the dank little space to life. An oil lamp was by the door and he adjusted the flame.

Pipes were bare along the ceiling, and the cracks in the walls spread out in a topography of tiny stream-lets and rivers. The smell of mold and decay was matched only by the stench of urine. A mattress—long past its prime—lay in the corner. Hovering above it stood a large metal trunk. Hoffner wondered what it was to have the remnants of one's life always at arm's reach.

"Landlord doesn't know I'm here," said Jogiches, as if the point wasn't obvious. "You take the mattress. I don't sleep much these days."

Exhaustion had been tracking Hoffner like a marksman; he could feel the squeezing of the trigger from behind him. He moved across to the mattress.

Jogiches rested his back against the wall and slid down to the floor. "You'll be taking that when this is done." Hoffner looked over and saw Jogiches nod-ding toward the trunk. "Her papers. All of them. Everything she had." Jogiches kept the lamp between his knees. "Not much chance of revolution now, is there, general strikes notwithstanding? Even I know it. But that"—Jogiches again nodded to the trunk—"that has to live beyond this."

Hoffner knelt down and opened the trunk's lid. He pulled back a thick blanket that had been placed across the top: Jogiches was keeping the contents warm and dry despite his own squalor. Even in shadow, Hoffner could make out the stacks of books and loose pages that were piled high to the edge.

Jogiches said, "We both know I won't be here long enough to make sure of that." He pulled his coat tighter around his chest and seemed to lose himself for a moment. "To make sure of any of it, I suppose." He looked back at Hoffner. "Put the blanket over it and close the lid."

The irony of a trunk as Rosa's final resting place was not lost on Hoffner. He did as he was told. "And the cause lives on," he murmured under his breath.

There was a snort of acknowledgment from across the room. Hoffner turned, surprised that Jogiches had heard: the eyes were barely open; the head was cocked to one side; the shadow above seemed to paint him in the pose of a hanging man. Jogiches nodded slowly, his eyes still closed: "The cause," he echoed. "She wanted to take her life. Did you know that? Just before the war. She said it was finished, that the workers had betrayed themselves by voting for the rearmament. One day a united proletariat, the next enemies at war. She was right, of course." His head tilted back as if he were remembering something. "I said we should go together, a final noble act, but she managed to see something else in it. A prelude, she said. The last slap to the workers' faces. Then they would see how they had been used. Then they would climb from their trenches and tear down the world that had imprisoned them for so long." He stopped and his eyes opened. He stared distantly into the dark. "'I am, I was, I shall be.'" His gaze was almost wistful. He looked over at Hoffner. "She wrote that the day before they took her. Not about herself but about the revolution. Yes, I know—cause, truth—you find it all absurd, but that's not what's in that trunk. What's there is faith, hope—even in moments of greatest despair—that she could see beyond herself, beyond the corruption and human frailty, and imagine what could be." His head fell back against the wall and again he shut his eyes. "And if you find that naïve, Inspector, then you haven't nearly understood what it is you're now up against."

Here at last was the humanity, thought Hoffner. Jogiches had recognized in Rosa something more vital than his own cold conviction, and it was that, and that alone, that he was now desperate to save. Hoffner said, "You surprise me."

Jogiches kept his eyes closed. "How so?"

"A romantic at the end?"

Jogiches found a smile somewhere. "And what is it for you, then, Inspector? Loose ends? A detective's need to mop things up? I don't believe that, and neither, I suspect, do you."

Hoffner had no reason to disagree. He said, "So what would she have done now?"

Jogiches opened his eyes and peered over at Hoffner—that familiar, impenetrable gaze. "She would have gotten some sleep," he said.

Hoffner needed no more by way of encouragement. The lamp flared out and they slipped off into quiet darkness.

Later, Hoffner had a dream. He was in the water of Wannsee, staring out into the endless blue, when he heard the sound of splashing coming out toward him. He turned, but the sun was too much in his eyes and he saw only the outline of a figure, a woman—Martha—drawing closer. He put up his hand to shield his eyes, but he could barely make her out. He turned back to the blue and waited for her to join him.

"You raced so far ahead," she said when she was almost to him.

Hoffner ran his hands through the water and he turned to see Rosa standing next to him.

"I've brought you this," she said as she handed him the pebble.

Hoffner took it and rubbed his thumb across its smoothness. It suddenly felt like sand and began to crumble in his palm.

"That's all right," she said. "I can bring you another." She started to go, but Hoffner reached out and took her arm.

"Why?" he said.

"Why?" she said with a kind smile. She pulled away and her face became Lina's. "Because it's enough that you want it." He felt himself losing his footing. He fell back into the water and his eyes opened.

It was several moments before Hoffner realized where he was. He heard Jogiches's breathing from somewhere across the room and he brought himself up to his elbows. Dreams usually exhausted him: they required unpacking. This one, however, had left him strangely refreshed.

It was true: he had raced too far ahead and had let himself get lost in things that were still too much for him—sacrifice and redemption, nobility and despair—and while he had been forced to confront and ultimately concede to them in the world of Martha and his boys and Lina—all of it beyond his control—he had also let them seep into the one place where they had no right to be: his case. He had gotten caught up in the larger ideas—Thulian or socialist, it made no difference—and had let them color his perception. They were clouding the details, and the one detail that had forever been out of place—the one that had stood apart from the very start—was Rosa. Everything led to her. It was only now that Hoffner recognized why that had never been the point. What mattered—what he had failed to grasp all along—was that these men wanted her: they had wanted her from the start. And if they wanted her, then he needed to take her from them. It was as simple as that. Let them come to him, then, and explain why.

"Jogiches," he said as he got to his feet. "What do you say to a bath?" He heard movement from across the room.

An anxious whisper followed: "Who's . . . ?" Jogiches caught himself; he, too, had been drifting elsewhere. A match flared and the lamp lit up. Hoffner checked his watch. Three-fifteen. "Is it safe to leave the trunk here?" he said.

Jogiches needed another moment to find his focus. "The trunk?" he said. "I imagine. Yes. As safe as anywhere." It was only when he was on his feet that he thought to ask, "A bath?" Jogiches looked genuinely puzzled. "What about a bath?"

It took them nearly half an hour to get across town to the Admiral's Palace, even at this time of night. The steam rooms were a common destination for Berlin's night-crawl crowd—open once again through the night now that the city had come back to its senses—and where a few marks and forty minutes were all that was needed to rejuvenate any set of tired bones or aching heads. For the most devoted— those who saw the pools and steam baths only by first light—it was known as the "clean break," the stop between bar and desk. It was remarkable how a few minutes sweating out the booze could make a day at the office seem almost bearable.

Hoffner paid for both himself and Jogiches and, after a quick stop at the locker stalls, emerged to the common lounge decked out in slippers and a

Turkish towel; Jogiches had opted for the full robe and hood: he looked like a slightly bedraggled Druid.

It was an impressive place, two stories high, with a colonnade of black and white marble columns under an open balcony that ran the perimeter of the four walls. A few of the denizens were peering down, catching a breath before returning to their self-imposed swelter boxes. Others sat below in thick leather chairs, reading papers or talking casually to one another. A series of Persian rugs dotted the floor. One might have guessed that this was the setting for an afternoon tea, had each of the men not been in various states of undress. The fattest invariably sat au naturel. Hoffner wondered if it was a lack of towel girth or simply pride that had prompted the choices.

He led Jogiches up the stairs and toward the last of the rooms on the right. A large, powerfully built man stood at the door in nothing but white socks: he had little to be ashamed of. He held a cigarette in the corner of his mouth and was showing extreme care each time he removed it to flick away the ash.

"Private room," he said through a cloud of smoke.

"Tell him Nikolai Hoffner wants to see him."

The man glanced over at Jogiches. "And?"

"Just tell him Hoffner."

The man sized them up again, and then knocked once over his shoulder. A moment later a plume of steam billowed from the half-opened door to reveal a second, equally impressive titan, who was drenched in sweat. "Nikolai Hoffner," said the first man. The door closed and the three stood staring at each other while they waited. "Drop the robe and the towel," said the man. "And the slippers. Nothing goes in." Jogiches and Hoffner did as they were told: they were now three naked silent men.

The knock came and the man nodded them through.

The sting of hot, moist air was instantaneous, as was the hiss of gushing steam. As far as Hoffner could make out, the room was all white tile, including the floor: he had to steady himself against the wall to keep from slipping. His skin had gone instantly slick, and the puffed air made it impossible to see more than a half-meter in front of him.

"Watch yourself there, Inspector," came a voice from across the room. "Let's see that you make it across alive." It was joined by a small chorus of laughter. "Turn it down, Zenlo," said the voice. Hoffner heard the squeal of a valve being spun. Instantly the hiss choked off and the steam began its slow descent to the floor. As the air cleared, Hoffner saw the six or seven men who were seated across the room on two step-levels. They might have passed for a klatch of well-fed businessmen if not for the collection of odd scars and discolorations on their cheeks, arms, and chests. Marks of the trade, thought Hoffner. No wonder they liked the baths: a nightly chance to wash away their sins.

On the topmost step, and in the far corner, sat an equally naked Alby Pimm.

Pimm was small and pale by comparison to the rest, with a shock of curly jet-black hair that made him look almost boyish. His face, however, said otherwise. It had that weathered look of forty-odd years living off the streets, time spent climbing to the top ranks of the **Immertreu,** one of Berlin's more notorious syndicates. Just now Pimm was enjoying a rather charmed relationship with the Kripo. He had proved himself useful during the war—keeping an eye on undesirables and foreigners—and had thus earned himself something of a free hand when it came to his less-violent enterprises: black-market trade, a little extortion—these passed without too much interference. Anything more serious, however, was still fair game.

Pimm said with a smile, "Not with us in an official capacity, are you, Inspector?" The men laughed again, and Hoffner pointed to a spot on the lower step. "Be my guest," said Pimm. "And this is . . ." Pimm needed another moment to find the name. "Herr Jogiches, isn't it?" Jogiches said nothing as the two men sat. "Odd little pairing." More laughter.

Hoffner said, "I need to talk to you."

"You are talking to me."

"Alone."

"Ah." Pimm was enjoying this. He took a drink from a small wooden box that sat at his side. "A bull and a Red," he said. "What times we live in." He took a second drink and then bobbed his head toward the door: the men began to take their towels and file out. The last in line was a long, lanky fellow with the most angular face Hoffner had ever seen: there looked to be just enough skin on the cheeks and nose to cover the bone, although the eye sockets seemed to be wanting a bit more. "Zenlo," Pimm said. The man turned. "Stay by the door." The man nodded and stepped outside.

Hoffner was now dripping with sweat. He pulled his hand across his face to clear his eyes. Pimm slid the box across the tile toward him and said, "That's how the Japanese drink their water. The wood keeps it cool. Clever little people."

"I could do with something a bit stronger," said Hoffner.

"Not in here you couldn't. That's what you're pissing out. Trust me, take the water." Pimm watched as Hoffner reached up for the box and drank; he then said, "I don't know who's doing all the killing, if that's why you're here. Bad for business all around. I thought you'd finished it with the Belgian."

Hoffner slid the box back. "Bad for more than business."

Pimm nodded slowly. "Yah." He picked up a bowl of water and, leaning forward, tipped it over his head. "I was sorry to hear about that." He remained stooped over. "That revolution of yours didn't do me much good, either, Herr Spartakus."

Jogiches was feeling the heat in his beard. He dabbed a bit of water onto his cheeks. "My apologies," he said.

Pimm laughed to himself and spat. He tipped a second bowl over himself and sat up. "So, what is it you gentlemen want?"

Hoffner had propped his elbows on his knees. He felt the sweat drip from his chin, and watched as it splattered on the tile between his feet. "I want you to break into the fourth floor of the Alex and steal a body." Hoffner took a bowl of his own and tipped it over his head.

Again Pimm laughed. "You want what?" Hoffner remained bent over in silence. It took Pimm another few seconds to realize that Hoffner was serious. The laughter stopped. "And why would I do that?"

Hoffner continued to gaze at the floor. "Because it would be good for business."

Five minutes later Pimm was no more convinced. "No one's going to believe that," he said.

Hoffner agreed. "You're probably right."

"I don't believe it." Pimm was picking at something on his chest. "You've been spending too much time with your friend here." Pimm looked over at Jogiches. "You don't say much, do you, Herr Spartakus?"

Jogiches returned the stare.

Pimm said, "You know, I've always wondered— why are so many of you Reds Jews? Why make people hate you twice?"

Jogiches answered without hesitation: "Persistence."

Pimm smiled and flicked something onto the floor. He said, "Trust me, I want to see Weigland hanging by his balls as much as anyone—"

Hoffner cut in. "I never said it was Weigland."

Pimm nodded. "No. You never did." He stood and moved over to the valve. He turned it twice and the steam hissed back into action. "You cramp up without it," he said. "The Japanese have girls who rub your legs while you sit. Keeps the blood moving. We tried it, but German girls sweat too much and stink up the place. Plus they thought it was for sex. They didn't understand the aesthetic." He was back at his towel. "And you're sure it's her? Our little Rosa?" Hoffner nodded. Pimm tugged at his ear. "And this helps me how, again?"

"How much sugar are you planning to move with the **Freikorps** breathing down your neck?" said Hoffner. "Ebert makes things a good deal easier."

"Order makes things easier," Pimm said bluntly. The steam was already beginning to rise; he waved a cloud from his face. "That's something your second-story safecracker doesn't follow. A little anarchy works just fine for him; the bulls are occupied elsewhere and he makes a killing. But an organization—that needs routine. That needs people settled, safe. Right, left—makes no difference to me."

"Then why chance another bump in the road when things are moving so smoothly now?"

Pimm bobbed his head as if conceding the point. He then took a towel and wiped his face. When he spoke, it was with a focus that was wholly unexpected: "The reason so many of you Reds are Jews, Herr Spartakus, is that a Jew is told to create heaven on earth. The next world, messiahs, fear of hell— never really been the point, has it? The Jew is meant to do it here, now. And the ones who get tired of waiting become Reds because for them, socialism **is** heaven on earth. The perfect world, and with no God telling them what to do this time. Everyone just as good as the rest. Everyone looking out for the rest. The Red can't tell you how you're supposed to get there—in fact, all he can tell you is what you're **not** supposed to do and what **won't** be there—but, still, he thinks he can build it. Sound familiar, does it?" Pimm paused. "Your Red never loses what makes him a Jew; he simply shifts his focus." Pimm held Jogiches's gaze and then turned to Hoffner. "You get my help, Inspector, not because it's good for business, or because the devil I know is better than the devil I don't, but because, even if nothing else of what you're saying is true, I have no interest in having one more lunatic tell me that my elimination is part of his grand plan." He shouted to the door. "Zenlo." The man appeared instantly. "We're going east. Tell the boys."

Pimm a Jew, and a political one at that, thought Hoffner: the world was full of surprises. At least this one was working in their favor.

Back at Pimm's offices—two large rooms above a

repair garage, furniture, a telephone—Pimm produced a series of remarkably accurate layouts of the Alex's third and fourth floors. He had had enough boys inside for a night or two, he explained. Someone was bound to remember something.

Equally remarkable was the ease with which Pimm and Jogiches got down to the planning of the thing. For Hoffner, it was like listening to a book being read in reverse: they were beginning where he always ended—with the inception of a crime—and they were leading to the moment that was his first. Hoffner was too tired to reconfigure his mind. He found a couch, sat back, and let it all pass in front of him.

The sun was just coming up, and a stream of men began to make their way up the stairs and into the offices. They were an odd collection of shapes and sizes—swindlers and thieves—and each with something to show for a night's work. Most carried a battered cigar box, the telltale appendage of Berlin's underbelly. Not that any of these men could have afforded the fine Dutch tobacco advertised on the top flaps. No, these boxes were filled with "jimmies" and "little aldermen"—always arranged in order of size— and, most important, a few S-hooks. After all, even housebreakers' tools deserved their nicknames: a jimmy your crowbar, a little alderman your picklock. An S-hook needed no such distinction. It was what it was, and could have you through a door in close to ten seconds if you knew what you were doing. For the less adept, a "ripper"—that ancient drilling tool—would get you in, but it was never as elegant. Those who worked for Pimm were S-hook men: they walked with a certain swagger.

Odder still was the businesslike efficiency with which everything was managed: one of the titans from the steam baths was behind a desk writing out slips for money and goods received, the men patiently waiting in line, all with a deferential nod for Pimm, who was too busy with Jogiches across the room to take any notice. The titan passed on the slips to a man who was tallying them up, who then passed them to a third who was writing feverishly into a ledger. No doubt those who were missing this morning's accounting would be visited later, but for now the process seemed far removed from the world that these men usually inhabited. Hoffner recognized a face here and there: it was nice to see that the men had found steady work.

Jogiches called over: "Which room on the floor?" Hoffner realized the question was for him, and he pushed himself up and stepped over to the table that was already thick with sheets of paper filled with diagrams and notes: they might just as well have been in Chinese for all that Hoffner could make of them. Jogiches pulled over one of the layouts and repeated the question.

"I don't know," said Hoffner.

Pimm and Jogiches exchanged a glance. Pimm said, "That's something we have to know."

Hoffner understood.

Jogiches said, "You can't go back in yourself, you know."

Hoffner nodded. Even he had known that from the start.

Kriminaldirektor Gerhard Weigland kept himself buttoned up to the neck as he peered out from the rear seat of his Daimler sedan. The automobile was an older model—a gift to himself on the occasion of his daughter's wedding—but it was still in excellent condition. Weigland had made sure to hire a good man to see to its upkeep: a former mechanic with the Kripo. A man to be trusted. That man was now seated behind the wheel and in full chauffeur's attire, awaiting instructions.

"You're sure you saw her go in?" said Weigland. He had arrived by cab five minutes ago after getting the call.

The man had been very clear on the telephone. He was no less certain now. "Yes, **mein Herr.**"

"And she hasn't come out?"

"No, **mein Herr.**"

The car was parked at the edge of a narrow alleyway. Weigland's eyes were fixed on the side mirror, which had been reangled so as to keep the building behind them in its sites. "Maybe we turn the motor on to get a bit of heat, don't you think?"

The man in the front seat pressed the starter and the car came to life.

"Much better," said Weigland.

"Yes, **mein Herr.**"

They sat in silence for another ten minutes before Weigland saw the front door to the building pull open. The girl appeared. Weigland hitched forward on his seat, but waited until she was out of view before reaching for the handle. "Take the car home," he said as he pushed the door open. He stepped to the cobblestones and quietly shut the door behind him. He then made his way to the edge of the alley and peered out. Finding the girl halfway down the street, Weigland began to follow.

It was a quarter to seven when Hoffner stepped from the tram. The fruit and vegetable carts were already up and running, as was a tinker's stand that was directly in front of Fichte's building. The man was hammering away at an old pot as a woman looked on: unlikely that Fichte was sleeping through that.

Hoffner bought an apple and remained by the carts. Fichte had picked a nice spot, just right for a bachelor detective. The street denizens probably felt safer knowing that a young Kripo man was living here; or at least they had felt that way until this week.

Hoffner was tossing away his third core when he saw Fichte emerge at the top of his stoop. The boy was a shadow of himself, his face pale and sunken, his eyes wrecked from nights without sleep. Hoffner waited until Fichte had reached the bottom of the steps before making his way over. Fichte was keeping his head down as he walked. He nearly walked past Hoffner, but for some reason looked up at the last moment. He stopped.

Hoffner thought he saw a moment of relief in the boy's eyes, as if Fichte had finally found someone with whom to share his burdens. An equally quick flash of disgust followed, then pity, all of which dissolved into a look of resigned exhaustion. Fichte hadn't the energy to feel anything lasting for Hoffner.

"Hello, Nikolai."

"Hans."

They stood silently until Fichte said, "She hasn't been in touch with me, if that's what you want. I don't know where she is." He began to move off, but Hoffner stopped him.

"That's not why I'm here, Hans."

Fichte was too tired to find the reason. He said, "Look, I was sorry . . . I mean, I **am** sorry . . . about all of that . . . your Martha. . . ." Fichte was floundering.

Hoffner cut him off. "Can we get a coffee somewhere?"

Fichte hesitated. "I don't think that's a good idea."

"Why? Because your Herr Braun might disapprove?"

Fichte looked as if he might answer; instead he reached into his coat pocket and pulled out his inhaler. He took a quick suck.

"That bad, is it?" said Hoffner.

Fichte coughed once and spat. "It's not that simple."

"I've been reading the papers, Hans. It looks pretty simple to me."

Fichte said nothing; he hadn't the will to argue.

They found a café and settled in at a table amid the morning rush, men behind papers, girls lost in chatter. No one was taking any notice of the two detectives.

"This is what they had in mind all along, isn't it?" said Fichte. He kept his hands cupped around his coffee for warmth.

Hoffner had no reason to make the boy feel any worse than he already did. He shrugged and said, "Maybe. I don't know."

"It's all the second carver, you know." Fichte spoke in a hushed tone. "Braun won't let me release it. He says it would only make things worse. I don't understand that. It wouldn't make things worse for you or me." Hoffner took a sip of his coffee and let Fichte talk. "It's all going to fall on me, isn't it? The idiot in the papers. The bull who's been covering up something. I don't even know what they're talking about." Fichte was slowly unraveling. "A member of the Reichs Ministry was by to have a chat with me. There might have to be formal charges if things don't get wrapped up quickly." Again Fichte shook his head to himself. "Formal charges."

"They won't do that," said Hoffner with as much reassurance as he could. "They'd come after me first." He saw a glimmer of hope in Fichte's eyes and said,

"The minister's name wasn't Nepp by any chance, was it?"

Surprise quickly turned to relief. The glimmer grew. "Yes," said Fichte. "Why?"

Hoffner nodded. There was no point in rattling the boy further. He said, "Where are they keeping her?" Fichte was too tired to follow. "Rosa," said Hoffner. "Where is she?"

The pain returned to Fichte's eyes; he shook his head. "I don't know."

Hoffner had expected Braun to toss the boy at least this bone. "Can you find out?"

"Why are they doing this?" Fichte said with a child's incredulity. "If they want me to look stupid, I can do that just fine on my own."

"It's not you, Hans."

"Then, what?"

Even now it was all beyond Fichte; Braun had chosen wisely. Hoffner wondered if in fact that choice had been made as early as last November: had Präger been encouraged to assign Fichte to him all those months ago? Hoffner said, "Can you find out where she is?" Fichte thought for a moment and then nodded. "No heroics, Hans. Just the room."

Again Fichte nodded. "Where do I send the information?"

"You don't. You bring it in person." Hoffner checked his watch. "Two hours. Rücker's bar." He stood and left a coin on the table. "She's gone to live with an uncle in Oldenburg." Hoffner saw the hope in the boy's eyes. "You go and find her when this is over." Hoffner placed his hat on his head and made his way to the door.

Twenty minutes later he stood on the tree-lined Sterner Strasse. It was over a year since he had seen the place, the pleasant little street, the playful curtains in the windows. It was not the Berlin he knew. Here, life actually sprouted in the flowerpots; there might even have been friends among the neighbors, an accountant's wife, a bachelor schoolteacher with whom to share a tea or a chocolate now and then. No doubt Giselle and Eva had long ago given up trying to find the man a wife: he preferred the company of his students. They had left it at that.

Giselle had come to Kreuzberg on the afternoon of the funeral to take the boys. By then, Sascha had already gotten to her, and even if Giselle might have known more about her sister's marriage than she had been willing to let on, death had a way of hardening the heart. The exchanges had been brief.

Hoffner pulled a wire cord and heard a bell ringing beyond. Half a minute later he heard the sound of several locks being unbolted, then a second series of locks, and finally the door coming open.

Giselle stood in a tile foyer, a glass-paned door behind her that was opened to a hallway. Her skirt and bodice were thick wool, with just a hint of cotton creeping out at the stiff neckline.

"You look dreadful, Nikolai," she said.

"Thank you. May I come in?"

With a certain reluctance she motioned him through; she then went back to her locks before joining him in the hall. "Georgi's asleep," she said. "I don't want to wake him."

Hoffner had expected as much; it was not why he had come. "Your lawyer is making do without you?"

"Herr Schmidt has been most kind, yes. He understands the situation." She corrected herself. "Not the entirety of the situation. Herr **Doktor** Keubel has been equally considerate with Eva. Until Georgi returns to school, we are to be here with him."

"Good," said Hoffner. "Then I need you to take the boys away for a few days. Into the country." He gave her no time to respond. "Not to friends or relatives. A train, an hour away. It doesn't need to be more than that. Find a small hotel and sign with a different name, not your own. Do you understand?"

Confusion registered as disdain in her face. "What are you talking about, Nikolai?"

Hoffner had no interest in pacifying her. "What wasn't clear in what I just said?" He had never spoken to her in this tone; her shock stifled any further questions. "You need to go this morning. Wake Georgi, get Sascha." She blanched at the suggestion. "What?" he said briskly.

For several seconds, she seemed uncertain how to respond. Finally the resolve drained from her. "I have something for you," she said. "Wait here." She left him in the hall and half a minute later returned with an envelope, which she handed to him. His full name was written across the front in Sascha's hand. "He left one for us, as well," she said, trying to explain. "Two days ago. We tried to find you—"

Hoffner put up a hand to stop her. He continued to stare at the envelope. "Two days ago?" he said, more to himself than her.

"Yes."

Hoffner tore open the envelope and read:

There is no reason for you to come after me if that is something that is even in your mind. I would not come home with you and you would not want to have me back, so let us save ourselves that unpleasantness.

I have signed on with a unit of the volunteer corps. I have decided this because I know a few more months of school will be of no use to me when I can be of greater use to my country. These are things you have never understood because you do not see anything but yourself. The Germany I am fighting for will have no place for people like that.

You will say that I am still not yet sixteen, but Krieger's uncle has been of great help in securing a place for me even though I am still a few weeks away from proper age. Herr Kommissar Tamshik has been a true friend to me and has called on a colleague from his army days on my behalf.

I am telling you this so that when my brother wishes to visit me he knows where I am. You are not to accompany him when he decides to do this, nor are you to influence his decision in any way. I have tried to explain to Georg what you have done and why I have acted as I have, but, because of you, he is still unable to understand. He has said things to me that are confused and entirely untrue because his mind has been so harmed by the death of our mother. He might never recover from this and you will be the only one to take the blame for that.

I am sure you are hoping that I despise you for this, but I have no such feelings. I am without them because you are in my mind no longer a person. It is the same way you have thought about me and my brother and my mother for so long, and now you know what that is like, as well.

This will be our last communication. Do not consider me your son. I no longer consider you my father.

Alexander Kurtzman

Hoffner stared at the page. Kurtzman. Sascha had taken his mother's family name just in case the message had not been clear enough.

The paragraphs were precisely spaced, the letters

exact. How many drafts had the boy written before completing this perfect page, Hoffner wondered. There was only one flaw: a slight swelling of ink at the end of the word "untrue." Had a moment of conscience prompted the hesitation with the pen? Hoffner hoped not. It would be better for Sascha to forget his own last moments with his mother. The same might not be so easy for Georgi.

An anxious Giselle said, "Does he tell you where he's gone?"

Hoffner was still with the letter. He turned to her: Tamshik would have to wait. He said calmly, "I need you to wake Georgi and get to the station." He folded the letter and dug it into his pocket.

She pressed, "All he said was that he was leaving."

Hoffner was growing impatient. "He'll be fine."

She said more pointedly, "He said he saw you with a girl." When Hoffner's silence became too much, she began to shake her head angrily. "Fine. Yes. We'll take him out of the city. Now get out of this house." She ushered him toward the door.

Hoffner stopped her. "I need to see Georgi."

Her eyes went wide. "You are some piece of work." She began to push him into the foyer, when a voice broke through at the far end of the hall. "Let him be, Giselle."

Both turned to see Eva holding Georgi by the hand. The boy was gazing at his father. He showed almost no reaction, such emptiness on so small a face. Hoffner walked over and went down on a knee. He watched as the vacant little eyes stared back at him. In a soft voice, Hoffner said, "Hello there, Georgi."

They stood like this for perhaps half a minute before the boy's brow furrowed and his eyes became heavy with tears; still he stood staring. When his lips pursed, Hoffner reached out and pulled him in. He felt the little body shake as Georgi's face wedged deep into his neck. He felt the sobbing in the boy's tiny-ribbed back, the small hands clasped tightly around his neck. Hoffner picked him up and began to walk slowly, back and forth, whispering in his ear, over and over, until Georgi began to catch his breath, his body calming, his head resting back on Hoffner's shoulder. The boy's cheeks were streaked and red. Hoffner felt the wetness on his own neck. A little hand came up and rested on Hoffner's cheek, and Georgi said, "Are we going home, Papi?"

The boy's hope was like an island in the current. Hoffner could see it: real, graspable, and completely uncharted. It was simply a matter of will to carry himself to it. Hoffner placed his hand over the boy's and said, "Soon." He pulled Georgi in tight and kissed him, the taste of tears on his cheek. Hoffner turned and saw a kindness in Eva's gaze, and he handed him to her.

She said brightly, "So how about a little trip today, Georgi?"

The boy kept his eyes on his father. "Are you coming, Papi?"

The current was growing stronger. Hoffner said, "Tomorrow. I'll come tomorrow."

"And then we'll go home?"

For just a moment, Hoffner let himself imagine something beyond the frailty, something of what could be. Surprisingly, it carried no hint of self-disgust. He placed a hand on the boy's cheek and then turned for the door.

Fichte tried the handle. It was locked and oddly cold, which gave him hope.

His choices had been limited: he needed something large enough for an examining table and storage, but isolated enough to keep it beyond the flow of every-day business. Two archive halls and a conference room later, he arrived at this, an office at the end of a long corridor at the back of the building. The spacing between its door and the next was sufficiently wide. Fichte scanned the corridor and then went to work. The lock was proving a bit more difficult than the others, but he finally managed to get it open. He had kept an S-hook as a souvenir from one of his first arrests: such things were always going missing from the evidence room, badges of honor among the junior officers. Fichte was now pleased to have found a use for it. It also made him feel better about what he was doing: things happened for a reason; no other way to explain why he had taken the hook in the first place, he thought.

The room was pitch black and much colder than

the hallway, but it was the odor of formaldehyde that told him he had found her. Fichte shut the door and flicked on the light, and a dull yellow filled the white-tiled space. The windows had been bricked in and, although it was a good deal smaller, the place had the same look and feel of the morgue rooms in the basement: an examining table, shelves for instruments and bottles. The only additions were a woman's apparel—skirt, bodice, shoes—that hung on various hooks across the room, and a single metal tank that stood against the far wall, underneath one of the absent windows. It was there that Fichte turned his attention.

Resembling an enormous pressure cooker, the tank sported several circular valves on its lid. As Fichte turned the last of them, the hiss of a releasing vacuum—along with an ungodly smell that struck him as rotting cabbage—seeped from the tank. Bringing the tail of his jacket up to his nose and mouth, Fichte pushed open the lid and saw a naked Rosa lying on several planks of wood, which were in turn set atop a bed of ice. Her skin was still remarkably intact and, save for a few tiny decayed bits on her thigh, she looked as if she had been dead for three days at most, not the seven weeks Fichte knew to be the case. Her entire body was covered in a thick layer of grease; even her hair was matted down in the stuff.

It was only then that Fichte thought to examine more closely the contents of the shelves across the room. Almost at once he noticed the collection of jars filled with what he knew to be the same grease. He stepped over and took one. It was labeled AS-COMYCETE 4, and had the eagle crest of the army medical corps stamped above it. A few days ago he might have been surprised, even overwhelmed, to find it here; the greater shock would have been the link to the military corps, but Fichte was beyond such reactions. Instead he opened the jar and sniffed at its contents. It was the same as they had found on Mary Koop, except that this batch had a bit more bite to it: it was in its pure form, having yet to be applied to the skin. Fichte thought of taking a jar for Hoffner, but he knew that would be too dangerous. He closed the lid, placed the jar back on the shelf, and then wrote the name in his notebook, making sure to copy it letter for letter. He then sketched the medical corps insignia and wrote down the number of bottles. Hoffner would be pleased with the work.

Fichte stepped again to the tank. There was really nothing to examine: Rosa was pale and slick and seemed peaceful enough. Fichte closed the lid and re-sealed the valves. He then took one final look at the room and realized that the label on the jar that he had taken was out of line with the rest. He stepped over and adjusted it. Another nice touch, he thought. Half a minute later he was pulling the door shut as he checked the area around the latch: only someone looking for them would have noticed the hair-line scratches. Even so, Fichte licked his thumb—the faint stink of the grease on it—and rubbed a bit of saliva over the wood.

He was feeling quite good about himself as he headed down the corridor: no heroics or missteps, and he had uncovered the name of the grease along with a connection to the army corps. Maybe there was a way out of this, after all?

Any sense of redemption, however, was short-lived, as Herr **Oberkommissar** Braun appeared at the top of the stairs, coming up from the third floor. Fichte did what he could with a casual nod.

"Herr **Bezirkssekretär**," said Braun, with a tight-lipped smile. "Were you looking for me?"

Fichte waited a moment too long to sound convincing. "Yes . . . Yes, I was, Herr **Oberkommissar**." Braun waited for more. Fichte said, "I was hoping to go over the second-carver theory again—"

Braun cut him off with a frustrated hand. "We've been through all of this, Herr **Bezirkssekretär**. As I said, when that information is necessary you will be told."

Fichte had no interest in lingering. "Certainly, Herr **Oberkommissar**," he said. "I won't trouble you with it again."

"And this was the only reason you came up to see me?"

"Yes, Herr **Oberkommissar**."

Braun was about to answer when it seemed as if something had just occurred to him—a wince for something he couldn't quite place—but he dismissed it quickly. "Fine. Any word from Herr Hoffner?"

"No, Herr **Oberkommissar**. Nothing."

"And you'll tell me when he contacts you?"

"Of course, Herr **Oberkommissar.**"

"Good." Braun nodded. Fichte offered a clipped bow and headed down the stairs.

It was only when Braun was halfway down the corridor that he realized what it was that had struck him: he had recognized the smell.

At just after eleven, Lina stepped onto the platform. She had done as Hoffner had asked: the train was due to leave in another eight minutes.

Hoffner had been standing in shadow for the past twenty-five—the corridor to the men's toilet offering an ideal vantage point—when he saw her. She was holding two small valises and was again wearing the blue hat. A porter took her bags and then helped her up. At the top step, she glanced around once, perhaps hoping to see him, and then stepped into the car.

Safe, he thought: he had needed to see it.

Hoffner began to move off when he saw another familiar figure on the platform. **Kriminaldirektor** Gerhard Weigland had been trailing after her and was now making his way to the train.

Hoffner's first reaction was to run out and stop him, but Weigland seemed less interested in Lina than in the surrounding crowds. Hoffner pressed farther back into the shadow as Weigland glanced nervously along the platform. It was obvious whom he was looking for; what was less clear was why he had come alone: Hoffner could see no one who looked even remotely like a Polpo detective anywhere on the platform.

Weigland now entered the front car of the train. Again, Hoffner stayed where he was: if Weigland had been interested in taking her, he would have done so already. More likely he was scanning the seats to see if Hoffner had been waiting for her on board. Weigland made quick work of it and emerged from the last of the cars just as the stationmaster was signaling the train's departure. Weigland looked disappointed. It was an odd reaction, thought Hoffner. Frustration, perhaps, but why disappointment? The train began to make its way out of the station and both men stared after it.

For nearly a minute, neither moved. Finally, Weigland made one more sweep of the platform and then began to head off. Hoffner followed.

One behind the other, they moved through to the main atrium and over to the station entrance. The place was thick with people, and Hoffner had to struggle to narrow the gap between them. When Weigland was almost to the doors, Hoffner drew to within half a meter of him and, pressing up to his side, discreetly took his arm and twisted it back. It was a pleasure to see the momentary wince in the old, bearded face.

Hoffner continued to propel them forward. "Hello, **Kriminal-direktor.**"

Remarkably, Weigland showed no surprise: in fact, he seemed only too happy to submit. "I was hoping you'd put in an appearance, Nikolai," he said calmly as he let himself be moved along. "You know this is really quite unnecessary."

"No one outside these doors, is there, Herr **Kriminaldirektor**?"

"I came alone, if that's what you mean."

"Good." Hoffner took them out into the morning sun. He needed an isolated spot. Most everyone was heading across the plaza and away from the river. Hoffner instead moved Weigland along the side of the station and toward the water. There were a few odd looks from passersby, but everyone was in too much of a hurry to take more than a cursory interest. Thirty meters on, Hoffner directed Weigland off the pavement and into the snow: they headed for the embankment. Weigland slipped once or twice for lack of balance, but Hoffner kept him upright as they moved down the slope. At the bottom, and with no one else in sight, Hoffner tossed the contents of Weigland's pockets and released him. He had expected to find a pistol. There was none.

The air was much colder here, directly off the water: Hoffner felt it at once on his face. A low wall stood as a barrier against the current, but it was little obstacle for anyone interested in throwing someone in. Both men kept well back of it. Weigland was stretching out his shoulder when he said, "You enjoyed that, did you?"

"How did you find her?"

"A man at her flat."

"She wasn't at her flat."

"Not for the last week, no, but she was there this morning. Six a.m."

Hoffner recalled the money he had given her: rent for Elise. Lina had been foolish. "Why?" he said.

Weigland looked momentarily puzzled. "So we could have this little chat. Why do you think?"

"The head of the Polpo trails a girl to find a Kripo detective? Why not just have one of your thugs pick me up?"

Again, Weigland seemed surprised by the question. "Because, **a,** I didn't know where you were, and **b,** I don't trust many of them. Is that the answer you were looking for?" Hoffner said nothing; he had never heard this tone from Weigland. "Now give me a cigarette. It's damned cold out here." Hoffner picked up Weigland's pack and flung it over. "And a light," said Weigland. Hoffner dug out his own matches and tossed the box over. "I told you to let this go," said Weigland as he lit up. He shook his head in frustration. "I told you to solve the case and move on. Why couldn't you do that?"

"Because the case wasn't over."

"Yes, yes it was," said Weigland more emphatically. "Your case was over the moment that little Belgian got shot. Why is it that you always have to know better?"

"The little Belgian wasn't working alone and we both know that. He was brought here for a reason. He also killed only six women. Someone else killed

Luxemburg and the prostitute at the zoo. The same someone who's killed two more women in the last week." Hoffner paused. "The same person who killed my wife." Hoffner waited for Weigland to look directly at him. "The case wasn't over."

Weigland's frustrations came to a boil. "It was for you. And your wife would still be alive if you had understood that."

Hoffner lashed back. "So why didn't the great Herr Polpo **Direktor** do anything to stop it?"

"Because," Weigland barked, "we needed to find out who was funding all of this activity under our noses." Weigland realized his voice was carrying: he spoke in a sharp whisper. "You don't think Braun and his cronies would have willingly volunteered that information, do you? It wasn't enough to have scum like this in my department. No. They were being told what to do by someone, or some group, that we had yet to find. This isn't a little criminal case, Nikolai. This isn't something that ties up neatly and gets folded away in a map when it's done."

Hoffner now realized how far he had underestimated Weigland all along. "When?"

"When what?" snapped Weigland.

"When did you know about Braun?"

"Christ, Nikolai. Months ago. Before your case ever began."

"And Munich?"

Weigland seemed reluctant to say. He took a long pull on his cigarette and glanced out over the river.

Hoffner waited through the silence. "It wouldn't have been when I made the trip, would it?"

Weigland hesitated before turning to Hoffner. "We were getting close. We would have found it eventually."

"And in the meantime, a few more bodies pile up?"

"Don't lecture me, Nikolai. Yes. You did some very clever work. Remarkable even. But you can see where it's gotten you."

"You were the one who had the Commissioner remove me from the case, weren't you? Once, of course, you had the information you needed." Weigland said nothing. Hoffner added, "Another Hoffner career ambushed at your hands. Well done."

Weigland snapped back, "Is that what you think?" Weigland waited before unleashing his final volley: "Your father also liked maps, Nikolai, but he wasn't as clever with them as you are—a great deal of ambition but not a lot of talent, cheap little medals notwithstanding. So, when it was clear that he wasn't going to make it into the Polpo, it was **his** idea to leak your mother's background. He knew what it would do. Let that take the blame instead of the truth." Weigland paused: he seemed to be lost in a string of long-forgotten arguments. "The trouble was, over the years, he began to believe it himself." Anger drained out of him. "He was a good friend," Weigland said absently. "I suppose I let myself believe it, as well."

Hoffner stared across at Weigland. He couldn't believe what he had just heard. All those years listening to his father rail against the injustice—the betrayal when he had chosen the Kripo over the Polpo, his mother standing meekly by, condemning him with her silence—all of it meaningless. And Weigland had been there, trying to shield him from it all along. Hoffner felt a sudden, distant rage. **All those years.** He had trouble masking his anger as he spoke: "So why the need to find me? Another trinket you've been keeping for me?"

Weigland spoke plainly: "Get yourself out of the city, Nikolai. Until this is done. I won't be able to protect you anymore."

"Protect me? You can't even control your own men." Before Weigland could answer, Hoffner said, "It ends tonight. Just keep yourself away from the Alex." Without so much as a nod, Hoffner turned to go.

Weigland called after him. "Why? What happens tonight?"

Hoffner stopped and looked back. "Tonight I relieve you of your burden, Herr **Direktor.**" He then turned and headed up the embankment.

Fichte was busy with a plate of noodles and sausage—the first time in a week he had found his appetite—when Hoffner stepped into the bar. Only the barkeep seemed to take any notice. The man reached for a bottle of brandy and a glass, but Hoffner shook him off and headed over to Fichte's table.

"You look better," said Hoffner.

Fichte swallowed. "You don't. I'll get you a plate."

Hoffner stopped him from calling the man over. "Did you find it?" Fichte nodded and scooped up another helping as Hoffner sat. "And?"

"You'll be amazed."

Fichte spoke through mouthfuls, bringing out his notebook and sliding it across the table. Surprisingly, Fichte offered no theories of his own. He simply stated where she was and what he had seen. He might have expected more of a reaction, but was happy enough not to be corrected along the way. When Hoffner remained silent, Fichte grew bolder. "They were supplying Wouters, weren't they? With the grease, I mean."

"It looks that way."

"So they knew what he was doing."

"Or worse," said Hoffner.

Fichte understood at once. "You think they brought him here." Hoffner saw the concentration in Fichte's eyes. "So why Luxemburg?" Fichte asked.

"That's why I needed you to find out where she was."

"You're going to take her, aren't you?"

"Yes."

"When?"

"Tonight. You don't have to be involved with this, Hans."

Fichte's eyes went wide. "They were the ones who killed your wife, weren't they?" Fichte realized too late the tactlessness of the comment. When Hoffner said nothing, Fichte continued, "I am involved in this."

Hoffner thought as he spoke: "All right, but I don't know what that means, yet. I'll telephone you when I do. Two rings and I'll disengage. We'll meet here." Hoffner stood. "And nothing foolish between now and then, Hans. You understand?"

Fichte nodded. He waited until Hoffner was out the door before reaching for his inhaler.

Pimm's offices were empty, save for a large, lounging man, when Hoffner got back. The man was reading a paper and looked up: the boss would be back soon; Hoffner was supposed to get some sleep; they had all agreed he looked terrible. Too tired to disagree, Hoffner found a sofa in the back and slept.

It might have been two or three hours later when he opened his eyes. He felt no less exhausted and his wrist had cramped from its angle under his chest. He tried to twist it loose as he sat up, and realized that he had somehow slept through the arrival of perhaps a dozen men who were around the far table with Pimm and Jogiches. These weren't the same breed as this morning, though they were just as identifiable: hobnail boots and balloon caps were the costume of Berlin's working class—the self-proclaimed proletariat in these circles. Hand any of them a cigar box—or clip a bit of facial scruff, thought Hoffner—and they might just have passed for Pimm's minions, except perhaps for the sour look of commitment in each of their eyes. That was Jogiches's work: he was transformed in front of them, feeding off their quiet reverence. Hoffner doubted that Jogiches had had more than a few hours of sleep—pockets here and there—over the last month. There was no telling it, though, in front of his disciples.

Hoffner's mouth was stale; he went in search of something and found a bottle of beer. It was warm, but he knew it would settle his stomach. He made his way over to the table and listened.

". . . between eight and eight-fifteen." Jogiches had a map of Berlin on the table and was pointing to various streets around the Alex. "Any earlier than that will do us no good." He noticed Hoffner. "You're with us again, then?" Hoffner mock-toasted with the bottle and let Jogiches carry on. Jogiches addressed the men: "How you get them there is up to you, but it's absolutely crucial that they avoid any sort of scuffle until they get to Alexanderplatz. You have to make this clear."

Jogiches took a stab at something inspirational, but it was too late for such gestures: the men had been given something to do. It was enough for them to do it.

When the last of them had gone, Hoffner said, "I thought the time for revolution had passed."

Jogiches was gathering up the papers. "It has."

"Do they know that?" said Hoffner.

Jogiches looked up, but it was Pimm who answered. "Does it matter?" he said. "Theft always needs a bit of misdirection, and now we have it."

Hoffner didn't see the logic. "First sign of trouble and Braun will get her out of there. He's too clever for that."

Jogiches answered, "Not if the bait is too good to pass up." Hoffner wasn't following. It was only when Jogiches continued to stare at him that Hoffner understood.

"They'll kill you if they take you," said Hoffner.

Jogiches nodded. "More than likely, yes. But they'll all want to be there when they do, just to find out how much of it I know, how much you know." Before Hoffner could answer, Jogiches said, "You'll have Rosa, they'll have me. Seems a fair trade."

Hoffner couldn't help his cynicism. "And you'll have your final noble act."

Jogiches shook his head; he seemed strangely at peace. "Nothing so grand," he said quietly. He went back to the pages. "It's only a matter of days before they track me down. We both know that." He picked up the last of the stacks and looked at Hoffner. "I can't choose when or how I die, Inspector, but I can choose why. And that, in the end, will have to be enough."

Fichte had been up in Braun's office ever since getting back from Rücker's. For some reason, Braun had chosen today to take him through the various methods of interrogation that the Polpo employed.

Fichte had tried to move things along and was praying that he hadn't missed the telephone call when he finally got back to his office. He called down to the switchboard and, to his relief, was told that nothing had come in.

It was nearly four when the phone finally rang. Fichte counted ten before calling the operator.

"**Bezirkssekretär** Fichte here," he said. "Was there an error made just now?"

A woman answered quickly. "I don't believe so, Herr **Bezirkssekretär,**" she said. "I put the call through, but the party must have disengaged."

"Thank you, Fräulein."

Fichte grabbed his coat and moved down the corridor: his heart was racing. He felt a momentary twinge in his chest and reached into his coat pocket: nerves always worked their worst. He took two quick sucks on his inhaler and then headed down the stairs. Things were about to be set right, he thought. Fichte permitted himself a momentary wave of exhilaration.

He was nearly to the landing when he noticed a sweet metallic taste in his mouth, followed by a sudden heat in his lungs. He stopped and placed his hand on the banister. For a moment he thought it was simply overexcitement, but his chest suddenly convulsed and he began to choke for breath. It felt as if his throat had sealed entirely. He dropped down and struggled to bring his inhaler up to his mouth, but he was losing focus, and there was a drumming in his ears as if he were about to faint. Frantically he wrapped his lips around the nozzle; he pressed down on the cap, but it was too late. Hans Fichte was already dead by the time the mist had passed his tongue.

⊶ THE ALEX ⊷

The rain had returned, and the streets around the square ran with melting snow.

Hoffner gazed out from the darkness and into the drizzled lamplight. They had chosen a small storefront, its display window offering a perfect view of the side entrances to the Alex. A few soldiers were wandering aimlessly up by the square; another two had positioned themselves inside a doorway across the street and were doing what they could to keep dry: these were the only signs of life. One of Pimm's men pulled out a cigarette and a voice by the door whispered, "You light that and you lose a finger." Pimm had placed Zenlo in charge; he was little more than a skeleton's shadow skulking by the door as he stared out, listening and watching.

Hoffner had waited nearly an hour at Rücker's. When Fichte had failed to show, Hoffner had told himself that the boy had simply lost his nerve; anything other than that was too much to consider. Across town, Pimm had not been pleased: he had wanted Hoffner nowhere near the Alex tonight, but the best-laid plans . . . "And you're sure they'll come for her?"

Hoffner had been sure. "As long as you have every-one in place."

Pimm had nodded. "He's done work for me before. He'll do what he's told."

Now it was just after eight, and the first echoes were beginning to rise up from beyond the square, a distant bellowing as if the streets themselves were sucking in for air. No one who had lived through December or January could have mistaken the sound for anything other than an approaching throng. The bodies were massing on the other side of the Platz. The soldiers had heard it as well, and began to head up the street.

"Forty minutes," said Zenlo. He turned back to the men. "Now you can have your cigarette, idiot."

There was hardly room to breathe.

Jogiches had forgotten the feel of a surging mob, the pulse of bodies all around him. He had forgotten the mood that comes with a column of arms and legs striding as one, the song in the footfall, the rhythm that drains each man of his singularity. It was nearly fifteen years since he had stepped from the shadows and onto the line: then there had been possibility, purpose—Warsaw, Rosa; now he marched alone, drifting within the current, yet no part of it. He gazed up into the night sky and felt the rain on his face, the taste of moist air in his lungs, and he breathed in with a sense of finality. The men around him strode with no such appreciation. For Jogiches, these were the only sensations left to him.

The column turned and the bodies poured out into the square. Jogiches felt the tempo rise. He saw the swarms spilling out from across the square and he ran, faster and faster, just as the first cracks of gunfire echoed into the night.

Zenlo led Hoffner across the cobblestones and over to the gate. Somewhere beyond the building the battle raged on, but here—on the side street and less than a hundred meters from it—there was an eerie stillness. The army reserves had yet to be called in: only the square had been engaged. Hoffner pulled out his key and opened the outer lock. Zenlo struck a match, and within half a minute the five men were inside the Alex.

The walk to the back stairs was uneventful: all activity was taking place on the other side of the building. What shouts and scampering they heard continued to move away from them. Even so, Hoffner paused at each landing as he led the men up.

At the fourth floor, he stopped again. There was no reason for it: the place felt as deserted as the rest. He began to move, when Zenlo grabbed him from behind and pulled him back down the steps. The grip was remarkable and utterly immobilizing. A moment later, Hoffner heard the faint sound of footfalls rising from down the corridor. He had been completely unaware of it until this moment: clearly these were men who knew their business. Hoffner pressed himself up against the wall with the rest and listened as Zenlo pulled a short blade from his pocket and held it flat against his leg.

The sound grew closer, and a shadow appeared on the corridor wall. From this angle, Hoffner could make out only the top of a head as it passed. He thought it might have been **Kommissar** Braun making his way to the front of the building, but it was only a guess. Hoffner said nothing and waited in the silence. Half a minute passed before Zenlo quietly pocketed the knife. He then motioned for Hoffner to lead them up to the landing.

The corridor was equally still, the door handle as cold as Fichte had described it. At once, one of the men went to work on the lock and within seconds had it open. He stepped back and let Hoffner push open the door. When all five men were inside, Zenlo closed the door behind them and flicked on the light.

The precision of the next few minutes astounded Hoffner. He had always attributed a certain recklessness to theft: this had the grace of a choreographed ballet, two men with the burlap tarp for her body, two others at the tank. Hoffner focused on the jars. Taking them one by one to the sink, he turned on the faucet and began to dump out the contents. The stink of the grease forced him to place his handkerchief up to his face; even with it, he felt a momentary wooziness and had to turn away: this was no time for hallucinations.

Only then did he notice a second examining table up against the wall on the far side of the door. A sheeted body lay on top, one of its hands having slipped out. Hoffner placed the bottle on the counter and stepped over. There was no reason to wonder what he would find: Hoffner knew who lay beneath.

Fichte's cold stare gazed up into the light as Hoffner pulled back the sheet: Braun hadn't even bothered to shut the boy's eyes. Hoffner did so, and saw the slight discoloring on the lips and tongue. He bent over and smelled the faint metallic scent that lingered in the mouth. Hoffner guessed prussic, maybe oxalic acid: in Fichte's lungs, either would have been instantly fatal.

There was nothing serene in the face, no peace at the end. The boy looked as muddled by his own death as by those he had investigated and had never fully understood. Hoffner tried not to think of those last moments, Fichte clinging to the hope that things could be made right, only to be brought face-to-face with his own futility. Perhaps Fichte had made it only to confusion. That was Hoffner's hope for the boy.

He reached down and repositioned the hand on the chest, then stood there a moment longer before pulling the sheet over the face. Hoffner turned back to the counter, took the next jar, and began to empty it.

Jogiches's jaw was already swollen, and his lip badly cut, by the time Braun stepped into the cell.

It was a damp, soulless place, set off from the rest of the cells with just these sorts of interviews in mind. Jogiches sat cuffed to a chair, his arms pulled tight behind his back. Tamshik had been going at him for a good twenty minutes; Hermannsohn had been battering away with an endless array of questions: neither had produced any results.

Tamshik stepped back as Braun pulled over a second chair and placed it in front of Jogiches. Braun sat. "It looks like it's all falling apart up there, **mein Herr,**" said Braun with a goading sympathy. "The barracks guards in the square. A tank from the Schloss armory. We might even see a flamethrower or two." Braun curled a smile even as Jogiches stared beyond him. "A bit of a waste, wasn't it?" Braun reached out his arm and Hermannsohn handed him a file: Braun began to flip through the pages as he spoke. "Not really like you to put in an appearance at one of these things, is it, **mein Herr**? And to be taken in the first wave of arrests. Now, that was sloppy." Braun paused on a page. "Next time you'll have to be a bit more careful, won't you?" Braun looked up. "At least with your friends, we were forced to track them down." Jogiches continued to stare ahead as Braun's gaze hardened. "And now you're going to tell me exactly what Herr Hoffner knows about Munich, what he knows about the Hotel Eden, and anything else you think I might want to hear."

The room fell silent. Jogiches let his eyes drop to Braun's. He waited before speaking: "Remarkable," said Jogiches, "how one little Jewess has caused you such problems, Herr **Oberkommissar.** Letting her fall into the canal . . . now, that was the mistake, wasn't it?" Jogiches saw the momentary tensing in Braun's jaw. Jogiches spat a string of blood onto the floor and asked, "Do you have the time, Herr **Oberkommissar**?" He spoke as if he were at a café, sharing a coffee with a friend.

Braun hesitated. "The time?"

Jogiches enjoyed watching the wheels spin behind the callous expression. "Around nine, nine-thirty, is it?" Jogiches nodded to himself. "I'd just like to know how long Rosa's been out of the building, that's all." He saw the momentary flash in Braun's eyes and continued: "I suppose I **will** have to be a bit more careful next time, Herr **Oberkommissar,** try not to be so sloppy." Jogiches paused and then added, "As, I imagine, will you."

Braun stifled his reaction. "You think you've done something clever, do you?" When Jogiches said nothing, Braun stood, adding with a too-practiced calm, "It won't make any difference."

Jogiches again locked his eyes on the far wall. "Oh, I think we both know that's not true." She was safe, he thought; he could let her go. He closed his eyes.

Now, thought Jogiches, I am absolutely alone.

Braun stared at the unnervingly serene face. He looked across at Tamshik and said, "Make sure the prisoner doesn't try to escape." Braun then turned and headed out of the cell.

Jogiches waited for the touch of the steel on his skin. He listened for the squeeze of the trigger. Both came more quickly than he expected.

The car was waiting outside, its exhaust puffing like a cigar in the cold and damp. The door opened and Hoffner stepped up to the front seat as the men laid Rosa across the back floorboards. With a quick release, Pimm put the car into gear and jolted them down the nearest side street.

"No problems?" said Pimm as he glanced into his mirror.

"Nothing on our end," said Hoffner.

"Good. Then our friend must have been successful." Pimm took a quick turn; the buildings peeled past in a gray wash of stone and glass. "You know my associate?"

Little Franz was seated between them. The boy had found himself a scarf and was smoking a cigarette. A nice bit of wool, thought Hoffner. "Stepping up in the world, eh, Franz?"

Franz continued to gaze out the windshield, his tiny fingers wrapped around his cigarette as he exhaled a thin stream of smoke. In Pimm's presence, Franz was a much tougher prospect. "I was told to come along," said the boy, the "Herr **Oberkommissar**" conspicuously absent.

Pimm said, "He needs to learn sometime. You won't hold it against him, will you?"

Hoffner nodded at the cigarette. "You have another?" Franz fished one from his pocket and handed it to Hoffner. "We'll call it even, then." Hoffner lit up.

Pimm took them west, making sure to keep clear of any residual scuff-ups along the way. The government had reacted quickly: armored cars and light artillery—vast metal rhinos standing sentry—had already cordoned off the streets leading into the square. It was difficult to tell just how many troops Ebert had sent in; at every turn there seemed to be another unit marching in formation: it was more than enough to conjure memories of early January.

"They're going to make quick work of this," said Pimm. "Wouldn't want to be back in that square."

"Yah," Hoffner grunted. He continued to gaze out. "So . . . what do you think, Franz? Was it worth it to get her out?" The boy seemed surprised to be asked; he shrugged lazily. Hoffner nodded to himself and then spoke across to Pimm. "I'd love to see the look on Braun's face when they find she's gone missing. Wouldn't that be nice?"

Pimm shifted gears and said, "Just so long as you keep the Kripo out of my back pocket for the next few weeks, we're settled." He took another quick turn and Hoffner put a hand to the roof so as to keep from flattening the boy. "That was the agreement," said Pimm as the car straightened. "You want to gum up the works with your friends in the Polpo, not my business. You don't keep up your end with me, and I'll bring her right back."

Hoffner laughed quietly. "Fair enough." He was glad to see little Franz following every word.

It was nearly ten when they pulled up to the construction fencing outside the Rosenthaler station, Pimm having doubled back when they had gotten far enough north to avoid any trouble. Even here, the sounds of Alexanderplatz crackled overhead through the rain: no one was venturing out, which made for a very private transport of the body up the ramp. At the ladder down into the site, the largest of the men hoisted Rosa onto his shoulder. He steadied his grip on the slick rungs and headed down. Three minutes later the small group, including Franz, stood in the main cavern. Pimm had set it up nicely with a few torches to brighten up the place.

"Perfect," said Hoffner. "The last place Braun would look."

Pimm nodded to his man to set her down; he then turned to Hoffner. "So we're good here?" he said impatiently. Pimm had his hat in his hand and was fingering the water from the brim. "We've done our bit?"

Hoffner said, "I need to get her into one of the back caverns."

Pimm motioned his men to the ladder. "Well, you enjoy that, then." He placed his hat on his head as his men began to climb.

"Hold on," Hoffner said with surprise. "I can't do that on my own, not with my ribs."

Pimm grabbed on to the ladder. "We're on a schedule, Inspector. We got her here. You want her someplace else, that's up to you." He waved over to the boy. "You, too, Franz. Let's go."

Franz began to follow. Hoffner said, "At least leave me the boy. Forty minutes, an hour at the most. I'll get someone. I need him to stay with the body."

Pimm let out a frustrated breath. He turned to Hoffner. "All right. Fine. Forty minutes." He took a step up the first rung and looked back at the boy. "You come by the office afterward. We'll square it." He waited for a nod from Franz and then headed up.

Five minutes later, Hoffner joined Pimm and his men in an alley across from the site. They all stood in the shadows, eyes fixed on the ramp.

"You could have had a career on the stage," said Hoffner as he watched and waited.

"I'll keep that in mind," said Pimm. "You're sure he's—"

Franz appeared at the top of the ramp. He slipped on the wood and then bounded out into the square before heading south toward Alexanderplatz.

Hoffner stepped from the shadows and said, "I'm sure."

⇥ A HERO OF THE REPUBLIC ⇤

Rosa lay quietly in the outline that had once been Mary Koop's. They had done their best to scrub her clean of the grease. They had even clothed her. Even so, her hair was still slick, and her face had an odd shine to it, especially in the torchlight: she looked as if she had been swimming.

Hoffner was kneeling by her side, his coat heavy from the rain. He had been like this for several minutes, replaying the dream and the pebble and the sun in his eyes as he had tried to find her. Odd, he thought, to be alone with her now. She had been words to him, an image in his head, alive and defiant: here, she seemed so much less than that. This was death, a body—a tool—nothing more. She was being used again, and for that, Hoffner felt his only remorse.

He heard the sound of footsteps approaching from beyond the cavern's opening, and he slowly tightened the grip around his pistol: he kept it low, hidden behind Rosa's torso. From the sound of it, there were several men making their way back. Hoffner tried to pick out the exact number: it was the only way he knew to keep his mind focused.

A light began to grow, the beam bobbing to the rhythm of the steps as they drew closer. Hoffner heard a whispering of voices, indistinct words dulled by the wood and dirt. A single "There" broke through, and a moment later two young soldiers— **Freikorps** from their uniforms—stepped into the shadowed chamber. Immediately they raised their rifles, keeping Hoffner in their sights. Braun was directly behind them; he stepped past them as a second man appeared at the opening. The man had a strikingly handsome face and carried a small jar in his hands.

Braun spoke with his usual charm: "What a surprising sense of symmetry you have, Herr **Oberkommissar.** The Rosenthaler Platz. Wouters's den. One might even say there's a sentimental side to you." Hoffner said nothing.

The second man now stepped forward. His focus was on Rosa. He seemed agitated. "They've removed the unguent."

Braun put up a hand to stop him. "Step away from the body, Herr **Oberkommissar.**"

Hoffner remained where he was. "You can tell Herr **Doktor** Manstein that I'm quite harmless, Herr Braun. Especially when I've got two rifles aimed at my chest."

Braun showed only a moment's surprise. "And what else did you learn on your trip to Munich, Herr **Oberkommissar?**"

Hoffner spoke across to Manstein. "Your father-in-law did excellent work creating this little haven for Wouters, Herr **Doktor.** Naturally the idea was yours."

Manstein studied Hoffner. He said nothing.

"I'm guessing the engineer Sazonov wasn't much of an expense," Hoffner continued. "Or his family. No reason to pay the dead." Hoffner saw a glimmer of confirmation in the eyes. "Must have been difficult being away from Munich all that time. The only one who knew how to apply the Ascomycete 4 to

Fräulein Koop, the only one who could placate Wouters with the appropriate injections between escapades, though I'm sure Herr **Direktor** Schumpert was delighted to have his daughter and grandchildren in the city for such an extended period of time."

Manstein stared at him without a trace of emotion. "Am I meant to be impressed?"

"But that's not all you were good for, was it, Herr **Doktor**?" said Hoffner.

Manstein's gaze grew colder still. "Can we shoot him now and get on with this?"

Hoffner looked at Braun. "That would make it quite a day for you, wouldn't it, Herr Braun?"

"Even with your back up against it," said Braun. "I will give you that." Braun unclipped his holster. "You're going to be my second carver, Herr Hoffner. Quite a story for the papers. Killing your own wife. Now, what kind of mind does that?" Braun began to pull out his pistol.

Without warning, six of Pimm's men emerged from the shadows, their guns drawn. Two had appeared from just outside the opening and now had their pistols pressed up against each of the soldiers' necks. The rifles were quickly handed over. Braun had turned at the sudden movement, and when he looked back, the barrel of Hoffner's pistol was staring him in the face. Hoffner reached over and took Braun's gun. He then nodded him over to a pair of chairs that Pimm was placing at the center of the cavern. Braun showed remarkable restraint as he made his way over.

"So tell me," said Braun as Zenlo tied off his hands behind him. "How **is** little Franz?"

"Don't worry," said Hoffner. "He still thinks he was helping you."

"Which means he'll know you were the one to pull the trigger when I end up dead, won't he?"

Hoffner holstered his gun and said, "Now, why would I want to do that?"

Pimm nodded over to the men by the soldiers. "Get the two of them out of here. Keep them busy for a few hours. Shoot them if you have to."

Hoffner waited until the **Freikorps** boys were gone before speaking. He picked up the jar and said, "Your private stash, Herr **Doktor**?" Manstein remained silent. "It was the only way I could think of getting you back here. How long do you think before she needs another slathering?"

Braun said, "If you're not going to kill us, Herr **Oberkommissar,** then this is going to be a very long night."

Hoffner nodded as if in agreement. "I said **I** wasn't going to kill you, Herr Braun. I can't speak for my friends, here." Hoffner hurled the jar against the wall and watched as the glass and grease shattered to the ground. "Wouters," he said, again nodding to himself. "That was such a clever choice, wasn't it? Old women and lace. Luxemburg and Jew-baiting, all in one." He turned to Manstein. "It must have taken you months to find him . . . all the way back to June of '18. But then, you were already familiar with Sint-

Walburga and their intriguing new patient, weren't you?" Hoffner saw a moment of recognition in Manstein's otherwise implacable stare. "Did they call you in to consult on the original case? Or was it a letter from a colleague that introduced you to Herr Wouters?" Manstein's silence was confirmation enough. "Very impressive, Herr **Doktor.** You knew the war was lost, the Kaiser was on shaky ground. And we were suddenly at peace with the Russians— who knew what to expect from the socialists after that? But to see all the way through to November, to revolution . . ." Hoffner looked across at Pimm. "That was very impressive, don't you think?"

Pimm perked up at being included. "Oh yes," he said with a nod. "Very."

Manstein snorted dismissively.

"It **wasn't** very impressive, **mein Herr**?" said Hoffner.

Manstein refused to look at Hoffner. "Just because you don't understand a thing doesn't mean it isn't possible." His voice had a refined quality: schools, breeding, a sense of entitlement. Manstein did nothing to hide his contempt. "It was a precautionary measure." He now looked up. "Evidently it was a precaution worth taking."

Hoffner said, "So you did all of this just to cover up killing Luxemburg?"

Manstein looked genuinely perplexed by the question. "Is that what you think, Herr Policeman?"

It wasn't, but Hoffner needed to engage the man.

Braun saw what Hoffner was after and tried to stop it. "Herr **Doktor,** you don't have to say anything—"

"Shut up, Braun." Manstein continued to stare up at Hoffner.

Braun held his own. "You'd be wise to let me take care of this."

"I'm tied to a chair in an excavation pit. I think you've done all you can."

Braun insisted: "He hasn't an inkling of what's going on here."

"He has **her,**" Manstein cut in. "And I don't think he'll be giving her back." It was a cold, unflappable stare that now peered at Hoffner. "You won't be giving her back to us, will you, Herr **Oberkommissar?**"

Evidently the marriage between the Thulians and the Polpo had been one of convenience. Hoffner knew he needed to take full advantage of that. "Did you enjoy the work, Herr **Doktor?**" he asked.

For the first time, uncertainty flashed through Manstein's eyes. "Excuse me?"

Hoffner gave Braun no time to interrupt: "It's a shame you didn't study your patient more closely. I imagine you were a bit too clever there, as well." Hoffner watched as the uncertainty grew. "For the longest time, I couldn't understand why Wouters's knife work was so smooth while the second carver's was so jagged and angled. I assumed it was someone like Tamshik, or even Braun here, but then the accuracy of the lines on the back was too good—too close to the original—not to be someone who actually had some skill with a knife. But to make it look too good, that would have been a problem, wouldn't it? So you had to alter your hand. After all, Wouters was mad, and didn't madness imply a kind of frenzy with the cutting? You must have watched him, seen him slice up the backs of those women, so you'd know how to re-create the pattern. But you didn't watch him closely enough, did you? This was an art for him. Battered and bloody hands hadn't stopped him as a boy from creating the most delicate lace patterns. His work was pristine." Hoffner paused. "Unlike yours."

Manstein stared coldly ahead.

"The Tiergarten whore," said Hoffner. "You got impatient. The Polpo wanted you to wait, but that was unacceptable. Wouters wasn't killing fast enough, and he was staying in the wrong part of town. You needed him in the Westend so you could get the kind of hysteria you wanted. Such a perfect spot, the U-Bahn station at the zoo. The threat of east coming west. Tell me, Herr **Doktor,** was it only the carving, or did you do the killing, as well?"

Braun had heard enough: "Don't let him do this."

Manstein ignored Braun: "More efficient that way, wouldn't you say, Herr **Oberkommissar**?"

With sudden venom, Hoffner cracked the back of his hand across Manstein's face. Manstein showed almost no reaction, while Braun flinched. Manstein's lip began to bleed and he licked at it with his tongue. "Does that make you feel better, Herr **Oberkommissar**?"

Hoffner was doing all he could to maintain his self-control: how easy it would be to beat this man to death, he thought. "Why Luxemburg?" he said.

Manstein spat a wad of blood. "You seem to be doing so well on your own. Why don't you tell me?"

Braun tried again. "This is exactly what he wants. How is it that you're incapable of seeing that?"

Manstein spat again. "Never the larger picture with you, Braun, is it?" Manstein wiped his chin on his shoulder and then looked up at Hoffner. "Go on, Detective. See if you can figure this out before Herr Braun here manages it."

It was clear that Manstein wanted to be pressed: that Hoffner had yet to figure out why was no reason to disappoint him. "She was a means to an end," he said.

Manstein offered another snort of contempt. "If we're going to state the obvious, I'd prefer the bullet."

Hoffner was inclined to grant the request, but that wasn't why he was here; instead, he tried to imagine where Jogiches might have taken things now. "All right," he said. "Berlin on edge . . . Rosa's body discovered . . . not much of a stretch to stir up fear of a Red reprisal for her killing. The Reds ready to strike . . ." Hoffner was building momentum. "Enter the **Freikorps.** Naturally the government gives them free rein to eliminate the problem—we can thank your former General Nepp in Defense for that—and you kill two birds with one stone. The socialists are purged, and your military wing gets a foothold in the

political door, and all in the name of reestablishing order." Hoffner knew there were too many holes in the
theory to count. His only hope was that Manstein had
found it equally unimpressive.

"A **dead** Luxemburg?" said Manstein. "Triggering
socialist reprisals with the design etched onto her
back? And that makes sense to you, Herr **Oberkommissar**?" Ego was always so transparent with men
like this. "Wouldn't that, in fact, have done just the
opposite—allow the Reds to stop worrying about
who had killed their beloved Rosa because, now, she
would have been nothing more than another unfortunate victim of some madman?" Manstein seemed
almost disappointed by Hoffner's attempt. "Nothing
gained there. No one to blame, Herr **Oberkommissar.** No reason to bring in the **Korps**."

It was an odd choice—the word "blame"—thought
Hoffner. He tried to see beyond it. If not Wouters,
then who? Even Manstein had to admit that the Jews
were too vague a target, lace designs notwithstanding. No. Manstein had made it clear that someone
else was meant to take responsibility for her death.
That was the key. That was why the bodies were pil-
ing up all over again. Someone who could . . .

Hoffner stopped. **Of course.** He looked across at
Pimm, and the words came back to him. This was a
crime like any other, no matter how intricate its planning: and like all crimes, misdirection lay at its core.

Hoffner suddenly understood where he had gone
wrong. He had been focusing on what these men had

been trying to keep hidden, the layers to be peeled away: that was what made for conspiracy. But what if it was the other way round? What if the key was in what they wanted revealed?

Hoffner looked again at Manstein. "You wanted the Kripo to dig deep, didn't you, Herr **Doktor**?"

Mantein's expression seemed to soften. "Dig, Herr **Oberkommissar**?" He sounded almost encouraging. "And what was it that you were meant to find?"

Hoffner began to see it. "It's really quite brilliant, isn't it? Because it's exactly what it appears to be. Wouters unleashed on the city. The murders as a ruse to create hysteria. All to cover up Luxemburg's killing. You wanted it all to come out because it was all meant to lead back to one place. Nepp. Your man in the Defense Ministry."

"**Very** good, Herr **Oberkommissar**."

Hoffner plowed on. "Nepp was the one to give the orders to separate Luxemburg and Liebknecht that night." Another flash of clarity. "And he was the one responsible for getting Wouters out of Belgium, wasn't he?" When Manstein said nothing, Hoffner continued, "Oster's orders. The ones to get him over the border. They were signed by **General** Nepp, weren't they?"

Manstein was actually enjoying this. "Excellent." Again Braun made a motion to speak, and again Manstein stopped him. "Go on, Herr **Oberkommissar**."

"You created the conspiracy with the sole purpose of laying it all at Ebert's feet. The tragedy of the last two months—it was all meant to be seen as little more than a highly elaborate scheme by the government to get rid of one of its more dangerous enemies. Rosa. Innocent women killed—"

"The city terrorized," Manstein added with a strange satisfaction.

"Except it's not you and your Thulian friends who get the blame. The conspiracy comes to light, and it's Herr Nepp who makes certain to implicate the Social Democrats when he falls on his sword. The government is sent reeling and the **Freikorps** steps in to bring us all back from the brink."

"No wonder you managed it so quickly with Wouters," Manstein said.

Backhanded compliments aside, Hoffner needed to fill in the missing pieces. "So why hold on to her?" he said. "Why not have Rosa's body discovered in late January? Everything else was in place."

"Why not indeed?" said Manstein. "Perhaps Herr Braun would like to answer that one?" Braun had given up trying: he sat with a vacant stare. Manstein continued: "Braun underestimated you. He convinced us it would take you several months to find Wouters. By then the city would be in a panic, the murders would be front-page news every day. You had managed to keep the case hidden throughout the revolution. We needed time to build the hysteria, to let Fräulein Luxemburg be our crowning jewel, the focus of the conspiracy to come. Unfortunately, you tracked down Wouters too quickly."

"So why not stop Wouters from taking his victim to the **Ochsenhof** that night?" Hoffner pressed. "I don't catch him and the killings go on." Manstein waited for Hoffner to put it together himself. "You didn't **have** Wouters by then, did you?"

"The Koop girl," Manstein said. "Once you took her, there was nothing to bring him back to the site. The little engineer Sazonov was cleverer than we thought. And once Wouters was gone, he needed to be dead. Tossing Luxemburg out after that, without a captivated public—and with you a hero—would have meant nothing. She would have been the victim of a crime already solved, and without any link to Nepp."

Something didn't sit right. "But she **was** tossed out. The Kripo found her floating in the Landwehr Canal."

Hoffner had hit a nerve. Again Manstein's expression soured. "You can thank Rifleman Runge for that." Manstein shook his head. "The boy got overexcited. Killed her too quickly. The knife work had to be done directly after death, otherwise the skin would have lost its elasticity. I managed to get to him in time, but then that mob you've been hearing so much about actually stumbled upon us. Down by the river. No choice but to find an embankment and hide her. Your comrades discovered her before we could get back. Braun was actually something of a help there."

Hoffner's mind was racing. Everything to set up

Ebert's government. Everything to place the blame where it least belonged.

"And Eisner?" said Hoffner. "The assassination? Berlin hysteria wasn't enough? You had to bring it home to Munich, as well?"

"That," said Manstein, "had nothing to do with us. We wouldn't have sent a Jew to do our dirty work."

No need for a coup, thought Hoffner. No need for an assassin's bullet. With Nepp in place, it had all been much subtler than that. Hoffner said, "And then the digging went too far."

"Yes," said Manstein, lingering with the word. "Your trip to Munich was something of an eye-opener. Not that it was as much of a problem as you might think. It was time to start leaving bodies again, build up the hysteria." Manstein peered directly into Hoffner's eyes. "That was where we managed two birds with one stone, Herr **Oberkommissar.** Your wife seemed the perfect choice."

There was something dead inside Hoffner, and no amount of goading could stir it to life. He said, "You're taking this all very calmly, Herr **Doktor.**"

"As are you, Herr **Oberkommissar.**"

Hoffner said nothing.

"In fact," Manstein added, "if you think about it, I'm **handing** it to you, Detective, not taking it."

Again, Manstein was leading him. "And why is that?" said Hoffner.

"And here I thought you were so much cleverer than Herr Braun and his Polpo." When Hoffner remained silent, Manstein spoke more deliberately: "As I said, you have her. And without Frau Luxemburg—"

"Yes. No conspiracy," said Hoffner. "I understand that."

"Yes, I think you do." Manstein waited before adding, "But if you arrest us . . ."

Hoffner listened to the tone in Manstein's voice, and allowed himself to see beyond all of this: to the press meetings, the newspapers, Manstein paraded out in front of all of them. And it suddenly became clear. "Too many questions," Hoffner said, almost to himself. "And ones you'd be only too happy to answer. Either way it would lead them back to Nepp."

"Precisely," said Manstein. "And from Nepp to Ebert. The larger picture, Herr **Oberkommissar.** Obviously, you're going to dispose of Fräulein Luxemburg, so you and I seem to be at an impasse. My friends and I have nothing to ignite our scheme, and you can't take the risk that exposing us wouldn't ultimately fall in Ebert's lap. Your finding all this out— or, rather, your having it spoon-fed to you—stops you from doing anything. Too much to lose. A final safeguard, if you will, even if Herr Braun here didn't quite understand that. Shame it had to come to this."

Hoffner thought for a moment. "So why not kill you?"

Manstein was no less poised. "You're not going to do that, Herr **Oberkommissar.** It's not who you are." Manstein waited. He then let out a long breath and, with surprising candor, said, "So I think we're done here." He turned to Zenlo. "You can remove the ropes now." Manstein jiggled his wrists in Zenlo's direction.

Hoffner said, "You're forgetting we still have a murderer on the loose."

"Oh, you'll find someone to take the fall for that, Herr **Oberkommissar.** The Kripo always does. And it's not as if it would be the first time, now would it?" Manstein turned again to Zenlo. "A knife, please. It's becoming uncomfortable."

Hoffner watched as Pimm and Zenlo shared a glance. They were no better prepared for this than Hoffner was. Hoffner said, "And everything goes on as it was? Is that the idea, Herr **Doktor**?"

For a moment, Manstein looked truly baffled by the question. "'Goes on as it . . . ?' Let me ask you this, Herr **Oberkommissar**—how long do you think the German people will suffer a Friedrich Ebert Germany? The man's already talking about running away from Berlin and setting up shop in Weimar. Everything as it was? Does that seem possible to you anymore? All you've done here is to delay the inevitable."

The cavern became uncomfortably quiet. Hoffner tried to find something to say, but he had no answer. If the men in Munich had come this close, this time . . . Manstein had him either way. What choice was there?

Hoffner looked over at Zenlo and held out his hand. "Give me your knife," he said. Again Zenlo looked to Pimm, and again Pimm said nothing.

"Your knife," Hoffner repeated. With no recourse, Zenlo stepped over and placed the knife in Hoffner's hand. Hoffner was now directly in front of Manstein. He knelt down and said, "You're right, Herr **Doktor.**" Without so much as a nod, Hoffner plunged the blade deep into Manstein's gut. "I do need someone to take the fall."

Manstein's expression was less anguish than shock. He coughed once, and Hoffner twisted the knife as he drove it higher and deeper into the flesh. He watched as the eyes searched his own for an answer, the throat choked and silent. "Very few things are inevitable, Herr **Doktor.** This happens to be one of them." Hoffner held him there, waiting for the life to drain from him. Manstein's body jerked once and became still.

Hoffner turned to Braun. The man sat cowering in disbelief as Hoffner let go of the knife and said, "Congratulations, Herr **Oberkommissar.**" There was nothing in Hoffner's tone. "You've just caught your second carver. What a proud day it is for the Polpo."

Braun managed to find his voice. "What have you done?"

Strangely, Hoffner felt nothing: no relief, no sense of retribution. All he noticed was a tackiness on his hand—a bit of blood that had caught between his knuckles—and he pulled out his handkerchief. "I've made you a hero of the Republic," he said as he concentrated on the stain. "You'll have to be careful how much you let out. How far you let the press dig. Otherwise, who knows what they might discover?"

Fighting to find his composure, Braun said, "And why would I do any of this?"

"Because," came a voice from across the cavern, "you could always be a dead hero, Herr **Oberkommissar**." **Kriminaldirektor** Gerhard Weigland stood just outside the opening to the tunnel. He was alone. He looked over at Pimm and said casually, "Hello, Alby."

Pimm and the rest watched in silence as Weigland moved slowly into the cavern. It was unclear how long Weigland had been there, although he seemed unmoved by the sight of Manstein's body. "Sorry to have missed all the festivities, Nikolai. It took a bit of time, convincing the boy to tell us where everyone had gone."

Once again Hoffner had underestimated Weigland: the warning to stay away from the Alex had done just the opposite. Hoffner stood and said, "Not much to see, Herr **Direktor.**"

Weigland again peered over at Manstein. "Yes," he said. "I can see that." He turned to Braun. "It seems your friend Hermannsohn chose to swallow the end of his gun rather than answer any of our questions about the late Herr Fichte. Herr Tamshik showed less courage. We have him in a cell."

Braun said defiantly, "I'll take the gun, if it's all the same."

Weigland kept his eyes on Braun. "No . . . I think

Nikolai's right. Alive and a hero will be far worse for you. All those eyes keeping a watch on you and your friends." Weigland had been waiting a long time for this moment: he was making sure to enjoy it. He turned to Hoffner. "But it's up to you, Nikolai." Weigland glanced again at Braun, his eyes narrowing for just a moment. "Shoot him if you want." Weigland then turned and headed out to the tunnel. "I'll be in the square."

Hoffner understood. It would make no difference. Weigland simply couldn't be here to see how things came out.

The footfalls receded and Hoffner reached over and pulled the knife from Manstein's chest. He began to wipe the blood on his handkerchief. "Shoot you," he said, thinking for a moment and then peering directly into Braun's eyes. "Not exactly who I am now, is it?" Hoffner stuffed the handkerchief into Braun's breast pocket and added, "You're about to have your picture in all the papers, Herr **Oberkommissar.** One day, you'll have to tell me what that's like."

⇥ ROSA ⇤

Two hours later, Pimm and Hoffner stood staring out across the coal-black current that was the Landwehr Canal. The sound of lapping water against the stone made raw the already biting air. Mercifully, the rain had let up.

Pimm breathed in deeply: he had been trying to

make conversation for the past half hour, to no avail. "Weigland's no idiot," he said; Hoffner remained silent with a cigarette. "He'll manage it. Save his own hide. He always does."

Hoffner nodded distantly. He knew Pimm was right: Weigland would find a way to sell it to the papers, give Berlin what she wanted: a mad doctor from Munich always brought satisfaction. And just in case Braun had missed something in the cavern, Weigland had been crystal clear back at the Alex: "You're out from under your rock, **mein Herr.** And that means you can be crushed at any time. It's going to be a very tight leash." Deputy Minister Nepp was to serve as the reminder: news of his fatal riding accident would be reaching the back pages a few days from now.

That had left Rosa, who was now wrapped in a tarp and propped up against a tree. Pimm and Hoffner had lugged her nearly half a kilometer through thick snow and wood, and Pimm was still recovering. He coughed up something and spat. "Shall we?" he said.

Hoffner took a last drag on his cigarette, then flicked it to the ground. Without a word, he stepped over and, laying the tarp on the snow, slowly began to unroll her. He had insisted on somewhere remote, close to where she had been dropped all those weeks ago. Out in the west. This seemed as good a place as any.

"Odd, dumping her back in," said Pimm as he knelt down to help.

Hoffner flipped her on her back. "Not so odd," he said.

Pimm showed only a moment's surprise at the return of Hoffner's voice. "Yah."

The rumors were already out there: the canal was where the mob had tossed her. More than that, Hoffner knew that the water would bloat her skin, distort the scarring, and leave her back unrecognizable. She would float up eventually—a month, maybe two—but better that than to have her off somewhere plotting her return with Herr Lenin. Rosa needed to float up so that she could be put to rest. It was the least he could do for her.

Hoffner reached into his coat and pulled out the pebble Martha had saved. He held it in his palm for a moment and then tucked it into one of Rosa's pockets. He stood.

"All right," he said.

Pimm brought himself up, and together they carried her to the edge of the embankment. With a nod from Hoffner, they heaved her body back and then tossed her in. The splash echoed—the patter against the wall more frantic—and then stillness. Both men stood watching as she floated out, her small face glistening in the moonlight.

Pimm's breathing softened. "You and I aren't all that different," he said. "The world throws something at us, and we manage it. We don't look too deeply. In the end, things take care of themselves."

Hoffner continued to watch her. He wanted to believe Pimm: he wanted to find something in this that said, yes, this is where it is meant to be. He knew that the city would right itself, that the chisel murders would drift quickly into some forgotten past, that even Rosa herself—when she finally came round again—would sparkle for only a moment before being overtaken and left behind. That was Berlin's saving grace, her incessant movement forward, her sense of promise in what was to come. Now, however, that promise seemed somehow out of reach. Too much had been lost—too much remained hidden beneath the surface—to make her future any more certain than his own.

There was a sudden swirling of water and Rosa's legs began to dip down; her torso followed, and finally her face. In a matter of moments, she was gone. Hoffner continued to stare out at the silent water.

"We've managed nothing with this," he said quietly. "Except perhaps a little time." His eyes followed what he imagined to be her path beneath the current. "These men will come again. And when they do . . . we'll look back at Rosa and her revolution and see how naïve we really were."

The air grew static. Hoffner felt suddenly stifled by the place. He needed the east and the Berlin he still knew: somewhere there—and there alone—he would find a way to keep moving. He turned to Pimm, and together they headed into the long night.

≈ AUTHOR'S NOTE ≈

Rosa did, in fact, float up on May 31, 1919. By then, Lieutenant Vogel and Rifleman Runge had been brought up on charges, but the trial was as much of a sham as the investigation had been. Vogel was sentenced to two years and four months for committing a misdemeanor—illegally disposing of a corpse while on duty, and for filing an incorrect report; Runge received two years and two weeks for attempted manslaughter. The presiding magistrate—a man who would go on to hold a prominent position in the Nazi People's Court—referred to extenuating circumstances, and the men's excellent war records, as justification for the light sentences. In 1933, Runge petitioned the Ministry of Justice for compensation for his unjust imprisonment, and for his early contribution to the cause of Nazi Germany. After all, his

Führer "had also paid for his ideals with prison." Runge was awarded six thousand marks.

A detective named Ernst Tamshik was, for a time, held responsible for Leo Jogiches's death: the official report stated that Jogiches had been shot in the back "while attempting to escape." No charges were ever brought.

Dietrich Eckart continued to preach from his wine-cellar perch, and came to be known as Hitler's mentor. Along with fellow Thulian Anton Drexler, he designed the philosophy and policies of the German Workers' Party, which eventually changed its name to the National Socialists under Hitler's leadership. Eckart died of liver failure in 1923, and thus failed to see the full potential of his work. The rag of a paper that he had purchased with Drexler in 1918 became the **Volkischer Beobachter** (**National Observer**), the central organ of Nazi Germany.

The **Freikorps,** which had played so pivotal a role in crushing the revolution, went on to even greater fame in the 1920s. Under the command of Ernst Roehm, the **Korps** became Hitler's Brownshirts—the SA. They, too, however, missed out on the fruits of their labors. On June 30, 1934, Hitler had the SA leadership purged during "the Night of the Long Knives" in order to placate the army's High Command. The **Wehrmacht,** as it turned out, wanted nothing to do with a bunch of thugs.

As for Albert Einstein, Käthe Kollwitz, and Leo Jogiches, they were all in Berlin during the revolution of 1919 (Einstein had, in fact, been the director of the Kaiser Wilhelm Institute since 1914); the remaining characters in the book were not.

All excerpts from Rosa's letters are authentic and can be found in either **The Letters of Rosa Luxemburg** (Humanities Press, 1993) or **Comrade and Lover** (MIT Press, 1979). The Shelter Registration Form that appears in chapter four is a reprint of a Weimar document, the text of which can be found in the collection of Joseph Roth's feuilletons titled **What I Saw** (W. W. Norton & Company, 2003).

✦ A BRIEF BIOGRAPHY ✦

Rosa Luxemburg was born on March 5, 1870, to a middle-class family of assimilated Jews in the small town of Zamosc on the easternmost edge of Poland. Shunned by the predominantly Orthodox and Hasidic communities, the family moved to Warsaw in 1873, where, for the next fifteen years, Rosa did everything she could to distance herself from the petit-bourgeois lifestyle her parents tried to emulate; even their stifled Judaism embarrassed her. Life was not made any easier when, at the age of five, she was misdiagnosed with a tubercular hip and forced to bind her legs in a cast for nearly a year. When she emerged, Rosa was left with a severe limp, a deformity she would struggle to conceal for the rest of her life.

Intellectually, Rosa also began to stand apart. Under an 1879 Russian law, classes in Polish literature and the humanities were strictly forbidden; remarkably, Polish could be taught only as a second language. The Russification of education in Warsaw began to force Rosa and other young Polish intellectuals to go underground, lending a conspiratorial aura to their studies. Figures such as the Romantic poet Adam Mickiewicz, with talk of equality and social justice, became inspirations for these new radicals. For some, however, such ideas had an influence beyond the classroom: at just seventeen, Rosa joined Proletariat, an illegal socialist group, whose goal was to build a worker's party. Thrilling as it must have been, it was also very dangerous, as the authorities suddenly began to take notice of her. At this point, it was her ideas and actions, not her physical limitations, that were drawing attention. It was time for Rosa to leave Warsaw.

Fear of prison, however, was not the only reason she needed to go. At the time, women—especially Jewish women—had no access to Polish universities. In February 1889, not quite nineteen, Rosa was smuggled out of the country in the back of a hay cart, then left to find her way to Zurich and its open university. Luckily, she was well at home there. A thriving band of Polish émigrés had set up shop at the university, among them a fellow conspirator named Leo Jogiches. Over the next fifteen years, the two would become lovers—to Rosa's mind it was a marriage, although there were never any official papers to say so—as well as comrades, plotters, prisoners, and rabble-rousers, all in the name of socialism. And while she would get her doctorate and publish countless articles—thus making a name for herself in the Polish and German parties—Jogiches would never manage to get out more than a few pages. She became the face of young socialism, while he remained only a shadow.

The tension eventually tore them apart. Rosa was left to struggle on her own, taking on both the German establishment and the less radical elements of her own Social Democratic Party. Where they wanted reform, Rosa wanted revolution. Her polemics isolated her still further, leaving her—by 1912—as the sole voice of the radical left. And while, for a time, she was allowed to teach at the Party's school in Berlin—her work on Marxist economy was too innovative to be ignored—men like Friedrich Ebert and Philipp Scheidemann were now taking the socialists in a far more moderate direction. Only something of drastic proportions could bring Rosa back to the fore.

Sadly, the war proved her final undoing. When the workers of Germany, Russia, England, and France voted for rearmament, it was the end of the International. It was also the end of her freedom: Rosa spent all but a few months of the war in prison—under the hollow euphemism of "protective custody"—writing and waiting. And when her release finally came in November 1918, it ushered in the last cruel hope of her life. The revolution was here. Her old comrade, Karl Liebknecht, had managed to sweep the workers up into a frenzy, building on the unrest in Kiel and the rest of Germany. Rosa returned to Berlin in triumph on November 11, and for the next eight weeks watched as the Social Democrats thwarted her every attempt at genuine socialist revolution. In a last, desperate effort to lay claim to the revolution, she and Jogiches—reunited again—along with Liebknecht, formed the first German Communist Party, under the banner of Spartakus, and took to the streets. They were crushed.

Her last days were spent on the run, moving from one safe house to the next, the press branding her a traitor—the Devil Jewess—until, on the night of January 15, the soldiers came, took her to the Hotel Eden, and killed her. Four months later, her body appeared floating in the Landwehr Canal, almost unrecognizable after being in the water for so long a time. And so began her legend.

ABOUT THE AUTHOR

Jonathan Rabb is the author of **The Overseer** and **The Book of Q.** He lives in New York with his wife and two children.